COMMUNICATIONS IN THE WORLD OF BUSINESS AND INDUSTRY

APPLIED EDUCATION

Pearson Custom Publishing

Cover Art: "Hand Jive," by Angela Sciaraffa.

Excerpts taken from:

Technical Writing: Process and Product, Second Edition,
by Sharon J. Gerson and Steven M. Gerson

A Pearson Education Company
Upper Saddle River, New Jersey 07458

Human Relations: Interpersonal, Job-Oriented Skills, Sixth Edition,
by Andrew J. DuBrin

Keys to Success: How to Achieve Your Goals, Second Edition,
by Carol Carter, Joyce Bishop, and Sarah Kravits

This special edition published in cooperation with
Pearson Custom Publishing

Printed in the United States of America

10 9 8 7 6 5 4 3 2 1

Please visit our website at www.pearsoncustom.com

ISBN 0-536-02834-6

BA 990453

PEARSON CUSTOM PUBLISHING
160 Gould Street/Needham Heights, MA 02494
A Pearson Education Company

Contents

PREFACE

GENERAL POLICIES FOR APLED

AMERICANS WITH DISABILITIES ACT

PLAGIARISM

BOARD POLICIES

GRADING SYSTEM

SCC STUDENT PROFILE PORTFOLIO

Evaluation sheets for APLED 121 and 123 are included

GENERAL POLICIES FOR APLED

Student Information
The *Americans with Disabilities Act* is designed to ensure that students with disabilities have an equal opportunity to access academic programs and successfully complete their educational goals. Spokane Community College is committed to providing accessibility to all students. Any students with disabilities who have accommodation needs must contact Disability Support Services located in the Learning Resource Center (Library) or call Laura at 533-8872 to make an appointment to complete the intake process. This information will remain strictly confidential.

Excerpts from *Regulations and Policies Concerning Student Conduct*
published by Affirmative Action/Administrative Services
Community Colleges of Spokane

PLAGIARISM **WAC 132Q-04-061**

Any student who presents the words or ideas of another in direct quotation, indirect quotation, or close paraphrase, must provide acknowledgment. Failure to do so shall constitute plagiarism. Plagiarism shall be cause for disciplinary action.

NOTE: The SCC Applied Education department has established the following policy.

- Deliberate plagiarism will result in 0.0 for the paper/project.
- Deliberate plagiarism can result in the failure of the course
- References/Resources must be available upon instructor's request.

Newspapers	Internet	Books
Brochures	Magazines	Handbooks
Trade Journals	Encyclopedia	Encarta
Text Books	Pamphlets	

ANTI-HARASSMENT **BOARD POLICY 1.70.01**
It is the intent of the board of trustees that all individuals shall be provided an environment free from any form of harassment, as defined below, in all faculties, events of activities directly or indirectly under the control of the Community Colleges of Sp0okane. Therefore, it shall be the policy of the board that harassment directed to any individual of group on the basis of race, creed, color, national origin, age, sex, marital status, sexual orientation, or the presence of a physical, sensory or mental disability is a violation of the mission and purpose of the Community Colleges of Spokane as an institution of higher education and shall not be tolerated, and pursuant to this policy, shall be prohibited.

Prohibited harassment shall include verbal and written comments, slurs, jokes, innuendoes, cartoons, pranks, and any and all other physical or non-physical conduct or activity that can be construed as derogatory, intimidating, hostile or offensive; or any behavior or action, either physical or verbal, which is sexual in nature and unwelcomed, unwanted or uninvited.

It shall be the responsibility of the chief executive officer to develop and implement an internal complaint procedure which shall provide individuals with valid reason to believe they implement an educational program for employees and student detailing specific behaviors constituting such prohibited harassment.

NON-DISCRIMINATION **BOARD POLICY 1.70.02**
The Community Colleges of Spokane, both as a public institution of higher education and as an employer, recognizes its responsibility in providing cultural and social leadership and to uphold the laws of the United States and the State of Washington regarding non-discrimination. In that regard, the fostering and developing of values that promote open-mindedness, awareness, sensitivity and respect for differences including perspectives of those of a different race, sex, social class or disability will be encouraged.

The understanding of social and culture traditions of different minority groups, women and disabled persons in both classroom and working environments is a fundamental role of this college district.

Prejudice and bigotry, including racism, sexism and any other bias that creates barriers, perpetuates stereotypes or promotes ignorance, is contrary to the mission and obligations of the Community Colleges and has no value or place in this academic community.

Confirmed violations of this policy by any student or academic, classified or administrative employee may lead to corrective discipline including suspension and dismissal.

DRUG-FREE WORKPLACE **BOARD POLICY 1.70.03**
It is the intent of the board of trustees that the unlawful manufacture, distribution, dispensing, possession or use of a controlled substance in all facilities, events, or activities directly or indirectly under the control of the Community Colleges of Spokane shall not be tolerated and, pursuant to this policy, shall be prohibited. Employees or students engaging in such prohibited activities shall be subject to disciplinary action, pursuant to applicable rules, regulations and employment contracts, which may result in suspension or termination.

CLASSROOM CONDUCT

- Each faculty member has the right to suspend up to three class days any student who by any actual misconduct disrupts any college class by engaging in conduct that renders it difficult or impossible to maintain the decorum of the class (see WAC 132 Q-04-067: and see WAC Q-04-170(2)).

GRADING SYSTEM for APLED CLASSES

GRADING SCALE

% POINTS		NUMERIC GRADE	LETTER GRADE EQUIVALENT*
100 - 4.0	75 - 2.5	3.8 - 4.0	A (Superior Achievement)
99 - 4.0	74 - 2.4	3.5 - 3.7	A-
98 - 3.9	73 - 2.3	3.2 - 3.4	B+
97 - 3.9	77 - 2.2	2.9 - 3.1	B (Above Average)
96 - 3.8	71 - 2.1	2.6 - 2.8	B-
95 - 3.8	70 - 2.0	2.3 - 2.5	C+
94 - 3.7	69 - 1.9	2.0 - 2.2	C (Average Achievement)
93 - 3.7	68 - 1.8	1.6 - 1.9	C-
92 - 3.6	67 - 1.7	1.3 - 1.5	D+
91 - 3.6	66 - 1.6	1.0 - 1.2	D
90 - 3.5	65 - 1.5	0.7 - 0.9	D- (Minimum Achievement)
89 - 3.5	64 - 1.4	0.0 - 0.6	Failing
88 - 3.4	63 - 1.3		
87 - 3.4	62 - 1.2		
86 - 3.3	61 - 1.1		
85 - 3.3	60 - 1.0		
84 - 3..2	59 - .9		
83 - 3.2	58 - .8		
82 - 3.1	57 - .7		
81 - 3.1	56 - .6		
80 - 3.1	55 - .5		
79 - 2.9	54 - .4		
78 - 2.8	53 - .3		
77 - 2.7	52 - .2		
76 - 2.6	51 - .1		

Below .7 is considered failing by the Registrar's Office.

GRADING POLICY: The Community Colleges of Spokane grading system is consistent with the general philosophy of the college by providing a system which indicates a student's performance and achievement in a variety of skills and programs. The system provides for permanent record of grade evaluations that reflect in various ways, successful course and program completion. The colleges operate on a quarter system. The quarter hour of credit is the unit of instruction.

***NUMERIC GRADES: Grades at the community Colleges of Spokane are reported in numerical fractions to the nearest tenth. The numerical grades are based on the letter grade system used prior to the 1986-87 academic year.**

THE SCC STUDENT PROFILE PORTFOLIO

WHAT
THE PORTFOLIO!!! Designed by members of the SCC faculty, the portfolio is intended for graduates to use in a job interview.

WHY
JOBS!!! If a company has openings for five new employees, they will usually interview ten to fifteen people for the jobs. As an SCC graduate, you already have some pluses going for you–the reputation of the school, the quality of instruction you received, and the networking many of your instructors do in the professional/technical areas. **PLUS,** now you have one more point in your favor–**the portfolio.**

WHO
SCC STUDENTS!!! All students graduating from SCC should have a completed portfolio to take with them on job interviews or to the next school they plan on attending.

WHERE
IN THE PORTFOLIO!!! The sections of the portfolio that deal with responsibility, work ethic, attitude, problem solving, global awareness, and personal communications will be filled out as you near graduation. However, in the meantime, you can be setting aside documents that show what you can do and how well you can do it.

Throughout your SCC career, you will be completing assignments, entering competitions, and earning certificates or awards that will show what a valuable employee you will be.

Example:	VICA competition	Spring Fling car show
	building a gingerbread house	building a can crusher
	lab jobs	resumes
	letters of recommendation	media coverage

WHEN
START NOW!!! Without fail, the advisory boards for SCC professional/technical programs have stressed the need for written communication skills. With this in mind, it is suggested that you save the following:

feasibility report	values/ethics report	progress report
research/Internet report	lab report	incident report

all documents that demonstrate your written communication skills

HOW
WRITE IT AND SAVE IT!!! It goes without saying, you wouldn't collect something that shows you in a poor light. So remember, in this class, you always ask at least three other people to edit a document before you turn it in. That way, you'll produce technical documents showcasing your written communication skills.

Chapter 1

READING AND STUDYING: Maximizing Written Resources

The society you live in revolves around the written word. Although the growth of computer technology may seem to have made technical knowledge more important than reading, the focus on word processing and computer handling of documents has actually *increased* the need for employees who function at a high level of literacy. As the *Condition of Education 1996* report states, "In recent years, literacy has been viewed as one of the fundamental tools necessary for successful economic performance in industrialized societies. Literacy is no longer defined merely as a basic threshold of reading ability, but rather as the ability to understand and use printed information in daily activities, at home, at work, and in the community."[1]

Two crucial keys to your college success are reading and studying. If you read thoroughly and understand what you read, and if you achieve your study goals, you can improve your capacity to learn and understand. In this chapter you will learn how you can overcome barriers to successful reading and benefit from defining a purpose each time you read. You will explore the PQ3R study technique and see how critical reading can help you maximize your understanding of any text. Finally, the chapter will provide an overview of your library's resources.

WHAT ARE SOME CHALLENGES OF READING?

Whatever your skill level, you will encounter challenges that make reading more difficult, such as an excess of reading assignments, difficult texts, distractions, a lack of speed and comprehension, and insufficient vocabulary. Following are some ideas about how to meet these challenges. Note that if you have a reading disability, if English is not your primary language, or if you have limited reading skills, you may need additional support and guidance. Most colleges provide services for students through a reading center or tutoring program. Take the initiative to seek help if you need it. Many accomplished learners have benefited from help in specific areas.

Dealing With Reading Overload

Reading overload is part of almost every college experience. On a typical day, you may be faced with reading assignments that look like this:

An entire textbook chapter on the causes of the Civil War (American history).

An original research study on the stages of sleep (psychology).

Pages 1–50 in Arthur Miller's play *Death of a Salesman* (American literature).

Reading all this and more leaves little time for anything else unless you read selectively and skillfully. You can't control your reading load. You can, however, improve your reading skills. The material in this chapter will present techniques that can help you read and study as efficiently as you possibly can, while still having time left over for other things.

Working Through Difficult Texts

While many textbooks are useful teaching tools, some can be poorly written and organized. Students using texts that aren't well written may blame themselves for the difficulty they're experiencing. Because texts are often written with the purpose of challenging the intellect, even well-written and organized texts may be difficult and dense to read. Generally, the further you advance in your education, the more complex your required reading is likely to be. For example, your sociology professor may assign a chapter on the dynamics of social groups, including those of dyads and triads. When is the last time you heard the terms *dyads* and *triads* in normal conversation? You may feel at times as though you are reading a foreign language as you encounter new concepts, words, and terms.

Assignments can also be difficult when the required reading is from primary sources rather than from texts. *Primary sources* are original documents rather than another writer's interpretation of these documents. They include:

- historical documents
- works of literature (novels, poems, and plays)

- scientific studies, including lab reports and accounts of experiments
- journal articles

The academic writing found in journal articles and scientific studies is different from other kinds of writing. Some academic writers assume that readers understand sophisticated concepts. They may not define basic terms, provide background information, or supply a wealth of examples to support their ideas. As a result, concepts may be difficult to understand.

Making your way through poorly written or difficult reading material is hard work that can be accomplished through focus, motivation, commitment, and skill. The following strategies may help.

Approach your reading assignments head-on. Be careful not to prejudge them as impossible or boring before you even start to read.

Accept the fact that some texts may require some extra work and concentration. Set a goal to make your way through the material and learn, whatever it takes.

When a primary source discusses difficult concepts that it does not explain, put in some extra work to define such concepts on your own. Ask your instructor or other students for help. Consult reference materials in that particular subject area, other class materials, dictionaries, and encyclopedias. You may want to make this process more convenient by creating your own mini-library at home. Collect reference materials that you use often, such as a dictionary, a thesaurus, a writer's style handbook, and maybe an atlas or computer manual. You may also benefit from owning reference materials in your particular areas of study. "If you find yourself going to the library to look up the same reference again and again, consider purchasing that book for your personal or office library," advises library expert Sherwood Harris.[2]

> "No barrier of the senses shuts me out from the sweet, gracious discourse of my book friends. They talk to me without embarrassment or awkwardness."
>
> Helen Keller

Look for order and meaning in seemingly chaotic reading materials. The information you will find in this chapter on the PQ3R reading technique and on critical reading will help you discover patterns and achieve a greater depth of understanding. Finding order within chaos is an important skill, not just in the mastery of reading, but also in life. This skill can give you power by helping you "read" (think through) work dilemmas, personal problems, and educational situations.

Managing Distractions

With so much happening around you, it's often hard to keep your mind on what you are reading. Distractions take many forms. Some are external: the sound of a telephone, a friend who sits next to you at lunch and wants to talk, a young child who asks for help with homework. Other distractions come from within. As you try to study, you may be thinking about your parent's health, an argument you had with a friend or partner, a paper due in art History, or a site on the Internet that you want to visit.

REAL WORLD PERSPECTIVE

How can I cope with a learning disability?

Clacy Albert, Washington State University—Pullman, Washington, Communications Major

All my life I've felt different. I just couldn't seem to learn the way other kids did. I felt stupid and afraid that other people would think I couldn't do anything right. I wouldn't raise my hand in class because I was afraid of being laughed at. I wouldn't volunteer for games because I was afraid I'd let my team down. Study groups were impossible for me. I didn't want anyone to know that I was different. Because of this, my self-esteem really suffered. I became very quiet.

It wasn't until I was a sophomore in high school that a teacher recognized something was wrong with the way I learned. It was my math teacher who saw that I couldn't recognize certain patterns. I would see things in reverse or not be able to recognize a pattern at all. He sat down with my parents and helped them understand something was wrong. Unfortunately, the school I attended didn't have any testing for learning disabilities, so I let it go until I was in college. When I enrolled at WSU they told us about the learning disability resource center. My mom suggested I finally get the testing I needed. I'm glad I did, because now I know that I have dyslexia and need special assistance to handle my studies. I wish there was mandatory testing for this disability in grade school. If there had been I wouldn't have suffered so deeply all these years. What suggestions do you have for helping me cope with this disability?

Edith Hall, Senior Sales Representative—Prentice Hall

I have a different disability but one that causes similar problems. I have Attention Deficit Hyperactivity Disorder and the fact that it was undiagnosed and untreated for many years has caused lots of problems in my life. It wasn't until I was six years out of college that I was diagnosed ADHD. And the great thing about it is I don't feel crazy anymore. Now I know why I can't sit still for long periods and why I can't complete large and/or long projects like other non-ADHD people can.

I think acknowledging that I had a disorder and then accepting it were the biggest steps to coping and living with this disorder. The other thing I have done is to get educated. I have read almost anything I can get my hands on. I am also involved in a support group. Having other people I can talk with about how my brain affects my behavior and my life truly is one of the best coping strategies I know.

Having a disability or disorder is not a bad thing. Ennis Cosby, slain son of comedian Bill Cosby, said of his dyslexia, "The day I found out I had dyslexia was the best day of my life." Finding out he had dyslexia relieved him of the belief that he was dumb or stupid or slow. For me, like Ennis Cosby, finding out I had ADHD was a great day in my life because I now had tools and help to be different . . . and I no longer felt alone.

Identify the Distraction and Choose a Suitable Action

Pinpoint what's distracting you before you decide what kind of action to take. If the distraction is *external* and *out of your control*, such as construction outside your building or a noisy group in the library, try to move away from it. If the distraction is *external* but *within your control*, such as the television, telephone, or children, take action. For example, if the television or phone is a problem, turn off the TV or unplug the phone for an hour. Figure 5-1 explores some ways that parents or other people caring for children may be able to maximize their study efforts.

FIGURE 5-1

Managing Children While Studying

Explain what your education entails. Tell them how it will improve both your life and theirs. This applies, of course, to older children who can understand the situation and compare it to their own schooling.

Keep them up to date on your schedule. Let them know when you have a big test or project due and when you are under less pressure, and what they can expect of you in each case.

Keep them active while you study. Give them games, books, or toys to occupy them. If there are special activities that you like to limit, such as watching videos on TV, save them for your study time.

Find help. Ask a relative or friend to watch your children or arrange for a child to visit a friend's house. Consider trading baby sitting hours with another parent, hiring a sitter to come to your home, or using a day care center that is private or school-sponsored.

Offset study time with family time and rewards. Children may let you get your work done if they have something to look forward to, such as a movie night, a trip for ice cream, or something else they like.

Study on the phone. You might be able to have a study session with a fellow student over the phone while your child is sleeping or playing quietly.

Special Notes for Infants

- Study at night if your baby goes to sleep early, or in the morning if your baby sleeps late.
- Study during nap times if you aren't too tired yourself.
- Lay your notes out and recite information to the baby. The baby will appreciate the attention, and you will get work done.
- Put baby in a safe and fun place while you study, such as a playpen, motorized swing, or jumping seat.

If the distraction is *internal*, there are a few strategies to try that may help you clear your mind. You may want to take a break from your studying and tend to one of the issues that you are worrying about. Physical exercise may relax you and bring back your ability to focus. For some people, studying while listening to music helps to quiet a busy mind. For others, silence may do the trick. If you need silence to read or study and cannot find a truly quiet environment, consider purchasing sound-muffling headphones or even earplugs.

Find the Best Place and Time to Read

Any reader needs focus and discipline in order to concentrate on the material. Finding a place and time that minimize outside distractions will help you achieve that focus. Here are some suggestions:

Read alone unless you are working with other readers. Family members, friends, or others who are not in study mode may interrupt your concentration. If you prefer to read alone, establish a relatively interruption-proof place and time, such as an out-of-the-way spot at the library or an after-class hour in an empty classroom. If you study at home and live with other people, you may want to place a "Quiet" sign on the door. Some students benefit from reading with one or more other students. If this helps you, plan to schedule a group reading meeting where you read sections of the assigned material and then break to discuss them.

Find a comfortable location. Many students study in the library on a hard-backed chair. Others prefer a library easy chair, a chair in their room, or even the floor. The spot you choose should be comfortable enough for hours of reading, but not so comfortable that you fall asleep. Also, make sure that you have adequate lighting and aren't too hot or too cold.

Choose a regular reading place and time. Choose a spot or two you like and return to them often. Also, choose a time when your mind is alert and focused. Some students prefer to read just before or after the class for which the reading is assigned. Eventually, you will associate preferred places and times with focused reading.

If it helps you concentrate, listen to soothing background music. The right music can drown out background noises and relax you. However, the wrong music can make it impossible to concentrate; for some people, silence is better. Experiment to learn what you prefer; if music helps, stick with the type that works best. A personal headset makes listening possible no matter where you are.

Turn off the television. For most people, reading and TV don't mix.

Building Comprehension and Speed

Most students lead busy lives, carrying heavy academic loads while perhaps working a job or even caring for a family. It's difficult to make time to study at all, let alone handle the enormous reading assignments for your different classes. Increasing your reading comprehension and speed will save you valuable time and effort.

Rapid reading won't do you any good if you can't remember the material or answer questions about it. However, reading too slowly can be equally inefficient because it often eats up valuable study time and gives your mind space to wander. Your goal is to read for maximum speed *and* comprehension. Focus on comprehension first, because greater comprehension is the primary goal and also promotes greater speed.

Methods for Increasing Reading Comprehension

Following are some specific strategies for increasing your understanding of what you read:

Continually build your knowledge through reading and studying. More than any other factor, what you already know before you read a passage will determine your ability to understand and remember important ideas. Previous knowledge, including vocabulary, facts, and ideas, gives you a context for what you read.

Context, Written or spoken knowledge that can help to illuminate the meaning of a word or passage.

Establish your purpose for reading. When you establish what you want to get out of your reading, you will be able to determine what level of understanding you need to reach and, therefore, on what you need to focus.

Remove the barriers of negative self-talk. Instead of telling yourself that you cannot understand, think positively. Tell yourself: *I can learn this material. I am a good reader.*

Think critically. Ask yourself questions. Do you understand the sentence, paragraph, or chapter you just read? Are ideas and supporting examples clear to you? Could you clearly explain what you just read to someone else?

Methods for Increasing Reading Speed

The following suggestions will help increase your reading speed.

Try to read groups of words rather than single words.

Avoid pointing your finger to guide your reading, since this will slow your pace.

Try swinging your eyes from side to side as you read a passage, instead of stopping at various points to read individual words.

Source: CALVIN AND HOBBES ©1987 Bill Watterson. Dist. by UNIVERSAL PRESS SYNDICATE. All rights reserved.

Vocalization, The practice of speaking the words and/or moving your lips while reading.

- When reading narrow columns, focus your eyes in the middle of the column and read down the page. With practice, you'll be able to read the entire column width.
- Avoid vocalization when reading.
- Avoid thinking each word to yourself as you read it, a practice known as *subvocalization*. Subvocalization is one of the primary causes of slow reading speed.

Expanding Your Vocabulary

Lifelong learners consider their vocabulary a work in progress, because they never finish learning new words. A strong vocabulary increases reading speed and comprehension—when you understand the words in your reading material, you don't have to stop as often to think about what they mean. No matter how strong or weak your vocabulary is, you can improve it by using a dictionary, reading and writing words in context, and learning common prefixes and suffixes.

Use a Dictionary

When reading a textbook, the first "dictionary" to search is the text glossary. Textbooks often include an end-of-book glossary that explains technical words and concepts. The definitions there are usually limited to the meaning of the term as it is used in the text.

Standard dictionaries provide a broader treatment. They give you all kinds of information about each word, including its origin, pronunciation, part of speech, synonyms (words that are similar), antonyms (words with opposite meanings), and multiple meanings. By using a dictionary whenever you read, you will increase your general comprehension. Buy a standard dictionary and keep it nearby. Don't hesitate to make notations in it when you need to. Consult your dictionary when you need help understanding a passage that contains unfamiliar key words.

You may not always have time for the following suggestions, but when you can use them, they will make your dictionary use as productive as possible.

Read every meaning of a word, not just the first. Think critically about which meaning suits the context of the word in question and choose the one that makes the most sense to you.

Substitute a word or phrase from the definition for the word. Use the definition you have chosen. Imagine, for example, that you encounter the following sentence and do not know what the word *indoctrinated* means:

> The cult indoctrinated its members to reject society's values.

When you search the dictionary, you find several alternate definitions, including *brainwashed, instructed*, and *trained exhaustively*. You decide that the definition closest to the correct meaning is *brainwashed*. Substituting this term, the sentence reads:

> The cult brainwashed its members to reject society's values.

Keep a journal of every new word you learn, including definitions. Review the journal on a regular basis and watch your vocabulary grow.

Reading and Writing Words in Context

Most people learn words best when they read and use them in written or spoken language. Although reading a definition tells you what a word means, you may have difficulty remembering that definition because you have no former knowledge, or context, to which to connect or compare it. Using a word in context after defining it will help to anchor the information so that you can continue to build upon it.

Here are some strategies for using context to solidify your learning of new vocabulary words.

Use new words in a sentence or two right away. Do this immediately after reading their definitions, while everything is still fresh in your mind.

Reread the sentence where you originally saw the word. Go over it a few times to make sure that you understand how the word is used.

Use the word over the next few days whenever it may apply. Try it while talking with friends, writing letters or notes, or in your own thoughts.

Consider where you may have seen or heard the word before. When you learn a word, going back to sentences you previously didn't understand may help you to broaden your understanding of its meaning. For example, when most children learn the Pledge of Allegiance, they memorize the words by rote without understanding exactly what "allegiance" means. Later, when they learn the definition of "allegiance," the pledge provides a context for the word that helps them understand it more fully.

Seek knowledgeable advice. If after looking up a word you still have trouble with its meaning, ask your instructor or a friend if they can help you figure it out.

If you keep a vocabulary journal, include sentences that place the word in context. Write sentences near the word's definition.

Root,
The central part or basis of a word, around which prefixes and/or suffixes can be added to produce different words.

Learn Prefixes and Suffixes

Often, if you understand part of a word, you will be able to figure out what the entire word means. Particularly helpful is a working knowledge of common prefixes and suffixes. *Prefixes* are word parts that are added to the beginning of a root, while *suffixes* are added to the end of the root. Table 5.1, on page 170, contains prefixes and suffixes you may encounter.

Facing the challenges of reading is only the first step. The next important step is to examine why you are reading any given piece of material.

WHY DEFINE YOUR PURPOSE FOR READING?

As with all other aspects of your education, asking important questions will enable you to make the most of your efforts. When you define your purpose, you ask yourself *why* you are reading a particular piece of material. One way to do this is by completing this sentence: "In reading this material,

TABLE 5.1 COMMON PREFIXES AND SUFFIXES

PREFIX	PRIMARY MEANING	EXAMPLE
a, ab	from, away	abstain, avert
ad, af, at	to	adhere, affix, attain
con, cor, com	with, together	convene, correlate, compare
di	apart	divert, divorce
il	not	illegal, illegible
ir	not	irresponsible
post	after	postpone, post-partum
sub, sup	under	subordinate, suppose

SUFFIX	PRIMARY MEANING	EXAMPLE
-able	able	recyclable
-arium	place for	aquarium, solarium
-cule	very small	molecule
-ist	one who	pianist
-meter	measure	thermometer
-ness	state of	carelessness
-sis	condition of	hypnosis
-y	inclined to	sleepy

I intend to define/learn/answer/achieve . . . " With a clear purpose in mind, you can decide how much time and what kind of effort to expend on various reading assignments. Nearly 375 years ago, Francis Bacon, the English philosopher, recognized that . . .

> Some books are to be tasted, others to be swallowed, and some few to be chewed and digested; that is, some books are to be read only in parts, others to be read but not curiously; and some few to be read wholly, and with diligence and attention.

Achieving your reading purpose requires adapting to different types of reading materials. Being a flexible reader—adjusting your reading strategies and pace—will help you to adapt successfully.

Purpose Determines Reading Strategy

With purpose comes direction; with direction comes a strategy for reading. Following are four reading purposes, examined briefly. You may have one or more for each piece of reading material you approach.

Purpose 1: Read to Evaluate Critically. Critical evaluation involves approaching the material with an open mind, examining causes and effects, evaluating ideas, and asking questions that test the strength of the writer's argument and that try to identify assumptions. Critical reading is essential for you to demonstrate an understanding of material that goes beyond basic recall of information. You will read more about critical reading later in the chapter.

Purpose 2: Read for Comprehension. Much of the studying you do involves reading for the purpose of comprehending the material. The two main components of comprehension are *general ideas* and *specific facts/examples*. These components depend on one another. Facts and examples help to explain or support ideas, and ideas provide a framework that helps the reader to remember facts and examples.

General Ideas. General-idea reading is rapid reading that seeks an overview of the material. You may skip entire sections as you focus on headings, subheadings, and summary statements in search of general ideas.

Specific Facts/Examples. At times, readers may focus on locating specific pieces of information—for example, the stages of intellectual development in young children. Often, a reader may search for examples that support or explain more general ideas—for example, the causes of economic recession. Because you know exactly what you are looking for, you can skim the material at a rapid rate. Reading your texts for specific information may help before taking a test.

> "In books, I could travel anywhere, be anybody, understand worlds long past and imaginary colonies in the future."
>
> Rita Dove

Purpose 3: Read for Practical Application. A third purpose for reading is to gather usable information which you can apply toward a specific goal. When you read a computer software manual, an instruction sheet for assembling a gas grill, or a cookbook recipe, your goal is to learn how to do something. Reading and action usually go hand in hand.

Purpose 4: Read for Pleasure. Some materials you read for entertainment, such as *Sports Illustrated* magazine or the latest John Grisham courtroom thriller. Entertaining reading may also go beyond materials that seem obviously designed to entertain. Whereas some people may read a Jane Austen novel for comprehension, as in a class assignment, others may read Austen books for pleasure.

Purpose Determines Pace

George M. Usova, senior education specialist and graduate professor at The Johns Hopkins University, explains: "Good readers are flexible readers. They read at a variety of rates and adapt them to the reading *purpose* at hand, the *difficulty* of the material, and their *familiarity* with the subject area."[3] As Table 5.2 shows, good readers link the pace of reading to their reading purpose.

TABLE 5.2 LINKING PURPOSE TO PACE

TYPE OF MATERIAL	READING PURPOSE	PACE
ACADEMIC READINGS • textbooks • original sources • articles from scholarly journals • on-line publications for academic readers • lab reports • required fiction	• Critical analysis • Overall mastery • Preparation for tests	• Slow, especially if the material is new and unfamiliar
MANUALS • instructions • recipes	• Practical application	• Slow to medium
JOURNALISM AND NONFICTION FOR THE GENERAL READER • nonfiction books • newspapers • magazines • on-line publications for the general public	• Understanding of general ideas, key concepts, and specific facts for personal understanding and/or practical application	• Medium to fast
NONREQUIRED FICTION	• Understanding of general ideas, key concepts, and specific facts for enjoyment	• Variable, but tending toward the faster speeds

Source: Adapted from Nicholas Reid Schaffzin, *The Princeton Review Reading Smart.* New York: Random House, 1996, p. 15.

So far, this chapter has focused on reading. Recognizing obstacles to effective reading and defining the various purposes for reading lay the groundwork for effective *studying*—the process of mastering the concepts and skills contained in your texts.

How Can PQ3R Help You Study Reading Materials?

When you study, you take ownership of the material you read. You learn it well enough to apply it to what you do. For example, by the time students studying to be computer-hardware technicians complete their coursework, they should be able to assemble various machines and analyze hardware problems that lead to malfunctions.

Studying also gives you mastery over *concepts*. For example, a dental hygiene student learns the causes of gum disease, a biology student learns what happens during photosynthesis, and a business student learns about marketing research.

This section will focus on a technique that will help you learn and study more effectively as you read your college textbooks.

PREVIEW-QUESTION-READ-RECITE-REVIEW (PQ3R)

PQ3R is a technique that will help you grasp ideas quickly, remember more, and review effectively and efficiently for tests. The symbols P-Q-3-R stand for *preview, question, read, recite,* and *review* — all steps in the studying process. Developed more than 55 years ago by Francis Robinson, the technique is still being used today because it works.[4] It is particularly helpful for studying texts. When reading literature, read the work once from beginning to end to appreciate the story and language. Then, reread it using PQ3R to master the material.

Moving through the stages of PQ3R requires that you know how to skim and scan. Skimming involves rapid reading of various chapter elements, including introductions, conclusions, and summaries; the first and last lines of paragraphs; boldface or italicized terms; pictures, charts, and diagrams. In contrast, scanning involves the careful search for specific facts and examples. You will probably use scanning during the *review* phase of PQ3R when you need to locate and remind yourself of particular information. In a chemistry text, for example, you may scan for examples of how to apply a particular formula.

Skimming, Rapid, superficial reading of material that involves glancing through to determine central ideas and main elements.

Scanning, Reading material in an investigative way, searching for specific information.

Preview P

The best way to ruin a "whodunit" novel is to flip through the pages to find out how everything turned out. However, when reading textbooks, previewing can help you learn and is encouraged. *Previewing* refers to the process of surveying, or pre-reading, a book before you actually study it. Most textbooks include devices that give students an overview of the text as a whole as well as of the contents of individual chapters. As you look at Figure 5-2, on the following page, think about how many of these devices you already use.

Question Q

Your next step is to examine the chapter headings and, on your own paper, write questions linked to those headings. These questions will focus your attention and increase your interest, helping you relate new ideas to what you already know and building your comprehension. You can take questions from the textbook or from your lecture notes, or come up with them on your own when you preview, based on what ideas you think are most important.

FIGURE 5-2 TEXT AND CHAPTER PREVIEWING DEVICES

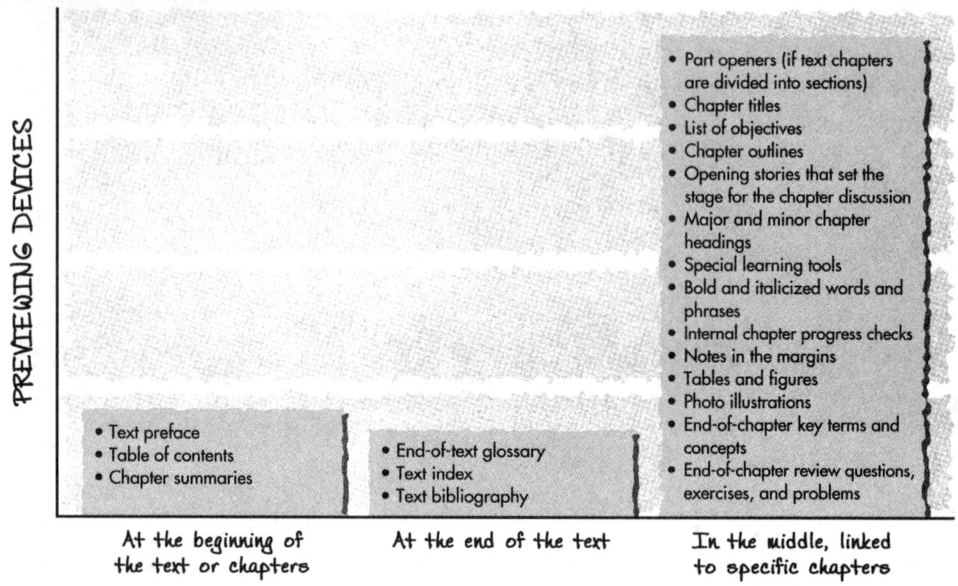

I. THE CONSUMER BUYING PROCESS	I. WHAT IS THE CONSUMER BUYING PROCESS?
A. Problem/Need Recognition	A. Why must consumers first recognize a problem or need before they buy a product?
B. Information Seeking	B. What is information seeking and who answers consumers questions?
C. Evaluation of Alternatives	C. How do consumers evaluate different products to narrow their choices?
D. Purchase Decision	D. Are purchasing decisions simple or complex?
E. Postpurchase Evaluations	E. What happens after the sale?

Here is how this technique works. The column on the left contains primary- and secondary-level headings from a section of *Business*, an introductory text by Ricky W. Griffin and Ronald J. Ebert. The column on the right rephrases these headings in question form.

There is no "correct" set of questions. Given the same headings, you would create your own particular set of questions. The more useful kinds of questions are ones that engage the critical-thinking mind actions and processes found in Chapter 4.

Read *R*

Your questions give you a starting point for *reading,* the first *R* in PQ3R. Read the material with the purpose of answering each question you raised. Pay special attention to the first and last lines of every paragraph, which should tell you what the paragraph is about. As you read, record key words, phrases, and concepts in your notebook. Some students divide the notebook into two columns, writing questions on the left and answers on the right. This method, known as the Cornell note-taking system, is described in more detail in Chapter 6.

If you own the textbook, marking it up — in whatever ways you prefer — is a must. The notations that you make will help you to interact with the material and make sense of it. You may want to write notes in the margins, circle key ideas, or highlight key sections. Some people prefer to underline, although underlining adds more ink to the lines of text and may overwhelm your eye. Although writing in a textbook makes it difficult to sell it back to the bookstore, the increased depth of understanding you can gain is worth the investment.

Highlighting may help you pinpoint material to review before an exam. Here are some additional tips on highlighting:

Get in the habit of marking the text *after* you read the material. If you do it while you are reading, you may wind up marking less important passages.

Highlight key terms and concepts. Mark the examples that explain and support important ideas. You might try highlighting ideas in one color and examples in another.

Highlight figures and tables. They are especially important if they summarize text concepts.

Avoid overmarking. A phrase or two is enough in most paragraphs. Set off long passages with brackets rather than marking every line.

Write notes in the margins with a pen or pencil. Comments like "main point" and "important definition" will help you find key sections later on.

Be careful not to mistake highlighting for learning. You will not necessarily learn what you highlight unless you review it carefully. You may benefit from writing the important information you have highlighted into your lecture notes.

One final step in the reading phase is to divide your reading into digestible segments. Many students read from one topic heading to the next, then stop. Pace your reading so that you understand as you go. If you find you are losing the thread of the ideas you are reading, you may want to try smaller segments, or you may need to take a break and come back to it later.

Recite *R*

Once you finish reading a topic, stop and answer the questions you raised about it in the *Q* stage of PQ3R. You may decide to recite each answer aloud, silently speak the answers to yourself, tell the answers to another person as though you were teaching him or her, or write your ideas and answers in brief notes. Writing is often the most effective way to solidify what you have read. Use whatever techniques best suit your learning-style profile (see Chapter 2).

After you finish one section, move on to the next. Then repeat the question-read-recite cycle until you complete the entire chapter. If during this process you find yourself fumbling for thoughts, it means that you do not yet "own" the ideas. Reread the section that's giving you trouble until you master its contents. Understanding each section as you go is crucial because the material in one section often forms a foundation for the next.

Review *R*

Review soon after you finish a chapter. Here are some techniques for reviewing.

- Skim and reread your notes. Then try summarizing them from memory.
- Answer the text's end-of-chapter review, discussion, and application questions.
- Quiz yourself, using the questions you raised in the *Q* stage. If you can't answer one of your own or one of the text's questions, go back and scan the material for answers.
- Review and summarize in writing the sections and phrases you have highlighted.
- Create a chapter outline in standard outline form or think-link form.
- Reread the preface, headings, tables, and summary.
- Recite important concepts to yourself, or record important information on a cassette tape and play it on your car's tape deck or your Walkman.
- Make flashcards that have an idea or word on one side and examples, a definition, or other related information on the other. Test yourself.
- Think critically: Break ideas down into examples, consider similar or different concepts, recall important terms, evaluate ideas, and explore causes and effects.
- Make think links that show how important concepts relate to one another.

Remember that you can ask your instructor if you need help clarifying your reading material. Your instructor is an important resource. Pinpoint

FIGURE 5-3 STUDY GROUP TECHNIQUES

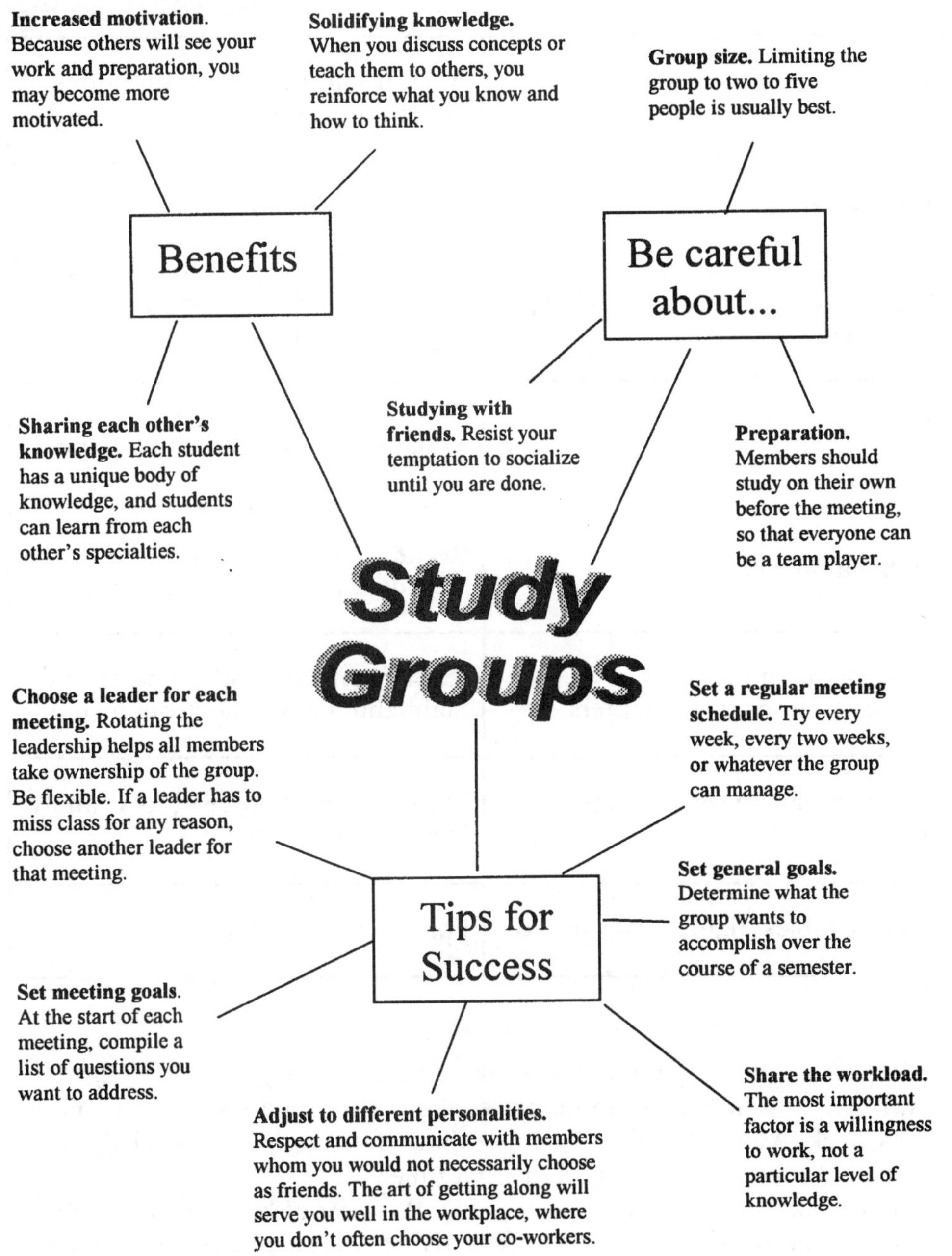

the material you want to discuss, schedule a meeting with him or her during office hours, and come prepared with a list of questions. You may also want to ask what materials to focus on when you study for tests.

If possible, you should review both alone and with study groups. Reviewing in as many different ways as possible increases the likelihood of retention. Figure 5-3 shows some techniques that will help a study group maximize its time and efforts.

TABLE 5-3 USE PQ3R TO BECOME AN ACTIVE READER

ACTIVE READERS TEND TO . . .

Divide material into manageable sections	Answer end-of-chapter questions and applications
Write questions	Create chapter outlines
Answer questions through focused note-taking	Create think links that map concepts in a logical way
Recite, verbally and in writing, the answers to questions	Make flashcards and study them
Highlight key concepts	Recite what they learned into a tape recorder and play the tape back
Focus on main ideas found in paragraphs, sections, and chapters	Rewrite and summarize notes and highlighted materials from memory
Recognize summary and support devices	Explain what they read to a family member or friend
Analyze tables, figures, and photos	Form a study group

Repeating the review process renews and solidifies your knowledge. That is why it is important to set up regular review sessions — for example, once a week. As you review, remember that refreshing your knowledge is easier and faster than learning it the first time.

As you can see in Table 5-3, using PQ3R is part of being an active reader. Active reading involves the specific activities that help you retain what you learn.

Putting PQ3R to Work

The following is an excerpt from *Principles of Microeconomics* by Karl E. Case and Ray C. Fair. Apply the PQ3R technique as you read it. Think through the major points of the passage and use the margins and/or the space provided on page 180 to make any notes, comments, or questions.

FIRMS AND HOUSEHOLDS: THE BASIC DECISION-MAKING UNITS

firm *An organization that transforms resources (inputs) into products (outputs). Firms are the primary producing units in a market economy.*

Throughout this book, we discuss and analyze the behavior of two fundamental decision-making units: *firms*—the primary producing units in an economy—and *households*—the consuming units in an economy. Both are made up of people performing different functions and playing different roles. In essence, then, what we are developing is a theory of human behavior.

A **firm** exists when a person or a group of people decides to reproduce a product or products by transforming *inputs* (that is, resources in the broadest sense) into *outputs* (the products that are sold in the market). Some firms produce goods; others produce services. Some are large, some are small, and some are in between. But all firms exist to transform resources into things that people want. The Colorado Symphony Orchestra takes labor, land, a building, musically talented people, electricity, and other inputs and combines them to produce concerts. The production process can be extremely complicated. The first flutist in the orchestra, for example, uses training, talent, previous performing experience, a score, an instrument, the conductor's interpretation, and her own feelings about the music to produce just one contribution to an overall performance.

Most firms exist to make a profit for their owners, but some do not. Columbia University, for example, fits the description of a firm: It takes inputs in the form of labor, land, skills, books, and buildings and produces a service that we call education. Although it sells that service for a price, it does not exist to make a profit, but rather to provide education of the highest quality possible.

Still, most firms exist to make a profit. They engage in production because they can sell their product for more than it costs to produce it. The analysis of firm behavior that follows rests on the assumption that *firms make decisions in order to maximize profits.*

entrepreneur *A person who organizes, manages, and assumes the risks of a firm, taking a new idea or a new product and turning it into a successful business.*

An **entrepreneur** is one who organizes, manages, and assumes the risks of a firm. It is the entrepreneur who takes a new idea or a new product and turns it into a successful business. All firms have implicit in them some element of entrepreneurship. When a new firm is created—whether a proprietorship, a partnership, or a corporation—someone must organize the new firm, arrange financing, hire employees, and take risks. That person is an entrepreneur. Sometimes existing companies introduce new products, and sometimes new firms develop or improve an old idea, but at the root of it all is entrepreneurship, which some see as the core of the free enterprise system.

At the root of the debate about the potential of free enterprise in formerly socialist Eastern Europe is the question of entrepreneurship. Does an entrepreneurial spirit exist in that part of the world? If not, can it be developed? Without it the free enterprise system breaks down.

households *The consuming units in an economy.*

The consuming units in an economy are **households.** A household may consist of any number of people: a single person living alone, a married couple living with four children, or 15 unrelated people sharing a house. Household decisions are presumably based on the individual tastes and preferences of the consuming unit. The household buys what it wants and can afford. In a large, heterogeneous, and open society such as the United States, wildly different tastes find expression in the marketplace. A six-block walk in any direction on any street in Manhattan or a drive from the Chicago loop south into rural Illinois should be enough to convince anyone that it is difficult to generalize about what people like and do not like.

Even though households have wide-ranging preferences, they also have some things in common. All—even the very rich—have ultimately limited incomes, and all must pay in some way for the things they consume. While households may have some control over their incomes—they can work more or less—they are also constrained by the availability of jobs, current wages, their own abilities, and their accumulated and inherited wealth (or lack thereof).

After reading the excerpt using PQ3R, answer the following questions. Try not to look back at the material. Instead, examine whether the PQ3R system helped you remember the key points of the passage.

1. What are the two decision-making units called?

2. Most firms exist to make a profit. True or false?

3. Someone who organizes, manages, and assumes risks is called a(n):

4. A household:
   a. is the consuming unit in an economy.
   b. may consist of any number of people.
   c. has ultimately limited incomes.
   d. is constrained by the availability of jobs.
   e. all of the above.

HOW CAN YOU READ CRITICALLY?

Your textbooks will often contain features that highlight important ideas and help you determine questions to ask while reading. As you advance in your education, however, many reading assignments will not be so clearly marked, especially if they are primary sources. You will need critical-reading skills in order to select the important ideas, identify examples that support them, and ask questions about the text without the aid of any special features or tools.

Critical reading enables you to consider reading material carefully, developing a thorough understanding of it through evaluation and analysis. A critical reader is able to discern what in a piece of reading material is true or useful, such as when using material as a source for an essay. A critical reader can also compare one piece of material to another and evaluate which makes more sense, which proves its thesis more successfully, or which is more useful for the reader's purpose.

Critical reading is reading that transcends taking in and regurgitating material. You can read critically by using PQ3R to get a basic idea of the material, asking questions based on the critical-thinking mind actions, and engaging your critical-thinking processes.

Use PQ3R to "Taste" Reading Material

Sylvan Barnet and Hugo Bedau, authors of *Critical Thinking, Reading, and Writing—A Brief Guide to Argument*, suggest that the active reading of PQ3R will help you form an initial idea of what a piece of reading material is all about. Through previewing, skimming for ideas and examples, highlighting and writing comments and questions in the margins, and reviewing, you can develop a basic understanding of its central ideas and contents.[6]

Summarizing, part of the review process in PQ3R, is one of the best ways to develop an understanding of a piece of reading material. To construct a summary, focus on the central ideas of the piece and the main examples that support those ideas. A summary does *not* contain any of your own ideas or your evaluation of the material. It simply condenses the material, making it easier for you to focus on the structure of the piece and its central ideas when you go back to read more critically. At that point, you can begin to evaluate the piece and introduce your own ideas. Using the mind actions will help you.

Summary,
A concise restatement of the material, in your own words, that covers the main points.

Ask Questions Based on the Mind Actions

The essence of critical reading, as with critical thinking, is asking questions. Instead of simply accepting what you read, seek a more thorough understanding by questioning the material as you go along. Using the mind actions of the Thinktrix to formulate your questions will help you understand the material.

What parts of the material you focus on will depend on your purpose for reading. For example, if you are writing a paper on the causes of World War II, you might spend your time focusing on how certain causes fit your thesis. If you are comparing two pieces of writing that contain opposing arguments, you may focus on picking out their central ideas and evaluating how well the writers use examples to support these ideas.

You can question any of the following components of reading material:

- The central idea of the entire piece
- A particular idea or statement
- The examples that support an idea or statement
- The proof of a fact
- The definition of a concept

Following are some ways to critically question your reading material, based on the mind actions. Apply them to any component you want to question by substituting the component for the words "it" and "this."

<u>Similarity:</u> What does this remind me of, or how is it similar to something else I know?

<u>Difference:</u> What different conclusions are possible?
How is this different from my experience?

<u>Cause and Effect:</u> Why did this happen, or what caused this?
What are the effects or consequences of this?
What effect does the author want to have, or what is the purpose of this material?
What effects support a stated cause?

<u>Example to Idea:</u> How would I classify this, or, what is the best idea to fit this example(s)?
How would I summarize this, or what are the key ideas?
What is the thesis or central idea?

<u>Idea to Example:</u> What evidence supports this, or what examples fit this idea?

<u>Evaluation:</u> How would I evaluate this? Is it valid or pertinent?
Does this example support my thesis or central idea?

Engage Critical-Thinking Processes

Certain thinking processes from Chapter 4 can help to deepen your analysis and evaluation of what you read. These processes are establishing truth, constructing an argument, and shifting perspective. Within these processes you will ask questions that use the mind actions.

Establishing Truth

With what you know about how to seek truth, you can evaluate any statement in your reading material, identifying it as fact, opinion, or assumption and challenging how it is supported. Evaluate statements, central ideas, or entire pieces of reading material using questions such as the following:

- Is this true? How does the writer know?
- How could I test the validity of this?
- What assumptions underlie this?
- What else do I know that is similar to or different from this?
- What information that I already know supports or disproves this?
- What examples disprove this as fact or do not fit this assumption?

For example, imagine that a piece of writing states, "The dissolving of the family unit is the main cause of society's ills." You may question the truth of this statement by looking at what facts and examples support it. You may question the writer's sources of information. You may investigate its truth by reading other materials. You could discern that some hidden assumptions underlie this statement, such as an assumed definition of what a family is or of what constitutes "society's ills." You could also find examples that do not fit this assumption, such as successful families that don't fit the definition of "family" used by the writer.

Constructing an Argument

When your reading material contains one or more arguments, you can use what you know about arguments to evaluate whether the writer has constructed his or her argument effectively. Ask questions like the following:

- What is the purpose of the writer's argument?
- Do I believe this? How is the writer trying to persuade me?
- If the author uses cause-and-effect reasoning, does it seem logical?
- Do the examples adequately support the central idea of the argument?
- What different and perhaps opposing arguments seem just as valid?
- If I'm not sure whether I believe this, how could I construct an opposing argument?

Don't rule out the possibility that you may agree wholeheartedly with an argument. However, use critical thinking to make an informed decision, rather than accepting it outright.

Shifting Perspective

Your understanding of perspective will help you understand that many reading materials are written from a particular perspective. Perspective often has a strong effect on how the material is presented. For example, if a recording artist and a music censorship advocate were to each write a piece about a controversial song created by that artist, their different perspectives would result in two very different pieces of writing.

To analyze perspective, ask questions like the following:

What perspective is guiding this? What are the underlying ideas that influence this material?

Who wrote this, and what may be the author's perspective? For example, a piece on a new drug written by an employee of the drug manufacturer may differ from a doctor's evaluation of the drug.

What does the title of the material tell me about its perspective? For example, a piece entitled "New Therapies for Diabetes" may be more informational, and "What's Wrong With Insulin Injections" may intend to be persuasive.

How does the material's source affect its perspective? For example, an article on health management organizations (HMOs) published in an HMO newsletter may be more favorable and one-sided than one published in *The New York Times*.

Seek Understanding

Reading critically allows you to investigate what you read so that you can reach the highest possible level of understanding. Think of your reading process as an archaeological dig. The first step is to excavate a site and uncover the artifacts. In reading, that corresponds to your initial preview and reading of the material. As important as the excavation is, the process would be incomplete if you stopped there and just took home a bunch of items covered in dirt. The second half of the process is to investigate each item, evaluate what all of those items mean, and to derive new knowledge and ideas from what you discover. Critical reading allows you to complete that crucial second half of the process.

As you work through all of the different requirements of critical reading, remember that critical reading takes *time* and *focus*. Finding a time, place, and purpose for reading, covered earlier in the chapter, is crucial to successful critical reading. Give yourself a chance to gain as much as possible from what you read.

No matter where or how you prefer to study, your school's library (or libraries) can provide many useful services to help you make the most of classes, reading, studying, and assignments.

WHAT DOES YOUR LIBRARY OFFER?

> "With one day's reading a man may have the key in his hands."
>
> Ezra Pound

Your library can help you search for all kinds of information. First, learn about your library, its resources, and its layout. While some schools have only one library, other schools have a library network that includes one or more central libraries and smaller, specialized libraries that focus on specific academic areas. Take advantage of library tours, training sessions, and descriptive pamphlets. Spend time walking around the library on your own. If you still have questions, ask a librarian. A simple question can save hours of searching. The following sections will help you understand how your library operates.

General Reference Works

General reference works give you an overview and lead you to more specific information. These works cover topics in a broad, nondetailed way. General reference guides are found in the front of most libraries and are often available on CD-ROM, a compact disk that contains millions of words and images. You access this information by inserting the disk into a specially designed computer. Among the works that fall into this category are:

- encyclopedias—for example, the multivolume *Encyclopedia Britannica*
- almanacs—*The World Almanac and Book of Facts*

- dictionaries—*Webster's New World College Dictionary*
- biographical reference works—*Webster's Biographical Dictionary*
- bibliographies—*Books in Print*

Specialized Reference Works

Look at *specialized reference works* to find more specific facts. Specialized reference works include encyclopedias and dictionaries that focus on a narrow field. The short summaries you will find there focus on critical ideas. Bibliographies that accompany the articles point you to the names and works of recognized experts. Examples of specialized references include the *International Encyclopedia of Film*, the *Encyclopedia of Computer Science and Technology*, and the *Dictionary of Education*.

Library Book Catalog

Found near the front of the library, the *book catalog* lists every book the library owns. The listings usually appear in three separate categories: authors' names, book titles, and subjects. Not too long ago, most libraries stored their book catalog on index-sized cards in hundreds of small drawers. Today, many libraries have replaced these cards with computers. Using a terminal that has access to the library's computer records, you can search by specific author, title, and subject.

The computerized catalog in your college library is probably connected to the holdings of other college and university libraries. This gives you an on-line search capacity, which means that if you don't find the book you want in your local library, you can track it down in another library and request it through an interlibrary loan. *Interlibrary loan* is a system used by many colleges to allow students to borrow materials from a library other than the one at their school. Students request materials through their own library, where the materials are eventually delivered by the outside library. When you are in a rush, keep in mind that interlibrary loan may take a substantial amount of time.

Periodical Indexes

Periodicals are magazines, journals, and newspapers which are published on a regular basis throughout the year. Examples include *Time, Business Week*, and *Science*. Many libraries display periodicals that are a year or two old and convert older copies to microfilm or microfiche (photocopies of materials reduced greatly in size and printed on film readable in a special reading machine—*microfilm* is a strip of film, and *microfiche* refers to individual leaves of film). Finding articles in publications involves a search of periodical indexes. The most widely used general index is the *Reader's Guide to Periodical Literature*, which is available on CD-ROM and in book form. The *Reader's Guide* indexes articles in more than 100 general-interest magazines and journals.

Electronic Research

You will also find complete source material through a variety of electronic sources, including the Internet, on-line services, and CD-ROM. Here is a sampling of the kind of information you will find:

- complete articles from thousands of journals and magazines
- complete articles from newspapers around the world
- government data on topics as varied as agriculture, transportation, and labor
- business documents, including corporate annual reports

Your library is probably connected to the *Internet*, a worldwide computer network that links government, university, research, and business computers along the Information Superhighway. Tapping into the *World Wide Web*—a tool for searching the huge libraries of information stored on the Internet—gives you access to billions of written words and graphic images. The Internet is so vast that this book contains an Internet Research Appendix to help you explore it. After reading this Appendix, you will have many tools to aid you on your journeys along the Information Superhighway. If your college has its own Internet home page, start by spending some time browsing through it.

Although most libraries do not charge a fee to access the Internet, they may charge when you connect to commercial on-line services, including Nexis, CompuServe, and Prodigy. Ask your librarian about all fees and restrictions. Libraries also have electronic databases on CD-ROM. A database is a collection of data—or, in the case of most libraries, a list of related resources that all focus on one specific subject area—arranged so that you can search through it and retrieve specific items easily. For example, the DIALOG Information System includes hundreds of small databases in specialized areas. CD-ROM databases are generally smaller than on-line databases and are updated less frequently. However, there is never a user's fee.

читать

This word may look completely unfamiliar to you, but anyone who can read the Russian language and alphabet will know that it means "read." People who read languages that use different kinds of characters, such as Russian, Japanese, or Greek, learn to process those characters as easily as you process the letters of your native alphabet. Your mind learns to process individually each letter or character you see. This ability enables you to move to the next level of understanding—making sense of those letters or characters when they are grouped to form words, phrases, and sentences.

Think of this concept when you read. Remember that your mind is an incredible tool, processing unmeasurable amounts of information so that you can understand the concepts on the page. Give it the best opportunity to succeed by reading as often as you can and by focusing on all of the elements that help you read to the best of your ability.

Applications

Name Date

Key Into Your Life: Opportunities to Apply What You Learn

Exercise 1: Studying a Text Page

The following page is from the Groups and Organizations chapter in the sixth edition of John J. Macionis's *Sociology*, a Prentice Hall text.[7] Using what you learned in this chapter about study techniques, complete the questions on page 188:

SOCIAL GROUPS

Virtually everyone moves through life with a sense of belonging; this is the experience of group life. A **social group** refers to *two or more people who identify and interact with one another.* Human beings continually come together to form couples, families, circles of friends, neighborhoods, churches, businesses, clubs, and numerous large organizations. Whatever the form, groups encompass people with shared experiences, loyalties, and interests. In short, while maintaining their individuality, the members of social groups also think of themselves as a special "we."

Groups, Categories, and Crowds

People often use the term "group" imprecisely. We now distinguish the group from the similar concepts of category and crowd.

Category

A *category* refers to people who have some status in common. Women, single fathers, military recruits, homeowners, and Roman Catholics are all examples of categories.

Why are categories not considered groups? Simply because, while the individuals involved are aware that they are not the only ones to hold that particular status, the vast majority are strangers to one another.

Crowd

A *crowd* refers to a temporary cluster of individuals who may or may not interact at all. Students sitting together in a lecture hall do engage one another and share some common identity as college classmates; thus, such a crowd might be called a loosely formed group. By contrast, riders hurtling along on a subway train or bathers enjoying a summer day at the beach pay little attention to one another and amount to an anonymous aggregate of people. In general, then, crowds are too transitory and too impersonal to qualify as social groups.

The right circumstances, however, could turn a crowd into a group. People riding in a subway train that crashes under the city streets generally become keenly aware of their common plight and begin to help each other. Sometimes such extraordinary experiences become the basis for lasting relationships.

Primary and Secondary Groups

Acquaintances commonly greet one another with a smile and the simple phrase "Hi! How are you?" The response is usually a well-scripted "Just fine, thanks. How about you?" This answer, of course, is often more formal than truthful. In most cases, providing a detailed account of how you are *really* doing would prompt the other person to beat a hasty and awkward exit.

Sociologists classify social groups by measuring them against two ideal types based on members' level of genuine personal concern. This variation is the key to distinguishing *primary* from *secondary* groups.

According to Charles Horton Cooley (1864–1929), who is introduced in the box, a **primary group** is *a small social group whose members share personal and enduring relationships.* Bound together by *primary relationships,* individuals in primary groups typically spend a great deal of time together, engage in a wide range of common activities, and feel that they know one another well. Although not without periodic conflict, members of primary groups display sincere concern for each other's welfare. The family is every society's most important primary group.

Cooley characterized these personal and tightly integrated groups as *primary* because they are among the first groups we experience in life. In addition, the family and early play groups also hold primary importance in the socialization process, shaping attitudes, behavior, and social identity.

Source: Sociology, 6/E by John J. Macionis, ©1997. Reprinted by permission of Prentice-Hall, Inc., Upper Saddle River, NJ.

1. Identify the headings on the page and the relationship among them. Which headings are primary-level headings; which are secondary; which are tertiary (third-level heads)? Which heading serves as an umbrella for the rest?

2. What do the headings tell you about the content of the page?

3. Identify the boldfaced and italicized terms. How do boldfaced terms differ from italicized terms?

4. After reading the chapter headings, write three study questions. List the questions below:

5. Using a marker pen, highlight key phrases and sentences. Write short marginal notes to help you review the material at a later point.

6. After reading this page, list four key concepts that you will need to study:

a.

b.

c.

d.

Exercise 2: Building Your Vocabulary

Look again at the textbook page you just worked with. Are there any words that are new to you? If so, write them below and look them up in the dictionary. Write the definition next to the word and then include the word in your own sentence. If there are no unfamiliar words in this page, choose three words from any reading assignment you have this week.

1.

2.

3.

Exercise 3: Focusing on Your Purpose for Reading

Read the following paragraphs on kinetic and potential energy and the first law of thermodynamics taken from *Life On Earth* by Teresa Audesirk and Gerald Audesirk. When you have finished, answer the questions below.

Among the fundamental characteristics of all living organisms is the ability to guide chemical reactions within their bodies along certain pathways. The chemical reactions serve many functions, depending on the nature of the organism: to synthesize the molecules that make up the organism's body, to reproduce, to move, even to think. Chemical reactions either require or release **energy**, which can be defined simply as *the capacity to do work*, including synthesizing molecules, moving things around, and generating heat and light. In this chapter we discuss the physical laws that govern energy flow in the universe, how energy flow in turn governs chemical reactions, and how the chemical reactions within living cells are controlled by the molecules of the cell itself. Chapters 7 and 8 focus on photosynthesis, the chief "port of entry" for energy into the biosphere, and glycolysis and cellular respiration, the most important sequences of chemical reactions that release energy.

Energy and the Ability to Do Work

As you learned in Chapter 2, there are two types of energy: **kinetic energy** and **potential energy**. Both types of energy may exist in many different forms. Kinetic energy, or *energy of movement*, includes light (movement of photons), heat (movement of molecules), electricity (movement of electrically charged particles), and movement of large objects. Potential energy, or *stored energy*, includes chemical energy stored in the bonds that hold atoms together in molecules, electrical energy stored in a battery, and positional energy stored in a diver poised to spring (Fig. 4-1). Under the right conditions, kinetic energy can be transformed into potential energy, and vice versa. For example, the diver converted kinetic energy of movement into potential energy of position when she climbed the ladder up to the platform; when she jumps off, the potential energy will be converted back into kinetic energy.

To understand how energy flow governs interactions among pieces of matter, we need to know two things: (1) the quantity of available energy and (2) the usefulness of the energy. These are the subjects of the laws of thermodynamics, which we will now examine.

The Laws of Thermodynamics Describe the Basic Properties of Energy

All interactions among pieces of matter are governed by the two **laws of thermodynamics**, physical principles that define the basic properties and behavior of energy. The laws of thermodynamics deal with "isolated systems," which are any parts of the universe that cannot exchange either matter or energy with any other parts. Probably no part of the universe is completely isolated from all possible exchange with every other part, but the concept of an isolated system is useful in thinking about energy flow.

The First Law of Thermodynamics States That Energy Can Neither Be Created nor Destroyed

The **first law of thermodynamics** states that within any isolated system, energy can neither be created nor destroyed, although it can be changed in form (for example, from chemical energy to heat energy). In other words, within an isolated system *the total quantity of energy remains constant.* The first law is therefore often called the **law of conservation of energy.** To use a familiar example, let's see how the first law applies to driving your car (Fig. 4-2). We can consider that your car (with a full tank of gas), the road, and the surrounding air roughly constitute an isolated system. When you drive your car, you convert the potential chemical energy of gasoline into kinetic energy of movement and heat energy. The total amount of energy that was in the gasoline before it was burned is the same as the total amount of this kinetic energy and heat.

An important rule of energy conversions is this: Energy always flows "downhill," from places with a high concentration of energy to places with a low concentration of energy. This is the principle behind engines. As we described in Chapter 2, temperature is a measure of how fast molecules move. The burning gasoline in your car's engine consists of molecules moving at extremely high speeds: a high concentration of energy. The cooler air outside the engine consists of molecules moving at much lower speeds: a low concentration of energy. The molecules in the engine hit the piston harder than the air molecules outside the engine do, so the piston moves upward, driving the gears that move the car. Work is done. When the engine is turned off, it cools down as heat is transferred from the warm engine to its cooler surroundings. The molecules on both sides of the piston move at the same speed, so the piston stays still. No work is done.

Source: Life on Earth by Audesirk/Audesirk, ©1997. Reprinted by permission of Prentice-Hall, Inc., Upper Saddle River, NJ.

a. *Reading for critical evaluation.* Evaluate the material by answering these questions:

Were the ideas clearly supported by examples? If you feel one or more were not supported, give an example.

Did the author make any assumptions that weren't examined? If so, name one or more.

Do you disagree with any part of the material? If so, which part, and why?

Do you have any suggestions for how the material could have been presented more effectively?

b. *Reading for practical application.* Imagine you have to give a presentation on this material the next time the class meets. On a separate sheet of paper, create an outline or think link that maps out the key elements you would discuss.

c. *Reading for comprehension.* Answer the following questions to determine the level of your comprehension.

Name the two types of energy.

Which one "stores" energy?

Can kinetic energy be turned into potential energy?

What is the term that describes the basic properties and behaviors of energy?

Mark the following statements as true (T) or false (F).

_____ Within any isolated system, energy can be neither created nor destroyed.

_____ Energy always flows downhill, from high concentration levels to low.

_____ All interactions among pieces of matter are governed by two laws of thermodynamics.

_____ Some parts of the universe are isolated from other parts.

Key to Cooperative Learning: Building Teamwork Skills

Reading and Group Discussion Divide into small groups, ideally groups of four. Take five minutes to independently read the excerpt from *Tools For Life* on page 192. Each person should select one of the following questions to focus on while reading. If your group is smaller than four, eliminate unselected questions. If your group is larger than four, some questions may have to be shared between two group members.

1. What role do internships play in today's corporate hiring process?
2. If you were a manager for a company, why would you want to hire someone who had had one or two internships during college?
3. What did Dan Kosta gain from taking a semester off from school for his internship?
4. How would an intern learn about business from the bottom up?

Use your critical-reading skills to achieve your purpose of exploring your selected question. Focus on finding ideas that help to answer the question and examples that support those ideas. Consider other information you know, relevant to your question, that may be similar to or different from the material in the passage. If your questions look for causes or effects, scan for them in the passage. Be sure to make notes as you write.

From "The New Rung on the Corporate Ladder," by Emma J. Taylor.

Gone are the days of the entry-level jobs; the internship has replaced it as the low rung on the corporate ladder. Summer internships have long been the de facto third semester of school, adding ballast and diversity to otherwise short résumés, but these days even three summer stints aren't always enough to secure you the right position. Recent grads are now turning to year-long postcollege internships, and undergrads are taking time off from school to fill low-paying or unpaid positions, all in the effort to prove they're ready to face the responsibility of full-time jobs. And employers are taking note.

"Work experience has a higher value than most educational experiences," says Patrick Scheetz, author of a nationwide hiring survey and director of the Collegiate Employment Research Institute at Michigan State University. "It is the employer's expectation," he explains. "If you went into heart surgery, you would ask if the surgeon had ever operated on a heart before. Why wouldn't an employer ask the same question of you?" Of last year's new hires, according to the survey, nearly 50 percent had completed career-related internships. "Work plays a big part in your development as a prospective employee," Scheetz says.

In other words, employers like to see you pay your dues.

Dan Kosta paid his when he took a semester off to intern with Paul Shaffer on *The Late Show with David Letterman*. He dealt with a lot of downtime and pulled some gofer details, but in the entertainment industry, as in many others, the mudsucking internship is virtually a prerequisite.

"It's backroom to backstage," Kosta says of his experience at *The Late Show*. "It's really about being there. I learned more about the entertainment industry in the first two weeks I was there than I could have taking any kind of class or reading any kind of book. It's just hands-on knowledge. You see how everything works, from the top to the bottom. And you're the bottom."[9]

Source: An excerpt from "The New Rung on the Corporate Ladder"

When you have finished reading critically, gather as a group. Each person (or pair) should take a turn presenting the question, the response and/or answer to the question that was derived through critical reading, and any other ideas that came up while reading. The group then has an opportunity to present any other ideas they want to add to the discussion of that question. Continue until each person has had a chance to present what they worked on.

Key to Self-Expression: Discovery Through Journal Writing

To record your thoughts, use a separate journal or the lined pages at the end of the chapter.

Reading Challenges What is your most difficult challenge when reading assigned materials? A challenge might be a particular kind of reading material, a reading situation, or the achievement of a certain goal when reading. Considering the tools that this chapter presents, make a plan that addresses this challenge. What techniques might be able to help you most? How and when will you try them out? What positive effects do you anticipate they may have on you?

Key to Your Personal Portfolio: Your Paper Trail to Success

Evaluate Your Reading and Study Skills On a separate sheet of paper, evaluate your current reading and studying skills. Analyze the current status of each of the following skill areas, what you are doing to improve your performance in each area, and your long-term and short-term goals for skill improvement. Define your short-term goal in terms of what you hope to accomplish after one month and your long-term goal in terms of what you hope to accomplish in one year.

Skill Areas

- Ability to define your reading purpose
- Progress in increasing your reading speed
- Progress in increasing your reading comprehension
- Vocabulary building
- Use of PQ3R
- Identification and use of text-previewing devices
- Participation in a study group
- Ability to understand and use visual aids

Use your item-by-item analysis as an action plan that will help you improve your skills. For example, if you currently spend no time building your vocabulary, your short-term goal may be to add five new words a week to your vocabulary, with your end-of-year goal the "ownership" of more than 200 new words. To accomplish this, you could do more reading and upgrade the quality of your reading material. One way to do this is to start reading a national paper like *The New York Times, Washington Post*, or *Wall Street Journal*, all of which are available on line and at your library. You may also want to keep a list of the unfamiliar words you encounter as you read, look them up in a dictionary, and use them in a sentence.

As part of your plan, prioritize the items on the list. For example, you may decide that your number-one priority is perfecting the use of PQ3R, while the item of least importance is forming a study group, since you study best alone.

As the year progresses, monitor your accomplishments in each area. You may decide to modify your action plan based on how the elements of the plan affect your school performance. If you work as well as attend class, consider the reading that you have to do on the job—newspapers, journals, or any other information—along with your school reading when you activate your plan and monitor your progress.

Name ______________________________ Date __________

Journal Entry

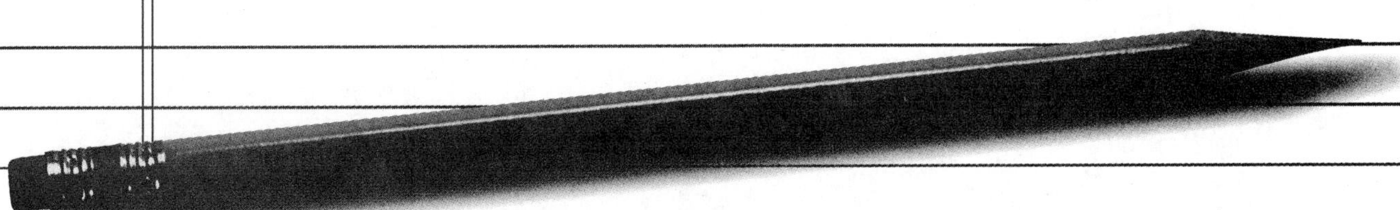

Chapter 2

NOTE-TAKING AND WRITING:

Harnessing the Power of Words and Ideas

Words, joined to form ideas, are tools that have enormous power. Whether you write an essay, a memo to a supervisor, or a love letter over e-mail, words allow you to take your ideas out of the realm of thought and give them a form that other people can read and consider. You can harness their power for your own. Set a goal for yourself: Strive continually to improve your knowledge of how to use words to construct understandable ideas.

This chapter will teach you the note-taking skills you need to record information successfully. It will show you how to express your written ideas completely and how good writing is linked to clear thinking. In class or at work, taking notes and writing well will help you stand out from the crowd.

HOW DOES TAKING NOTES HELP YOU?

Notes help you learn when you are in class, doing research, or studying. Since it is virtually impossible to take notes on everything you hear or read, the act of note-taking encourages you to decide what is worth remembering. Looking at the positive effects of note-taking will help you see why good note-taking is a useful habit (see Table 6-1).

TABLE 6-1 THE VALUE OF NOTES

✓ Your notes provide material that helps you study information and prepare for tests.
✓ When you take notes, you become an active, involved listener and learner.
✓ Notes help you think critically and organize ideas.
✓ The information you learn in class may not appear in any text; you will have no way to study it without writing it down.
✓ If it is difficult for you to process information while in class; having notes to read and make sense of later can help you learn.
✓ Note-taking is a skill for life that you will use on the job and in your personal life.

Recording Information In Class

Your notes have two purposes: First, they should reflect what you heard in class, and second, they should be a resource for studying, writing, or comparing with your text material.

Preparing to Take Class Notes

Taking good class notes depends on good preparation, including the following:

- ➤ If your instructor assigns reading on a lecture topic, you may choose to complete the reading before class so that the lecture becomes more of a review than an introduction.
- ➤ Use separate pieces of 8 1/2-by-11-inch paper for each class. If you use a three-ring binder, punch holes in papers your instructor hands out and insert them immediately following your notes for that day.
- ➤ Take a comfortable seat where you can easily see and hear, and be ready to write as soon as the instructor begins speaking.

- ➤ Choose a note-taking system that helps you handle the instructor's speaking style. While one instructor may deliver organized lectures at a normal speaking rate, another may jump from topic to topic or talk very quickly.
- ➤ Set up a support system with a student in each class. That way, when you are absent, you can get the notes you missed.

What to Do During Class

Because no one has the time to write down everything he or she hears, the following strategies will help you choose and record what you feel is important, in a format that you can read and understand later.

Date each page. When you take several pages of notes during a lecture, add an identifying letter or number to the date on each page: 11/27 A, 11/27 B, . . . or 11/27—1 of 3, 11/27—2 of 3.

Add the specific topic of the lecture at the top of the page. For example:

11/27A—<u>U.S. Immigration Policy After World War II</u>

If your instructor jumps from topic to topic during a single class, try starting a new page for each new topic.

Ask yourself critical-thinking questions as you listen: Do I need this information? Is the information important or is it just a digression? Is the information fact or opinion? If it is opinion, is it worth remembering? (Chapter 4 offers ideas about how to distinguish between fact and opinion.)

Record whatever an instructor emphasizes (see Figure 6-1 for details).

Continue to take notes during class discussions and question-and-answer periods. What your fellow students ask about may help you as well.

Leave one or more blank spaces between points. This white space will help you review your notes, because information will appear in self-contained sections.

Draw pictures and diagrams that help illustrate ideas.

Indicate material that is especially important with a star, with underlining, with a highlighter pen, or by writing words in capital letters.

If you cannot understand what the instructor is saying, leave a space and place a question mark in the margin. Then ask the instructor to explain it again after class or discuss it with a classmate. Fill in the blank when the idea is clear.

Take notes until the instructor stops speaking. Students who stop writing a few minutes before the class is over can miss critical information.

Make your notes as legible, organized, and complete as possible. Your notes are only useful if you can read and understand them.

FIGURE 6-1 HOW TO PICK UP ON INSTRUCTOR CUES

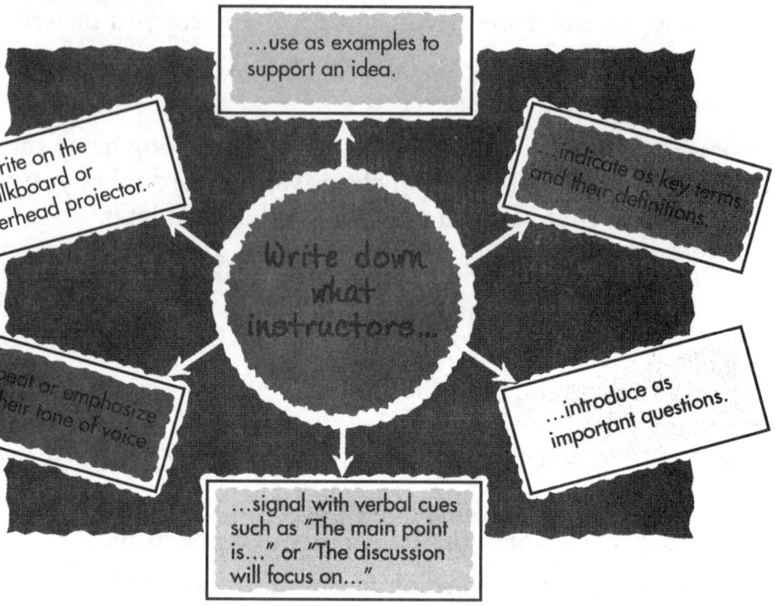

"Omit needless words. . . . This requires not that the writer make all his sentences short, or that he avoid all detail and treat his subjects only in outline, but that every word tell."

William Strunk, Jr.

(*Source:* William Strunk, Jr. and E.B. White. *The Elements of Style*, 3rd Edition. Copyright © 1979. All rights reserved. Reprinted by permission from Allyn & Bacon.)

Make Notes a Valuable After-Class Reference

Class notes are a valuable study tool when you review them regularly. Try to begin your review within a day of the lecture. Read over the notes to learn the information, clarify abbreviations, fill in missing information, and underline or highlight key points. Try to review each week's notes at the end of that week. Think critically about the material, in writing, study group discussions, or quiet reflective thought, using the following questions.

- What do these ideas mean? What examples support or negate them?
- How do I evaluate these ideas? Why are they important?
- How do these ideas, facts, and statements fit together? Is there any missing information?

Summarizing your notes is another important review technique. Summarizing involves critically evaluating which ideas and examples are most important and writing them in a condensed form. You may prefer to summarize as you review your notes, although you might also try summarizing your notes from memory after you review them.

You can take notes in many ways. Different note-taking systems suit different people and situations. Explore each system and choose what works for you.

WHAT NOTE-TAKING SYSTEM SHOULD YOU USE?

You will benefit most from the system that feels most comfortable to you. As you consider each system, remember the learning-styles profile you compiled in Chapter 2. The most common note-taking systems include outlines, the Cornell system, and think links.

Taking Notes in Outline Form

When a reading assignment or lecture seems well organized, you may choose to take notes in outline form. *Outlining* shows the relationships among ideas and their supporting examples through the use of line-by-line phrases set off by varying indentations.

Formal outlines indicate ideas and examples using Roman numerals, capital and lower-case letters, and numbers. When you are pressed for time, such as during class, you can use an informal system of consistent indenting and dashes instead. Formal outlines also require at least two headings on the same level—that is, if you have a II A you must also have a II B. Figure 6-2 on the following page shows an outline on civil rights legislation.

Guided Notes

From time to time, an instructor may give you a guide, usually in the form of an outline, to help you take notes in the class. This outline may be on a page that you receive at the beginning of the class, on the board, or on an overhead projector.

Although *guided notes* help you follow the lecture and organize your thoughts during class, they do not replace your own notes. Because they are more of a basic outline of topics than a comprehensive coverage of information, they require that you fill in what they do not cover in detail. If you tune out in class because you think that the guided notes are all you need, you will most likely miss important information.

When you receive guided notes on paper, write directly on the paper if there is room. If not, use a separate sheet and write on it the outline categories that the guided notes suggest. If the guided notes are on the board or overhead, copy them down, leaving plenty of space in between for your own notes.

Using the Cornell Note-Taking System

The *Cornell note-taking system*, also known as the T-note system, was developed more than 45 years ago by Walter Pauk at Cornell University.[1] The system is successful because it is simple—and because it works. It consists of three sections on ordinary note paper:

FIGURE 6-2 SAMPLE FORMAL OUTLINE

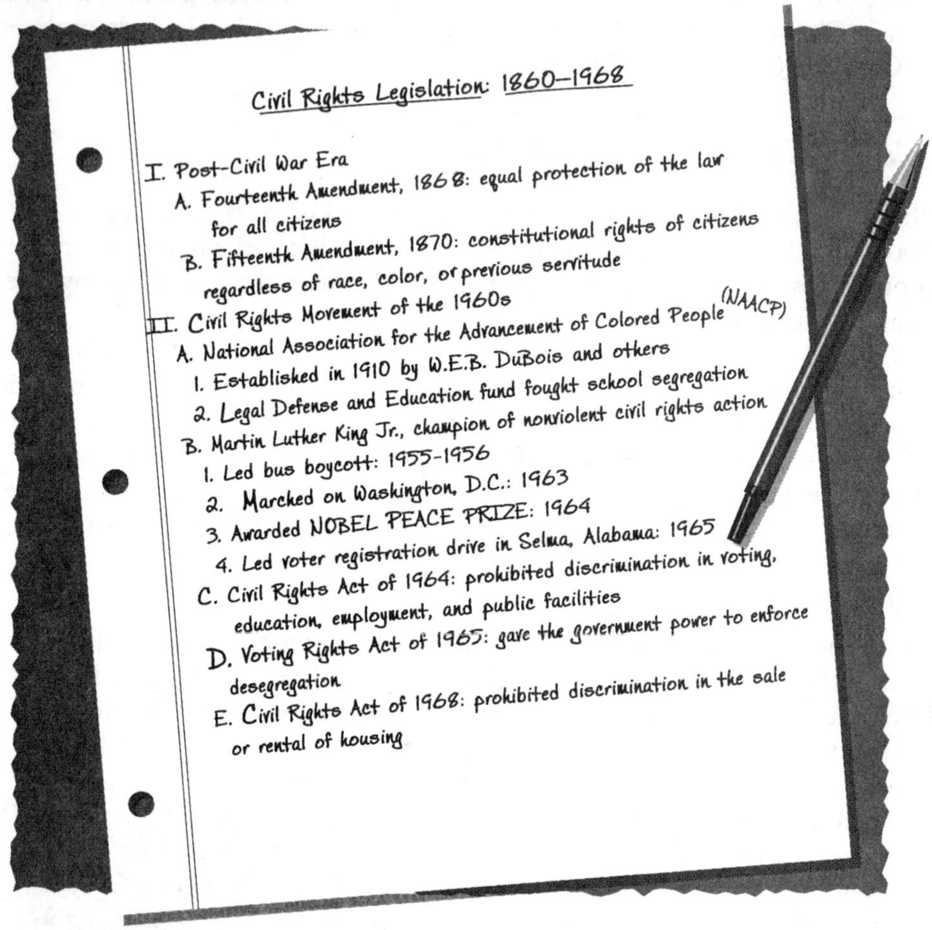

- *Section 1*, the largest section, is on the right. Record your notes here in informal outline form.
- *Section 2*, to the left of your notes, is the *cue column*. Leave it blank while you read or listen, then fill it in later as you review. You might fill it with comments that highlight main ideas, clarify meaning, suggest examples, or link ideas and examples. You can even draw diagrams.
- *Section 3*, at the bottom of the page, is the *summary area*, where you summarize the notes on the page. When you review, use this section to reinforce concepts and provide an overview.

When you use the Cornell system, create the note-taking structure before class begins. Picture an upside-down letter T and use Figure 6-3 as your guide. Make the cue column about 2 ½ inches wide and the summary area 2 inches tall. Figure 6-3 shows how a student used the Cornell system to take notes in an introduction-to-business course.

FIGURE 6-3 NOTES TAKEN USING THE CORNELL SYSTEM

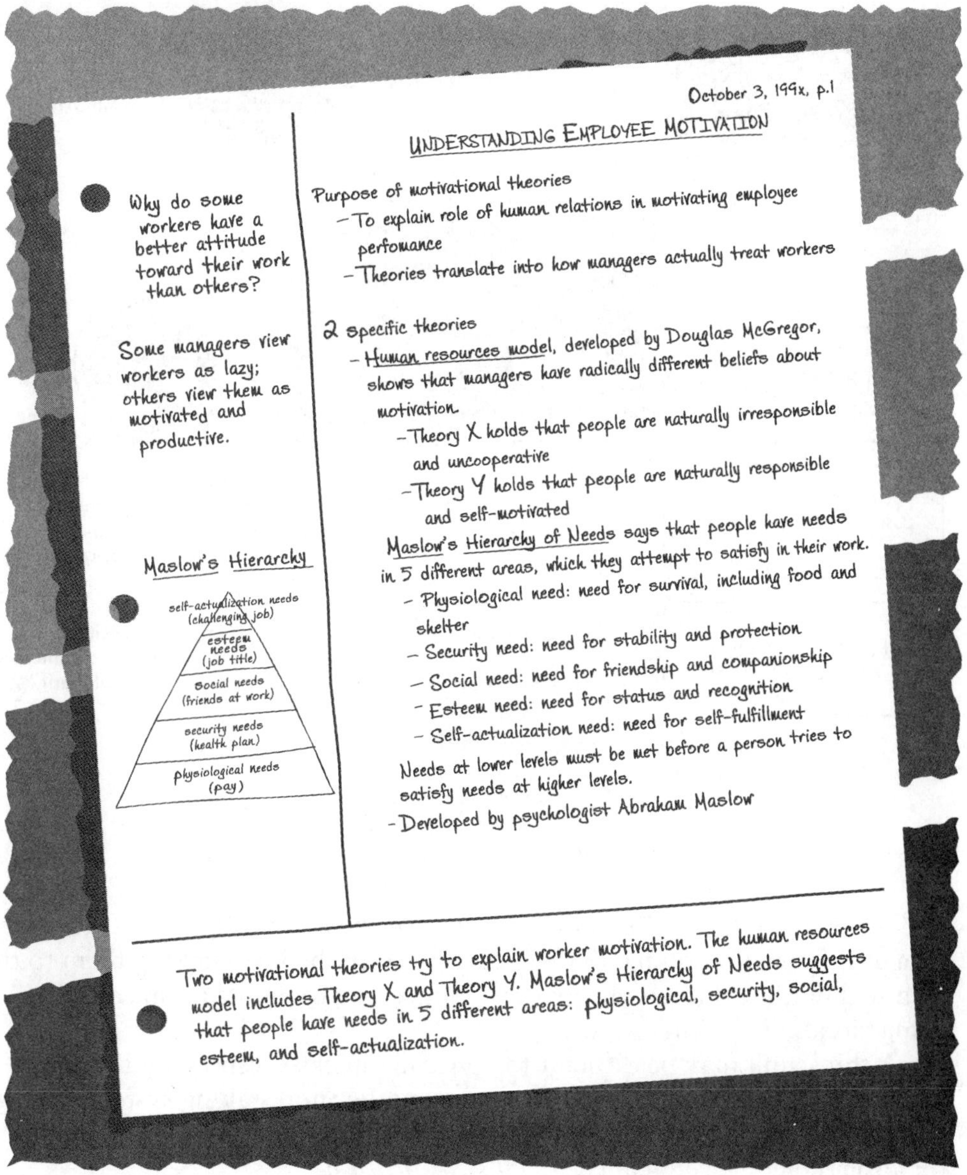

Creating a Think Link

A *think link*, also known as a mind map, is a visual form of note-taking. When you draw a think link, you diagram ideas using shapes and lines that link ideas and supporting details and examples. The visual design makes the connections easy to see, and the use of shapes and pictures extends the material beyond just words. Many learners respond well to the power of visualization. You can use think links to brainstorm ideas for paper topics as well.

Visualization, The interpretation of verbal ideas through the use of mental visual images.

One way to create a think link is to start by circling your topic in the middle of a sheet of unlined paper. Next, draw a line from the circled topic

FIGURE 6-4 SAMPLE THINK LINK

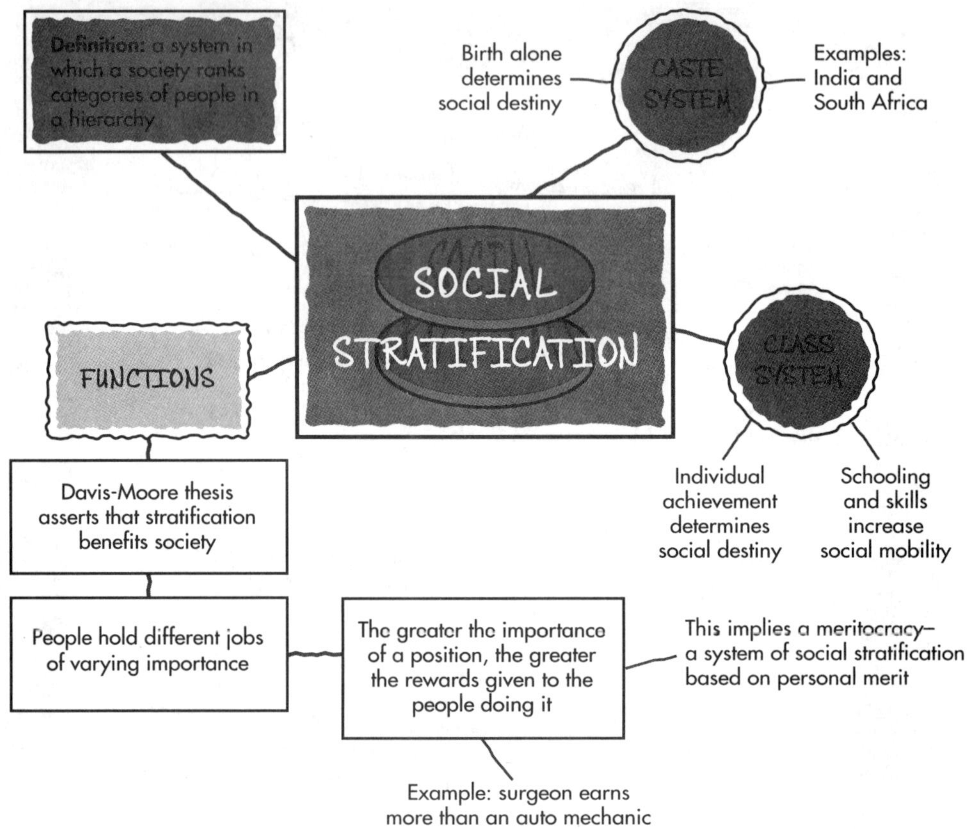

and write the name of the first major idea at the end of that line. Circle the idea also. Then jot down specific facts related to the idea, linking them to the idea with lines. Continue the process, connecting thoughts to one another using circles, lines, and words.

A think link may be difficult to construct in class, especially if your instructor talks quickly. In this case, use another note-taking system during class. Then make a think link as you review. Figure 6-4 shows a think link on a sociology concept called *social stratification*.

Once you choose a note-taking system, your success will depend on how well you use it. Personal shorthand will help you make the most of whatever system you choose.

HOW CAN YOU WRITE FASTER WHEN TAKING NOTES?

When taking notes, many students feel they can't keep up with the instructor. Using some personal shorthand (not standard secretarial shorthand) can help to push the pen faster. *Shorthand* is writing that shortens words or replaces them with symbols. Because you are the only intended reader, you can misspell and abbreviate words in ways that only you understand.

The only danger with shorthand is that you might forget what your writing means. To avoid this problem, review your shorthand notes while your abbreviations and symbols are fresh in your mind. If there is any confusion, spell out words as you review.

Here are some suggestions that will help you master this important skill:

1. Use the following standard abbreviations in place of complete words:

w/	with	cf	compare, in comparison to
w/o	without	ff	following
→	means; resulting in	Q	question
←	as a result of	p.	page
↑	increasing	*	most importantly
↓	decreasing	<	less than
∴	therefore	>	more than
∵	because	=	equals
≈	approximately	%	percent
+ OR &	and	Δ	change
—	minus; negative	2	to; two; too
NO. OR #	number	vs	versus; against
i.e.	that is,	eg	for example
etc.	and so forth	c/o	care of
ng	no good	lb	pound

2. Shorten words by removing vowels from the middle of words:

   prps = purpose
   Crvtte = Corvette (as on a vanity license plate for a car)

3. Substitute word beginnings for entire words:

   assoc = associate; association
   info = information

4. Form plurals by adding s:

   prblms = problems
   prntrs = printers

5. Make up your own symbols and use them consistently:

   b/4 = before
   2thake = toothache

6. Learn to rely on key phrases instead of complete sentences ("German—nouns capitalized" instead of "In the German language, all nouns are capitalized.")

While note-taking focuses on taking in ideas, writing focuses on expressing them. Next you will explore the roles that writing can play in your life.

HOW CAN YOU BECOME A GOOD WRITER?

Good writing depends upon and reflects clear thinking. Therefore, a clear thought process is the best preparation for a well-written document, and a well-written document shows the reader a clear thought process. Good writing also depends on reading. The more you expose yourself to the work of other writers, the more you will develop your ability to express yourself well. Not only will you learn more words and ideas, but you will also learn about all the different ways a writer can put words together in order to express ideas. In addition, critical reading generates new ideas inside your mind, ideas you can use in your writing.

In school, almost any course you take will require you to write essays or papers in order to communicate your knowledge and thought process. In order to express yourself successfully in those essays and papers, you need good writing skills. Knowing how to write and express yourself is essential outside of school as well, as the following example demonstrates. Imagine that you run a summer internship program at a major television network. You have two qualified student candidates who are vying for one internship position. Parts of both student's letters to you are shown in Figures 6-5 and 6-6. Read both figures before continuing with the text at the bottom of the page.

FIGURE 6-5 FIRST STUDENT'S WRITING SAMPLE

I am a capible student who'se interests are many. I like the news business so much so that I want you to offer me the internship with your company.

My experience will impress you, as I'm sure you will agree I am a reporter for the college news station, and I can be a reporter for you as well. If you let me try. Instructers who know my work like my style. I prefer to think of myself as an individuel with a unique style that nothing can match.

Which candidate would you choose? The second student's letter is well written, persuasive, logical, and error free. In contrast, the first student's letter is not thought through clearly and has technical errors. Good writing quality gives the edge to student number two.

Instructors, supervisors, and other people who see your writing judge your thinking ability based on what you write and how you write it. Over the next few years you may write papers, essays, answers to essay test questions, job application letters, résumés, business proposals and reports, memos to co-workers, and letters to customers and suppliers. Good writing skills will help you achieve the goals you set out to accomplish with each writing task.

FIGURE 6-6 SECOND STUDENT'S WRITING SAMPLE

From the time I was 8 years old, I was hooked on the news. Instead of watching cartoons on television, I watched Tom Brokaw, Dan Rather, and Peter Jennings. I celebrated the day that CNN started a 24-hour all-news network.

It seemed like a natural step to go into the news business. I started in high school as a reporter, and then I became editor-in-chief of the school paper. As a college freshman, I am majoring in broadcast journalism, and I am also working at the school TV station. Even though I'm starting at the bottom, I believe that there's a learning opportunity around every corner. By the time I take on my first reporting assignment next year, I feel that my knowledge and experience will have grown. I hope it will be enough to make me a competent journalist.

WHAT ARE THE ELEMENTS OF EFFECTIVE WRITING?

Every writing situation is different, dependent upon three elements. Your goal is to understand each element before you begin to write:

Your purpose: What do you want to accomplish with this particular piece of writing?

Your topic: What is the subject about which you will write?

Your audience: Who will read your writing?

Figure 6-7 shows how these elements are inter-dependent. As a triangle needs three points to be complete, a piece of writing needs these three elements.

FIGURE 6-7 THE THREE ELEMENTS OF WRITING

Writing Purpose

Writing without having set your purpose first is like driving without deciding where you want to arrive. You'll get somewhere, but chances are it won't be where you needed to go. Therefore, when you write, always define what you want to accomplish before you start.

There are many different purposes for writing. However, the two purposes you will most commonly use in classwork and on the job are to inform and to persuade.

The purpose of *informative writing* is to present and explain ideas. A research paper on how hospitals use donated blood to save lives informs readers without trying to mold opinion. The writer presents facts in an unbiased way, without introducing a particular point of view. Most newspaper articles, except on the opinion and editorial pages, are examples of informative writing.

Persuasive writing has the purpose of convincing readers that your point of view is correct. Often, persuasive writing seeks to change the mind of the reader. For example, as a member of the student health committee, you write a newspaper column attempting to persuade readers to give blood. Examples of persuasive writing include newspaper editorials, business proposals, and books and magazine articles with a point of view.

Additional possible writing purposes include *entertaining* the reader and *narrating* (describing an image or event to the reader). Although most of your writing in school will inform or persuade, you may occasionally need to entertain or narrate as well. Sometimes purposes will even overlap—you might write an informative essay that entertains at the same time.

Knowing Your Audience

In almost every case, a writer creates written material so that it can be read by others. The two partners in this process are the writer and the audience. Knowing who your audience is will help you communicate successfully.

Audience, The reader or readers of any piece of written material.

Key Questions About Your Audience

In school, your primary audience is your instructors. For many assignments, instructors will want you to assume that they are typical readers rather than informed instructors. Writing for typical readers usually means that you should be as complete as possible in your explanations.

At times you may write papers that intend to address informed instructors or a specific reading audience other than your instructors. In such cases, you may ask yourself some or all of the following questions, depending on which are relevant to your topic.

- What are my readers' ages, cultural backgrounds, interests, and experiences?
- What are their roles? Are they instructors, students, employers, customers?
- How much do they know about my topic? Are they experts in the field or beginners?

REAL WORLD PERSPECTIVE

How can I improve my writing?

Erica Epstein, Ithaca College—Ithaca, New York, Education Major

I don't know if it was the school's fault or mine, but by the time I was in high school, I didn't do homework or reading. I just stopped paying attention. The classes were too boring. Fifteen weeks of the same topic was redundant. I think education should be interesting. The material should be tied in with something else so it has meaning. Instead, the teacher feeds you the information so you don't really have to put much effort in. But now, even though I do all right, I have to work really hard to write a good paper. I think if I'd had a better start I wouldn't have to spend so much time rewriting my papers.

My teachers say the main problem is with my grammar. I tend to go from the past tense to the present tense in the wrong places. I just don't make proper sentences. I also have trouble organizing my material. I jump in and start writing. But I end up starting somewhere in the middle when I should be somewhere else. This is really frustrating. I had to take the writing class twice because I didn't get a high enough score the first time. I passed it this semester. I go to the writing center. They help me outline what I'm going to write. But I still end up rewriting my work before it's what I want. It's been really helpful but I know I still need to do more. What suggestions do you have?

Tom Smith, University of Wyoming, Administration of Justice

First of all, just like you, I get help from the writing center at my school. They know a lot about what the different teachers expect of you, particularly the technical stuff like footnote and bibliography requirements. They also give great advice about phrasing and punctuation. I also ask several of my friends to edit my papers. Usually, they'll focus in on the weaker points and then I can make the changes and strengthen my work. If your papers are sounding too chatty, this would probably be the best thing for you to do. They'll be able to show you where you've gotten off the point. I'm never bothered by their comments. In fact, I'm grateful because it helps my papers be more professional. By the time three or four people have read my work, I'm usually pretty sure I've handled the problems. I also personally edit my papers about three or four times before I turn them in. I make sure I got my point across. I also try and look at my paper from an opposing perspective or different viewpoint. That way I can be sure my arguments are clear. Finally, if you don't have a reference book for writers, I suggest you go to your college bookstore and get one. And don't forget to use your spell-check and thesaurus. That way you'll be sure your spelling is correct and you can increase your vocabulary with every paper you write.

- Are they interested, or do I have to convince them to read what I write?
- Can I expect my audience to have an open or closed mind?

After you answer the questions about your audience, take what you have discovered into consideration as you write.

Your Commitment to Your Audience

Your goal is to organize your ideas so that readers can follow them. Suppose, for example, you are writing an informative research paper for a non-expert audience on using on-line services to get a job. One way to accomplish your goal is to first explain what these services are and the kinds of help they offer, then describe each service in detail, and finally conclude with how these services will change job hunting in the twenty-first century.

Effective and successful writing involves following the steps of the *writing process.*

WHAT IS THE WRITING PROCESS?

The writing process provides an opportunity for you to state and refine your thoughts until you have expressed yourself as clearly as possible. Critical thinking plays an important role every step of the way. The four main parts of the process are planning, drafting, revising, and editing.

Planning

Planning gives you a chance to think about what to write and how to write it. Planning involves brainstorming for ideas, defining and narrowing your topic by using prewriting strategies, conducting research if necessary, writing a thesis statement, and writing a working outline. Although the steps in preparing to write are listed in sequence, in real life the steps overlap one another as you plan your document.

Open Your Mind Through Brainstorming

Whether your instructor assigns a partially defined topic (novelist Toni Morrison) or a general category within which you make your own choice (women authors), you should brainstorm to develop ideas about what you want to write. Brainstorming is a creative technique that involves generating ideas about a subject without making judgments. You may want to look at the section on creativity in Chapter 4 for more details.

First, let your mind wander! Write down anything on the assigned subject that comes to mind, in no particular order. Then, organize that list into an outline or think link that helps you see the possibilities more clearly. To make the outline or think link, separate list items into general ideas or categories and sub-ideas or examples. Then associate the sub-ideas or examples with the ideas they support or fit. Figure 6-8 shows a portion of an outline that the student editor for this book, Michael B. Jackson, constructed from

FIGURE 6-8 PART OF A BRAINSTORMING OUTLINE

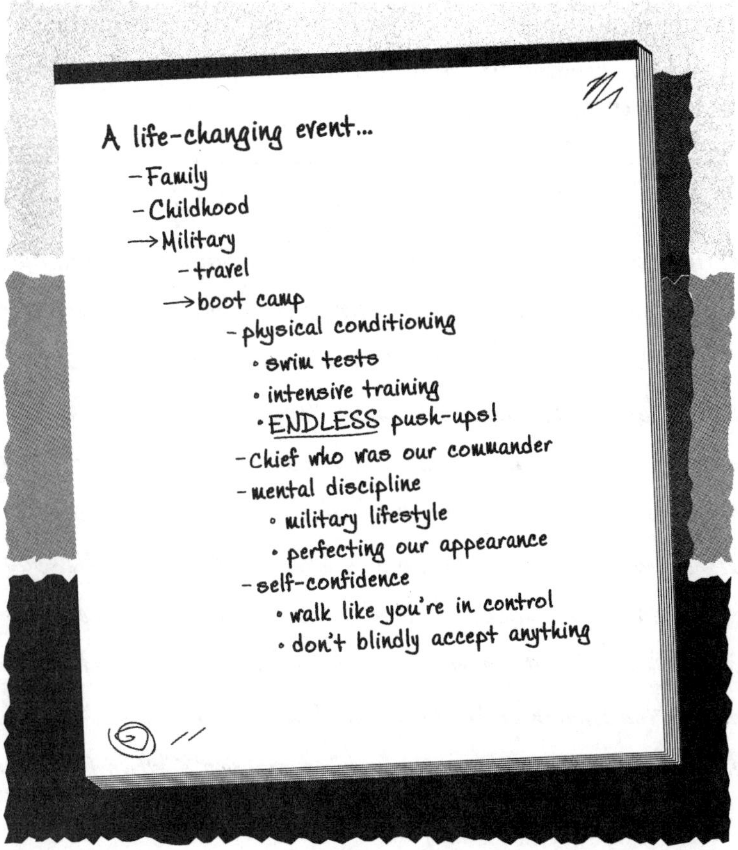

his brainstorming list. The assignment is a five-paragraph essay on a life-changing event. Here, only the subject that Michael eventually chose is shown broken down into different ideas.

Narrow Your Topic Through Prewriting Strategies

When your brainstorming has generated some possibilities, you can narrow your topic. Focus on the sub-ideas and examples from your initial brainstorming session. Because they are relatively specific, they will be more likely to point you toward possible topics.

Choose one or more sub-ideas or examples that you like and explore them using prewriting strategies such as brainstorming, freewriting, and asking journalists' questions.[2] Prewriting strategies will help you decide which of your possible topics you would most like to pursue.

Prewriting strategies, Techniques for generating ideas about a topic and finding out how much you already know before you start your research and writing.

Brainstorming The same process you used to generate ideas will also help you narrow your topic further. Generate thoughts about the possibility you have chosen and write them down. Then, organize them into categories, noticing any patterns that appear. See if any of the sub-ideas or examples seem as if they might make good topics.

Freewriting Another stream-of-consciousness technique that encourages you to put down ideas on paper as they occur to you is called *freewriting.* When you freewrite, you write whatever comes to mind without censoring your ideas or worrying about grammar, spelling, punctuation, or organization. Freewriting helps you think creatively and gives you an opportunity to begin weaving in information that you know. Freewrite on the sub-ideas or examples you have created to see if you want to pursue any of them. Here is a sample of freewriting:

> Boot camp for the Coast Guard really changed my life. First of all, I really got in shape. We had to get up every morning at 5 A.M., eat breakfast, and go right into training. We had to do endless military-style push-ups—but we later found out that these have a purpose, to prepare us to hit the deck in the event of enemy fire. We had a lot of aquatic tests, once we were awakened at 3 A.M. to do one in full uniform! Boot camp also helped me to feel confident about myself and be disciplined. Chief Marzloff was the main person who made that happen. He was tough but there was always a reason. He got angry when I used to nod my head whenever he would speak to me, he said that made it seem like I was blindly accepting whatever he said, which was a weakness. From him I have learned to keep an eye on my body's movements when I communicate. I learned a lot more from him too.

Asking journalists' questions When journalists start working on a story, they ask themselves Who? What? Where? When? Why? and How? You can use these *journalists' questions* to focus your thinking. Ask these questions about any sub-idea or example to discover what you may want to discuss. For example:

Who?	Who was at boot camp? Who influenced me the most?
What?	What about boot camp changed my life? What did we do?
When?	When in my life did I go to boot camp, and for how long? When did we fulfill our duties?
Where?	Where was camp located? Where did we spend our day-to-day time?
Why?	Why did I decide to go there? Why was it such an important experience?
How?	How did we train in the camp? How were we treated? How did we achieve success?

As you prewrite, don't forget to focus on the paper length, due date of your assignment, and any other requirements (such as topic area or purpose). These requirements influence your choice of a final topic. For example, if you had a month to write an informative 20-page paper on learning disabilities, you might choose to discuss the symptoms, diagnosis, effects, and treatment of Attention Deficit Disorder. If you were given a week to write a five-page persuasive essay, you might write about how elementary students with ADD need special training.

Prewriting will help you develop a topic broad enough to give you something with which to work but narrow enough to be manageable. Prewriting also helps you see what you know and what you don't know. If your assignment requires more than you already know, you may need to do research.

Conduct Research

Much of the writing you do in college, such as when you must write a short essay for freshman composition or for an exam, will rely on what you already know about a subject. In these cases, prewriting strategies may generate all the ideas and information you need. In other writing situations, outside sources are necessary. Try doing your research in stages. In the first stage, look for a basic overview that can help you write a thesis statement. In the second stage, go into more depth in your research, tracking down information that will help you fill in the gaps and complete your thoughts.

Write a Thesis Statement

Your work up until this point has prepared you to write a *thesis statement*, the central message you want to communicate. The thesis statement states your subject and point of view, reflects your writing purpose and audience, and acts as the organizing principle of your paper. It tells your readers what they should expect to read. Here is an example from Michael's paper:

Topic	Coast Guard boot camp
Purpose	To inform and narrate
Audience	Instructor with unknown knowledge about the topic
Thesis statement	Chief Marzloff, our Basic Training Company Commander at the U.S. Coast Guard Basic Training Facility, shaped my life through physical conditioning, developing our self-confidence, and instilling strong mental discipline.

A thesis statement is just as important in a short document, such as a letter, as it is in a long paper. For example, when you write a job application letter, a clear thesis statement will help you tell the recruiter why you deserve the job.

Write a Working Outline

The final step in the preparation process involves writing a working outline. Use this outline as a loose guide instead of a finalized structure. As you draft your paper, your ideas and structure may change many times. Only through allowing changes and refinements to happen can you get closer and closer to what you really want to say. Some students prefer a more formal outline structure, while others like to use a think link. Choose whatever form suits you best.

Create a Checklist

Use the checklist in Table 6-2 to make sure your preparation is complete. Under "Date Due," create your own writing schedule, giving each task an intended completion date. Work backwards from the date the assignment is due and estimate how long it will take to complete each step. Refer to Chapter 3 for time-management skills that will help you schedule your writing process.

As you develop your schedule, keep in mind that you'll probably move back and forth between tasks. You might find yourself doing two and even three things on the same day. Stick to the schedule as best you can, while balancing the other demands of your busy life, and check off your accomplishments on the list as you complete them.

TABLE 6-2 PREPARATION CHECKLIST

DATE DUE	TASK	IS IT COMPLETE?
	Brainstorm	
	Define and narrow	
	Use prewriting strategies	
	Conduct research if necessary	
	Write thesis statement	
	Write working outline	
	Complete research	

Drafting

Some people aim for perfection when they write a first draft. They want to get everything right—from word choice to tone to sentence structure to paragraph organization to spelling, punctuation, and grammar. Try to resist this tendency, because it may lead you to shut the door on ideas before you even know they are there.

A *first draft* involves putting ideas down on paper for the first time—but not the last! You may write many different versions of the assignment until you like what you see. Each version moves you closer to communicating exactly what you want to say in the way you want to say it. The process is like starting with a muddy pond and gradually clearing the mud away until your last version is a clear body of water, showing the rocks and the fish underneath the surface. Think of your first draft as a way of establishing the pond before you start clearing it up.

The elements of writing a first draft are freewriting, crafting an introduction, organizing the ideas in the body of the paper, formulating a conclusion, and citing sources. When you think of drafting, it might help you to imagine that you are creating a kind of "writing sandwich." The bottom slice of bread is the introduction, the top slice is the conclusion, and the sandwich stuffing is made of central ideas and supporting examples (see Figure 6-9).

"Clear a space for the writing voice. . . .you cannot will this to happen. It is a matter of persistence and faith and hard work. So you might as well just go ahead and get started."

Anne Lamott

(*Source: Bird by Bird* by Anne Lamott, © 1994, Pantheon Books, a division of Random House, Inc.)

Freewriting Your Draft

If the introduction, body, and conclusion are the three parts of the sandwich, freewriting is the process of searching the refrigerator for the ingredients and laying them all out on the table. Take everything that you have developed in the planning stages and freewrite a very rough draft. Don't censor yourself. For now, don't consciously think about your introduction, conclusion, or structure within the paper body. Focus on getting your ideas out of the realm of thought and onto the paper, in whatever form they prefer to be at the moment.

When you have the beginnings of a paper in your hands, you can start to shape it into something with a more definite form. First, work on how you want to begin your paper.

Writing an Introduction

The introduction tells your readers what the rest of the paper will contain. Including the thesis statement is essential. Here, for example, is a draft of an

FIGURE 6-9 CREATE A "WRITING SANDWICH" IN YOUR FIRST DRAFT

introduction for Michael's paper about the Coast Guard. The thesis statement is underlined at the end of the paragraph:

> Chief Marzloff took on the task of shaping the lives and careers of the youngest, newest members of the U.S. Coast Guard. During my eight weeks in training, he was my father, my instructor, my leader, and my worst enemy. He took his job very seriously and demanded that we do the same. <u>The Chief was instrumental in conditioning our bodies, developing our self-confidence, and instilling mental discipline within us</u>.

Hooks, Elements—including facts, quotes, statistics, questions, stories, or statements—that catch the reader's attention and encourage him or her to want to continue to read.

When you write an introduction, you might try to draw the reader in with an anecdote—a story that is directly related to the thesis. You can try other hooks, including a relevant quotation, dramatic statistics, and questions that encourage critical thinking. Whatever strategy you choose, be sure it is linked to your thesis statement. In addition, try to state your purpose without referring to its identity as a purpose. For example, in your introductory paragraph, state "Computer technology is infiltrating every aspect of business," instead of, "In this paper, my purpose is to prove that computer technology is infiltrating every aspect of business."

After you have an introduction that seems to set up the purpose of your paper, work on making sure the body fulfills that purposc.

Creating the Body of a Paper

The body of the paper contains your central ideas and supporting evidence. *Evidence*—proof that informs or persuades—consists of the facts, statistics, examples, and expert opinions that you know or have gathered during research.

Look at the array of ideas and evidences within your draft in its current state. Think about how you might group certain items of evidence with the particular ideas they support. Then, when you see the groups that form, try to find a structure that helps you to organize them into a clear pattern. Here are some strategies to consider.

Arrange ideas by time. Describe events in order or in reverse order.

Arrange ideas according to importance. You can choose to start with the idea that carries the most weight and move to ideas with less value or influence. You can also move from the least important to the most important idea.

Arrange ideas by problem and solution. Start with a specific problem, then discuss one or more solutions.

Writing the Conclusion

Your conclusion is a statement or paragraph that provides closure for your paper. Aim to summarize the information in the body of your paper, as well as to critically evaluate what is important about that information. Try one of the following devices:

- a summary of main points (if material is longer than three pages)
- a story, a statistic, a quote, a question that makes the reader think
- a call to action
- a look to the future

As you work on your conclusion, try not to introduce new facts or restate what you feel you have proved ("I have successfully proven that violent cartoons are related to increased violence in children.") Let your ideas as they are presented in the body of the paper speak for themselves. Readers should feel that they have reached a natural point of completion.

Crediting Authors and Sources

When you write a paper using any materials other than your own thoughts and recollections, the ideas you gathered in your research become part of your own writing. This does not mean that you can claim these ideas as your own or fail to attribute them to someone. You need to credit authors for their ideas and words in order to avoid **plagiarism.**

Plagiarism, The act of using someone else's exact words, figures, unique approach, or specific reasoning without giving appropriate credit.

Writers own their writings just as a computer programmer owns a program that he or she designed or a photographer owns an image that he or she created. A piece of writing and its ideas are the writer's products, or "intellectual property." Using an idea, phrase, or word-for-word paragraph without crediting its author is the same as using a computer program without buying it or printing a photograph without paying the photographer. It is just as serious as any other theft, and may have unfavorable consequences. Most colleges have stiff penalties for plagiarism as well as for any other cheating offense.

To avoid plagiarism, learn the difference between a quotation and a paraphrase. A *quotation* refers to a source's exact words, which are set off from the rest of the text by quotation marks. A *paraphrase* is a restatement of the quotation in your own words, using your own sentence structure. Restatement means to completely rewrite the idea, not just to remove or replace a few words. A paraphrase may not be acceptable if it is too close to the original. Figure 6-10 on the next page demonstrates these differences.

Plagiarism often begins by accident when you research. You may forget to include quotation marks around a word-for-word pickup from the source, or you may intend to cite or paraphrase but never find the time to do it. To avoid forgetting, try writing something like "Quotation from original; rewrite later" next to quoted material, and note at that time the specifics of the original document (title, author, source, page number, etc.), so you don't spend hours trying to locate it later.

Even an acceptable paraphrase requires a citation of the source of the ideas within it. Take care to credit any source that you quote, paraphrase,

FIGURE 6-10 AVOID PLAGIARISM BY LEARNING HOW TO PARAPHRASE[5]

QUOTATION

> "The most common assumption that is made by persons who are communicating with one another is . . . that the other perceives, judges, thinks, and reasons the way he does. Identical twins communicate with ease. Persons from the same culture but with a different education, age, background, and experience often find communication difficult. American managers communicating with managers from other cultures experience greater difficulties in communication than with managers from their own culture."[4]

UNACCEPTABLE PARAPHRASE
(the underlined words are taken directly from the quoted source)

> When we communicate, we assume that the person to whom we are speaking <u>perceives, judges, thinks, and reasons the way</u> we do. This is not always the case. Although <u>identical twins communicate with ease, persons from the same culture but with a different education, age, background, and experience often</u> encounter communication problems. Communication problems are common among American managers as they attempt to <u>communicate with managers from other cultures</u>. They experience greater communication problems than when they communicate <u>with managers from their own culture</u>.

ACCEPTABLE PARAPHRASE

> Many people fall into the trap of believing that everyone sees the world exactly as they do and that all people communicate based on the same assumptions. This belief is difficult to support even within our own culture as African-Americans, Hispanic-Americans, Asian-Americans, and others often attempt unsuccessfully to find common ground. When intercultural differences are thrown into the mix, such as when American managers working abroad attempt to communicate with managers from other cultures, clear communication becomes even harder.

or use as evidence. To credit sources, write a footnote or endnote that describes the source. Use the format preferred by your instructor. Writing handbooks such as the *MLA Handbook* contain acceptable formats.

Continue Your Checklist

Create a checklist for your first draft (see Table 6-3). The elements of a first draft do not have to be written in order. In fact, many writers prefer to write the introduction after they complete the body of the paper, so the introduction will accurately reflect the paper's content and tone. Whatever

TABLE 6-3 FIRST DRAFT CHECKLIST

DATE DUE	TASK	IS IT COMPLETE?
	Freewrite a draft	
	Plan and write the introduction	
	Organize the body of the paper	
	Include research evidence in the body	
	Plan and write the conclusion	
	Check for plagiarism and rewrite passages to avoid it	
	Credit your sources	

order you choose, make sure your schedule allows adequate time to get everything done—with enough time left over for revisions.

Revising

When you *revise,* you critically evaluate the word choice, paragraph structure, and style of your first draft to see how it works. Any draft, no matter how good, can always be improved. Be thorough as you add, delete, replace, and reorganize words, sentences, and paragraphs. You may want to print out your draft and then spend time making notes and corrections on that hard copy before you make changes on a typewritten or computer printed version. Figure 6-11 on the next page shows a paragraph from Michael's first draft, with revision comments added.

In addition to revising on your own, some of your classes may include peer review (having students read each other's work and offer suggestions). A peer reviewer can tell you what comes across well and what may be confusing. Having a different perspective on your writing is extremely valuable. Even if you don't have an organized peer-review system, you may want to ask a classmate to review your work as a favor to you.

The elements of revision include being a critical writer, evaluating paragraph structure, and checking for clarity and conciseness.

Being a Critical Writer

Critical thinking is as important in writing as it is in reading. Thinking critically when writing will help you move your papers beyond restating what

FIGURE 6-11

Of the changes that ~~happened to us,~~ the physical transformation is the ~~biggest.~~ ~~When we arrived at the training facility, it was January, cold and cloudy. At the time,~~ I was a little thin, but I had been working out and thought that I could physically do anything. Oh boy, was I wrong! The Chief said to us right away: "Get down, maggots!" Upon this command, we all to drop to the ground and do military-style push-ups. Water survival tactics were also part of the training ~~that we had to complete.~~ Occasionally, my dreams of home were interrupted at 3 a.m. when we had a surprise aquatic test. Although we ~~didn't feel too happy about~~ this sub-human treatment at the time, we learned to appreciate how the conditioning was turning our bodies into fine-tuned machines.

military recruits undergo

most evident

Too much.

Maybe— upon my January arrival at the training facility,

his trademark phrase

were

endless

unnecessary

resented

mention how Chief was involved

say more about this (swimming in uniform incident?)

you have researched and learned. Of course, your knowledge is an important part of your writing. What will make your writing even more important and unique, however, is how you use critical thinking to construct your own new ideas and knowledge from what you have learned.

The key to critical writing is asking the question, "So what?" For example, if you were writing a paper on nutrition, you might discuss a variety of good eating habits. Asking "So what?" could lead you into a discussion of *why* these habits are helpful, or, what positive effects they have. If you were writing a paper on egg imagery in the novel *All the King's Men* by Robert Penn Warren, you might list all the examples you noticed of that imagery. Then, asking "So what?" could lead you to evaluate why that imagery is so strong and what idea you think those examples convey.

As you revise, ask yourself questions that can help you think through ideas and examples, come up with your own original insights about the material, and be as complete and clear as possible. Use the mind actions to guide you. Here are some examples of questions you may ask:

Are these examples clearly connected to the idea?

Are there any similar concepts or facts I know of that can add to how I support this?

What else can I recall that can help to support this idea?

In evaluating any event or situation, have I clearly indicated the causes and effects?

What new idea comes to mind when I think about these examples or facts?

How do I evaluate any effect/fact/situation? Is it good or bad, useful or not?

What different arguments might a reader think of that I should address here?

Finally, critical thinking can help you evaluate the content and form of your paper. As you start your revision, ask yourself the following questions.

- Will my audience understand my thesis and how I've supported it?
- Does the introduction prepare the reader and capture attention?
- Is the body of the paper organized effectively?
- Is each idea fully developed, explained, and supported by examples?
- Are my ideas connected to one another through logical transitions?
- Do I have a clear, concise, simple writing style?
- Does the paper fulfill the requirements of the assignment?
- Does the conclusion provide a natural ending to the paper?

Evaluating Paragraph Structure

Think of your individual paragraphs as mini-versions of your paper as a whole, each with an introduction, a body, and a conclusion. Make sure each paragraph has a *topic sentence* that states the paragraph's main idea (a topic sentence does for a paragraph what a thesis statement does for an entire paper). The rest of the paragraph should support that idea by presenting examples and other evidence. Although some topic sentences may occur just after the first sentence of a paragraph, or even at the end, most of them occur at the beginning. For example:

> Chief Marzloff played an integral role in the development of our self-confidence. He taught us that anything less than direct eye contact was disrespectful to both him and ourselves. He encouraged us to be confident about our own beliefs and to think about what was said to us before we decided whether to accept it. Furthermore, the Chief reinforced self-confidence through his own example. He walked with his chin up and chest out, like the proud parent of a newborn baby. He always gave the appearance that he had something to do and that he was in complete control.

Transitions,
Words and phrases that connect thoughts, helping readers move from one idea or paragraph to the next.

Examine how your paragraphs flow one into the other by evaluating your use of transitions. For example, words like *also, in addition*, and *next* indicate that another idea is coming. Similarly, *finally, as a result*, and *in conclusion* tell readers a summary is on its way.

Check for Clarity and Conciseness

Aim to say what you want to say in the clearest, most efficient way possible. A few well-chosen words will do your ideas more justice than a flurry of language. Try to eliminate extra words and phrases. Rewrite wordy phrases in a more concise, conversational way. For example, you can write "if" instead of "in the event that," or "now" instead of "this point in time." "Capriciously, I sauntered forth to the entryway and pummeled the door that loomed so majestically before me," might become, "I skipped to the door and knocked loudly."

"See revision as 'envisioning again.' If there are areas in your work where there is a blur or vagueness, you can simply see the picture again and add the details that will bring your work closer to your mind's picture."

Natalie Goldberg

(*Source:* From *Writing Down the Bones* by Natalie Goldberg, © 1986. Reprinted by arrangement with Shambhala Publications, Inc., 300 Massachusetts Avenue, Boston, MA 02115)

Editing

In contrast to the critical thinking of revising, *editing* involves correcting technical mistakes in spelling, grammar, punctuation, as well as checking style consistency for elements such as abbreviations and capitalizations. Editing comes last, after you are satisfied with your ideas, organization, and style of writing. If you use a computer, you might want to use the grammar-check and spellcheck functions to find mistakes. A spell-checker helps, but you still need to check your work on your own. While a spell-checker won't pick up the mistake in the following sentence, someone who is reading for sense will:

They are not hear on Tuesdays.

Look also for *sexist language*, which characterizes people based on their gender. Sexist language often involves the male pronoun *he* or *his*. For example "An executive often spends hours each day going through his electronic mail" implies that executives are always men. A simple change will eliminate the sexist language: "Executives often spend hours each day going through their electronic mail," or, "An executive often spends hours each day going

through his or her electronic mail." Try to be sensitive to words that leave out or slight women. *Mail carrier* is preferable to *mailman; student* to *coed.*

Proofreading is the last stage of editing, occurring when you have a final version of your paper. Proofreading means reading every word and sentence in the final version to make sure they are accurate. Look for technical mistakes, run-on sentences, and sentence fragments. Look for incorrect word usage and references that aren't clear.

Teamwork can be a big help as you edit and proofread, because another pair of eyes may see errors that you didn't notice on your own. If possible, have someone look over your work. Ask for feedback on what is clear and what is confusing. Then ask the reader to edit and proofread for errors.

A Final Checklist

You are now ready to complete your revising and editing checklist. All the tasks listed in Table 6-4 should be complete when you submit your final paper.

Your final paper reflects all the hard work you put in during the writing process. Figure 6-12 shows the final version of Michael's paper.

TABLE 6-4 REVISING AND EDITING CHECKLIST

DATE DUE	TASK	IS IT COMPLETE?
	Check the body of the paper for clear thinking and adequate support of ideas	
	Finalize introduction and conclusion	
	Check word spelling and usage	
	Check grammar	
	Check paragraph structure	
	Make sure language is familiar and concise	
	Check punctuation	
	Check capitalization	
	Check transitions	
	Eliminate sexist language	

FIGURE 6-12

March 19, 1997
Michael B. Jackson

BOYS TO MEN

His stature was one of confidence, often misinterpreted by others as cockiness. His small frame was lean and agile, yet stiff and upright, as though every move were a calculated formula. For the longest eight weeks of my life, he was my father, my instructor, my leader, and my worst enemy. His name is Chief Marzloff, and he had the task of shaping the lives and careers of the youngest, newest members of the U.S. Coast Guard. As our Basic Training Company Commander, he took his job very seriously and demanded that we do the same. Within a limited time span, he conditioned our bodies, developed our self-confidence, and instilled within us a strong mental discipline.

Of the changes that recruits in military basic training undergo, the physical transformation is the most immediately evident. Upon my January arrival at the training facility, I was a little thin, but I had been working out and thought that I could physically do anything. Oh boy, was I wrong! The Chief wasted no time in introducing me to one of his trademark phrases: "Get down, maggots!" Upon this command, we were all to drop to the ground and produce endless counts of military-style push-ups. Later, we found out that exercise prepared us for hitting the deck in the event of enemy fire. Water survival tactics were also part of the training. Occasionally, my dreams of home were interrupted at about 3 a.m. when our company was selected for a surprise aquatic test. I recall one such test that required us to swim laps around the perimeter of a pool while in full uniform. I felt like a salmon swimming upstream, fueled only by natural instinct. Although we resented this sub-human treatment at the time, we learned to appreciate how the strict guidance of the Chief was turning our bodies into fine-tuned machines.

Beyond physical ability, Chief Marzloff also played an integral role in the development of our self-confidence. He would often declare in his raspy voice, "Look me in the eyes when you speak to me! Show me that you believe what you're saying!" He taught us that anything less was an expression of disrespect. Furthermore, he appeared to attack a personal habit of my own. It seemed that whenever he would speak to me individually, I would nervously nod my head in response. I was trying to demonstrate that I understood, but to him, I was blindly accepting anything that he said. He would roar, "That is a sign of weakness!" Needless to say, I am now conscious of all bodily motions when communicating with others. The Chief also reinforced self-confidence through his own example. He walked with his square chin up and chest out, like the proud parent of a newborn baby. He always gave the appearance that he had something to do, and that he was in complete control. Collectively, all of the methods that the Chief used were all successful in developing our self-confidence.

Perhaps the Chief's greatest contribution was the mental discipline that he instilled in his recruits. He taught us that physical ability and self-confidence were nothing without the mental discipline required to obtain any worthwhile goal. For us, this discipline began with adapting to the military lifestyle. Our day began promptly at 0500 hours, early enough to awaken the oversleeping roosters. By 0515 hours, we had to have showered, shaved, and perfectly donned our uniforms. At that point, we were marched to the galley for chow, where we learned to take only what is necessary, rather than indulging. Before each meal, the Chief would warn, "Get what you want, but you will eat all that you get!" After making good on his threat a few times, we all got the point. Throughout our stay, the chief repeatedly stressed the significance of self-discipline. He would calmly utter, "Give a little now, get a lot later." I guess that meant different things to all of us. For me, it was a simple phrase that would later become my personal philosophy on life. The Chief went to great lengths to ensure that everyone under his direction possessed the mental discipline required to be successful in boot camp or in any of life's challenges.

Chief Marzloff was a remarkable role model and a positive influence on many lives. I never saw him smile, but it was evident that he genuinely cared a great deal about his job and all the lives that he touched. This man single-handedly conditioned our bodies, developed our self-confidence, and instilled a strong mental discipline that remains in me to this day. I have not seen the Chief since March 28, 1992, graduation day. Over the years, however, I have incorporated many of his ideals into my life. Above all, he taught us the true meaning of the U.S. Coast Guard slogan, "Semper Peratus" (Always Ready).

Suà

Suà is a Shoshone Indian word, derived from the Uto-Aztecna language, meaning "think."While much of the Native American tradition in the Americas focuses on oral communication, written languages have allowed Native American perspectives and ideas to be understood by readers outside the Native American culture. The writings of Leslie Marmon Silko, J. Scott Momaday, and Sherman Alexis have expressed important insights that all readers can consider.

Think of *suà*, and of how thinking can be communicated to others through writing, every time you begin to write. The power of writing allows you to express your own insights so that others can read them and perhaps benefit from knowing them. Explore your thoughts, sharpen your ideas, and remember the incredible power of the written word.

Applications

Name ______________________________ Date ______________

Key Into Your Life: Opportunities to Apply What You Learn

Exercise 1: Evaluate Your Notes

Choose one particular class period from the last two weeks. Have a classmate photocopy his or her notes from that class period for you. Then evaluate your notes by comparing them with your classmate's. Think about:

- Do your notes make sense?
- How is your handwriting?
- Do the notes cover everything that was brought up in class?
- Are there examples to back up ideas?
- What note-taking system is used?
- Will these notes help you study?

Write your evaluation here ______________________________

What ideas or techniques from your classmate's notes do you plan to use in the future? ______________________________

Exercise 2: Class vs. Reading

Pick a class for which you have a regular textbook. Choose a set of class notes on a subject that is also covered in that textbook. Read the textbook section that corresponds to the subject of your class notes, taking notes as you go. Compare your reading notes to the notes you took in class.

Did you use a different system with the textbook, or the same as in class? Why? ______________________________

Which notes can you understand better? Why do you think that's true?

What did you learn from your reading notes that you want to bring to your class note-taking strategy?

Exercise 3: Audience Analysis

As a reporter for your college newspaper, you have been assigned the job of writing a story about some part of campus life. The choice is yours, and you submit the following suggestions to your editor-in-chief:

- The campus parking lot squeeze: Too many cars and too few spaces
- Diversity: How students accept differences and live and work together
- Drinking on campus: Is the problem getting better or worse?

Your editor-in-chief asks you the following questions about reader response. Consider that your readers may include students, faculty and administrators, and community members.

1. Would readers care enough about each subject to read the entire article?

2. How would you adjust your writing according to whether readers know or don't know about the subject?

3. Which article idea is likely to have the greatest appeal to all the audiences? Why?

4. For each topic, name the audience (or audiences) that you think would be most interested. If you think one audience would be equally interested in more than one topic, you can name an audience more than once.

Campus parking lot

Student diversity

Drinking on campus

5. How can you make a specific article interesting to a general audience?

Exercise 4: Prewriting

Choose a topic you are interested in and know something about—for example, college sports, handling stress in a stressful world, our culture's emphasis on beauty and youth, or child rearing. Narrow your topic, then use the following prewriting strategies to discover what you already know about the topic and what you would need to learn if you had to write an essay about the subject for one of your classes. (If necessary, continue this prewriting exercise on a separate sheet of paper.)

Brainstorm your ideas:

Freewrite:

Ask journalists' questions:

Exercise 5: Writing a Thesis Statement

Write two thesis statements for each of the following topics. The first statement should try to inform the reader, while the second should try to persuade. In each case, writing a thesis statement will require that you narrow the topic:

- *The rising cost of a college education*
  Thesis with an informative purpose

Thesis with a persuasive purpose

➤ *Taking care of your body and mind*
Thesis with an informative purpose

Thesis with a persuasive purpose

➤ *Career choice*
Thesis with an informative purpose

Thesis with a persuasive purpose

Key to Cooperative Learning: Using Teamwork Skills

Collaborative Writing In many jobs, you may be asked to work with other employees to produce written documents, including reports, proposals, procedure manuals, and even important letters and memos. Writing in groups, also known as *collaborative writing*, involves planning, drafting, revising, and editing.

To see what collaborative writing is like, join with three classmates and choose a general topic you are all interested in—for example, "What Colleges Can Do to Help Students Juggle School, Work, and Family" or "Teaching Safer Sex in an Age When Sex Isn't Safe." Now imagine that you and other group members have to write a persuasive paper on some aspect of this topic. Writing the paper involves the following steps:

- ➤ Each group member should spend an hour in the library to get an overview of the topic so that everyone is able to write about it in general terms.
- ➤ The group should come together to brainstorm the topic, narrow its focus, and come up with a thesis. Use your research and thesis to write a working outline that specifies what the paper

will say and the approach it will take. Divide the writing assignment into parts and assign a part to each group member.

- Each group member should *draft* his or her portion of the paper. Each section should be about two to three paragraphs long.
- Photocopy each draft and give a copy to each group member. Working independently, each person should use the suggestions in this chapter to *evaluate and revise* each section. Afterwards, come together as a group to hammer out differences and prepare a final, unedited version.
- Photocopy this version and distribute it to group members. Have everyone *edit* the material, looking for mistakes in spelling, grammar, punctuation, and usage. Incorporate the group's changes into a final version you all agree on, and ask every group member to read it. The group's goal is to produce a finished paper that satisfies the thesis and also looks good.
- Working alone, each group member should answer the following questions. Finally, compare your responses with those of other group members:

1. What do you see as the advantages and disadvantages of collaborative writing? Is it difficult or easy to write as a team member? ____________

2. What part of the collaborative writing project worked best? Where did you encounter problems? ____________

3. What did you learn from this experience that will make you a more effective collaborative writer on the next project? ____________

KEY TO SELF-EXPRESSION: DISCOVERY THROUGH JOURNAL WRITING

To record your thoughts, use a separate journal or the lined pages at the end of the chapter.

Your Relationship With Words Some people love to work with words—writing them, reading them, speaking them—while others would rather do anything else. Do you enjoy writing in school, or does writing intimidate you? Do you write anything outside of school? Discuss how you feel about writing.

KEY TO YOUR PERSONAL PORTFOLIO: YOUR PAPER TRAIL TO SUCCESS

Writing Sample: A Job Interview Letter To get a job interview, you may have to write a letter describing your background and value to the company. (Remember how the sample letters that opened this chapter affected the internship choice.) Practice writing this letter, and make the result part of your portfolio. Write a one-page, three-paragraph cover letter to a prospective employer. (The letter will accompany your résumé.) Be creative—you may use fictitious names, but select a career and industry that interest you. Use the following business letter format:

Firstname Lastname
1234 Your Street
Your, ST 12345

January 1, 1998

Ms. Prospective Employer
Prospective Company
5432 Their Street
Them, ST 54321

Dear Ms. Employer:

First paragraph . . .

Second paragraph . . .

Third paragraph . . .

Sincerely,

sign your name here

Firstname Lastname

Enclosure(s) (*use this notation if you have included a résumé or other item with your letter)*

Introductory paragraph: Start with an attention getter—a statement that convinces the employer to read on. For example, name a person the employer knows who told you to write, or refer to something positive about the company that you read about in the paper. Identify the position for which you are applying and tell the employer that you are interested in working for the company.

Middle paragraph: Sell your value. Try to convince the employer that hiring you will help the company in some way. Center your "sales effort" on your experience in school and the workplace. If possible, tie your qualifications to the needs of the company. Refer indirectly to your enclosed résumé.

Final paragraph: Close with a call to action. Ask the employer to call you, or tell the employer to expect your call to arrange an interview.

Exchange first drafts with a classmate. Read each other's letters and make notes in the margins. Discuss each letter, and make whatever corrections are necessary to produce a well-written, persuasive letter. Create a final draft for your portfolio.

Name ______________________ Date ________

Journal Entry

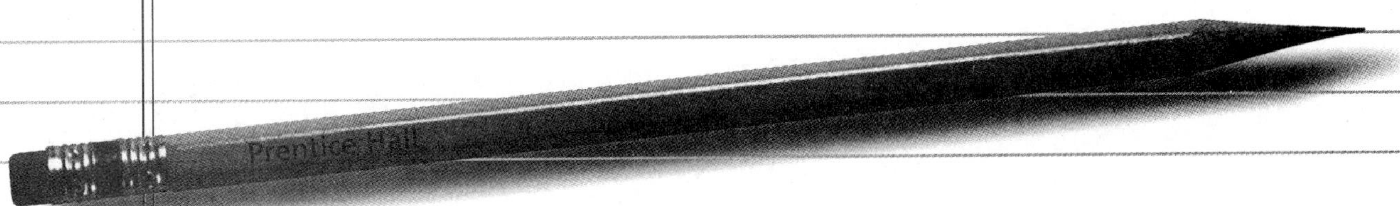

Chapter 3

LISTENING, MEMORY, AND TEST TAKING:
Taking In, Retaining, and Demonstrating Knowledge

College exposes you daily to facts, opinions, and ideas. It is up to you to take in, retain, and demonstrate knowledge of what you learn, for use in or out of school. You can accomplish these goals through active listening, focused use of your memory skills, and thorough preparation for taking tests.

Listening is one of the primary ways of taking in information. You listen as instructors discuss concepts, as members of a study group share ideas, or as friends share their thoughts. Memory skills can help you retain what you've listened to so that you can recall it for a paper, a discussion, or a test. After you've listened and remembered, test taking is your key to demonstrating what you have learned to your instructor or others. Test taking demands preparation and strategy. In this chapter, you will learn strategies to improve your ability to take in, remember and show knowledge of what you have learned.

WHY IS LISTENING A SKILL?

The act of hearing isn't quite the same as the act of listening. While *hearing* refers to sensing spoken messages from their source, *listening* involves a complex process of communication. Successful listening results in the speaker's intended message reaching the listener. In school, and at home, poor listening results in communication breakdowns and mistakes, and skilled listening promotes progress and success.

Ralph G. Nichols, a pioneer in listening research, studied 200 students at the University of Minnesota over a nine-month period. His findings, summarized in Table 7-1, demonstrate that effective listening depends as much on a positive attitude as on specific skills.[1]

To overcome barriers, explore what the listening process is and the reasons it can be hard to listen well.

TABLE 7-1 WHAT HELPS AND HINDERS LISTENING

LISTENING IS HELPED BY ...	LISTENING IS HINDERED BY ...
...making a conscious decision to work at listening; viewing difficult material as a listening challenge.	...caring little about the listening process; tuning out difficult material.
...fighting distractions through intense concentration.	...refusing to listen at the first distraction.
...continuing to listen when a subject is difficult or dry, in the hope that one might learn something interesting.	...giving up as soon as one loses interest.
...withholding judgment until hearing everything.	...becoming preoccupied with a response as soon as a speaker makes a controversial statement.
...focusing on the speaker's theme by recognizing organizational patterns, transitional language, and summary statements.	...getting sidetracked by unimportant details.
...adapting note taking style to the unique style and organization of the speaker.	...always taking notes in outline form, even when a speaker is poorly organized, leading to frustration.
...pushing past negative emotional responses and forcing oneself to continue to listen.	...letting an initial emotional response shut off continued listening.
...using excess thinking time to evaluate, summarize, and question what one just heard and anticipating what will come next.	...thinking about other things and, as a result, missing much of the message.

FIGURE 7-1 STAGES OF LISTENING

The Stages of Listening

Listening is made up of four stages that build on one another: sensing, interpreting, evaluating, and reacting. These stages take the message from the speaker to the listener and back to the speaker (see Figure 7-1).

During the *sensation stage* (also known as *hearing*), your ears pick up sound waves and transmit them to the brain. For example, you are sitting in class and hear your instructor say, "The only opportunity to make up last week's test is Tuesday at 5 P.M."

In the *interpretation stage*, listeners attach meaning to a message. This involves understanding what is being said and relating it to what you already know. For example, when you hear this message, you relate it to your knowledge of the test, whether you need to make it up, and what you are doing on Tuesday at 5 P.M.

In the *evaluation stage* of listening, you decide how you feel about the message—whether, for example, you like it or agree with it. This involves considering the message as it relates to your needs and values. In this example, if you do need to make up the test but have to work Tuesday at 5 P.M., you evaluate that you aren't thrilled with the message.

The final stage of listening involves a *reaction* to the message in the form of direct feedback. Your reaction, in this example, may be to raise your hand or stick around after class and ask the instructor if there is any alternative to that particular makeup test time.

HOW CAN YOU IMPROVE YOUR LISTENING SKILLS?

Listening is a teachable—and learnable—skill. Improving your learning skills involves managing listening challenges and becoming an active listener. Although becoming a better listener will help in every class, it is especially important in subject areas that are difficult for you.

Manage Listening Challenges

Classic studies have shown that immediately after listening, students are likely to recall only half of what was said. This is partly due to particular listening challenges, including divided attention and distractions, the tendency to shut out the message, the inclination to rush to judgment, and partial hearing loss or learning disabilities.[2] To help create a positive listening environment, in both your mind and your surroundings, explore how to manage these challenges.

Divided Attention and Distractions

Imagine you are talking with a friend at a noisy party when, suddenly, you hear your name mentioned across the room. You weren't consciously listening to anything outside your own conversation. Now, though, you strain to hear what someone might be saying about you, and listen with only half an ear to what your friend says. Chances are you hear neither person very well. This situation illustrates the consequences of divided attention. While you are capable of listening to more than one message at the same time, the usual result is that you may not completely hear or understand any of them.

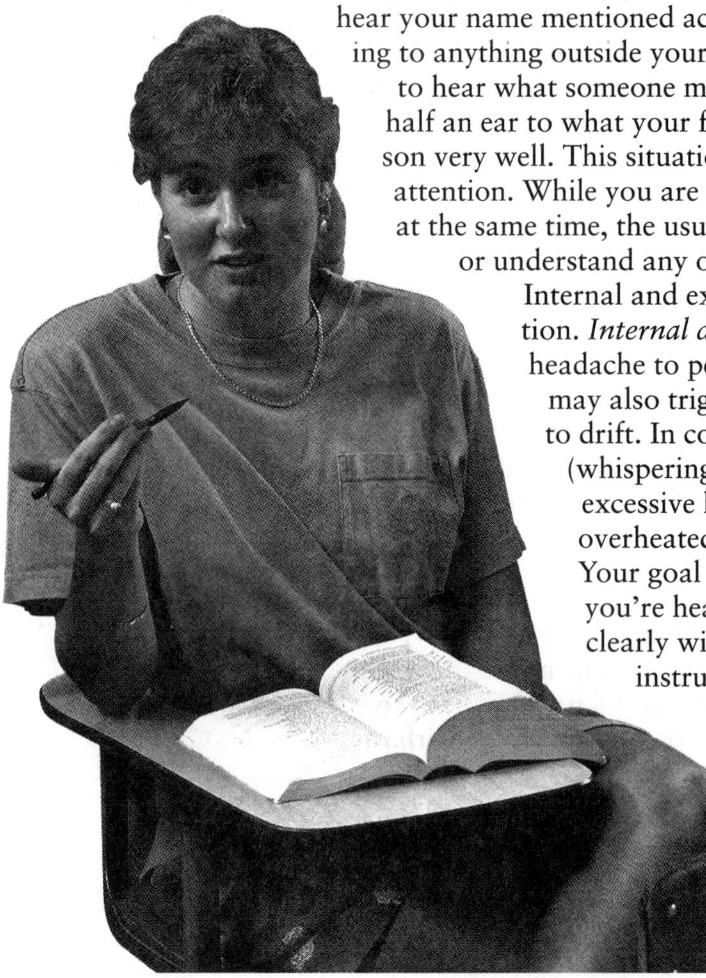

Internal and external distractions often divide your attention. *Internal distractions* include anything from hunger to headache to personal worries. Something the speaker says may also trigger a recollection that may cause your mind to drift. In contrast, *external distractions* include noises (whispering, honking horns, screaming sirens) and even excessive heat or cold. It can be hard to listen in an overheated room that is putting you to sleep.

Your goal is to reduce distractions and focus on what you're hearing. Sitting where you can see and hear clearly will help. When you can see and hear your instructors, you have a much better chance of being able to listen well, and you may be more likely to be willing to listen. In order to avoid activity that might divide your attention, you may want to sit away from people who might distract you by chatting or making noise.

Make sure you are as relaxed and alert as possible. Work to concentrate on class when you're in class and save worrying about personal problems for later. Try not to go to class hungry or thirsty. Dress comfortably. Bring a sweater or sweatshirt if you anticipate that the classroom will be too cold. If there's a chance you'll be too warm, wear a removable layer of clothing.

Shutting Out the Message

Instead of paying attention to everything the speaker says, many students fall into the trap of focusing on specific points and shutting out the rest of the message. Worse, if you perceive that a subject is too difficult or uninteresting, you may tune out everything. Shutting out the message makes it tough to listen well from that point on, since the information you miss may be the foundation for what goes on in future classes.

Creating a positive listening environment includes accepting responsibility for listening. While the instructor communicates information to you, he or she cannot force you to listen. You are responsible for taking in that information. One important motivator is believing that what your instructors say is valuable. As many students learn the hard way, instructors often cover material from outside the textbook during class and then test on that material. If you work to take in the whole message in class, you will be able to read over your notes later and think critically about what is most important.

The Rush to Judgment

People tend to stop listening when they hear something they don't like. If you rush to judge what you've heard, your focus turns to your personal reaction rather than the content of the speaker's message. Students who disagree during a lecture often spend a lot of thinking time figuring out how to word a question or comment for response.

Judgments also involve reactions to the speakers themselves. If you do not like your instructors or if you have preconceived notions about their ideas or cultural background, you may decide that their words have little value. Anyone whose words have ever been ignored because of race, background, gender, or disability understands how prejudice can interfere with listening (see Chapter 8 for more about how prejudice stifles listening).

Work to recognize and control your judgments. Being aware of what you tend to judge will help you avoid putting up a barrier against incoming messages that clash with your opinions or feelings. Keeping an open mind means being aware of the things you believe in as well as your prejudices. It also means defining education as a continuing search for evidence, regardless of whether it supports or negates your point of view.

Partial Hearing Loss and Learning Disabilities

Good listening techniques don't solve every listening problem. Students who have a partial hearing loss have a physical explanation for why listening is difficult. If you have some level of hearing loss, seek out special services that can help you listen in class. You may require special equipment or might benefit from tutoring. You may be able to arrange to meet with your instructor outside of class to clarify your notes.

Other disabilities, such as Attention Deficit Disorder (ADD) or a problem with processing heard language, can cause difficulties with both focusing on and understanding that which is heard. People with such disabilities have varied ability to compensate for and overcome them. If you have a disability, don't blame yourself for having trouble listening. Your counseling center, student health center, advisor, and instructors should be able to give you particular assistance in working through your challenges.

Become an Active Listener

"No one cares to speak to an unwilling listener. An arrow never lodges in a stone; often it recoils upon the sender of it."

St. Jerome

On the surface, listening seems like a passive activity; you sit back and listen as someone else speaks. Effective listening, however, is really an *active* process that involves setting a purpose for listening, asking questions, and paying attention to verbal signposts.

Set Purposes for Listening

Active listening is difficult if you don't know or care why you are listening. Think through why you listen in any situation. Establish what you want to achieve by listening, such as greater understanding of the material, a more direct connection with your instructor, staying awake in class, or better note taking. When you set a purpose, you have a goal that you can achieve only through active listening. A purpose for listening motivates you to listen.

Ask Questions

Asking questions is not a sign of stupidity or a reason to doubt your intelligence. In fact, a willingness to ask questions shows a desire to learn, and is the mark of an active listener and critical thinker. Some questions are *informational*—seeking information—such as any question beginning with the phrase, "I don't understand. . . . " Other *clarifying* questions state your understanding of what you just heard and ask if that understanding is correct. While some clarifying questions focus on a key concept or theme ("So, some learning disorders can be improved with treatment?"), others highlight specific facts ("Is it true that dyslexia can cause people to reverse letters and words?").

If for whatever reason you don't have an opportunity to ask your questions in class, jot them down and ask them during a discussion period or during a talk with your instructor.

Pay Attention to Verbal Signposts

You can identify important facts and ideas and predict test questions by paying attention to the speaker's specific choice of words. *Verbal signposts* often involve transition words and phrases that help organize information, connect ideas, and indicate what is important and what is not. Let phrases like those in Table 7-2 direct your attention to the material that follows.

Effective listening will enable you to acquire knowledge. You also need a good memory, however, so that you can remember what you've heard.

TABLE 7-2 PAYING ATTENTION TO VERBAL SIGNPOSTS

SIGNALS POINTING TO KEY CONCEPTS	SIGNALS OF SUPPORT
There are two reasons for this...	For example,...
A critical point in the process involves...	Specifically,...
Most importantly,...	For instance,...
The result is...	Similarly,...
SIGNALS POINTING TO DIFFERENCES	**SIGNALS THAT SUMMARIZE**
On the contrary,...	Finally,...
On the other hand,...	Recapping this idea,...
In contrast,...	In conclusion,...
However,...	As a result,...

Source: Adapted from George M. Usova, *Efficient Study Strategies: Skills for Successful Learning.* Pacific Grove, CA: Brooks/Cole Publishing Company, 1989, p. 69.

HOW DOES MEMORY WORK?

You need an effective memory in order to use the knowledge you take in throughout your life. Human memory works like a computer. Both have essentially the same purpose: to encode, store, and retrieve information.

> During the *encoding stage*, information is changed into usable form. On a computer, this occurs when keyboard entries are transformed into electronic symbols and stored on a disk. In the brain, sensory information becomes impulses that the central nervous system reads and codes. You are encoding, for example, when you study a list of chemistry formulas.
>
> During the *storage stage* information is held in memory (the mind's version of a computer hard drive) for later use. In this example, after you complete your studying of the formulas, your mind stores them until you need to use them.
>
> During the *retrieval stage*, memories are recovered from storage by recall, just as a saved computer program is called up by name and used again. In this example, your mind would retrieve the chemistry formulas when you had to take a test or solve a problem.

Memories are stored in three different storage banks. The first, called *sensory memory*, is an exact copy of what you see and hear, and lasts for a second or less. Certain information is then selected from sensory memory and moves into *short-term memory*, a temporary information storehouse that lasts no more than 10 to 20 seconds. You are consciously aware of material in your short-term memory. While unimportant information is quickly dumped, important information is transferred to *long-term memory*—the mind's more permanent storehouse.

Having information in long-term memory does not mean that you will be able to recall it when needed. Particular techniques can help you improve your recall.

HOW CAN YOU IMPROVE YOUR MEMORY?

THE FAR SIDE By GARY LARSON

"Mr. Osborne, may I be excused? My brain is full."

Source: The Far Side © 1986 Far Works, Inc. Used by permission of Universal Press Syndicate. All rights reserved.

Your accounting instructor is giving a test tomorrow on the use of bookkeeping programs. You feel confident, since you spent hours last week memorizing the material. Unfortunately, by the time you take the test, you may remember very little. That's because most forgetting occurs within minutes after memorization.

In a classic study conducted in 1885, researcher Herman Ebbinghaus memorized a list of meaningless three-letter words such as CEF and LAZ. Within one short hour he measured that he had forgotten more than 50 percent of what he learned. After two days, he knew fewer than 30 percent. Although his recall of the syllables remained fairly stable after that, the experiment shows how fragile memory can be, even when you take the time and energy to memorize information.[3]

People who have superior memories may have an inborn talent for remembering. More often, though, they have mastered techniques for improving recall. Remember that techniques aren't a cure-all for memory difficulties, especially for those who may have disabilities such as ADD. If you have a disability, the following memory techniques may help you but may not be enough. Seek specific assistance if you consistently have trouble remembering.

Memory Improvement Strategies

As a student, your job is to understand, learn, and remember information, from general concepts to specific details. The following suggestions will help improve your recall.

Develop a Will to Remember

Why can you remember the lyrics to dozens of popular songs but not the functions of the pancreas? Perhaps this is because you want to remember them, you connect them with a visual image, or you have an emotional tie to them. To achieve the same results at school or on the job, tell yourself that what you are learning is important and that you need to remember it. Saying these words out loud can help you begin the active, positive process of memory improvement.

Understand What You Memorize

Make sure that everything you want to remember makes sense. Something that has meaning is easier to recall than something that is gibberish. This basic principle applies to everything you study—from biology and astronomy to history and English literature.

Recite, Rehearse, and Write

When you *recite* material, you repeat it aloud in order to remember it. Reciting helps you retrieve information as you learn it and is a crucial step in studying (see Chapter 5). *Rehearsing* is similar to reciting, but is done in silence, in your mind. It involves the process of repeating, summarizing, and associating information with other information. *Writing* is rehearsing on paper. The act of writing solidifies the information in your memory.

Separate Main Points From Unimportant Details

If you use critical-thinking skills to select and focus on the most important information, you can avoid overloading your mind with extra clutter. To focus on key points, highlight only the most important information in your texts and write notes in the margins about central ideas. When you review your lecture notes, highlight or rewrite the most important information to remember.

Study During Short but Frequent Sessions

If you think you have mastered material after studying it once, you might be shortchanging yourself. Research shows that you can improve your chances of remembering material if you learn it more than once. The more you study, the more you are likely to remember at exam time.

To get the most out of your study sessions, spread them over time. A pattern of short sessions followed by brief periods of rest is more effective than continual studying with little or no rest. Even though you may feel as though you accomplish a lot by studying for an hour without a break, you'll probably remember more from three 20-minute sessions. Try sandwiching study time into breaks in your schedule, such as when you have time between classes.

When studying for several tests at a time, avoid studying two similar subjects back to back. You'll be less confused when you study history after biology rather than, for example, if you study chemistry after biology.

Separate Material Into Manageable Sections

When material is short and easy to understand, studying it start to finish may work. For longer material, you may benefit from dividing it into logical sections, mastering each section, putting all the sections together, and then testing your memory of all the material. Actors take this approach when learning the lines of a play, and it can work just as well for students.

Use Visual Aids

Any kind of visual representation of study material can help you remember. You may want to convert material into a think link or outline. Write material in any visual shape that helps you recall it and link it to other information.

FIGURE 7-2 FLASH CARDS HELP YOU MEMORIZE IMPORTANT FACTS

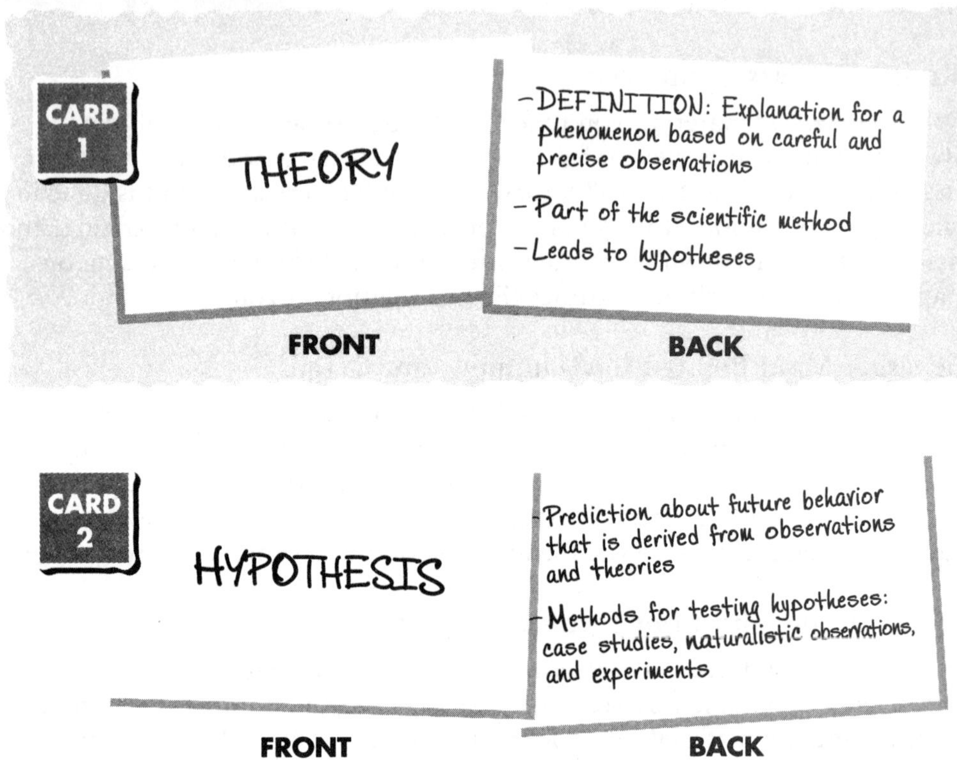

Flashcards are a great visual memory tool. They give you short, repeated review sessions that provide immediate feedback. Make them from 3-by-5-inch index cards. Use the front of the card to write a word, idea, or phrase you want to remember. Use the back side for a definition, explanation, and other key facts. Figure 7-2 shows two flashcards for studying psychology.

Here are some additional suggestions for making the most of your flash cards:

Use the cards as a self-test. Divide the cards into two piles: the material you know and the material you are learning. You may want to use rubber bands to separate the piles.

Carry the cards with you and review them frequently. You'll learn the most if you start using cards early in the course, well ahead of exam time.

Shuffle the cards and learn information in various orders. This will help avoid putting too much focus on some information and not enough on others.

Test yourself in both directions. First, look at the terms or ideas and provide definitions or explanations. Then turn the cards over and reverse the process.

Making the Most of Last-Minute Studying

Last-minute studying, or *cramming*, often results in forgetting much of the material learned. Study conditions, however, aren't always ideal. Sometimes a busy week may leave you only a few hours to prepare for a big exam. Nearly every student crams sometime during college. If you end up with a tight schedule, use these hints to make the most of your study time:

- *Go through your flashcards*, if you have them, one last time.
- *Resist going through your notes or textbook page by page.* Focus on crucial concepts; don't sweat the rest.
- *Create a last-minute study sheet with hard-to-remember material.* On a single sheet of paper, write down key facts, definitions, formulas, and so on. Try to keep the material short and simple. If you prefer visual notes, use think links to map out ideas and their supporting examples (see Chapter 6 for information on think links).
- *Arrive at the exam room a few minutes early.* Study the sheet or your flashcards until you are asked to clear your desk.
- *While it is still fresh in your mind, record any helpful information on a piece of scrap paper.* Do this before looking at any test questions.

After your exam, evaluate the effects cramming had on learning the material and what you will do to improve the situation next time. Set a goal and plan ahead.

Mnemonic Devices

Certain show business performers entertain their audiences by remembering the names of 100 strangers or flawlessly repeating 30 ten-digit phone numbers. These performers probably have superior memories, but genetics alone can't produce these results. They also rely on memory techniques, known as mnemonic devices (pronounced neh MAHN ick) to help them.

Mnemonic devices, Memory techniques that involve associating new information with information you already know.

Mnemonic devices work by connecting information you are trying to learn with simpler information or information that is familiar. Instead of learning new facts by rote (repetitive practice), associations give you a hook on which to hang these facts and retrieve them. Mnemonic devices make information familiar and meaningful through unusual, unforgettable mental associations and visual pictures.

Here's an example to prove the power of mnemonics. Suppose you want to remember the names of the first six presidents of the United States. The first letters of their last names—Washington, Adams, Jefferson, Madison, Monroe, and Adams—together read W A J M M A. To remember them, you might add an "e" after the "J" and create a short nonsense word, "wajemma." To remember their first names—George, John, Thomas, James, James, and John—you might set the names to the tune of "Happy Birthday" or any musical tune that you know.

Visual images, idea chains, and acronyms are a few of the more widely used kinds of mnemonic devices. Apply them to your own memory challenges.

Create Visual Images and Associations

Visual images are easier to remember than images that rely on words alone. In fact, communication through visual images goes back to the prehistoric era, when people made drawings that still exist on cave walls. It's no accident that the phrase "a picture is worth a thousand words" is so familiar. The best mental pictures often involve colors, three-dimensional images, action scenes, and disproportionate, funny, or ridiculous images.

"The true art of memory is the art of attention."
Samuel Johnson

Especially for visual learners, turning information into mental pictures helps improve memory. To remember that the Spanish artist Picasso painted "The Three Women," you might imagine the women in a circle dancing to a Spanish song with a pig and a donkey (pig-asso). Don't reject outlandish images—as long as they help you.

Use an Idea Chain to Remember Items in a List

An *idea chain* is a memory strategy that involves forming exaggerated mental images of a large group of items. The first image is connected to the second image, which is connected to the third image, and so on. Imagine, for example, that you want to remember the seven Thinktrix mind actions that appear in the critical-thinking discussion in Chapter 4: recall, similarity, difference, cause and effect, example to idea, idea to example, and evaluation. You can use the visual icons to form an idea chain that goes like this:

> The other end of a string tied around your finger (*recall*) leads to two pyramids (*similarity*) and ends at a black square office building next to one of the pyramids (*difference*). Inside the building there's a courtyard with a fountain dripping into a pool (*cause and effect*). On the wall, a painted "ex" and an arrow direct you to a light bulb (*example to idea*), which points to another "ex" (*idea to example*). Lit by the light bulb above, a set of scales weighs mail (*evaluation*).

Create Acronyms

Acronym,
A word formed from the first letters of a series of words, created in order to help you remember the series.

Another helpful association method involves the use of the acronym. The acronym "Roy G. Biv" often helps students remember the colors of the spectrum. Roy G. Biv stands for **R**ed, **O**range, **Y**ellow, **G**reen, **B**lue, **I**ndigo, **V**iolet. In history, you can remember the big-three Allies during World War II—Britain, America, and Russia—with the acronym BAR.

When you can't create a name like Roy G. Biv, create an acronym from an entire sentence, in which the first letter of each word in the sentence stands for the first letter of each memorized term. When science students want to remember the list of planets in order of their distance from the sun, they learn the sentence: My very elegant mother just served us nine pickles. (Mercury, Venus, Earth, Mars, Jupiter, Saturn, Uranus, Neptune, and Pluto.)

Improving your memory requires energy, time, and work. In school, it also helps to master PQ3R, the textbook study technique that was introduced in Chapter 5. By going through the steps in PQ3R and using the specific memory techniques described in this chapter, you will be able to learn more in less time—and remember what you learn long after exams are over.

HOW CAN TAPE RECORDERS HELP YOU LISTEN, REMEMBER, AND STUDY?

The selective use of a tape recorder can provide helpful backup to your listening and memory skills and to your study materials. It's important, though, not to let tape recording substitute for active participation. Not all students like to use tape recorders, but if you choose to do so, here are some guidelines and a discussion of potential effects.

Guidelines for Using Tape Recorders

Ask the instructor whether he or she permits tape recorders in class. Some instructors don't mind, while others don't allow students to use them.

Use a small, portable tape recorder. Sit near the front for the best possible recording.

Participate actively in class. Take notes just as you would if the tape recorder were not there.

Use tape recorders to make study tapes. Questions on tape can be like audio flashcards. One way to do it is to record study questions, leaving 10–15 seconds between questions for you to answer out loud. Recording the correct answer after the pause will give you immediate feedback. For example, part of a recording for a writing class might say, "The three elements of effective writing are . . . (10–15 seconds) . . . topic, audience, and purpose."

Potential Positive Effects of Using Tape Recorders

- You can listen to an important portion of the lecture over and over again.
- You can supplement or clarify sections of the lecture that confused you or that you missed.
- Tape recordings can provide additional study materials to listen to when you exercise or drive in your car.
- Tape recordings can help study groups reconcile conflicting notes.
- If you miss class, you might be able to have a friend record the lecture for you.

Potential Negative Effects of Using Tape Recorders

- You may tend to listen less in class.
- You may take fewer notes, figuring that you will rely on your tape.
- It may be time-consuming. When you attend a lecture in order to record it and then listen to the entire recording, you have taken twice as much time out of your schedule.

- If your tape recorder malfunctions or the recording is hard to hear, you may end up with very little study material, especially if your notes are sparse.

Think critically about whether using a tape recorder is a good idea for you. If you choose to try it, let the tape recorder be an additional resource for you instead of a replacement for your active participation and skills. Tape-recorded lectures and study tapes are just one study resource you can use in preparation for the tests that will often come your way.

HOW CAN PREPARATION HELP IMPROVE TEST SCORES?

Many people don't look forward to taking tests. If you are one of those people, try thinking of exams as preparation for life. When you volunteer, get a job, or work on your family budget, you'll have to apply what you know. This is exactly what you do when you take a test.

Like a runner who prepares for a marathon by exercising, eating right, taking practice runs, and getting enough sleep, you can take steps to master your exams. Your first step is to study until you know the material that will be on the test. Your next step is to use the following strategies to become a successful test taker: Identify test type, use specific study skills, prepare physically, and conquer test anxiety.

Identify Test Type and Material Covered

Before you begin studying, try to determine the type of test and what it will cover:

- Will it be a short-answer test with true/false and multiple-choice questions, an essay test, or a combination?
- Will the test cover everything you studied since the semester began or will it be limited to a narrow topic?
- Will the test be limited to what you learned in class and in the text or will it also cover outside readings?

Your instructors may answer these questions for you. Even though they may not tell you the specific questions that will be on the test, they might let you know what blocks of information will be covered and the question format. Some instructors may even drop hints throughout the semester about possible test questions. While some comments are direct ("I might ask a question on the subject of __________ on your next exam"), other clues are subtle. For example, when instructors repeat an idea or when they express personal interest in a topic ("One of my favorite theories is . . . "), they are letting you know that the material may be on the test.

Here are a few other strategies for predicting what may be on a test:

Use PQ3R to identify important ideas and facts. Often, the questions you write and ask yourself when you read assigned materials may be part of the test. In addition, any textbook study questions are good candidates for test material.

If you know people who took the instructor's course before, ask them about class tests. Try to find out how difficult the tests are and whether the test focuses more on assigned readings or class notes. Ask about instructor preferences. If you learn that the instructor pays close attention to detail such as facts or grammar, plan your work accordingly.

Examine old tests if instructors make them available in class or on reserve in the library. If you can't get copies of old tests, use clues from the class to predict test questions. After taking the first exam in the course, you will have a lot more information about what to expect in the future.

Use Specific Study Skills

Certain study skills are especially useful for test taking. They include choosing study materials, setting a study schedule, critical thinking, taking a pretest, and becoming organized.

Choose Study Materials

Once you have identified as much as you can about the subject matter of the test, choose the materials that contain the information you need to study. You can save yourself time by making sure that you aren't studying anything you don't need to. Go through your notes, your texts, any primary source materials that were assigned, and any handouts from your instructor. Set aside any materials you don't need so they don't take up your valuable time.

Set a Study Schedule

Use your time-management skills to set a schedule that will help you feel as prepared as you can be. Consider all the relevant factors—the materials you need to study, how many days or weeks until the test date, and how much time you can study each day. If you establish your schedule ahead of time and write it in your date book, you will be much more likely to follow it.

Schedules will vary widely according to situation. For example, if you have only three days before the test and no other obligations during that time, you might set two 2-hour study sessions for yourself during each day. On the other hand, if you have two weeks before a test date, classes during the day, and work three nights a week, you might spread out your study sessions over the nights you have off work during those two weeks.

Prepare Through Critical Thinking

Using the techniques from Chapter 4, approach your test preparation critically, working to understand rather than just to pass the test by repeating facts. As you study, try to connect ideas to examples, analyze causes and effects, establish truth, and look at issues from different perspectives. Although it takes work, critical thinking will promote a greater understanding of the subject and probably a higher grade on the exam. Using critical thinking is especially important for essay tests. Prepare by identifying potential essay questions and writing your responses.

Take a Pretest

Use questions from the ends of textbook chapters to create your own pretest. Choose questions that are likely to be covered on the test, then answer them under testlike conditions—in quiet, with no books or notes to help you, and with a clock telling you when to quit. Try to duplicate the conditions of the actual test. If your course doesn't have an assigned text, develop questions from your notes and from assigned outside readings.

Become Organized

A checklist, like the one in Figure 7-3 on the facing page, will help you get organized and stay on track as you prepare for each test.

Prepare Physically

When taking a test, you often need to work efficiently under time pressure. If your body is tired or under stress, you will probably not think as clearly or perform as well. If you can, avoid pulling an all-nighter. Get some sleep so that you can wake up rested and alert. If you are one of the many who press the snooze button in their sleep, try setting two alarm clocks and placing them across the room from your bed. That way you'll be more likely to get to your test on time.

Eating right is also important. Sugar-laden snacks will bring your energy up only to send it crashing back down much too soon. Similarly, too much caffeine can add to your tension and make it difficult to focus. Eating nothing will leave you drained, but too much food can make you want to take a nap. The best advice is to eat a light, well-balanced meal before a test. When time is short, grab a quick-energy snack such as a banana, some orange juice, or a granola bar.

Conquer Test Anxiety

A certain amount of stress can be a good thing. Your body is on alert, and your energy motivates you to do your best. For many students, however, the time before and during an exam brings a feeling of near-panic known as *test anxiety*. Described as a bad case of nerves that makes it hard to think or remember, test anxiety can make your life miserable and affect how you do on tests. When anxiety blocks performance, here are some suggestions:

Prepare so you'll feel in control. The more you know about what to expect on the exam, the better you'll feel. Find out what material will be covered, the format of the questions, the length of the exam, and the percentage of points assigned to each question.

FIGURE 7-3 PRETEST CHECKLIST[4]

Course: ____________________ Teacher: ______________________________

Date, time, and place of test: ______________________________________

Type of test (e.g., Is it a midterm or a minor quiz?): ________________

What the instructor has told you about the test, including the types of test questions, the length of the test, and how much the test counts in your final grade: ____

____

____

____

____

Topics to be covered on the test in order of importance:

1. ______________________________________
2. ______________________________________
3. ______________________________________
4. ______________________________________
5. ______________________________________

Study schedule, including materials you plan to study (e.g., texts and class notes) and date you plan to complete each source:

Source	Date of Completion
1. ______________________________	______________________
2. ______________________________	______________________
3. ______________________________	______________________
4. ______________________________	______________________
5. ______________________________	______________________

Materials you are expected to bring to the test (e.g., your textbook, a sourcebook, a calculator): ____

____

Special study arrangements (e.g., plan study group meetings, ask the instructor for special help, get outside tutoring): ______________________

____

____

Life management issues (e.g., make child-care arrangements, rearrange work hours): ____

____

____

Put the test in perspective. No matter how important it may seem, a test is only a small part of your educational experience and an even smaller part of your life. Your test grade does not reflect the kind of person you are or your ability to succeed in life.

Make a study plan. Divide the plan into a series of small tasks. As you finish each one, you'll feel a sense of accomplishment and control.

Practice relaxation. When you feel test anxiety coming on, take some deep breaths, close your eyes, and visualize positive mental images related to the test, like getting a good grade and finishing confidently with time to spare.

Test Anxiety and the Returning Adult Student

If you're returning to school after a layoff of five, ten, or even twenty years, you may wonder if you can compete with younger students or if your mind is still able to learn new material. To counteract these feelings of inadequacy, focus on how your life experiences have given you skills you can use. For example, managing work and a family requires strong time management, planning, and communication skills that can help you plan your study time, juggle school responsibilities, and interact with students and instructors.

In addition, your life experiences give you examples with which you can understand ideas in your courses. For example, your relationship experiences may help you understand concepts in a psychology course; managing your finances may help you understand economics or accounting practices; and work experience may give you a context for what you learn in a business management course. If you let yourself feel positive about your knowledge and skills, you may improve your ability to achieve your goals.

Coping With Math Anxiety

For many students there is a special anxiety associated with taking a math test. As Sheila Tobias, author of *Overcoming Math Anxiety*[5], explains, *math anxiety* is linked to the feeling that math is impossible:

> The first thing people remember about failing at math is that it felt like sudden death. Whether it happened while learning word problems in sixth grade, coping with equations in high school, or first confronting calculus and statistics in college, failure was instant and frightening. An idea or a new operation was not just difficult, it was impossible! And instead of asking questions or taking the lesson slowly, assuming that in a month or so they would be able to digest it, people remember the feeling as certain as it was sudden, that they would *never* go any further in mathematics.

Students who believe they are no good at math probably won't do well on math tests, even if they study. Their attitude creates a huge problem. If you are one of these students, here are some steps you can take to begin thinking about math—and math tests—in a different way.

See the value in learning to use your mind in a mathematical way. Mathematical thinking is another type of critical thinking. It can help you solve the little and big problems that are part of your world, including

REAL WORLD PERSPECTIVE

How can I prepare for exams?

Jeff Felardeau, Selkirk College—Nelson, B.C., Adult Basic Education

I've been out of school for quite a long time, so when I returned and had to memorize material for exams, I just wasn't prepared. The labor work I was doing didn't require me to use my memorization skills. I had the most difficulty memorizing for classes like biology and any of the sciences where you have to memorize a lot of facts. I'd work hard by repeating the information over and over in my mind, but I'd only be able to recall it for a short time afterwards—long-term learning wasn't there. Whenever I'd prepare for an exam, I'd find myself in a "cram" mode because I didn't remember any of the material from class. It was like learning the material all over again.

I took a class called College Success which gave me some good study tips. They taught me things like mind-mapping, listening skills, and note-taking styles. They also taught me to use word associations and visualization to help remember the material. It's helped me improve a lot but still, I get stuck in old habits and patterns and forget to apply the methods that that will really help me improve. I know that if I don't change these old study patterns and habits, I'll hit the wall sooner or later. I can't keep using methods that served me in the past but are no longer effective for where I am today. What do you suggest?

Miriam Kapner, New England Conservatory, Boston, MA., Junior in Oboe Performance

Even though you have a good understanding of what it takes to prepare for an exam, the key is to remain disciplined. If your mind is wandering in class and you find you're staring out the window looking at those clouds, remember that you have control of your mind. By staying focused in class you will not have to study so much when exam time rolls around. Although we all fall victim to daydreaming, try and gain control of your mind by thinking of your goals or by using simple mind tricks. Even if the class has a very dry teacher, there are ways to keep focused. One day a friend and I sat down and figured out exactly how much each class was costing us. When we realized the amount of money we were spending for that hour, it was a real eye-opener. If I'm really having a hard time, then I make sure I ask at least two questions per class. This forces me to pay attention.

In order to memorize, you need to be able to find some order. It helps if you have a reference point to begin with and then look for certain patterns or categories. I also use mnemonic devices to help me remember. In fact, I can still remember the ones I learned in elementary school: General Electric Lights Never Dim for the first five books of the Bible and of course, Every Good Boy Does Fine for the lines in the treble clef. But mainly, whatever steps you take to improve your preparation for exams, remember that you are in control of your mind—not the other way around.

how to measure the amount of wallpaper you need in a room, how to compare student loan programs, and even how to analyze the stock market.

Think of math as a tool that will help you land a good job. In fields such as engineering, accounting, banking, and the stock market, the ability to solve numerical problems is at the heart of the work. In real estate, retail sales, medicine, and publishing, you may use math for tasks such as writing budgets and figuring mortgage rates.

Turn negative self-talk into positive self-talk. Instead of telling yourself that a problem is too hard, tell yourself that if you take small, logical steps, you will succeed. Says Tobias, "If we can talk ourselves into feeling comfortable and secure, we may let in a good idea."[6]

Don't believe that women can't do math. Sheila Tobias says that when male students fail a math quiz, they don't think they worked hard enough; but when female students fail, they are three times more likely to feel that they just don't have what it takes.[7] Whether you are a man or a woman, work to overcome this stereotype.

Use the people and resources around you. Get to know your math instructor so you're comfortable asking for help. Join a math study group and make building confidence a group goal. Have a pep meeting right before a big test. Look for math-anxiety workshops. Seek out a tutor who can help you with your skills and build your confidence.

Become comfortable in the world of math. Find a computer program with math games or buy a paperback book with math puzzles. Do percentages and estimations in your head. Have fun with problems and enjoy solving them. Then transfer these feelings to class work and tests.

Understand math's relationship to your life success. Being at ease with numbers can serve you in day-to-day functions. Percentages can help you compare the financial benefits of different loan programs; adding and subtracting will allow you to balance a checkbook, and fractions will help you compare costs at work. Furthermore, working with numbers helps to develop general thinking skills. The precise calculation and problem solving involved in math help you develop precision, a focus on detail, patience, and a sense of order.

When you have prepared using the strategies that work for you, you are ready to take your exam. Focus on methods that can help you succeed when the test begins.

WHAT STRATEGIES CAN HELP YOU SUCCEED ON TESTS?

Even though every test is different, there are general strategies that will help you handle almost all tests, including short-answer and essay exams.

Write Down Key Facts

Before you even look at the test, write down any key information—including formulas, rules, and definitions—that you studied recently or even right before you entered the test room. Use the back of the question sheet or a piece of scrap paper for your notes (make sure it is clear to your instructor that this scrap paper didn't come into the test room already filled in!). Recording this information right at the start will make forgetting less likely.

Begin With an Overview of the Exam

Even though exam time is precious, spend a few minutes at the start of the test to get a sense of the kinds of questions you'll be answering, what kind of thinking they require, the number of questions in each section, and the point value of each section. Use this information to schedule the time you spend on each section. For example, if a two-hour test is divided into two sections of equal point value—an essay section with four questions and a short-answer section with sixty questions—you can spend an hour on the essays (fifteen minutes per question) and an hour on the short-answer section (one minute per question).

As you make your calculations, think about the level of difficulty of each section. If you think you can handle the short-answer questions in less than an hour and that you'll need more time with the essays, rebudget your time in a way that works for you.

Know the Ground Rules

A few basic rules apply to any test. Following them will give you the advantage.

Read test directions. While a test made up of 100 true/false questions and one essay may look straightforward, the directions may tell you to answer eighty, or that the essay is a optional bonus. Some questions or sections may be weighted more heavily than others. Try circling or underlining key words and numbers that remind you of the directions.

Begin with the parts or questions that seem easiest to you. Starting with what you know best can boost your confidence and help you save time to spend on the harder parts.

Watch the clock. Keep track of how much time is left and how you are progressing. You may want to plan your time on a scrap piece of paper, especially if you have one or more essays to write. Wear a watch or bring a small clock with you to the test room. A wall clock may be broken, or there may be no clock at all! Also, take your time. Rushing is almost always a mistake, even if you feel you've done well. Stay till the end so you can refine and check your work.

Master the art of intelligent guessing. When you are unsure of an answer, you can leave it blank or you can guess. In most cases, guessing will benefit you. First eliminate all the answers you know—or believe—are wrong. Try to narrow your choices to two possible answers; then, choose the one that makes more sense to you. When you recheck your work, decide if you would make the same guesses again, making sure there isn't a qualifier or fact that you hadn't noticed before.

Qualifier,
A word, such as *always, never,* or *often,* that changes the meaning of another word or word group.

Follow directions on machine-scored tests. Machine-scored tests require that you use a special pencil to fill in a small box on a computerized answer sheet. Use the right pencil (usually a number 2) and mark your answer in the correct space. Neatness counts on these tests, because the computer can misread stray pencil marks or partially erased answers. Periodically, check the answer number against the question number to make sure they match. One question skipped can cause every answer following it to be marked incorrect.

Use Critical Thinking To Avoid Errors

When the pressure of a test makes you nervous, critical thinking can help you work through each question thoroughly and avoid errors. Following are some critical-thinking strategies to use during a test.

Recall facts, procedures, rules, and formulas. You base your answers on the information you recall. Think carefully to make sure you recall it accurately.

Think about similarities. If you don't know how to attack a question or problem, consider any similar questions or problems that you have worked on in class or while studying.

Notice differences. Especially with objective questions, items that seem different from what you have studied may indicate answers you can eliminate.

Think through causes and effects. For a numerical problem, think through how you plan to solve it and see if the answer—the effect of your plan—makes sense. For an essay question that asks you to analyze a condition or situation, consider both what caused it and what effects it has.

Find the best idea to match the example or examples given. For a numerical problem, decide what formula (idea) best applies to the example or examples (the data of the problem). For an essay question, decide what idea applies to, or links, the examples given.

Support ideas with examples. When you put forth an idea in an answer to an essay question, be sure to back up your idea with an adequate number of examples that fit.

Evaluate each test question. In your initial approach to any question, evaluate what kinds of thinking will best help you solve it. For example, essay questions often require cause-and-effect and idea-to-example thinking, while objective questions often benefit from thinking through similarities and differences.

The general strategies you have just explored also can help you address specific types of test questions.

Master Different Types of Test Questions

Although the goal of all test questions is to discover how much you know about a subject, every question type has its own way of asking what you know. Objective questions, such as multiple choice or true/false, test your ability to recall, compare, and contrast information and to choose the right answer from among several choices. Subjective questions, usually essay questions, demand the same information recall but ask that you analyze the mind actions and thinking processes required, then organize, draft, and refine a written response. The following guidelines will help you choose the best answers to both types of questions.

Objective questions, Short-answer questions that test your ability to recall, compare, and contrast information and to choose the right answer from a limited number of choices.

Subjective questions, Essay questions that require you to express your answer in terms of your own personal knowledge and perspective.

Multiple-Choice Questions

Multiple-choice questions are the most popular type on standardized tests. The following strategies can help you answer these questions:

Read the directions carefully. While most test items ask for a single correct answer, some give you the option of marking several choices that are correct.

First read each question thoroughly. Then look at the choices and try to answer the question.

Underline key words and phrases in the question. If the question is complicated, try to break it down into small sections that are easy to understand.

Pay special attention to qualifiers such as *only, except,* etc. For example, negative words in a question can confuse your understanding of what the question asks ("Which of the following is *not* . . .").

If you don't know the answer, eliminate those answers that you know or suspect are wrong. Your goal is to narrow down your choices. Here are some questions to ask:

- Is the choice accurate in its own terms? If there's an error in the choice—for example, a term that is incorrectly defined—the answer is wrong.
- Is the choice relevant? An answer may be accurate, but it may not relate to the essence of the question.
- Are there any qualifiers, such as *always, never, all, none,* or *every*? Qualifiers make it easy to find an exception that makes a choice incorrect. For example, the statement that "children *always* begin talking before the age of two" can be eliminated as an answer to the question, "When do children generally start to talk?"

- Do the choices give you any clues? Does a puzzling word remind you of a word you know? If you don't know a word, does any part of the word (prefix, suffix, or root) seem familiar to you?

Look for patterns that may lead to the right answer, then use intelligent guessing. Test-taking experts have found patterns in multiple-choice questions that may help you get a better grade. Here is their advice:

> "A little knowledge that acts is worth infinitely more than much knowledge that is idle."
>
> Kahlil Gibran

- Consider the possibility that a choice that is more *general* than the others is the right answer.
- Look for a choice that has a middle value in a range (the range can be from small to large, from old to recent). This choice may be the right answer.
- Look for two choices with similar meanings. One of these answers is probably correct.

Make sure you read every word of every answer. Instructors have been known to include answers that are right except for a single word.

When questions are keyed to a long reading passage, read the questions first. This will help you focus on the information you need to answer the questions.

Here are some examples of the kinds of multiple-choice questions you might encounter in an Introduction to Psychology course[9] (the correct answer follows each question):

1. Arnold is at the company party and has had too much to drink. He releases all of his pent-up aggression by yelling at his boss, who promptly fires him. Arnold normally would not have yelled at his boss, but after drinking heavily he yelled because____________.
   a. parties are places where employees are supposed to be able to "loosen up"
   b. alcohol is a stimulant
   c. alcohol makes people less concerned with the negative consequences of their behavior
   d. alcohol inhibits brain centers that control the perception of loudness

   (The correct answer is C)

2. Which of the following has not been shown to be a probable cause of or influence in the development of alcoholism in our society?
   a. intelligence
   c. personality
   b. culture
   d. genetic vulnerability

   (The correct answer is A)

True/False Questions

True/false questions test your knowledge of facts and concepts. Read them carefully to evaluate what they truly say. Try to take these questions at face value without searching for hidden meaning. If you're truly stumped, guess (unless you're penalized for wrong answers).

Look for qualifiers in true/false questions—such as *all, only, always, because, generally, usually*, and *sometimes*—that can turn a statement that would otherwise be true into one that is false, or vice versa. For example, "The grammar rule, 'I before E except after C,' is *always* true" is *false*, whereas "The grammar rule, 'I before E except after C,' is *usually* true," is *true*. The qualifier makes the difference. Here are some examples of the kinds of true/false questions you might encounter in an Introduction to Psychology course.

> Are the following questions true or false?
>
> 1. Alcohol use is always related to increases in hostility, aggression, violence, and abusive behavior. (False)
> 2. Marijuana is harmless. (False)
> 3. Simply expecting a drug to produce an effect is often enough to produce the effect. (True)

Essay Questions

An essay question allows you to use writing to demonstrate your knowledge and express your views on a topic. Start by reading the questions and deciding which to tackle (sometimes there's a choice). Then focus on what each question is asking, the mind actions you will have to use, and the writing directions. Read the question carefully and do everything you are asked to do. Some essay questions may contain more than one part.

Watch for certain action verbs that can help you figure out what to do. Figure 7-4 on the next page, explains some words commonly used in essay questions. Underline these words as you read any essay question and use them as a guide.

Next, budget your time and begin to plan. Create an informal outline or think link to map your ideas and indicate examples you plan to cite to support those ideas. Avoid spending too much time on introductions or flowery prose. Start with a thesis idea or statement that states in a broad way what your essay will say (see Chapter 6 for a discussion of thesis statements). As you continue to write your first paragraph, introduce the essay's points, which may be subideas, causes and effects, or examples. Wrap it up with a concise conclusion.

Use clear, simple language in your essay. Support your ideas with examples, and look back at your outline to make sure you are covering everything. Try to write legibly. If your instructor can't read your ideas, it doesn't matter how good they are. If your handwriting is messy, try printing, skipping every other line, or writing on only one side of the paper.

Do your best to save time to reread and revise your essay after you finish getting your ideas down on paper. Look for ideas you left out and sentences that might confuse the reader. Check for mistakes in grammar, spelling, punctuation, and usage. No matter what subject you are writing

FIGURE 7-4 COMMON ACTION VERBS ON ESSAY TESTS

Analyze—Break into parts and discuss each part separately.
Compare—Explain similarities and differences.
Contrast—Distinguish between items being compared by focusing on differences.
Criticize—Evaluate the positive and negative effects of what is being discussed.
Define—State the essential quality or meaning. Give the common idea.
Describe—Visualize and give information that paints a complete picture.
Discuss—Examine in a complete and detailed way, usually by connecting ideas to examples.
Enumerate/List/Identify—Recall and specify items in the form of a list.
Explain—Make the meaning of something clear, often by making analogies or giving examples.
Evaluate—Give your opinion about the value or worth of something, usually by weighing positive and negative effects, and justify your conclusion.
ILLUSTRATE—Supply examples.
Interpret—Explain your personal view of facts and ideas and how they relate to one another.
OUTLINE—Organize and present the sub-ideas or main examples of an idea.
PROVE—Use evidence and argument to show that something is true, usually by showing cause and effect or giving examples that fit the idea to be proven.
Review—Provide an overview of ideas and establish their merits and features.
State—Explain clearly, simply, and concisely, being sure that each word gives the image you want.
SUMMARIZE—Give the important ideas in brief.
Trace—Present a history of the way something developed, often by showing cause and effect.

about, having a command of these factors will make your work all the more complete and impressive.

Here are some examples of essay questions you might encounter in your Introduction to Psychology course. In each case, notice the action verbs from Figure 7-4.

1. Summarize the theories and research on the causes and effects of daydreaming. Discuss the possible uses for daydreaming in a healthy individual.
2. Describe the physical and psychological effects of alcohol and the problems associated with its use.

Use Specific Techniques for Math Tests

Mathematical test problems present a special challenge to some students, especially those who suffer from math anxiety. These strategies may help you overcome any difficulties you might have:

Analyze problems carefully. Make sure that you take all the "givens" into account as you begin your calculations. Focus also on what you want to find or prove.

Write down any formulas, theorems, or definitions that apply to the problem. Do this before you begin your calculations.

Estimate before you begin to come up with a "ballpark" solution. Then work the problem and check the solution against your estimate. The two answers should be close. If they're not, recheck your calculations. You may have made a simple calculation error.

Break the calculation into the smallest possible pieces. Go step by step and don't move on to the next step until you are clear about what you've done so far.

Recall how you solved similar problems. Past experience can give you valuable clues as to how a particular problem should be handled.

Draw a picture to help you see the problem. This can be a diagram, a chart, a probability tree, a geometric figure, or any other visual image that relates to the problem at hand.

Take your time. Precision demands concentration and focus. Also, if you're using a calculator, one wrong keystroke can mean the difference between a right and wrong answer.

Be neat. When it comes to numbers, mistaken identity can mean the difference between a right and a wrong answer. A 4 that looks like a 9 or a 1 that looks like a 7 can make trouble.

Use the opposite operation to check your work. When you come up with an answer, work backwards to see if you are right. Use subtraction to check your addition; use division to check multiplication; and so on. Try to check every problem before you hand in your paper.

Look back at the questions to be sure you did everything that was asked. Did you answer every part of the question? Did you show all the required work? Be as complete as you possibly can.

HOW CAN YOU LEARN FROM TEST MISTAKES?

The purpose of a test is to see how much you know, not merely to achieve a grade. The knowledge that comes from attending class and studying should allow you to correctly answer test questions. Knowledge also comes when you learn from your mistakes. If you don't learn from what you get wrong on a test, you are likely to repeat the same mistake again on another test and in life. Learn from test mistakes just as you learn from mistakes in your personal and business life.

Try to identify patterns in your mistakes by looking for:

- *careless errors*—In your rush to complete the exam, did you misread the question or directions, blacken the wrong box, skip a question, or use illegible handwriting?
- *conceptual or factual errors*—Did you misunderstand a concept or never learn it in the first place? Did you fail to master certain facts? Did you skip part of the assigned text or miss important classes in which ideas were covered?

You may want to rework the questions you got wrong. Based on the feedback from your instructor, try rewriting an essay, recalculating a math problem, or redoing the questions that follow a reading selection. As frustrating as they are, remember that mistakes show that you are human, and they can help you learn. If you see patterns of careless errors, promise yourself that next time you'll try to budget enough time to double-check your work. If you pick up conceptual and factual errors, rededicate yourself to better preparation.

When you fail a test, don't throw it away. First, take comfort in the fact that a lot of students have been in your shoes and that you are likely to improve your performance. Then recommit to the process by reviewing and analyzing your errors. Be sure you understand why you failed. You may want to ask for an explanation from your instructor. Finally, develop a plan to really learn the material if you didn't understand it in the first place.

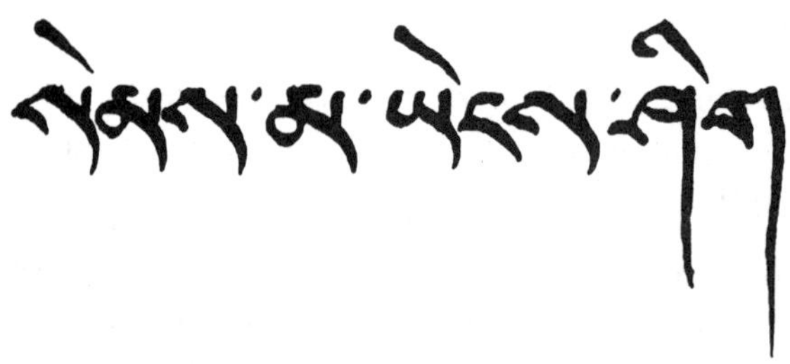

In Sanskrit, the written language of India and other Hindu countries, the characters above read *sem ma yeng chik*, meaning, "do not be distracted." This advice can refer to focus for a task or job at hand, the concentration required to critically think and talk through a problem, or the mental discipline of meditation.

Think of this concept as you strive to improve your listening and memory techniques. Focus on the task, the person, or the idea at hand. Try not to be distracted by other thoughts, other people's notions of what you should be doing, or any negative messages. Be present in the moment to truly hear and remember what is happening around you. Do not be distracted.

Applications

Name ____________________ Date ____________

Key Into Your Life: Opportunities to Apply What You Learn

Exercise 1: Optimum Listening Conditions

➤ Describe a recent classroom situation in which you had an easy time listening to the instructor:

Where are you? ____________________

What is the instructor discussing? ____________________

Is it a straight lecture or is there give-and-take between instructor and students? ____________________

____

What is your state of mind? (List factors that might affect your ability to listen.) ____________________

____

____

____

Are there any external barriers to communication? If yes, what are they, and how do they affect your concentration? ____________________

____

____

➤ Now describe a situation where you have found it more difficult to listen.

Where are you? ____________________

What is the instructor discussing? ____________________

Is it a straight lecture or is there give-and-take between instructor and students? ____________________

____

What is your state of mind? (List factors that might affect your ability to listen.) ____________________

____

____

____

Are there any external barriers to communication? If yes, what are they, and how do they affect your concentration? ____________________

____

____

➤ Examine the two situations. Based on your descriptions, name three conditions that are crucial for you to listen effectively.

1. ____________________

2. ____________________

3. ____________________

What steps can you take to recreate these conditions in more difficult situations like the second one you described? ____________________

____

____

Exercise 2: Create a Mnemonic Device

Look back at all the memory principles examined in this chapter. Using what you learned about mnemonic devices, create a mnemonic that allows you to remember these memory principles quickly. You can create a mental picture or an acronym. If you are using a mental picture, describe it here; if you are using an acronym, write it and then indicate what each letter stands for.

____

____

____

____

Think of other situations in which you used a mnemonic device to remember something. What was the device? How effective was it in helping you remember the information?

____

____

____

____

Exercise 3: Boost Your Memory

What do you have the most trouble remembering? Is it names, historic dates, scientific formulas, the actions in a sequence? Write it here. ________

____

Now spend a week trying to improve. For example, if you have trouble remembering the battles of World War II in order, you could recite and rehearse them, then associate each battle with an image and link the images in a chain. Indicate here the techniques that you try:

1. ______________________________

____

2. ______________________________

____

3. ______________________________

____

Did your skills improve? If so, what technique (or combination of techniques) helped the most? Explain how you think you can apply these techniques to other memory challenges.

____

____

____

____

Exercise 4: Test Analysis

When you get back your next test, take a detailed look at your performance.

- Start by writing what you think of your test performance and grade. Were you pleased or disappointed? If you made errors, were they careless or due to not knowing facts and concepts?

____

____

____

- Next, list the test-preparation activities that helped you do well on the exam and the activities you wish you had done—and intend to do—for the next exam:

Positive actions I took

____

____

____

Positive actions I intend to take next time

- Finally, list the activities you don't intend to repeat when studying for the next test.

Exercise 5 : Learning From Your Mistakes

For this exercise, use an exam on which you made one or more mistakes.

- Why do you think you answered the question(s) incorrectly?

- Did any qualifying terms, such as *always, sometimes, never, often, occasionally, only, no* and *not*, make the question(s) more difficult or confusing? What steps could you have taken to clarify the meaning?

- Did you try to guess the correct answer? If so, why do you think you made the wrong choice?

- Did you feel rushed? If you had had more time, do you think you would have gotten the right answer(s)? What could you have done to budget your time more effectively?

- If an essay question was a problem, what do you think went wrong? What will you do differently the next time you face an essay question on a test?

Key to Cooperative Learning: Building Teamwork Skills

Hone Your Listening Skills Improve listening through teamwork. Divide into groups of five to nine to play a game called *Celebrity*. Each group will have two or three teams, each with two or three people (for example, a group of seven will have two teams of two and one of three). Using small slips of paper, each person must write down the names of five well-known people, one on each slip. The people may be living or dead and can have achieved celebrity status in any field—sports, entertainment, politics, arts and literature, science and medicine, and so on. Each scrap of paper should be folded to conceal the name written on it. Put all of the scraps together in one container. The only other equipment you need is a watch with a second hand.

Within each team of two, there is a giver and a receiver (team members switch roles every time they have a new turn). Teams take turns guessing. While a member of a non-guessing team times the pair for one minute, the giver of the guessing team picks a piece of paper and describes the named celebrity to the receiver without saying any part of the person's name. The giver can use words, sounds, motion, singing, anything that will help the receiver. (For Jackie Robinson: "Famous baseball player, first black man on a pro team, first name is the same as President Kennedy's wife," etc.) If and when the receiver guesses correctly, the giver keeps that scrap and chooses another, continuing to go through as many names as possible before the minute is up. When time is called, the container of names (minus the names guessed) moves to the next team. (If a name remains unguessed when time is called, that paper has to go back into the container without the giver revealing the name.)

When all the names have been guessed, teams count their papers to learn their scores. Then come together as a class and take some time to exchange views about your experience. How did the time limit, teamwork atmosphere, or noise affect your ability to listen? Which names were you more able to guess? Which gave you trouble, and why? Evaluate your skills.

Key to Self Expression: Discovery Through Journal Writing

To record your thoughts, use a separate journal or the lined page at the end of the chapter.

Talk about how you feel about tests and how you generally perform when you take them.

As you walk into a room for a test, does your heart race or your mind go blank? Do you feel apprehensive? Does your performance on tests accurately reflect what you know or do your tests scores fall short of your knowledge? If there is a gap between your knowledge and your scores, why do you think this gap exists? What can you do to work through any test anxiety you have?

Key to Your Personal Portfolio: Your Paper Trail to Success

Apply Your New Study Skills Combine your study skills to create a study plan that will help you maximize your performance on any test. First, look at your memory skills. Which ones will help you most as you prepare for exams?

- understanding what you memorize
- reciting and rehearsing
- separating main points from unimportant details
- planning study sessions so that you remember the most from each session
- separating material into digestible chunks
- using flashcards
- using mnemonic devices

Rank the items from most helpful to least helpful. Then, discuss how you will use the five most helpful items.

Next, use the following checklist for any test to make sure that you have covered all your bases.

_____ I asked the instructor what will be covered on the exam and the format of the test questions.

_____ I tried to learn as much as I could about the kinds of tests the instructor gives by talking to former students and getting copies of old exams.

_____ I used critical thinking to explore difficult concepts that might be on the test.

_____ I took a pretest.

_____ I tried to prepare my body and mind to perform at their best.

_____ I used positive self-talk and other techniques to overcome negative thoughts that might affect my performance.

_____ I have gotten my personal life under control so I can focus on the exam.

_____ I have a plan of action that I will follow when I see the test for the first time. I'll try to get an overview of the test, learn test ground rules, schedule my time, and evaluate questions and choices in case I have to guess.

_____ I reviewed strategies for handling multiple-choice, true/false, and essay questions and feel comfortable with these strategies.

Finally, think back on what you learned in this chapter and in Chapter 5, the reading and studying chapter (you can refer to the material).

Now, develop a plan that shows how you will apply your new knowledge about study skills as you prepare for your next exam. Here are some of the items you can include:

- ➤ the specific critical-thinking techniques that will help you master the material
- ➤ the memory techniques that work best for you
- ➤ what you think about PQ3R as a study technique and whether you will try it
- ➤ the test-taking strategies that will help you prepare for and take your exams
- ➤ how to overcome what makes you anxious about tests

Using separate sheets of paper, construct your plan, using an outline or a think link.

To make the best plan, you have to know yourself and the techniques that will work best for you. Not every suggestion in this book is right for every person. Choose the skills that will work best for you and then use them to become a better student.

Name ______________________________ Date __________

Journal Entry

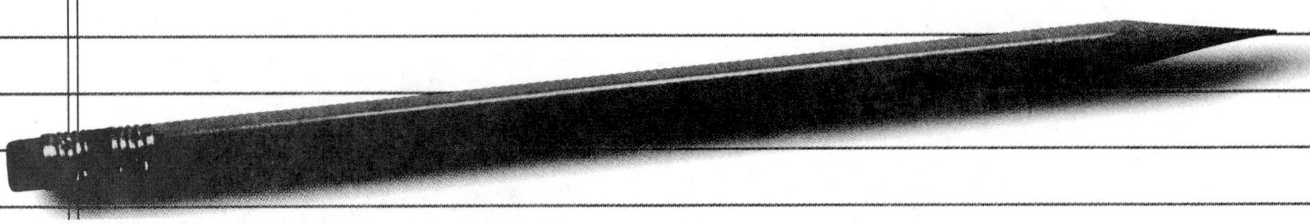

Chapter 4

RELATING TO OTHERS:
Appreciating Your Diverse World

The greater part of your waking life involves interaction with people—family and friends, peers, fellow students, co-workers, instructors, and many more. When you put energy into your relationships and open the lines of communication, you can receive much in return. Your relationships can also tell you a lot about the world and yourself. Having a strong network of relationships can help you grow and progress toward your goals.

This chapter will explore the issues of diversity that can hinder or help how you perceive others and relate to them. You will also explore communication styles, personal relationships, and the roles you can play in groups and on teams. Finally, you will read about various kinds of conflict and criticism, examining how to handle them so they benefit you instead of setting you back.

HOW CAN YOU UNDERSTAND AND ACCEPT OTHERS?

Human interaction is an essential element of life. In a diverse world, many people are different from what you are familiar with and perceive as "normal." In this section you will explore diversity in your world, the positive effects of accepting diversity, and how to overcome barriers to understanding. The first requirements for dealing with differences are an open mind and a willingness to learn.

Diversity in Your World

For centuries, travel to different countries was seen as part of a complete education. Edith Wharton, a nineteenth-century author, wrote a story called "False Dawn" in which a character named Mr. Raycie recommends travel to his son: "A young man, in my opinion, before setting up for himself, must see the world; form his taste; fortify his judgment. He must study the most famous monuments, examine the organization of foreign societies, and the habits and customs of those older civilizations . . . I believe he will be able to learn much."[1] When cultures were so separated, learning about differences was best accomplished through travel.

Diversity, The variety that occurs in every aspect of humanity, involving both visible and invisible characteristics.

Today, although traveling is still a valuable way to learn, different places and people often come to you. More and more, diversity is part of your community, on your television, on your Internet browser, at your school, in your workplace, and in your family. It used to be that most people lived in societies with others who seemed very similar to them. Now, differences are often woven into everyday life.

You may encounter examples of diversity like these:

- Communities with people from different stages of life
- Co-workers who represent a variety of ethnic origins
- Classmates who speak a number of different languages
- Social situations featuring people from various cultures, religions, and sexual orientations
- Individuals who marry a person or adopt a child from a different racial or religious background
- Diverse restaurants, services, and businesses in the community
- Neighborhoods with immigrants from a variety of social-class backgrounds
- Different lifestyles as reflected in books, magazines and newspapers, television, movies, music, the Internet, and other forms of popular culture
- People in the workplace who have a variety of disabilities—some more obvious than others

Each person has a choice about how to relate to others—or *whether* to relate to them. No one can force you to interact with any other person, or to adopt a particular attitude as being "right." Considering two important responsibilities may help you sort through your options.

Your responsibility to yourself lies in being true to yourself, in taking time to think through your reactions to other people. When you evaluate your thoughts, try to also consider their source: Have you heard these ideas from other people or organizations or the media? Do you agree with them, or does a different approach feel better to you? Through critical thinking you can arrive at decisions about which you feel comfortable and confident.

Your responsibility to others lies in treating people with tolerance and respect. No one will like everyone he or she meets, but acknowledging that others deserve respect and have a right to their opinions will build bridges of communication. The more people accept one another, the more all kinds of relationships will be able to thrive.

The Positive Effects of Diversity

More than just "a nice thing to do," accepting diversity has very real benefits to people in all kinds of relationships. Acceptance and respect form the basis for any successful interaction. As more situations bring diverse people into relationships, communication will become more and more dependent upon acceptance and mutual understanding.

Consider how positive relationships with diverse people may contribute to success. Relationships among family, friends, and neighbors affect personal life. Relationships among students, instructors, and other school personnel affect student life. Relationships among co-workers, supervisors, and customers/clients affect work life. Understanding and communication in these relationships can bring positive effects such as satisfying relationships, achievement, and progress. Failure to understand and communicate well can have negative effects.

For example, examine the potential effects of reactions to diversity in the following situations. Although each of these situations focuses on the reaction of only one person, it's important to note that both parties need to work together to establish mutual trust and openness.

> "Minds are like parachutes. They only function when they are open."
>
> Sir James Dewar

A male Hispanic employee has a female African-American supervisor. If the employee believes negative stereotypes about women or African-American people and resists taking directions from the supervisor, he may lose his job or be viewed as a liability. On the other hand, if the employee can respect the supervisor's authority and consider any different methods or ideas she has, their relationship is more likely to become supportive and productive. He may then be more likely to feel comfortable, perform well, and move up at work.

A learning-disabled student has an Asian instructor. If the student assumes that Asian people are superior and intimidating, letting that opinion lead her to resist the advice and directions her instructor gives her, she may do poorly in the class or drop the course. On the other hand, if the student stays open to what the instructor has to offer, the instructor may feel respected and may be more encouraging. The student may then be more likely to pay attention in class, work hard, and advance in her education.

A Caucasian man has a sister who adopts a biracial child. If the man cuts off contact with his sister because he fears racial differences and doesn't approve of racial mixing, he may deny himself her support and create a rift in the family. On the other hand, if the man can accept the new family member and respect his sister's choice, she may feel more supported and continue to support him in turn. The situation may help to build a close and rewarding family relationship.

Accepting others isn't always easy, and it's common to let perceptions about people block your ability to communicate. Following are some barriers that can hinder your ability to accept and understand others, and suggestions for how to overcome them.

Barriers to Understanding

You deserve to feel positive about who you are, where you come from, what you believe, and the others with whom you identify. However, problems arise when people use the power of group identity to put others down or cut themselves off from others. Table 8-1 shows how an open-minded approach can differ from an approach that is characterized by barriers.

Stereotypes, prejudice, discrimination, stereotype vulnerability, and fear of differences all can form barriers to communication.

Stereotypes

Stereotype, A standardized mental picture that represents an oversimplified opinion or uncritical judgment.

As you learned in Chapter 4, an assumption is an idea that you accept without looking for proof. A stereotype occurs when an assumption is made about a person or group of people, based on one or more characteristics. You may have heard stereotypical assumptions such as these: "Women are too emotional for business." "African-Americans can run fast and sing well." "Hispanics are Catholic and have tons of kids." "White people are cold and power-hungry." "Gay people sleep around." "Learning-disabled people can't hold down jobs." "Older people can't learn new things." Stereotypes are as common as they are destructive.

Why might people stereotype? Here are a few reasons:

People seek patterns and logic. Trying to make sense of a complex world is part of human nature. People often try to find order by using the labels and categories that stereotypes provide.

Stereotyping is quick and easy. Making an assumption about a person from observing an external characteristic is easier than working to know a person as a unique individual. Labeling a group of people based on a characteristic they seem to have in common takes less time and energy than exploring the differences and unique qualities within the group.

Movies, magazines, and other media encourage stereotyping. The more people see stereotypical images—the unintelligent blonde, the funny overweight person, the evil white businessman—the easier it is to believe that such stereotypes are universal.

TABLE 8-1 A CLOSED-MINDED APPROACH VS. AN OPEN-MINDED APPROACH

YOUR ROLE	SITUATION	CLOSED-MINDED APPROACH	OPEN-MINDED APPROACH
Team member on the job	A co-worker from from India observes a Hindu religious ritual at lunchtime.	You stare at the religious ritual, thinking it weird. You feel that this co-worker should just blend in and act like everyone else.	Your observe the ritual, respecting how the person expresses religious beliefs. You look up Hindu religion in your spare time to learn more.
Fellow student	For an assignment, you are paired up with a student old enough to be your mother.	You figure that the student will be closed off to the modern world. You think that she might also act like a parent and preach to you about how to do the assignment.	You avoid thinking that this student will act like your parents and get to know her as an individual. You stay open to what you can learn from her experiences and knowledge.
Friend	You are invited to dinner at a friend's house for the first time. When he introduces you to his partner, you realize that he is gay.	You are turned off by the idea of two men in a relationship and by gay culture in general. You are uncomfortable and make an excuse to leave early. You avoid your friend from then on.	You have dinner with your friend and his partner. You learn that they have a committed, supportive relationship. You take the opportunity to learn more about who they are and what their lives are like.
Employee	Your new boss is Japanese-American, hired from a competing company.	You assume that your new boss is very hard-working, expecting unrealistic things things from you and your co-workers. You assume she doesn't take time to socialize.	Your rein in your assumptions, knowing they are based on stereotypes, and approach your new boss with an open mind.

The ease of stereotypes comes at a high price. First and foremost, stereotypes can perpetuate harmful generalizations and falsehoods about others. These false ideas can promote discrimination. For example, if an employer believes that Vietnamese people cannot speak English well, he might not even bother to interview them. Secondly, stereotypes also communicate the message that you don't care about or respect others enough to discover who they really are. This may encourage others to stereotype you in return. Others may not give you a chance if they feel that you haven't given them a chance.

Addressing stereotypes.

Recall from the critical-thinking material in Chapter 4 the questions you can ask about an assumption in order to examine its validity. Apply these questions to stereotypes:

1. In what cases is this stereotype true, if ever? In what cases is it not true?
2. Has stereotyping others benefited me? Has it hurt me? In what ways?
3. If someone taught me this stereotype, why? Did that person think it over or just accept it?
4. What harm could be done by always accepting this stereotype as true?

Using these steps, think through the stereotypes you assume are true. When you hear someone else use a stereotype and you know some information that disproves it, volunteer that information. Encourage others to think through stereotypes and to reject them if they don't hold up under examination.

Give others the benefit of the doubt. Thinking beyond stereotypes is an important step toward more open lines of communication.

Prejudice

Prejudice, A preconceived judgment or opinion, formed without just grounds or sufficient knowledge.

Prejudice occurs when people "prejudge," meaning that they make a judgment before they have sufficient knowledge upon which to base that judgment. People often form prejudiced opinions on the basis of a particular characteristic—gender, race, culture, abilities, sexual orientation, religion, and so on. You may be familiar with the labels for particular kinds of prejudice, such as *racism* (prejudice based on race) or *ageism* (prejudice based on age). Any group can be subjected to prejudice, although certain groups have more often been on the receiving end of such closed-minded attitudes. Prejudice can lead people to disrespect, harass, and put down others. In some cases, prejudice may lead to unrealistic expectations of others that aren't necessarily negative, such as if someone were to judge all Jewish people as excelling in business.

Prejudice can have one or more causes. Some common causes include the following.

People experience the world through the lens of their own particular identity. You grow up in a particular culture and family and learn their attitudes. When you encounter different ideas and ways of life, you may react by categorizing them. You may also react with ethnocentrism—the idea that your group is better than anyone else's.

When people get hurt, they may dislike or blame anyone who seems similar to the person who hurt them. Judging others based on a bad experience is human, especially when a particular characteristic raises strong emotions.

Jealousy and fear of personal failure can lead a person to want to put others down. When people are feeling insecure about their own abilities, they might find it easier to devalue the abilities of others rather than to take risks and try harder themselves.

The many faces of prejudice often show on college campuses. A student may not want to work with an in-class group that contains people of another race. Campus clubs may tend to limit their membership to a particular group and exclude others. Religious groups may devalue the beliefs of other religions. Groups that gather based on a common characteristic might be harassed by others. Women or men may find that instructors or fellow students judge their abilities and attitudes based on their gender. All of these attitudes severely block attempts at mutual understanding.

Addressing Prejudice. Being critical of people who are different cuts you off from all kinds of perspectives and people that can enhance the quality of your life. Critical thinking is your key to changing prejudicial attitudes. For example, suppose you find yourself thinking that a certain student in your class isn't the type of person you want to get to know. Ask yourself: Where did I get this attitude? Am I accepting someone else's judgment? Am I making judgments based on how this person looks or speaks or behaves? How does having this attitude affect me or others? If you see that your attitude needs to change, have the courage to activate that change by considering the person with an open, accepting mind.

Another tactic, and often an extremely difficult one, is to confront people you know when they display a prejudiced attitude. It can be hard to stand up to someone and risk a relationship or, if the person is your employer, even a job. On the other hand, your silence may imply that you agree. Evaluate the situation and decide what choice is most suitable and is true to your values. Ask yourself if you can associate with a person if he or she thinks or behaves in a way that you do not respect.

You have a range of choices when deciding whether to reveal your feelings about someone's behavior. You can decide not to address it at all. You may drop a humorous hint and hope that you make your point. You may make a small comment to "test the waters" and see how the person reacts, hoping that later you can have a more complete discussion about it. Whatever you do, express your opinion respectfully. Perhaps the other person will take that chance to rethink the attitude; perhaps he or she will not. Either way, you have taken an important stand.

Discrimination

Discrimination occurs when people deny others opportunities because of their perceived differences. Prejudice often accompanies discrimination. Discrimination can mean being denied jobs or advancement, equal educational opportunities, equal housing opportunities, services, or access to events, people, rights, privileges, or commodities.

Discrimination happens in all kinds of situations, revolving around gender, language, race, culture, and other factors. A 32-year-old married woman may not win a job because the interviewer assumes that she will become pregnant. A Russian person may be fired from a restaurant job because his English is heavily accented. Sheryl McCarthy, an African-American columnist for *New York Newsday*, sees it on the street. "Nothing is quite so basic and clear as having a cab go right past your furiously waving body and pick up the white person next to you," she says in her book, *Why Are the Heroes Always White?*[2] "Sometimes you can debate whether racism was the motivating factor in an act; here there is no doubt whatsoever." Even so-called majority populations may now experience the power of discrimination. For example, a qualified white man may be passed up for a promotion in favor of a female or minority employee.

The disabled are often targets of discrimination because people may believe that they are depressed and incapacitated. John Hockenberry, a wheelchair-using paraplegic who travels the world in his work as an award-winning journalist, challenges the idea that disabled people lead lives of unproductive misery. "My body may have been capable of less, but virtually all of what it could do was suddenly charged with meaning. This feeling was the hardest to translate to the outside, where people wanted to believe that I must have to paint things in this way to keep from killing myself," he says in his memoir *Moving Violations*.[3]

Obesity can invite discrimination as well. People who are overweight may have trouble winning jobs or moving up at work. Even shopping for clothing can present limited options. Only recently have certain name-brand designers begun to create clothing in women's sizes above 12, and many designers still discriminate.

Addressing discrimination. U.S. federal law states that it is unlawful for you to be denied an education, work or the chance to apply for work, housing, or basic rights based on your race, creed, color, age, gender, national or ethnic origin, religion, marital status, potential or actual pregnancy, or potential or actual illness or disability (unless the illness or disability prevents you from performing required tasks, and unless accommodations for the disability are not possible). Unfortunately, the law is frequently broken, with the result that incidents go unnoticed. Many times people don't report incidents, fearing trouble from those they accuse. Sometimes people don't even notice their attitudes seeping through, such as in an interview situation.

First and foremost, be responsible for your own behavior. Never knowingly participate in or encourage discrimination. When you act on prejudicial attitudes by discriminating against someone, the barrier to communication this discrimination causes hurts you as well as anyone else involved. A person who feels denied and shut out may be likely to do the same to you, and may even encourage others to do so.

Second, if you witness a discriminatory act or feel that you have been discriminated against, decide whether you want to approach an authority about it. You may want to begin by talking to the person who can most directly affect the situation—an instructor, your supervisor, a housing authority. Don't assume that people know when they hurt or offend someone. For example, if you have a disability and you find that accommodations haven't been made for you at school, speak up. Meet with an advisor to discuss your needs for transport, equipment, or a particular schedule.

If you don't find satisfaction and change at that level, try the next level of authority (an administrator, your supervisor's boss, a government official). If that doesn't produce results, you can take legal action, although legal struggles can take a lot of time and drain a great deal of money out of your pocket. At each decision stage, weigh all the positive and negative effects and evaluate whether the action is feasible for you. Although keeping quiet may not bring change, you may not be able to act right away. In the long run, if you are able to stand up for what you believe, your actions may be worthwhile.

REAL WORLD PERSPECTIVE

How can I adjust to diversity?

Carrie Nelson, University of Guadalajara—Centro de Estudios para Extranjeros

Once I made the decision to study Spanish, the idea of studying abroad in a Spanish-speaking country was simultaneous. I have always been fascinated with learning about other cultures and being introduced to new ideas. Once I started filling out forms for the school in Mexico and buying my plane ticket, however, I began to question my decision. I wondered if I could really handle this big of a change in my life. But in my heart I knew that I had made the right decision.

Now that I am actually studying in Guadalajara, Mexico, I cannot imagine how I could have been nervous. This is one of the best decisions I have ever made, although I have had to adjust to living here. In some aspects the Mexican and American cultures are very similar but in other regards they can be very different. For example, in the U.S. the customer is considered the most important person and expects to be served very quickly. In Mexico the customer is important but the way of life is much more relaxed. Therefore if a clerk gets a personal phone call they will most likely talk to that person whether there is a customer waiting or not.

Every day I experience something new or begin to better understand the differences in our cultures. By learning about other people, I am learning more about myself and the beauty and complexity of people. Still, I would like to deepen my relationship with the people of Guadalajara. I realize I am just scratching the surface of this experience. Do you have any suggestions?

Tan Pham, Gonzaga University—Spokane, Washington

In 1981, I escaped from Vietnam after having tried unsuccessfully 13 different times. Like your experience in Guadalajara, I found being in a new country both wonderfully enriching and overwhelming at the same time.

When I first arrived in the U.S., I was amazed at the way the people value time. In Vietnam, as in Guadalajara, things are much slower. But here, time is seen as money. I learned it was very important to arrive at my appointments at the exact time they were scheduled. I was also amazed at the technology: the computers and the transportation.

When you visit another country there is so much to learn. My recommendation is that you stay open to the experience. Let go of your past and fully embrace the new life you have accepted. Remember not to isolate yourself. Talk to the people. Avoid socializing just with people from your own country. Try to immerse yourself fully in the new culture. Also, ask for help. Most people are very sincere in their desire to help you. Each land has unique opportunities. Take advantage of them as explore your new world.

Stereotype Vulnerability

When people feel that they are part of a certain group, they take pride from what they perceive to be good about that group. On the other hand, they may want to distance themselves from stereotypical qualities associated with that group, such as when a woman in a business situation wants to avoid seeming too emotional. *Stereotype vulnerability* happens when people avoid facing a problem because they think that admitting it will just perpetuate a stereotype.

An example of stereotype vulnerability is an immigrant to the United States who resists seeking English tutoring for fear of seeming like just another foreigner. Another example is a person in a wheelchair who avoids asking for help in scheduling class locations for fear of being identified as an angry, demanding disabled person. Such fears cut people off from communication that could improve their lives.

Another side of stereotype vulnerability occurs when people refuse help because they believe that others want to help them out of pity for their minority status. "She thinks I'm disadvantaged because I'm African-American." "He only wants to help because he looks down on my having a learning disability." "They want to give me charity." These refusals are based on assumptions. Sometimes, such assumptions may contain a grain of truth. Frequently, though, the person who offers help just wants to help another human being, and the person who refuses it loses out on what may be valuable assistance.

Addressing stereotype vulnerability. Don't let stereotypes prevent you from getting assistance. If you find yourself avoiding help because you don't want to be labeled, have the courage to overcome your hesitation. Your assumption that others will stereotype you may not be accurate. Approach someone who can help you and give that person a chance to get to know your individual needs and problems. Perhaps he or she will see you not as a representative of a group but as an individual who needs and deserves specific attention.

Curb your own tendencies to judge according to stereotypes. Even if someone fulfills a stereotype about the group to which he or she belongs, never assume this stereotype is true of everyone else in that group. Approach every person as a unique individual.

If you feel that someone has offered you help out of pity for you, think through your assumption. Consider the possibility that he or she simply wants to help you. You may even want to discuss the situation with the person. Often a person who offers help can offend without meaning to. If you don't need or want that kind of help, or you don't like the way it was offered, say so clearly and respectfully. In addition, if you are the one offering help, be respectful of the fact that others may not want your help.

> "I have a dream that one day on the red hills of Georgia the sons of former slaves and the sons of former slave owners will be able to sit down together at the table of brotherhood."
>
> Martin Luther King, Jr.

Fear of Differences

It's human instinct to fear the unknown. Many people stop long before they actually explore anything unfamiliar. They allow their fear to prevent them from finding out anything about what's outside their known world. As cozy as that world can be, it also can be limiting, cutting off communication from people who could enrich that world in many different ways.

The fear of differences has many effects. A young person who fears the elderly may avoid visiting a grandparent in a nursing home. A person of one religion might reject friendships with those of other religions out of a fear of different religious beliefs. Someone in a relationship may fear the commitment of marriage. A person might turn down an offer to buy a house in a neighborhood that is populated with people from a different ethnic group. In each case, the person has denied him or herself a chance to learn a new perspective, communicate with new individuals, and grow from new experiences.

Address fear of differences. Diversity doesn't mean that you have to feel comfortable with everyone or agree with what everyone else believes. The fear of differences, though, can keep you from discovering anything outside your own world. Challenge yourself by looking for opportunities to expose yourself to differences. Today's world increasingly presents such opportunities. You can choose a study partner in class who has a different ethnic background. You can expand your knowledge with books or magazines. You can visit a museum or part of town that introduces a culture new to you. You can attend an unfamiliar religious service with a friend. Gradually broaden your horizons and consider new ideas.

If you think others are uncomfortable with differences, encourage them to work through their discomfort. Explain the difference so that it doesn't seem so mysterious. Offer to help them learn more in a setting that isn't threatening. Bring your message of the positive effects of diversity to others.

Accepting and Dealing With Differences

Successful interaction with the people around you benefits everyone. The success of that exchange depends upon your ability to accept differences. How open can you be? Your choices range from rejecting all differences to freely celebrating them, with a range of possibilities in between. Ask yourself important questions about what course of action you want to take. Realize that the opinions of family, friends, the media, and any group with which you identify may sometimes lead you into perspectives and actions that you haven't thought through completely. Do your best to sort through outside opinions and make a choice that feels right.

At the forefront of the list of ways to deal with differences is mutual respect. Respect for yourself and others is essential. Admitting that other people's cultures, behaviors, races, religions, appearances, and ideas deserve as much respect as your own promotes communication and learning.

What else can you do to accept and deal with differences?

Avoid judgments based on external characteristics. These include skin color, weight, facial features, or gender.

Cultivate relationships with people of different cultures, races, perspectives, and ages. Find out how other people live and think, and see what you can learn from them.

Educate yourself and others. "We can empower ourselves to end racism through massive education," say Tamara Trotter and Joycelyn Allen in *Talking Justice: 602 Ways to Build and Promote Racial Harmony*.[4] "Take advantage of books and people to teach you about other cultures. Empowerment comes through education. If you remain ignorant and blind to the critical issues of race and humanity, you will have no power to influence positive change." Read about other cultures and people.

Be sensitive to the particular needs of others at school and on the job. Think critically about their situations. Try to put yourself in their place by asking yourself questions about what you would feel and do if you were in a similar situation.

Work to listen to people whose perspectives clash with or challenge your own. Acknowledge that everyone has a right to his or her opinion, whether or not you agree with it.

Look for common ground—parenting, classes, personal challenges, interests.

Help other people, no matter how different they may be. Sheryl McCarthy writes about an African-American man who, in the midst of the 1992 Los Angeles riots, saw a man being beaten and helped him to safety. "When asked why he risked grievous harm to save an Asian man he didn't even know, Williams said, 'Because if I'm not there to help someone else, when the mob comes for me, will there be someone there to save me?' "[5] Continue the cycle of kindness.

Explore your own background, beliefs, and identity. Share what you learn with others.

Cultivate your own personal diversity. You may be one of the growing population of people who have two, three, or ten different cultures in your background. Perhaps your father is Native American and Filipino and Scottish, and your mother is Creole (French, Spanish, and African-American). Respect and explore your heritage. Even if you identify only with one group or culture, there are many different sides of you.

Take responsibility for making changes instead of pointing the finger at someone else. Avoid blaming problems in your life on certain groups of people.

Learn from the atrocities of history like slavery and the Holocaust. Cherish the level of freedom you have and seek continual improvement at home and elsewhere in the world.

Teach your children about other cultures. Impress upon them the importance of appreciating differences while accepting that all people have equal rights.

Recognize that people everywhere have the same basic needs. Everyone loves, thinks, hurts, hopes, fears, and plans. People are united through their essential humanity.

Expressing your ideas clearly and interpreting what others believe are crucial keys to communicating within a diverse world. The following section examines how you can communicate most effectively with the people around you.

HOW CAN YOU EXPRESS YOURSELF EFFECTIVELY?

The only way for people to know each other's needs is to communicate as clearly and directly as possible. Successful communication promotes successful school, work, and personal relationships. Exploring communication styles, paying attention to body language, addressing specific communication problems, and using specific success strategies will help you express yourself effectively.

Adjusting to Communication Styles

Communication is an exchange between two or more people. The speaker's goal is for the listener (or listeners) to receive the message exactly as the speaker intended. Different people, however, have different styles of communicating. Problems arise when one person has trouble "translating" a message that comes from someone who uses a different style. There are at least four communication styles into which people tend to fit: the Intuitor, the Senser, the Thinker, and the Feeler. Of course, people may shift around or possess characteristics from more than one category, but for most people one or two styles are dominant. Recognizing specific styles in others will help you communicate more clearly.[6]

The Styles

The following are characteristics of each communication style.

A person using the *Intuitor* style is interested in ideas more than details, often moves from one concept or generalization to another without referring to examples, values insight and revelations, talks about having a vision, looks toward the future, and can be oriented toward the spiritual.

A person showing the style of *Senser* prefers details or concrete examples to ideas and generalizations, is often interested in the parts rather than the whole, prefers the here-and-now to the past or future, is suspicious of sudden insights or revelations, and feels that "seeing is believing."

A person using the *Thinker* style prefers to analyze situations, likes to solve problems logically, sees ideas and examples as useful if they help to figure something out, and becomes impatient with emotions or personal stories unless they have a practical purpose.

A person showing the style of *Feeler* is concerned with ideas and examples that relate to people, often reacts emotionally, is concerned with values and their effects on people and other living things, doesn't like "cold logic" or too much detail.

You can benefit from shifting from style to style according to the situation, particularly when trying to communicate with someone who prefers a style different from yours. Shifting, however, is not always easy or possible. The most important task is to try to understand the different styles and to help others understand yours. In general, no one style is any better than another. Each has its own positive effects that enhance communication and negative effects that can hinder it, depending on the situation.

Identifying Your Styles

These four styles are derived from the Myers-Briggs Type Indicator (MBTI). Because the learning style assessments are also in part derived from the MBTI, you will notice similarities between those assessments and these communication styles. Table 8-2 shows how some learning styles may correspond loosely to the communication styles. Not all individual learning styles within the assessments are mentioned, and the styles that are noted may correspond with different styles in different situations, but these matchups depict the most common associations. Finding where your learning styles fit may help you to determine your dominant communication style or styles.

Adjusting to the Listener's Style

When you are the speaker, you will benefit from an understanding of both your own style and the styles of your listeners. It doesn't matter how clear you think you are being if the person you are speaking to can't "translate" your message by understanding your style. Try to take your listener's style into consideration when you communicate.

Following is an example of how adjusting to the listener can aid communication.

An intuitor-dominant instructor to a senser-dominant student: "Your writing isn't clear." The student's reply: "What do you mean?"

- *Without adjustment:* If the intuitor doesn't take note of the senser's need for detail and examples, he or she may continue with a string of big-picture ideas that might further confuse and

TABLE 8-2 LEARNING STYLES AND COMMUNICATION STYLES

COMMUNICATION STYLE	LEARNING STYLES INVENTORY	PATHWAYS TO LEARNING (MULTIPLE INTELLIGENCES)	PERSONALITY SPECTRUM
Intuitor	Theoretical, Holistic	Intrapersonal	Adventurer
Senser	Factual	Bodily-Kinesthetic	Organizer
Thinker	Linear	Logical-Mathematical	Thinker
Feeler	Reflective	Interpersonal	Giver

turn off the senser. "You need to elaborate more. Try writing with your vision in mind. You're not considering your audience."

- *With adjustment:* If the intuitor shifts toward a focus on detail and away from his or her natural focus on ideas, the senser may begin to understand, and the lines of communication can open. "You introduced your central idea at the beginning but then didn't really support it until the fourth paragraph. You need to connect each paragraph's idea to the central idea. Also, not using a lot of examples for support makes it seem as though you are writing to a very experienced audience."

Adjusting to the Communicator's Style

As a facet of communication, listening is just as important as speaking. When you are the listener, try to stay aware of the communication style of the person who is speaking to you. Observe how that style satisfies, or doesn't satisfy, what a person of your particular style prefers to hear. Work to understand the speaker in the context of his or her style and translate the message into one that makes sense to you.

Following is an example of how adjusting to the communicator can boost understanding.

A feeler-dominant employee to a thinker-dominant supervisor: "I'm really upset about how you've talked down to me. I don't think you've been fair. I haven't been able to concentrate since our discussion and it's hurting my performance."

- *Without adjustment.* If the thinker becomes annoyed with the feeler's focus on emotions, he or she may ignore them, putting up an even stronger barrier between the two people. "There's no reason to be upset. I told you clearly and specifically what needs to be done. There's nothing else to discuss."
- *With adjustment.* If the thinker considers that emotions are dominant in the feeler's perspective, he or she could respond to those emotions in a way that still searches for the explanations and logic the thinker understands best: "Let's talk about how you feel. Please explain to me what has caused you to become upset, and we'll discuss how we can improve the situation."

Words are only one aspect of communication style. People also use their bodies in different ways to communicate messages to one another.

The Power of Body Language

Your actions—not your words—are the most basic form of communication. Even people who cannot speak each other's language can communicate ideas through gestures and facial expressions. Your gestures, eye movement, facial expression, body positioning and posture, touching behavior, and use of personal space are all types of nonverbal communication, also called *body language*. If you understand how it works, you can use body language to your advantage.

How Body Language Works

Body language can reinforce or contradict verbal statements. For example, if a jittery person on a date says he's nervous, his body language *reinforces* his statement. On the other hand, if he insists that he is relaxed and at ease, his jittery behavior *contradicts* his statement. When body language contradicts verbal language, the message conveyed by the body language is dominant. Consider, for example, if someone were to ask you how you feel, and you said "fine" although you don't feel fine at all. In such a case your posture, eye contact, and other body language would convey the real message loud and clear.

Nonverbal cues also color what you communicate. Consider this statement: "This is the best idea I've heard all day." If you were to say this three different ways—once in a loud voice while standing up, once quietly while sitting with arms and legs crossed and looking away, and once while maintaining eye contact and taking the receiver's hand—you might send three different messages.

Although differences occur from person to person and from culture to culture, some specific types of body language may have particular meanings. For example, a body turned away may signal lack of interest, while an "open" sitting posture with legs uncrossed may show agreement. Crossed arms may show disagreement or a desire to close off. Hands on the hips may show a toughness and readiness, and a firm, brief handshake may radiate capability and friendliness. Good posture and a brisk walking pace may indicate confidence. Eye contact speaks volumes and is often dependent on cultural tradition. In the United States, for example, direct and steady eye contact may show attention and respect, while in Asian countries, respect is often conveyed by avoiding direct eye contact.[7]

Nonverbal communication strongly influences a first impression. First impressions emerge from a combination of nonverbal cues, tone of voice, and words spoken. Usually, nonverbal elements (signals and tone) come across first and strongest. Think about it; when you meet someone, you tend to judge the person before either of you speaks a word. You make assumptions based on nonverbal behavior such as posture, eye contact, gestures, and speed and style of movement.

Using Body Language to Your Advantage

The following strategies can help you maximize your awareness and use of body language.

Become aware. Pay attention to what other people communicate nonverbally. If a friend compliments you with strong eye contact and a natural smile, you might feel flattered. If the same friend speaking the same words doesn't look you in the eye and is physically closed off from you, there might be something left unsaid. Also, be aware that your nonverbal communication affects your messages, and try to make sure that what you say nonverbally reinforces your words.

Try not to contradict your words with your body language. A nonverbal message that goes against what you speak can cause confusion and perhaps make you appear dishonest. The receiver, unsure of which to believe, may tend to go with the nonverbal message. If you say to your advisor, "That grade is fine with me," with a tense tone of voice and aggressive posture, the advisor may be confused about what you feel. If you tell a friend that he looks nice but don't look him in the eye, he may think you are lying to make him feel better.

Note cultural differences. In some cultures, casual acquaintances stand close together when speaking; in others, the same distance may be used only in very intimate, personal conversations. Some people shake hands readily and touch others when speaking. Others may feel that touching is invasive and should only be used with intimate friends. Within each conversation you have, you can discover what seems appropriate by paying attention to what the other person does.

Overcoming Communication Problems

Communication problems may occur when information is not clearly presented, or when those who receive information filter it through their own perspectives and interpret it in different ways. Some of the most common communication problems follow, along with strategies to help you combat them.

Problem: Unclear or incomplete explanation

Solution: Support ideas with examples

When you clarify a general idea with supporting examples that illustrate how it works and what effects it causes, you will help your receiver understand what you mean and therefore have a better chance to hold his or her attention.

For example, if you tell a friend to take a certain class, that friend might not take you seriously until you explain why. If you then communicate the positive effects of taking that class (progress toward a major, an excellent instructor, friendly study sessions), you may get your message across. The same principle applies to your attitude toward this course. If others communicate to you specific examples of how your work in the course will benefit your education, career, and personal life, you may be more likely to apply yourself.

Work situations benefit form explanation as well. As a supervisor, if you assign a task without explanation, you might get a delayed response or find mistakes in your employee's work. If, however, you explain the possible positive effects of the task, you'll have better results.

Problem: Limited knowledge of audience

Solution: Think about with whom you're communicating

As with writing a paper, considering your audience will improve communication. Ask yourself questions about what is appropriate for your audience. Tailor your words, tone, and level of formality to the person and the situation. Even with the same person, your communication style may change from situation to situation. For example, if you have a good relationship with a supervisor, you may have a more informal communication style when the two of you are alone than you have when you are with others in a work setting. People are also in different moods at different times. Be sensitive, stay aware, and make adjustments as necessary.

Problem: Faulty timing

Solution: Choose optimum listening conditions

Even a perfectly worded message won't get through to someone who isn't ready to receive it. If you try to talk to your instructor when she is rushing out the door, coat half on and briefcase in hand, your message probably won't come across too well. If you tell someone to come to your home when you are distracted with work or children, you may not hear accurately. Pay attention to mood as well. If a friend has had an exhausting and traumatic week, you might not want to choose that time to ask a favor.

People on both the sending and receiving ends of communication will benefit from good timing. Choose a time to talk or listen according to when you can best focus on your communication.

Source: ©Nina Paley

Problem: Stereotyping

Solution: Look past external appearances

In almost every student's life, there are people of diverse backgrounds—instructors, deans, employers, fellow students, neighbors—who offer helpful and important information. If you want to benefit from what the people around you have to offer, make your best attempt to look past appearance or identification with a group to really hear the words spoken. If your assumptions are affecting your ability to listen, use the methods you explored earlier in this chapter to evaluate their accuracy.

Problem: Attacking the receiver

Solution: Send "I" messages

When a conflict arises, often the first instinct is to pinpoint what someone else did wrong. "You didn't lock the door!" "You never called last night!" "You left me out!" Making an accusation, especially without proof, puts the other person on the defensive and shuts down the lines of communication.

Using "I" messages will help you communicate your own needs rather than focusing on what you think someone else did wrong or should do differently. "I felt uneasy when I came to work and the door was unlocked." "I became worried about you when I didn't hear from you last night." "I felt disappointed when I realized that I couldn't join the party." "I" statements soften the conflict by highlighting the *effects* that the other person's actions have had on you, rather than the person or the actions themselves. When you focus on your own response and needs, your receiver may feel more free to respond, perhaps offering help and even acknowledging mistakes.

If you often feel dissatisfied and tense after an exchange, you may benefit from focusing more on your own needs when you communicate. Translate your anger into an "I" statement before speaking. Ask the other person, "Can we decide together how to improve this situation? Here's how I feel about what has happened." Using "I" statements will bring better results.

Problem: Passive or aggressive communication styles

Solution: Become assertive

Among the three major communication styles—aggressive, passive, assertive—the one that conveys a message in the clearest, most productive way is the assertive style. The other two, while commonly used, throw the communication out of balance. An aggressive communicator often denies the receiver a chance to respond, while a passive communicator may have trouble getting the message out. Assertive behavior strikes a balance between aggression and passivity. If you can be an assertive communicator, you will be more likely to get your message across while assuring that others have a chance to speak as well. Table 8-3 on the following page, compares some characteristics of each kind of communicator.

Assertive, **Able to declare and affirm one's own opinions while respecting the rights of others to do the same.**

Aggressive communicators focus primarily on their own needs. They can become angry and impatient when those needs are not immediately satisfied. In order to become more assertive, aggressive communicators might try to take time to think before speaking, avoid ordering people around, use "I" statements, and focus on listening to what the other person has to say.

Passive communicators deny themselves the power that aggressive people grab. They focus almost exclusively on the needs of others instead of on their own needs, experiencing frustration and tension that remains unexpressed. In order to become more assertive, passive communicators might try to acknowledge anger or hurt more often, speak up when they feel strongly about something, realize that they have a right to make requests, and know that their ideas and feelings are as important as anyone else's.

Communication Success Strategies

These additional strategies can help improve your communication.

Think before you speak. Spoken too soon, ideas can come out sounding nothing like you intended them to. Taking time to think, or even rehearsing mentally, can help you choose the best combination of words. Think it through and get it right the first time.

TABLE 8-3 AGGRESSIVE, PASSIVE, AND ASSERTIVE STYLES

AGGRESSIVE	PASSIVE	ASSERTIVE
Loud, heated arguing	Concealing one's own feelings	Expressing feelings without being nasty or overbearing
Physically violent encounters	Denying one's own anger	Acknowledging emotions but staying open to discussion
Blaming, name-calling, and verbal insults	Feeling that one has no right to express anger	Expressing self and giving others the chance to express themselves equally
Walking out of arguments before they are resolved	Avoiding arguments	Using "I" statements to defuse arguments
Being demanding: "Do this"	Being noncommittal: "You don't have to do this unless you really want to . . . "	Asking and giving reasons: "I would appreciate it if you would do this, and here's why . . . "

Don't withhold your message for too long. One danger of holding back is that a problem or negative feeling may become worse. Speaking promptly has two benefits: (1) you solve the problem sooner, and (2) you are more likely to focus on the problem at hand than to spill over into other issues.

Communicate in a variety of ways, and be sensitive to cultural differences. Remember that words, gestures, and tones mean different things to different people.

Be clear, precise, and to the point. Say exactly what you need to say. Link your ideas to clear examples, avoiding any extra information that can distract.

Communication is extremely important for building and maintaining personal relationships. Explore the role those relationships play in who you are.

HOW DO YOUR PERSONAL RELATIONSHIPS DEFINE YOU?

The relationships you have with friends, family members, and significant others often take center stage. Jobs and schooling can come and go, but you rely on the people with whom you share your life.

In addition to being part of your life, the people around you help to define who you are. Since birth, you have learned by taking in information from verbal and nonverbal language. The chain of learning stretches back through time, each link formed by an exchange of information between people. Those with whom you live, play, study, and work are primary sources of ideas, beliefs, and ways of living. You grow and change as you have new experiences, evaluate them, and decide what to learn from them.

These influential relationships can affect other areas of your life. You have probably experienced conflict that caused you to be unable to sleep, eat, or get any work done. On the other hand, a successful relationship can have positive effects on your life, increasing your success at work or at school. Following are some strategies for improving your personal relationships.

Relationship Strategies

If you can feel good about your personal relationships, other areas of your life will benefit. Here are some suggestions.

Make personal relationships a high priority. Nurture the ones you have and be open to developing new ones. Life is meant to be shared. In some marriage ceremonies, the bride and groom share a cup of wine that symbolizes life. One of the reasons for this tradition is to double the sweetness of life by tasting it together, and to cut the bitterness in half by sharing it. Any personal relationship can benefit from the experience of this kind of sharing.

Invest time. You devote time to education, work, and the other priorities in your life. Relationships need the same investment. They are like plants in a garden, needing nourishment to grow and thrive. Your attention provides that nourishment. In addition, spending time with people you like can relieve everyday stress and strain. When you make time for others, everyone benefits.

Spend time with people you respect and admire. Life is too short to hang out with people who bring you down, encourage you to participate in activities you don't approve of, or behave in ways that upset you. Develop relationships with people whom you respect, whose choices you admire, and who inspire you to be all that you can be. This doesn't mean that you have to agree with everything that others do. For example, you may disagree with a friend who lets his child watch a lot of TV. However, you may severely disapprove of someone who disciplines a child violently, and you may choose to end your association with that person.

Work through tensions. Negative feelings can multiply when left unspoken. Unexpressed feelings about other issues may cause you to become disproportionately angry over a small issue. A small annoyance over dishes in the sink can turn into a gigantic fight about everything under the sun. Get to the root of the problem. Discuss it, deal with it, and move on.

Refuse to tolerate violence. It isn't easy to face the problem of violence or to leave a violent relationship. People may tolerate violence out of a belief that it will end, a desire to keep their families together, a self-esteem so low that they believe they deserve what they get, or a fear that trying to leave may lead to greater violence. No level of violence is acceptable. Someone who behaves violently toward you cannot possibly have your best interests at heart. If you find that you are either an aggressor or a victim, do your best to get help. See chapter 9 for more information on domestic violence.

Show appreciation. In this fast-moving world, people don't thank each other often enough. If you think of something positive, say it. Thank someone for a service, express your affection with a smile. A little positive reinforcement goes a long way toward nurturing a relationship.

If you want a friend, be a friend. The Golden Rule, "Do unto others as you would have them do unto you," never goes out of style. If you treat a friend with the kind of loyalty and support that you appreciate yourself, you are more likely to receive the same in return.

Take risks. It can be frightening to reveal your deepest dreams and frustrations, to devote yourself to a friend, or to fall in love. You can choose not to reveal yourself or give yourself to a friendship at all. However, giving is what feeds a relationship, bringing satisfaction and growth. If you take the plunge, you risk disappointment and heartbreak, but you stand to gain the incredible benefits of companionship, which for most people outweigh the risks.

Keep personal problems in their place. Solve personal problems with the people directly involved and no one else. If at all possible, try not to bring your emotions into class or work. Doing so may hurt your performance while doing nothing to help your problem. If you are overwhelmed by a personal problem, try to address it before you go to class or work. If it's impossible to address it at that time, at least make a plan that you can carry out later. Making some step toward resolving the problem will help you concentrate on other things.

If it doesn't work out, find ways to cope. Everyone experiences strain and breakups in intimate relationships, friendships, and family ties. Be kind to yourself and use coping strategies that help you move on. Some people need lots of time alone; others need to spend time with their friends and family. Some seek more formal counseling. Some people throw their energy into a project, a job, a class, a new workout regimen, or anything else that will take their mind off what hurts. Some just need to cry it out and be miserable for a while. Some write in a journal or write letters to the person that they never mail. Do what's right for you, and believe that sooner or later you can emerge from the experience stronger and with new perspective.

Now and again, your personal relationships will experience conflict. Following are ideas for how to deal with conflict and criticism in a productive and positive way.

HOW CAN YOU HANDLE CONFLICT AND CRITICISM?

Conflict and criticism, as unpleasant as they can often be, are natural elements in the dynamic of getting along with others. It's normal to want to avoid people or situations that cause distress. However, if you can face your fears and think through them critically, you can gain valuable insight into human nature—your own and that of others. You may be able to make important changes in your life based on what you learn.

Conflict Strategies

Conflicts both large and small arise when there is a clash of ideas or interests. You may have small conflicts with a housemate over food left out overnight, a door left unlocked, or a bill that needs paying. On the other end of the spectrum, you might encounter major conflicts with your partner about finances, with an instructor about a failing grade, or with a person who treats you unfairly because of your race, gender, age, or ethnic origin.

Conflict can create anger and frustration, shutting down communication. The two most destructive tendencies are to avoid the conflict altogether (a passive tactic) or to let it escalate into a blowout fight (an aggressive tendency). Avoidance doesn't make the problem go away—in fact, it will probably worsen. If you tend to be passive, assert yourself by acknowledging and expressing your feelings as soon as you can put them into words. On the other hand, a shouting match gives no one an opportunity or desire to listen. If you tend to be aggressive, give yourself time to cool down before you address a conflict. Try to express what you feel without letting your emotions explode.

If calmly and intelligently handled, conflict can shed light on new ideas and help to strengthen bonds between those involved. The primary keys to conflict resolution are calm communication and critical-thinking skills. Think through any conflict using what you know about problem solving.

Identify and analyze the problem. Determine the severity of the problem by looking at its effects on everyone involved. Then, find and analyze the causes of the problem.

Brainstorm possible solutions. Consider as many angles as you can, without judgment. Explore what ideas you can come up with from what you or others have done in a similar situation.

Explore each solution. Evaluate the positive and negative effects of each solution. Why might each work, or not work, or work partially? What would take into account everyone's needs? What would cause the least stress? Make sure everyone has a chance to express an opinion.

Choose, carry out, and evaluate the solution you decide is best. When you have implemented your choice, evaluate its effects. Decide whether you feel it was a good choice.

One more hint: Use "I" statements. Focus on the effects the problem has had on you rather than focusing on someone who caused it. Show that you are taking responsibility for your role in the exchange.

Dealing With Criticism and Feedback

Feedback, Evaluative or corrective information about an action or process.

No one gets everything right all the time. People use constructive criticism and feedback to communicate what went wrong and to suggest improvements.

Consider any criticism carefully. If you always interpret criticism as a threat, you will close yourself off from learning. Even if you eventually decide that you disagree, you can still learn from exploring the possibility. Know that you are strong enough to embrace criticism and become a better person because of it.

Constructive, Promoting improvement or development.

Criticism can be either constructive or unconstructive. Criticism is considered *constructive* when it is offered supportively and contains useful suggestions for improvement. On the other hand, *unconstructive* criticism focuses on what went wrong, doesn't offer alternatives or help, and is often delivered in a negative or harsh manner. Whereas constructive criticism can promote a sense of hope for improvement in the future, unconstructive criticism can create tension, bad feelings, and defensiveness.

Any criticism can be offered constructively or unconstructively. Consider a case where someone has continually been late to work. A supervisor can offer criticism in either of these ways:

> *Constructive:* The supervisor talks privately with the employee. "I've noticed that you have been late to work a lot. Other people have had to do some of your work. Is there a problem that is keeping you from being on time? Is it something that I or someone else can help you with?"
>
> *Unconstructive:* The supervisor watches the employee slip into work late. The supervisor says, in front of other employees, "Nice to see you could make it. If you can't start getting here on time, I might look for someone else who can."

If you can learn to give constructive criticism and deal with whatever criticism comes your way from others, you will improve your relationships and your productivity. When offered constructively and carefully considered, criticism can bring about important changes.

Giving Constructive Criticism

When you offer criticism, use the following steps to communicate clearly and effectively:

1. *Criticize the behavior rather than the person.* In addition, make sure the behavior you intend to criticize is changeable. Chronic lateness can be changed; a physical inability to perform a task cannot.
2. *Be strategic and discreet.* Carefully choose a convenient time and a private place to talk.
3. *Define specifically the behavior you want to change.* Try not to drag any side issues into the conversation.
4. *Limit the behaviors you will criticize to one.* If you have others, discuss them later, one at a time. People can hear criticism better if they are not hit with several issues at once.
5. *Balance criticism with positive words.* Alternate critical comments with praise in other areas.
6. *Stay calm and be brief.* Avoid threats, ultimatums, or accusations. Use "I" messages; choose positive, nonthreatening words, so the person knows that your intentions are positive.

7. *Explain the effects caused by the behavior that warrants the criticism.* Help the person understand why a change needs to happen, and talk about options in detail. Compare and contrast the effects of the current behavior with the effects of a potential change.
8. *Offer help in changing the behavior.* Lead by example.

> "Do not use a hatchet to remove a fly from your friend's forehead."
>
> Chinese proverb

Receiving Criticism

When you find yourself on the receiving end of criticism, use these coping techniques:

1. *Listen to the criticism before you speak up.* Resist the desire to defend yourself until you've heard all the details. Decide if the criticism is offered in a constructive or unconstructive manner.
2. *Think the criticism through critically.* Evaluate it carefully. While some criticism may come from a desire to help, other comments may have less honorable origins. People often criticize others out of jealousy, anger, frustration, or displaced feelings. In cases like those, it is best (though not always easy) to let the criticism wash right over you.
3. *If the criticism is constructive and you accept it, say so.* If you are unsure, take time to think. You may say, "I would like time to think about that. I'll get back to you." Remember that criticism heard from more than one person is more likely to be valid.
4. *If it is unconstructive, you may not want to respond at that moment.* Unconstructive criticism can inspire anger that might be destructive to express. Wait until you cool down and think about the criticism to see if there is anything important hiding under how it was presented. Then, tell the person that you see the value of the criticism, but also communicate to him or her how the delivery of the criticism made you feel. If he or she is willing to talk in a more constructive manner, continue with the following steps below. If not, your best bet may be to consider the case closed and move on.
5. *If it is constructive, ask for suggestions of how to change the criticized behavior.* You could ask, "How would you handle this if you were in my place?"
6. *Before the conversation ends, summarize the criticism and your response to it.* Repeat it back to the person who offered it. Make sure both of you understand the situation in the same way.
7. *If you feel that the criticism is valid, plan a specific strategy for correcting the behavior.* Think over what you might learn from changing your behavior. If you don't agree with the criticism even after the whole conversation, explain your behavior from your point of view.

Remember that the most important feedback you will receive in school is from your instructors, and the most important on-the-job feedback will come from your supervisors, more experienced peers, and occasionally clients. Making a special effort to take in this feedback and consider it carefully will help you learn many important lessons. Even when the criticism is not warranted, the way you respond is important. Furthermore, knowing how to handle conflict and criticism will help you define your role and communicate with others when you work in groups.

WHAT ROLE DO YOU PLAY IN GROUPS?

Group interaction is an important part of your educational, personal, and working life. With a team project at work or a cooperative learning exercise in school, for example, being able to work well together is necessary in order to accomplish a goal. If you are comfortable in your designated role and with the different types of people and styles within your group, you will help the group function more effectively because you will be more effective yourself.

A group or team can be co-workers, fellow students, a family, or any other people who need to accomplish a goal together. Everyone in the group has a vested interest in the outcome. Therefore, everyone should have the opportunity to voice opinions and to participate in the activities that the group decides will achieve the goal or goals.

Groups have their own chemistry and structure. The two major roles in the group experience are those of *participant* and *leader*. Any group needs both in order to function successfully. Become aware of the role you tend to play when relating to others. Try different roles to help you decide where you can be most effective. The following strategies (from *Contemporary Business Communication*, by Louis E. Boone, David L. Kurtz, and Judy R. Block) are linked to either participating or leading.[8] Keep in mind that for many groups, the lines may blur—members may perform some leadership tasks and some participant tasks at the same time, or the leadership of the group may shift frequently.

Being an Effective Participant

Some people are happiest when participating in group activities that someone else leads and designs. They don't feel comfortable in a position of control or having the power to set the tone for the group as a whole. They trust others to make those decisions, preferring to help things run smoothly by taking on an assigned role in the project and seeing it through. Participators need to remember that they are "part owners" of the process. Each team member has a responsibility for, and a stake in, the outcome. The following strategies will help a participant to be effective.

Participation Strategies

Get involved. If a decision you don't like is made by a group of which you are a member, and you stayed uninvolved in the decision, you have no one to blame but yourself for not speaking up. Put some energy into your participation and let people know your views. You are as important a team member as anyone else, and your views are likewise valuable.

Be organized. When you participate with the group as a whole, or with any of the team members, stay focused and organized. The more organized your ideas are, the more people will listen, take them into consideration, and be willing to try them.

Be willing to discuss. Everyone has an equal right to express his or her ideas. Even as you enthusiastically present your opinions, be willing to consider those of others. Keep an open mind and think critically about other ideas before you assume they won't work. If a discussion heats up, take a break or let a more neutral group member mediate.

Keep your word. Make a difference by doing what you say you're going to do. Let people know what you have accomplished. If you bring little or nothing to the process, your team may feel as if you weigh them down.

Focus on ideas, not people. One of the easiest ways to start an argument is for participants to attack group members themselves instead of discussing their ideas. Separate the person from the idea, and keep the idea in focus.

Play fairly. Give everyone a chance to participate. Be respectful of other people's ideas. Don't dominate the discussion or try to control or manipulate others.

Being an Effective Leader

Some people prefer to initiate the action, make decisions, and control how things proceed. They have ideas they want to put into practice and enjoy explaining them to others. They are comfortable giving direction to people and guiding group outcomes. Leaders often have a big-picture perspective; it allows them to see how all of the different aspects of a group project can come together. In any group setting the following strategies will help a leader succeed.

Leadership Strategies

Define and limit projects. One of the biggest ways to waste time and energy is to assume that a group will know its purpose and will limit tasks on its own. A group needs a leader who can define the purpose of the gathering and limit tasks so the group doesn't take on too much. Some common purposes are giving/exchanging information, brainstorming, making a decision, delegating tasks, or collaborating on a project.

Map out who will perform which tasks. A group functions best when everyone has a particular contribution to make. You don't often choose who you work with—in school, at work, or in your family—but you can help different personalities work together by exploring who can do what best. Give people specific responsibilities and trust that they will do their jobs.

Set the agenda. The leader is responsible for establishing and communicating the goal of the project and how it will proceed. Without a plan, it's easy to get off track. Having a written agenda to which group members can refer is helpful. A good leader invites advice from others when determining group direction.

Focus progress. Even when everyone knows the plan, it's still natural to wander off the topic. The leader should try to rein in the discussion when necessary, doing his or her best to keep everyone to the topic at hand. When challenges arise midstream, the leader may need to help the team change direction.

Set the tone. Different group members bring different attitudes and mental states to a gathering. Setting a positive tone helps to bring the group together and motivate people to peak performance. When a leader values diversity in ideas and backgrounds and sets a tone of fairness, respect, and encouragement, group members may feel more comfortable contributing their ideas.

Evaluate results. The leader should determine whether the team is accomplishing its goals. If the team is not moving ahead, the leader needs to make changes and decisions.

If you don't believe you fit into the traditional definition of a leader, remember that there are other ways to lead that don't involve taking charge of a group. You can lead others by setting an honorable example in your actions, choices, or words. You can lead by putting forth an idea that takes a group in a new direction. You can lead by being the kind of person whom others would like to be.

It takes the equal participation of all group members to achieve a goal. Whatever role works best for you, know that your contribution is essential. You may even play different roles with different groups. You might be a participator at school and a leader in a self-help group. You could enjoy leading a religious group but prefer to take a back seat at work. Finally, stay aware of group dynamics; they can shift quickly and move you into a new position you may or may not like. If you don't feel comfortable, speak up. The happier each group member is, the more effectively the group as a whole will function.

Kente

The African word *kente* means "that which will not tear under any condition." *Kente* cloth is worn by men and women in African countries such as Ghana, Ivory Coast, and Togo. There are many brightly colored patterns of *kente*, each beautiful, unique, and special.

Think of how this concept applies to being human. Like the cloth, all people are unique, with brilliant and subdued aspects. Despite any mistreatment or misunderstanding by the people you encounter in your life, you need to work to remain strong so that you don't tear and give way to disrespectful behavior. This strength can help you to endure, stand up against any injustice, and fight peacefully but relentlessly for the rights of all people.

Applications

Name ____________________ Date ____________________

Key Into Your Life: Opportunities to Apply What You Learn

Exercise 1: Diversity Discovery

Express your own personal diversity. Describe yourself in response to the following questions.

What ethnic background(s) do you have?

Name one or more facts about you that someone wouldn't know from simply looking at you.

Name two values or beliefs that govern how you live, what you pursue, and/or with whom you associate.

What other characteristics or choices define your uniqueness?

Now, join with a partner in your class. Try to choose someone you don't know well. Your goal is to communicate what you have written to your partner, and for your partner to communicate to you in the same way. Spend ten minutes talking together and take notes on what the other person says. At the end of that period, join together as a class. Each person will describe his or her partner to the class.

What did you learn about your partner that surprised you?

What did you learn that went against any assumptions you may have made about that person based on his or her appearance, background, or behavior?

Has this exercise changed the way you see this person or other people? Why or why not?

Exercise 2: Prejudice

Name an incorrect assumption others may have about you.

Why would others assume this? How can you help them reevaluate that assumption?

Now, describe one of your prejudices that is directed toward another group.

Think critically about this prejudice. In what cases might this not make sense?

What might you do to educate yourself about this other group?

Exercise 3: The "I"s Have It

In your quest for better communication, rewrite the following sentences so that they are in the less accusatory "I" message style. Check your answers with other students and/or with your instructor.

1. You blew it completely.

2. Why didn't you tell me the meeting time changed?

3. You always forget to pick me up.

4. What does it take for you to understand how this machine works?

5. Where did you put the stapler? Did you lose it?

6. You are impossible to understand when you talk like that.

Exercise 4: Your Communication Style

Look back at the four styles on p. 295: Intuitor, Thinker, Feeler, and Senser. Which describes you the best? Rank the four styles, listing first the one that fits most, and listing last the one that fits least.

1. ______
2. ______
3. ______
4. ______

Of the two styles that best fit you, which one has more positive effects on your ability to communicate? What are those effects?

Which style has more negative effects? What are they?

To determine whether you are primarily passive, aggressive, or assertive, read the following sentences and circle the ones that sound like something you would say to a peer.

1. Get me the keys.
2. Would you mind if I stepped out just for a second?
3. Don't slam the door.
4. I'd appreciate it if you would have this done by two o'clock.
5. I think maybe it needs a little work just at the end, but I'm not sure.
6. Please take this back to the library.
7. You will have a good time if you join us.
8. Your loss.
9. I don't know, if you think so. I'll try it.
10. Let me know what you want me to do.
11. Turn it this way and see what happens.
12. We'll try both our ideas and see what works best.
13. I want it on my desk by the end of the day.
14. Just do what I told you.
15. If this isn't how you wanted it to look, I can change it. Just tell me and I'll do it.

Aggressive communicators would be likely to use sentences 1, 3, 8, 13, and 14.

Passive communicators would probably opt for sentences 2, 5, 9, 10, and 15.

Assertive communicators would probably choose sentences 4, 6, 7, 11, and 12.

In which category did you choose the most sentences? __________

If you scored as an assertive communicator, you are on the right track. If you scored in the aggressive or passive categories, analyze your style. What are the effects? Give an example in your own life of the effects of your style.

____

____

Turn back to p. 301 to review suggestions for aggressive or passive communicators. What can you do to improve your skills?

____

____

Exercise 5: Criticism

Think about any criticism of yourself that you have ignored or rejected. Choose one item of criticism and write it here.

____

____

Now, be honest with yourself. Do you agree with this criticism? Why. How did the criticism make you feel? How was it delivered?

Based on what you are learning from exploring this criticism, name a change you plan to make in order to improve what was criticized or how you react to criticism.

KEY TO COOPERATIVE LEARNING: BUILDING TEAMWORK SKILLS

Problem Solving Close to Home Divide into small groups of two to five. Assign one group member to take notes. Discuss the following questions, one by one:

1. What are the three largest problems my school faces with regard to how people get along with and accept others?
2. What could my school do to deal with the three problems listed above?
3. What can each individual student do to deal with the three problems listed above? (Talk about what you specifically feel that you can do.)

When you are finished, gather as a class. Each group should share their responses with the class. Observe the variety of problems and solutions. Notice whether more than one group came up with one or more of the same problems. You may want to assign one person in the class to gather all of the responses together. That person, together with your instructor, could put these responses into an organized document that you can share with the upper-level administrators at your school.

KEY TO SELF-EXPRESSION: DISCOVERY THROUGH JOURNAL WRITING

To record your thoughts, use a separate journal or the lined page at the end of the chapter.

New Perspective[9] Imagine that you have no choice but to change either your gender (male/female) or your racial/ethnic/religious group. Which would you change, and why? What do you anticipate would be the positive and negative effects of the change—in your social life, in your family life, on the job, at school? How would what you know and experience before the change affect how you would behave after the change?

Key to Your Personal Portfolio: Your Paper Trail to Success

Letters of Recommendation It will be very important to have positive letters of recommendation from people who know and respect you. You can use them when you apply for jobs, internships, scholarships, or academic programs.

First, create a list of people who have served or could serve as references for you. Brainstorm names from all areas of your human resources:

Instructors	Friends	Present/Former employers
Administrators	Family Members	Mentors
Counselors	Present/former coworkers	Students

Make a chart that looks like the one that follows. Fill in the information for each reference.

Name	Address	Phone Number	Association
Jo Trenholm	727 Mercury Way Boston, MA	617/224-2808	Current supervisor

Update the information on this chart as you meet potential references or lose touch with old ones. Keep it on hand for the time that you need a new letter or want to cite a reference on a résumé.

Next, decide which three people you would like to approach to write a letter for you. Choose people who know you well and who have seen you in action, either in an academic or work situation. You will want your references to emphasize your strengths and to discuss qualities like open-mindedness, ability to be a team player, and interpersonal relations. Letters should also contain references to your specific skills, capabilities, and style of working and thinking.

If you have a specific purpose for your letter right now, ask your three references to write letters that suit that purpose. If you don't, keep the information on hand until you do.

When references write letters for you, be sure to thank them right away for their help and to keep them up to date on your activities. Always let a reference know when you have sent a letter out, so that he or she may be prepared to receive a call from the person/company/program to which you have applied.

Name ______________________ Date __________

Journal Entry

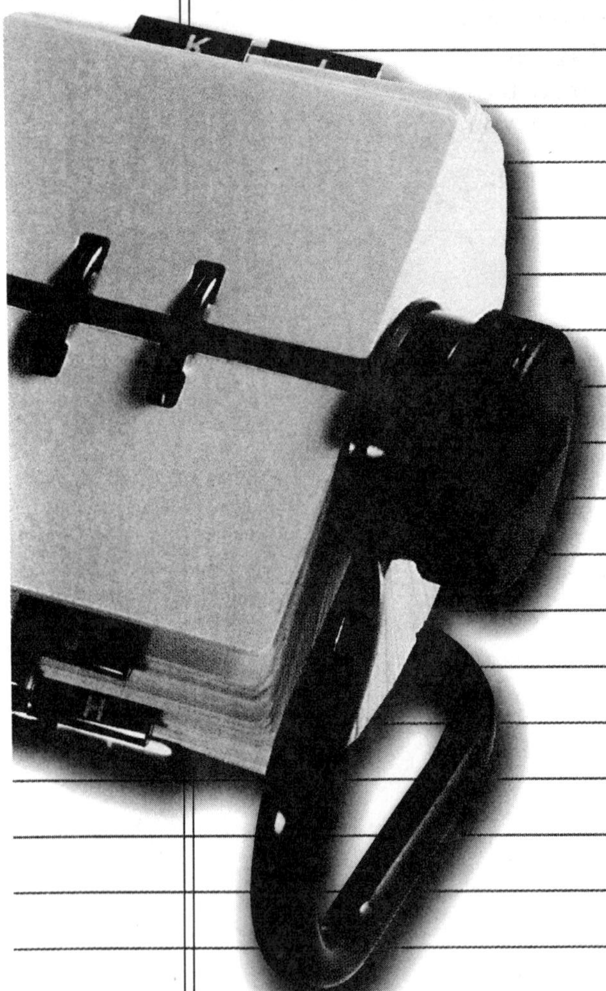

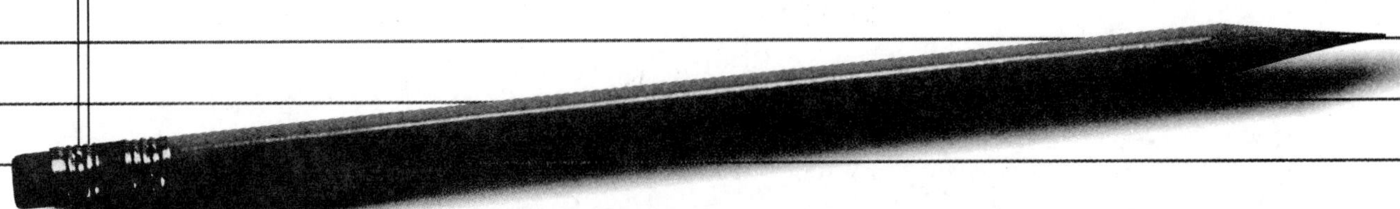

Chapter 5

OBJECTIVES IN TECHNICAL WRITING

- CLARITY
- CONCISENESS
- ACCURACY
- ORGANIZATION
- ETHICS

When you insert paper into your typewriter or turn on your PC, your goal is to write successful technical correspondence. But what is good technical writing? What are your primary objectives in the memo, letter, or report?

CLARITY

The ultimate goal of good technical writing is clarity. If you write a memo, letter, or report that is unclear to your readers, which your readers can't understand, then what have you accomplished? You've wasted time. First, your readers don't understand your point or can't follow your train of thought. They must write you a follow-up inquiry to determine your needs. This wastes *their* time. Once you receive the inquiry, you must rewrite your correspondence, trying to clarify your initial intentions. You've now written twice to accomplish the same goal. This wastes *your* time.

To avoid these time-consuming endeavors, write for clarity. But how do you do this?

PROVIDE SPECIFIC DETAIL

One way to achieve clarity is by supplying specific, quantified information. If you write using vague, abstract adjectives or adverbs, such as *some* or *recently,* your readers will interpret these words in different ways. The adverb *recently* will mean thirty minutes ago to one reader, yesterday to another, and last week to a third reader. This adverb, therefore, is not clear. The same applies to an adjective like *some*. You write, "I need some information about the budget." Your readers can only guess at what you mean by *some*. Do you want the desired budget increase for 1997, the budget expenditures for 1995, the allotted budget increase for 1996, the guidelines for implementing a budget increase, the budgeted allotment for travel, or the explanation for the budget decrease for training?

Look at the following example of vague writing caused by imprecise, unclear adjectives. (Vague word usage is underlined.) The flawed example is then followed by improvements wherein clarity is achieved by quantifying.

ACTIVITY REPORT DRAFT

Our latest attempt at molding preform protectors has led to some positive results. We spent several hours in Dept. 15 trying different machine settings and techniques. Several good parts were molded using two different sheet thicknesses. Here's a summary of the findings.

First, we tried the thick sheet material. At 240°F, this thickness worked well.

Next, we tried the thinner sheet material. The thinner material is less forgiving, but after a few adjustments we were making good parts. Still, the thin material caused the most handling problems.

The engineer who wrote this report realized that it was unclear. To solve the problem, she rewrote the report, quantifying the vague adjectives.

ACTIVITY REPORT REVISION

During the week of 10/4/96, we spent approximately twelve hours in Dept. 15 trying different machine settings, techniques, and thicknesses to mold preform mold protectors. Here's a report on our findings.

.030" Thick Sheet

At 240°F, this thickness worked well.

0.15" Thick Sheet

This material is less forgiving, but after decreasing the heat to 200°F, we could produce good parts. Still, material at .015" thick causes handling problems.

Your goal as a technical writer is to communicate clearly. To do so, state your exact meaning through specific, quantified word usage.

ANSWER REPORTERS' QUESTIONS

A second way to write clearly is to answer reporters' questions—who, what, when, where, why, and how. The best way we can emphasize the importance of answering these reporters' questions is by sharing with you the following memo, written by a highly placed executive to a newly hired employee.

```
DATE:     November 11, 1996
TO:       Mary Jane Post
FROM:     Don Goldenbaum
SUBJECT: TECHNICIAN MEETING
Please be prepared to plan a presentation on month-end
reports. Please be sure that your explanations are very
detailed. Thanks.
```

That's the entire memo. The questions are, "What doesn't the newly hired employee know?" "What additional information would that employee need to do the job?" "What needs clarifying?"

Simply, the employee needs answers to reporters' questions. For example, ***what*** is the subject of the presentation? If the answer is month-end reports, we still lack clarity. ***Which*** of the 12 month-end reports does Don want Mary Jane to discuss? ***Who*** is the audience? We read the word ***technician*** in the subject line, but is Don focusing on automotive technicians, electronic engineering technicians, or dental hygiene technicians? ***Why*** is this presentation being made? That is, what's the rationale or motivations for the meeting? ***When*** will the presentation be made, and ***how*** much detail is "very detailed"? ***Where*** will Mary Jane and the technicians meet for the presentation? Mary Jane has a right to ask for clarity on one more point: ***what*** exactly is she supposed to do? Is she being asked to make a presentation, plan a presentation, or merely prepare to plan a presentation?

This memo's lack of clarity, a result of its inability to answer reporters' questions, causes Mary Jane stress, anxiety, and tension. As a new hire, she wants to do her job well, but Don's unclear correspondence hinders her. You must write clearly to avoid causing your reader stress and to help your reader do the job effectively.

In contrast, the memo on the following page achieves clarity by answering reporters' questions.

Becky knows ***where*** the meetings will be held (Conference Room C); ***who*** selected her for the committee (her manager); ***what*** she will accomplish (writing a proposal about changes to the CIA system); ***when*** the meetings will occur (Friday, Monday, and

DATE: September 5, 1996
TO: Becky Stapleton
FROM: Dave Woodring
SUBJECT: CASH-IN ADVANCE (CIA) PROCEDURE TASK FORCE

You have been chosen by your manager to be a member of the CIA Task Force. This committee will assess current CIA procedures and revise the system.

The following is your schedule for Task Force activities:

Friday, September 12: 8:30-10:30 a.m.
Assess the current system and brainstorm new ideas.

Monday, September 15: 8:30-10:30 a.m.
Review the suggested changes, add new ideas, and test the adjusted system.

Wednesday, September 17: 8:30-10:30 a.m.
Review the adjusted system and write a proposal confirming your changes.

All meetings will be held in Conference Room C. Thank you for your involvement. If you have any questions, please call me at ext. 1849.

Wednesday); ***why*** she's involved (to assess and revise a current system); and ***how*** the work will be accomplished (the sequence of work during the three days of meetings).

Answering reporters' questions is a simple but effective way to write clearly.

USE EASILY UNDERSTANDABLE WORDS

Another key to clarity is using words which your readers can understand easily. Avoid ***obscure*** words, and be careful when you use ***acronyms, abbreviations,*** and ***jargon.***

Obscure Words

A good rule of thumb is to ***write to express, not to impress; write to communicate, not to confuse.*** If your reader must use a dictionary, you're not writing clearly.

Try to make sense of the following examples of unclear writing.

The following rules are to be used when determining whether or not to duplicate messages:

- Do not duplicate nonduplicatable messages.
- A message is considered nonduplicatable if it has already been duplicated.

Your job duties will be to assure that distributed application modifications will execute without abnormal termination through the creation of production JCL system testing.

It's hard to believe, but these examples were written by businesspeople who were trying to communicate *something*. However, the examples are filled with old-fashioned words. The words are too difficult to understand.

Following is a list of difficult, out-of-date terms and the modern alternatives.

Obscure Words	**Easy Words**
aforementioned	already discussed
initial	first
in lieu of	instead of
accede	agree
as per your request	as you requested
issuance	send
this is to advise you	I'd like you to know
subsequent	later
inasmuch as	because
ascertain	find out
pursuant to	after
forward	mail
cognizant	know
endeavor	try
remittance	pay
disclose	show
attached herewith	attached
pertain to	about
supersede	replace
obtain	get

Impressive writing is correspondence we can understand easily. A modern thrust in technical writing is to write the way you speak ... unless you speak poorly. Try to be casual, almost conversational. As shown in the preceding chart, replace obscure words with easy words.

Acronyms, Abbreviations, and Jargon

In addition to obscure words, a similar obstacle to readers is created by acronyms, abbreviations, and jargon.

We've all become familiar with common acronyms such as ***scuba*** (self-contained underwater breathing apparatus), ***radar*** (radio detecting and ranging), *NASA* (National Aeronautics Space Agency), *FICA* (Federal Insurance Contributions Act), and *MADD* (Mothers Against Drunk Drivers)—single words created from the first letters of multiple words. We're comfortable with abbreviations like ***FBI*** (Federal Bureau of Investigations), *JFK* (John F. Kennedy), *NFL* (National Football League), ***IBM*** (International Business Machines), and *L.A.* (Los Angeles). Some jargon (in-house language) has become so common that we reject it as a cliché. Baseball jargon is a good example. It's hard to tolerate sportscasters who speak baseball jargon, describing line drives as "frozen ropes" and fast balls as "heaters."

However, more often than not, acronyms, abbreviations, and jargon cause problems, not because they are too common but because no one understands them. Your technical writing loses clarity if you depend on them. You might think your readers understand them, but do they?

Try to guess the meaning of the following abbreviations and jargon:

- *CIA*—Your first guess was Central Intelligence Agency, wasn't it? Wrong! By this abbreviation we mean Cash in Advance.
- *Spaghetti*—Your first guess made you envision a romantic dinner at a candlelit pasta house, didn't it? Wrong! We are using fire prevention jargon. For firefighters, spaghetti is a term for various fire hoses and lines.
- *Fifo*—If you guessed that this is a natural, all-bran cereal, you're wrong, but don't worry. This is a confusing acronym, except for business office personnel, who immediately recognize it as meaning "first in, first out."

You have to decide when to use acronyms, abbreviations, and jargon and how to use them effectively. One simple rule is to define your terms. You can do so either ***parenthetically*** or in a *glossary*. Rather than just writing *CIA,* write *CIA (Cash in Advance)*. Such parenthetical definitions, which are only used once per correspondence, don't take a lot of time and won't offend your readers. Instead, the result will be clarity.

If you use many potentially confusing acronyms or abbreviations, or if you need to use a great deal of technical jargon, then parenthetical definitions might be too cumbersome. In this case, supply a separate glossary. (This point is discussed in greater detail in Chapter 15.) A *glossary* is an alphabetized list of terms, followed by their definitions, as in the following example:

CPA	Certified Public Accountant
FICA	Federal Insurance Contributions Act (Social Security taxes)
Franchise	Official establishment of a corporation's existence
Gross pay	Pay before deductions
Line of credit	Amount of money which can be borrowed
Net pay	Pay after all deductions
Profit and loss statement	Report showing all incomes and expenses for a specified time

USE VERBS IN THE ACTIVE VOICE VERSUS THE PASSIVE VOICE

It has been decided that Joan Smith will head our Metrology Department.

The preceding sentence is written in the *passive voice* (the primary focus of the sentence, ***Joan Smith,*** is acted on rather than initiating the action). Passive voice causes two problems.

1. Passive constructions are often unclear. After reading the preceding sentence, our question is, ***who*** decided that Joan Smith will head the department? To solve this problem and to achieve clarity, replace the vague indefinite pronoun ***it*** with a precise noun: "***Mike Handler*** decided that Joan Smith will head our Metrology Department."
2. Passive constructions are wordy. Passive sentences always require helping verbs ***(has been)***. When we revise the sentence to read "Mike Handler decided that Joan Smith will head our Metrology Department," the helping verb ***has been*** disappears.

The revision ("Mike Handler decided that Joan Smith will head our Metrology Department") is written in the *active voice.* When you use the active voice, your subject ***(Mike Handler)*** initiates the action.

Another common problem with passive voice construction concerns prepositions. Look at the following example:

Overtime is favored by hourly workers. (passive voice)

Again, this sentence, written in the passive voice, uses a helper verb ***(is),*** has the subject ***(hourly workers)*** acted on rather than initiating the action, but also includes a preposition ***(by)***. The sentence is wordy. Revised, the sentence reads as follows:

Hourly workers favor overtime. (active voice)

We've omitted the helper verb ***is,*** we've deleted the preposition ***by,*** and the subject, ***Hourly workers,*** initiates the action. The sentence is less wordy and more precise.

CONCISENESS

After clarity, your second major goal in technical writing is conciseness. Conciseness is important for at least two reasons.

First, remember how time consuming technical writing is in the work environment? American workers spend approximately eight hours per week writing and additional time reading and revising others' writing. Conciseness in writing can help reduce some of this time. If you write concisely, providing thorough detail in fewer words, you can save yourself time and take up less of your readers' time.

Second, concise writing can aid comprehension. If you dump an enormous number of words on your readers, they might give up before finishing your correspondence or skip and skim so much that they miss a key concept. Wordy writing will lead your readers to think, "Oh no! I'll never be able to finish that. Maybe I can skim through it. I'll probably get enough information that way." Conciseness, on the other hand, makes your writing more appealing to your readers. They'll think, "Oh, that's not too bad; I can read it easily." If they can read your correspondence easily, they will read it with greater interest and involvement. This, of course, will aid their comprehension.

Let's look at some poor writing—writing which is wordy, time consuming to read, and not easily comprehensible.

> Please prepare to supply a readout of your findings and recommendations to the officer of the Southwest Group at the completion of your study period. As we discussed, the undertaking of this project implies no currently known incidences of impropriety in the Southwest Group, nor is it designed specifically to find any. Rather, it is to assure ourselves of sufficient caution, control, and impartiality when dealing with an area laden with such potential vulnerability. I am confident that we will be better served as a company as a result of this effort.

Is that paragraph easy to understand? No, it's not. Why? What gets in your way? Do you have difficulty following it because you are an outsider and are not aware of the situation that generated it? That's only part of the problem. The reason you have difficulty understanding this paragraph is because it's poorly written. It causes difficulty for two reasons: (a) the paragraph is too long, and (b) the words and sentences in the paragraph are too long.

LIMIT PARAGRAPH LENGTH

The number of lines per paragraph or words per paragraph is arbitrary. Obviously, as the writer, you must decide what's best. Some paragraphs, due to the complexity of the subject matter, might require more development. Other paragraphs requiring less development can be shorter.

Nonetheless, an excessively long paragraph is ineffective. In a long paragraph, you force your reader to wade through many words and digest large amounts of information. This hinders comprehension. In contrast, short, manageable paragraphs invite reading and help your reader understand your content.

As a rule of thumb, a paragraph in a memo, letter, or short report should consist of (a) no more than four to six typed lines, or (b) no more than 50 words. Sometimes you can accomplish these goals by cutting your paragraphs in half; find a logical place to stop a paragraph and then start a new one. Even the foregoing difficult example can be improved in this way.

Please prepare to supply a readout of your findings and recommendations to the officer of the Southwest Group at the completion of your study period. As we discussed, the undertaking of this project implies no currently known incidences of impropriety in the Southwest Group, nor is it designed specifically to find any.

Rather, it is to assure ourselves of sufficient caution, control, and impartiality when dealing with an area laden with such potential vulnerability. I am confident that we will be better served as a company as a result of this effort.

The writing is still difficult to understand, but at least it's a bit more manageable. You can read the first paragraph, stop, and consider its implications. Then, once you have grasped its intent, you can read the next paragraph and try to tackle its content. The paragraph break gives you some room to breathe.

LIMIT WORD AND SENTENCE LENGTH

In addition to the length of the example paragraph, the writing is flawed. The paragraph is filled with excessively long words and sentences. This writer has created an impenetrable wall of haze—the writing is foggy. In fact, we can determine how foggy this prose is by assessing it according to Robert Gunning's Fog Index.

Here's his mathematical way of determining how foggy your writing is.

Fog Index

1. Count the number of words in successive sentences. Once you reach approximately one hundred words, divide these words by the number of sentences. This will give you an average number of words per sentence.
2. Now count the number of long words within the sentences you've just reviewed. Long words are those with three or more syllables. You can't count (a) proper names, like Leonardo DaVinci, Christopher Columbus, or Alexander DeToqueville; (b) long words that are created by combining shorter words, such as ***chairperson*** or ***policeperson;*** or (c) three-syllable verbs created by ***ed*** or ***es*** endings, such as ***united*** or ***arranges***. Discounting these exceptions, count the remaining multisyllabic words. (A good example of a multisyllabic word is the word ***mul-ti-syl-lab-ic***.)
3. Finally, to determine the fog quotient, add the number of words per sentence and the number of long words. Then multiply your total by 0.4.

Given this system, let's see how the original difficult paragraph (page 32) scores. The paragraph is composed of 92 words in 4 sentences. Thus, the average number of words per sentence is 23. The paragraph contains 16 multisyllabic words ***(recommendation, officer, completion, period, undertaking, currently, incidences, impropriety, specifically, sufficient, impartiality, area, potential, vulnerability, confident, and company)***.

23	(words per sentence)
+ 16	(multisyllabic words)
39	(total)

39	(total)
× .4	(fog factor)
15.6	(fog index level)

What does 15.6 mean? Look at the fog index reading level in Figure 3.1.

The paragraph is written at a level midway between college junior and senior, definitely above the danger line.

Why is this level of writing considered dangerous? A fog index of 15.6 enters the danger zone for two reasons:

- Approximately 18 percent of Americans graduate from college. Thus, if you're writing at a college level, you're alienating approximately 82 percent of your audience.
- Studies show that college graduates read at approximately a tenth-grade level. Thus, even if you're writing to college graduates, you can't assume their reading skills are proficient.

Given these facts, many businesses ask their employees to write at a sixth- to eighth-grade level. To accomplish this, you would have to strive for an average of

Fog Index Reading Level

	FOG INDEX	BY GRADE	BY MAGAZINE
	17	College graduate	No popular magazine scores this high.
	16	College senior	
	15	College junior	
	14	College sophomore	
Danger Line	13	College freshman	
	12	High school senior	*Atlantic Monthly*
	11	High school junior	*Time* and *Newsweek*
	10	High school sophomore	*Reader's Digest*
	9	High school freshman	*Good Housekeeping*
	8	Eighth grade	*Ladies' Home Journal*
	7	Seventh grade	Modern romances
	6	Sixth grade	Comics

Figure 3.1

approximately 15 words per sentence and no more than 5 multisyllabic words per 100 words.

15	(words per sentence)
+ 5	(multisyllabic words)
20	(total)

20	(total)
× .4	(fog factor)
8.0	(fog index level)

You can't always avoid multisyllabic words. Scientists would find it impossible to write if they could never use words like ***electromagnetism, nitroglycerine, telemetry,*** or ***trinitrotolulene***. The purpose of a fog index is to make you aware that long words and sentences create reading problems. Therefore, although you can't always avoid long words, you should be careful when using them.

Here are ways to lower a potentially high fog index.

USE THE MEAT CLEAVER THEORY OF REVISION

One way to limit the number of words per sentence is to cut the sentence in half or thirds. The following sentence, which contains 44 words, is too long:

> ***Version 1***
> To maintain proper stock balances of respirators and canister elements and to ensure the identification of physical limitations which may negate an individual's previous fit-test, a GBC-16 Respirator Request and Issue Record will need to be submitted for each respirator requested for use.

If we use the meat cleaver approach, we can make this sentence more concise and easier to understand.

> ***Version 2***
> Please submit a GBC-16 Respirator Request and Issue Record for each requested respirator. We then can maintain proper respirator and canister element stock balances. We also can identify physical limitations which may negate an individual's previous fit-test.

This sentence, now cut in thirds, is more digestible. Because we have less to swallow whole, we can understand the content more easily.

AVOID SHUN WORDS

In the preceding examples, the original sentence contains 44 words: the revised version is composed of 3 sentences, totaling 38 words. Where did those missing 6 words go?

One way to write more concisely is to shun words ending in *-tion* or *-sion*—words ending in a *shun* sound. For example, the original sentence reads "to ensure the identific*ation* of physical limitations." To revise this, we simply wrote "identify physical limitations." That's three words versus six in the original version. Deleting three words in this case reduces wordiness by 50 percent. Shun words are almost always unnecessarily wordy.

Let's try another example. Instead of writing "I want you to take into considera*tion* the following," you could write "consider the following." That's nine words versus three, a 66.6 percent savings in word count.

Look at the following shun words and their concise versions:

Shun Word	**Concise Version**
came to the conclu*sion*	concluded (or decided)
with the excep*tion* of	except for
make revi*sions*	revise
investiga*tion* of the	investigate
consider implementa*tion*	implement
utiliza*tion* of	use

AVOID CAMOUFLAGED WORDS

Camouflaged words are similar to shun words. In both instances, a key word is buried in the middle of surrounding words (usually helper verbs or unneeded prepositions). For example, in the phrase *with the exception of,* the key word *except* is camouflaged behind the unneeded *with, the, -tion,* and *of.* Once we prune away these unneeded words, the key word *except* is left, making the sentence less wordy.

Camouflaged words are common. Here are some examples and their concise versions:

Camouflaged Word	**Concise Version**
make an *amend*ment to	amend
make an *adjustment* of	adjust
have a *meet*ing	meet
*thank*ing *you* in advance	thank you
for the purpose of *discuss*ing	discuss
arrive at an *agree*ment	agree
at a *later* moment	later

AVOID THE EXPLETIVE PATTERN

Another way to write more concisely is to avoid the following expletives:

- *there* is, are, was, were, will be
- *it* is, was

Both these expletives (*there* and *it*) lead to wordy sentences.
For example, consider the following sentence:

There are three people who will work for Acme.

This sentence can be revised to read, "Three people will work for Acme." The original sentence contains nine words; the revision has six. We've omitted three words by deleting the expletive *there*. Your response to this revision could be "So what, who cares? What's the point of deleting three words?" Deleting three words doesn't seem like much. However, the omission equals a 33 percent savings in word count, helping us achieve conciseness. In one sentence, that might be a minimal achievement, but if you can delete three words from every sentence, the benefits will add up.

The expletive *it* creates similar wordiness, as in the following sentence:

It has been decided that ten engineers will be hired.

If we delete the expletive *it*, the sentence reads, "Ten engineers will be hired." The original sentence contained ten words; the revision has five. We've achieved a 50 percent savings in word count.

OMIT REDUNDANCIES

Redundancies are words that say the same thing. Conciseness is achieved by saying something once rather than twice. For example, in each of the following instances, the boldface words are redundant:

during **the year of** 1996
(1996 is obviously a year; the words *the year of* are redundant.)
in **the month of** December
(As in the preceding example, *the month of* is redundant; what else is December?)
needless to say
(If it's needless to say, why say it?)
The computer will cost **the sum of** $1,000.
(One thousand dollars *is* a sum.)
the results **so far achieved** prove
(A result, by definition, is something which has been achieved.)
our **regular** monthly status reports require
(Monthly status reports must occur every month; regularity is a prerequisite.)
We collaborated **together** on the project.
(One can't collaborate alone!)
the **other** alternative is to
(Every alternative presumes that some other option exists.)
This is a **new** innovation.
(As opposed to an old innovation?!)
the consensus **of opinion** is to
(The word *consensus* implies opinion.)

AVOID WORDY PHRASES

Sentences may be wordy not because you've been redundant or because you've used shun words, camouflaged words, or expletives. Sometimes sentences are wordy simply because you've used wordy phrases.

Here are examples of wordy phrases and their concise revisions:

Wordy Phrase	Concise Revision
in order to purchase	to purchase
at a rapid rate	rapidly (or state the exact speed)
it is evident that	evidently
with regard to	regarding
in the first place	first
a great number of times	often (or state the number of times)
despite the fact that	although
is of the opinion that	thinks
due to the fact that	because
am in receipt of	received
enclosed please find	enclosed is
as soon as possible	by 11:30 A.M.
in accordance with	according to
in the near future	soon
at this present writing	now
in the likely event that	if
rendered completely inoperative	broken

ACCURACY

Clarity and conciseness are primary objectives of effective technical writing. However, if your writing is clear and concise but incorrect—grammatically or textually—then you've wasted your time and destroyed your credibility. To be effective, your technical writing must be *accurate.*

Accuracy in technical writing requires that you *proofread* your text. The examples of inaccurate technical writing on page 39 are caused by poor proofreading (we've underlined the errors to highlight them).

First City Federal Savings and Loan
1223 Main
Oak Park, Montana

October 12, 1996

Mr. and Mrs. David Harper
2447 N. Purdom
Oak Park, Montana

Dear Mr. and Mrs. Purdom:

Note that the savings and loan incorrectly typed the customer's street rather than the last name.

National Bank
1800 Commerce Street
Houston, TX

September 9, 1996

Adler's Dog and Oat Shop
8893 Southside
Bellaire, TX

Dear Sr.:
In response to your request, your account with us has been close out. We are submitted a check in the amount of $468.72 (your existing balance). If you have any questions, please fill free to conact us.

In addition to all the other errors, it should be "Dog and Cat Shop," of course. All the errors make the writer look incompetent.

To ensure accurate writing, use the following proofreading tips:

1. *Let someone else read it.* We miss errors in our own writing for two reasons. First, we make the error because we don't know any better. Second, we read what we think we wrote, not what we actually wrote. Another reader might help you catch errors.
2. *Use the gestation approach.* Let your correspondence sit for a while. Then, when you read it, you'll be more objective.
3. *Read backwards.* You can't do this for content. You should only read backwards to slow yourself down and to focus on one word at a time to catch typographical errors.

4. *Read one line at a time.* Use a ruler or scroll down your PC to isolate one line of text. Again, this slows you down for proofing.
5. *Read long words syllable by syllable.* How is the word ***responsiblity*** misspelled? You can catch this error if you read it one syllable at a time (re-spon-si-bl-i-ty).
6. *Use technology.* Computer spell checks are useful for catching most errors. They might miss proper names, homonyms (***their, they're,*** or ***there***) or incorrectly used words such as *device* to mean *devise.*
7. *Check figures, scientific and technical equations, and abbreviations.* If you mean $400,000, don't write $40,000. Double check any number or calculations. If you mean to say HCl (hydrochloric acid), don't write HC (a hydrocarbon).
8. *Read it out loud.* Sometimes we can hear errors that we can't see. For example, we know that ***a outline*** is incorrect. It just sounds wrong. ***An outline*** sounds better and is correct.
9. *Try scattershot proofing.* Let your eyes roam around the page at random. Sometimes errors look wrong at a glance. If you wander around the page randomly reading, you often can isolate an error just by stumbling on it.
10. *Use a dictionary.* If you're uncertain, look it up.

If you commit errors in your technical writing, your readers will think one of two things about you and your company: (a) They'll either conclude that you are stupid, or (b) that you're lazy. In either situation, you lose. Errors create a negative impression at best; at worst, a typographical error relaying false figures, calculations, amounts, equations, or scientific/medical data can be disastrous.

ORGANIZATION

If you're clear, concise, and accurate, but no one can follow your train of thought because your text rambles, you still haven't communicated effectively. Successful technical writing must also be well organized.

Here's an analogy to explain the importance of organization. Most artists can't just dip a brush in paint and then splatter that paint on canvas. People want to make sense of what they see, and splattered images cause confusion. The same applies to technical writing. As the writer, you can't haphazardly throw words on the page and expect readers to understand you clearly. In contrast, you should order that information on the page logically, allowing your readers to follow your train of thought.

No one method of organization always works. Following are five patterns of organization which you can use to help clarify content.

SPATIAL

If you are writing to describe the parts of a machine or a plot of ground, you might want to organize your text spatially. You would describe what you see as it appears in space—left to right, top to bottom, inside to outside, or clockwise. These spatial sequences help your readers visualize what you see and, therefore, better understand the physical qualities of the subject matter. They can envision the layout of the land you describe or the placement of each component within the machine.

For example, let's say you are a contractor describing how you will refinish a basement. Your text reads as follows:

> At the basement's north wall, I will build a window seat 7' long by 2' wide by 2' high. To the right of this seat, on the east wall, I will build a desk 4' high by 5' long by 3' wide. On the south wall, to the left of the door, I will build an entertainment unit the height of the wall including four, 4' high by 4' wide by 2' deep shelving compartments. The west wall will contain no built-ins. You can use this space to display pictures and to place furniture.

Note how this text is written clockwise, uses points of the compass to orient the reader, and includes the transitional phrases "to the right" and "to the left" to help the reader visualize what the contractor will build. That's spatial organization.

CHRONOLOGY

Whereas you would use spatial organization to describe a place, you would use chronology to document time or the steps in an instruction. For example, an emergency medical technician reporting services provided during an emergency call would document those activities chronologically.

> At 1:15 P.M., we arrived at the site and assessed the patient's condition taking vitals (pulse, respiration, etc.). At 1:17 P.M., after stabilizing the patient, we contacted the hospital and relayed the vitals. By 1:20 P.M., the patient was on an IV drip and enroute to the hospital. Our vehicle arrived at the hospital at 1:35 P.M. where hospital staff took over the patient's care.

Chronology also would be used to document steps in an instruction. No times would be provided as in the EMT report. In contrast, the numbered steps would denote the chronological sequence a reader must follow.

IMPORTANCE

Your page of text is like real estate. Certain areas of the page are more important than others—location, location, location. If you bury key data on the bottom of a page, your reader might not see the information. In contrast, content placed approximately one-third from the top of the page and two-thirds from the bottom (eye level) garners more attention. The same applies to a bulletized list of points. Readers will focus their attention on the first several points more than on the last few.

By knowing this, you can decide which ideas you want to emphasize and then place that information on the page accordingly. Organize your ideas by importance. Place the more important ideas above the less important ones.

The following agenda is incorrectly organized.

Agenda

- Miscellaneous ideas
- Questions from the audience
- Refreshments
- Location, date, and time
- Subject matter
- Guest speakers

Which of these points is most important? Certainly not the first two. A better list would be organized by importance, as follows.

Agenda

- Subject matter
- Guest speakers
- Location, date, and time
- Refreshments
- Questions from the audience
- Miscellaneous ideas

COMPARISON/CONTRAST

Many times in business you will need to document options and/or ways in which you surpass a competitor. These would require that you organize your text by comparison/contrast. You compare similarities and contrast differences. For example, if you are writing a sales brochure, you might want to present your potential client alternatives regarding services, personnel, timetables, and fee structures. Table 3.1 shows how comparison/contrast provides the client options for cost and features. Each housing option is comparable in that the developer provides a 4-bedroom, 3 1/2-bath home with fully equipped kitchen. However, the homes contrast regarding garage size, deck availability, and basement. These options then affect the cost. The table, organized according to comparison/contrast, helps the reader understand these distinctions.

PROBLEM/SOLUTION

Every proposal and sales letter is problem/solution-oriented. When you write a proposal, for instance, you are proposing a solution to an existing problem. If your proposal focuses on new facilities, your reader's current building must be flawed. If your proposal focuses on new procedures, your reader's current approach to doing business must need improvement. Similarly, if your sales letter promotes a new product, your customers will only purchase it if their current product is inferior.

Table 3.1

Housing Costs

ITEM	FEATURES	COSTS
The Broadmoor	4 bedroom, 3 1/2 bath 2-car garage fully equipped kitchen	$180,000
The Aspen	4 bedroom, 3 1/2 bath finished basement 3-car garage fully equipped kitchen	$190,000
The Regency	4 bedroom, 3 1/2 bath patio deck finished basement with 1/2 bath 3-car garage fully equipped kitchen	$200,000

To clarify the value of your product or service, therefore, you should emphasize the readers' need (their problem) and show how your product is the solution. Note how the following executive summary from a proposal is organized according to problem/solution:

> ***Executive Summary***
> Your city's 20 year-old wastewater treatment plant does not meet EPA requirements for toxic waste removal or ozone depletion regulations. This endangers your community and lessens property values in their neighborhoods.
>
> Anderson and Sons Engineering Company has a national reputation for upgrading wastewater treatment plants. Our staff of qualified engineers will work in partnership with your city's planning commission to modernize your facilities and protect your community's values.

This summary's first paragraph identifies the problem. The second paragraph promotes the solution. Together, the problem/solution organization clarifies the writer's intent.

ETHICS

Here's the scenario. You're a technical writer responsible for producing a maintenance manual. Your boss tells you to include the following sentence.

> "NOTE: Our product has been tested for defects and safety by trained technicians."

When read literally, this sentence is true. The product has been tested, and the technicians are trained. However, you know that the product has only been tested for 24 hours by technicians trained on site without knowledge of international regulations.

So where's the problem? As a good employee, you're required to write what your boss told you ... aren't you? Even though the statement isn't completely true, you legally can include it in your manual ... can't you?

The answer to both questions is "No!" Actually, you have an ethical responsibility to write the truth. Your customers expect it, and it's in the best interests of your company. Of equal importance, including the sentence in your manual is illegal. Though the sentence is essentially true, it implies something that is false. Readers will assume that the product has been ***thoroughly*** tested by technicians who have been ***correctly*** trained. Thus, the sentence deceives the readers. Such comments are "actionable under law" if they lead to false impressions (Wilson WE-68). If you fail to properly disclose information, including dangers, warnings, cautions, or notes like the sentence in question, then your company is legally liable. (We discuss how to correctly write hazard alert messages in Ch. 11.)

Knowing this, however, doesn't make writing easy. Ethical dilemmas exist in corporations. The question is, "What do you do when confronted with such problems?"

One way to solve this dilemma is by checking your actions against these three concerns: legal, practical, and ethical. For example, if you plan to write operating instructions for a mechanism, will your text be

1. *Legal,* focusing on liability, negligence, and consumer protection laws?
2. *Practical,* since dishonest technical writing backfires and can cause the company to lose sales or to suffer legal expenses?
3. *Ethical,* written to promote customer welfare and avoid deceiving the end user? (Bremer et al. 76-77)

These are not necessarily three separate issues. Each interacts with the other. Our laws are based on ethics and practical applications.

LEGALITIES

If you're uncertain, that's what lawyers are for. When asked to write text that profits the company but deceives the customer, for instance, you might question where your loyalties lie. After all, the boss pays the bills, but your customers might also be your next-door neighbors. Such conflicts exist and challenge all employees. What do you do? You should trust your instincts and trust the laws. Suffice it to say that laws are written to protect the customer, the company, and you—the employee. If you believe you are being asked to do something illegal that will harm your community, seek legal counsel.

PRACTICALITIES

Though it might appear to be in the best interests of the company to hide potentially damaging information from customers, such is not the case. First, as technical writer, your goal is candor. That means that you must be truthful, stating the facts. It also means that you must not lie, keeping silent about facts that are potentially dangerous (Girill 178–9). Second, practically speaking, the best business approach is *good* business. The ultimate goal of a company is not just making a profit, but making money the right way—"good ethics is good business" (Guy 9). What good is it to earn money from a customer who will never buy from you again, or who will sue for reparation? That's not practical.

ETHICALITIES

Here's the ultimate dilemma. Defining ethical standards has been challenging for professional organizations. As Shirley A. Anderson-Hancock, manager for the Society for Technical Communication's Ethical Guidelines Committee, states, "Everyone who participates in discussions of ethical issues may offer a different perspective, and many viewpoints may be legitimate" (6). Due to the difficulty of clearly defining what is and what is not ethical, the Society for Technical Communication struggled for three years before publishing its guidelines in 1995 (see Figure 3.2).

These ethical guidelines, as the Society for Technical Communication Ethical Guidelines Committee admits, had to be "sufficiently broad to apply to different working environments for the next several years" (Anderson-Hancock 6).

One way to clarify these necessarily broad standards is by looking at the Society for Technical Communication's Code for Communicators, which reads as follows:

> As a technical communicator, I am the bridge between those who create ideas and those who use them. Because I recognize that the quality of my services directly affects how well ideas are understood, ***I am committed to excellence in performance and the highest standards of ethical behavior.***
>
> I value the worth of the ideas I am transmitting and the cost of developing and communicating ideas. I also value the time and effort spent by those who read or see or hear my communication.
>
> I therefore recognize my responsibility to communicate technical information truthfully, clearly, and economically.

STC Ethical Guidelines for Technical Communicators

Introduction

As technical communicators, we observe the following ethical guidelines in our professional activities. Their purpose is to help us maintain ethical practices.

Legality

We observe the laws and regulations governing our professional activities in the workplace. We meet the terms and obligations of projects we undertake. We ensure that all terms of our contractual agreements are consistent with the STC Ethical Guidelines.

Honesty

We seek to promote the public good in our activities. To the best of our ability, we provide truthful and accurate communications. We dedicate ourselves to conciseness, clarity, coherence, and creativity, striving to address the needs of those who use our products. We alert our clients and employers when we believe material is ambiguous. Before using another person's work, we obtain permission. In cases where individuals are credited, we attribute authorship only to those who have made an original, substantive contribution. We do not perform work outside our job scope during hours compensated by clients or employers, except with their permission; nor do we use their facilities, equipment, or supplies for personal gain. When we advertise our services, we do so truthfully.

Confidentiality

Respecting the confidentiality of our clients, employers, and professional organizations, we disclose business-sensitive information only with their consent or when legally required. We acquire releases from clients and employers before including their business-sensitive information in our portfolios or before using such material for a different client or employer or for demonstration purposes.

Quality

With the goal of producing high quality work, we negotiate realistic, candid agreements on the schedule, budget, and deliverables with clients and employers in the initial project planning stage. When working on the project, we fulfill our negotiated roles in a timely, responsible manner and meet the stated expectations.

Fairness

We respect cultural variety and other aspects or diversity in our clients, employers, development teams, and audiences. We serve the business interests of our clients and employers, as long as such loyalty does not require us to violate the public good. We avoid conflicts of interest in the fulfillment of our professional responsibilities and activities. If we are aware of a conflict of interest, we disclose it to those concerned and obtain their approval before proceeding.

Professionalism

We seek candid evaluations of our performance from clients and employers. We also provide candid evaluations of communication products and services. We advance the technical communication profession through our integrity, standards, and performance.

(*Approved by the STC Board of Directors, April 1995*)

Figure 3.2

My commitment to professional excellence and ethical behavior means that I will

- Use language and visuals with precision.
- Prefer simple, direct expression of ideas.
- Satisfy the audience's need for information, not my own need for self-expression.
- Hold myself responsible for how well my audience understands my message.
- Respect the work of colleagues, knowing that a communication problem may have more than one solution.
- Strive continually to improve my professional competence.
- Promote a climate that encourages the exercise of professional judgment and that attracts talented individuals to careers in technical communication.

Let's expand on each of the previously mentioned points separately. In doing so, we can achieve a working guide for ethical standards.

1. Use language and visuals with precision. In a recent survey comparing technical writers and teachers of technical writing, we discovered an amazing finding; professional technical writers rate grammar and mechanics higher than teachers do (Gerson and Gerson). On a 5-point scale (5 equaling "very important"), writers rated grammar and mechanics 4.67, whereas teachers only rated grammar and mechanics 3.54. That equals a difference of 1.13, which represents a 22.6 percent divergence of opinion.

Given these numbers, would we be precise in writing "teachers do not take grammar and mechanics as seriously as writers do"? The numbers accurately depict a difference of opinion, and the 22.6 percent divergence is substantial. However, these figures do not assert that teachers ignore grammar. To say so is imprecise and would constitute an ethical failure to present data accurately. Even though writers are expected to highlight their client's values and downplay their client's shortcomings, technical writers ethically cannot skew numbers to accomplish these goals (Bowman and Walzer MPD-93). Information must be presented accurately, and writers must use language precisely.

Precision also is required when you use visuals to convey information. Look at Figures 3.3 and 3.4. Both figures show that XYZ's sales have risen; however, Figure 3.3 is misleading. The scale used to show the company's growth is out of proportion, creating the imprecise image of meteoric growth. The width of the line graph's y-axis is constricted and overemphasizes the rate of growth. In contrast, Figure 3.4 depicts the same numerical growth but uses a different scale, which shows more accurately that the company experienced a gradual growth. As with language, the writer is ethically responsible for presenting visual information precisely.

2. Prefer simple, direct expression of ideas. While writing an instructional manual, you might be asked to use legal language to help your company avoid legal problems (Bowman and Walzer MPD-93). Here's a typically obtuse warranty that legally protects your company:

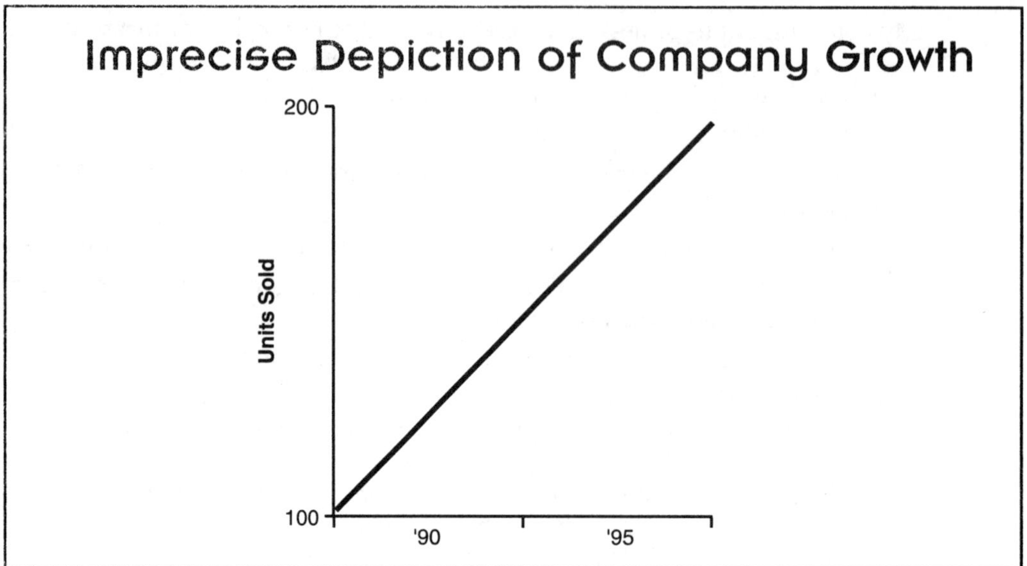

Figure 3.3

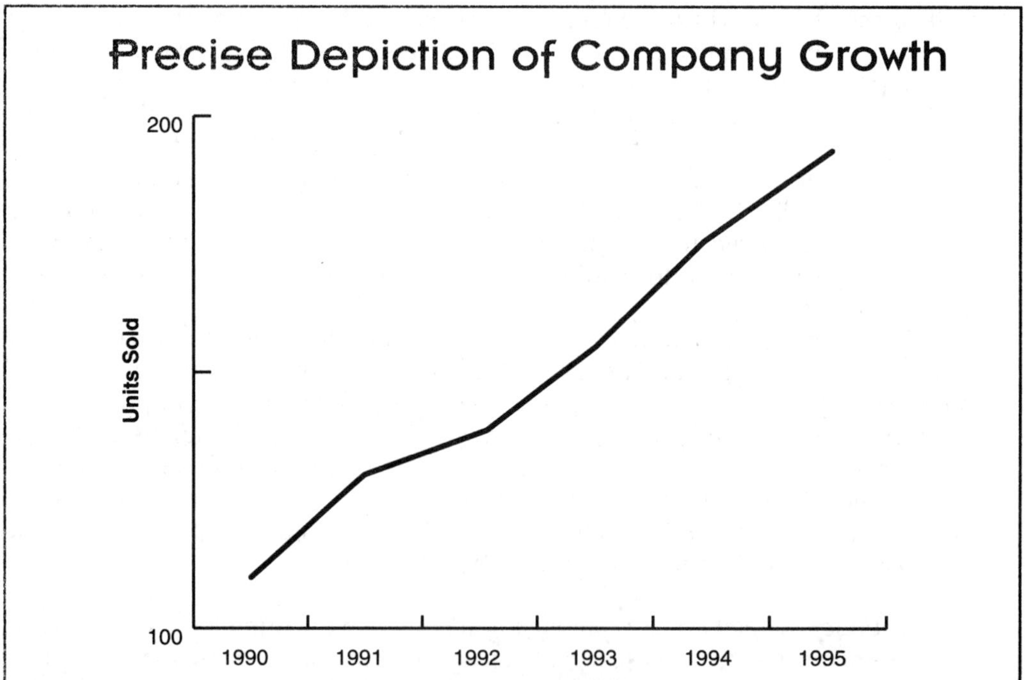

Figure 3.4

> Acme's liability for damages from any cause whatsoever, including fundamental breach, arising out of this Statement of Limited Warranty, or for any other claim related to this product, shall be limited to the greater of $10,000 or the amount paid for this product at the time of the original purchase, and shall not apply to claims for personal injury or damages to personal property caused by Acme's negligence, and in no event shall Acme be liable for any damages caused by your failure to perform your responsibilities under this Statement of Limited Warranty, or for loss of profits, lost savings, or other consequential damages, or for any third-party claims.

Can your audience easily grasp this warranty's lengthy sentence structure and difficult-to-understand words? No, the readers will become frustrated and fail to recognize what is covered under such a warranty. Although you are following your boss's directions, you are not fulfilling one of your ethical requirements to use simple and direct language.

Writing can be legally binding ***and*** easy to understand. The former does not negate the latter. As a successful technical writer who values "the time and effort spent by those who read or see or hear [your] communication," you want to aid communication by using simple words and direct expression of ideas whenever possible.

3. Satisfy the audience's need for information, not my own need for self-expression. The importance of simple language also encompasses the Society for Technical Communication's third point mentioned in its Code for Communicators: satisfying "the audience's need for information, not my own need for self-expression." The previously mentioned warranty might be considered poetic in its sentence structure and sophisticated in its word usage. It does not communicate what the audience needs, however. Such elaborate and convoluted writing will only satisfy one's need for self-expression: that's not the goal of effective technical writing.

Electronic mail (e-mail) presents another opportunity for unethical behavior. Because e-mail is so easy to use, many company employees use it too frequently. They write e-mail for business purposes, but they also use e-mail when writing to family and friends. Employees know not to abuse their company's metered mail by using corporate envelopes and stamps to send in their gas bills or write thank-you notes to Aunt Rose. These same employees, however, will overload the company's e-mail system (on company time) by writing e-mail messages to relatives coast to coast. They are not satisfying their business colleague's need for information; in contrast, they are using company-owned e-mail systems for their own self-expression (Hartman and Nantz 60). That's unethical.

4. Hold myself responsible for how well my audience understands my message. As a technical writer, you must place the audience first. When you write a precise proposal or instruction, using simple words and syntax, you can take credit for helping the reader understand your text. Conversely, you must also accept responsibility if the reader fails to understand.

Ethical standards for successful communication require the writer to always remember the readers—the real people who read manuals to put together their children's toys, who read corporate annual reports to understand how their stocks are doing, and who read proposals to determine whether to purchase a service. An ethical writer remembers that these real people will be frustrated by complex instructions, confused by inaccessible stock reports, and misled by inaccurate proposals. It's unethical to forget that your writing can frustrate people and even endanger them. It's unethical to incorrectly use your writing to mislead or to confuse. In contrast, as an ethical writer, you need to treat these readers like a neighbor, someone you care about, and then write accordingly. Take the time to check your facts, present your information precisely, and communicate clearly so that your readers—your friends, coworkers, and clients—are safe and satisfied. You are responsible for your message (Barker et al. 38–39).

5. *Respect the work of colleagues.* Each of the ethical considerations already discussed relates to your clients, the readers of your technical communication. This fifth point differs in two ways: first, it relates to coworkers or professional colleagues; second, it highlights the importance of online ethics, the ethical dilemmas presented by electronic communications on the Internet. We can discuss these two points simultaneously.

Much of today's technical writing takes place on-line, electronically (we discuss electronic communication in Chapter 9). This new venue for technical writing creates three unique reasons for an increased focus on ethics. As the technical writer, you must ethically consider ***confidentiality, courtesy,*** and ***copyright*** when working with the Internet or any private electronic network.

- *Confidentiality.* The 1974 Privacy Act allows "individuals to control information about themselves and to prevent its use without consent" (Turner 59). The Electronic Communication Privacy Act of 1986, which applies all federal wiretap laws to electronic communication, states that e-mail messages can only be disclosed "with the consent of the senders or recipients" (Turner 60). However, both of these laws can be abused easily on the Internet. First, neither law specifically defines "consent." Data such as your credit records can be accessed without your knowledge by anyone with the right hardware and software. Your confidentiality can be breached easily.

  Second, the 1986 Electronic Communication Privacy Act fails to define "the sender." In the workplace, a company owns the e-mail system, just as it owns other more tangible items such as desks, computers, and file cabinets. Companies have been held liable for electronic messages sent by employees. Thus, many corporations consider the contents of one's e-mail and one's e-mailbox company property, not the property of the employee. With ownership comes the right to inspect an employee's messages. Although you might write an e-mail message assuming that your thoughts are confidential, this message can be monitored without your knowledge (Hartman and Nantz 61).

  These instances might be legal, but are they ethical? Though a company can eavesdrop on your e-mail or access your life's history through databases, that doesn't mean they should. As an employee or corporate manager, you should respect another's right to confidentiality. Ethically, you should avoid the temptation to read someone else's e-mail or to access data about an individual without his or her consent.

- *Courtesy.* As already noted, e-mail is not as private as you might believe. Whatever you write in your e-mail correspondence can be read by others. Given this reality, you should be very careful about what you say in e-mail. Specifically, you don't want to offend coworkers by "flaming" (writing discourteous messages). Before you criticize a coworker's ideas or ability, and before your castigate your employer, remember that common courtesy, respect for others, is ethical (Adams et al. 328).
- *Copyright.* A final ethical consideration relates to copyright laws. Every English teacher you've ever had has told you to avoid ***plagiarism*** (stealing another writer's words and ideas). Plagiarism, unfortunately, is an even greater problem on the Internet. The Internet is perhaps the world's largest library without walls; it's almost a universal commons where anyone can set up a soap box and speak (or print) his or her opinion.

  This incredible ability to disseminate massive amounts of information presents problems. If you were an unethical technical writer, you could access data from the Internet and easily print it as your own. After all, it's hard to trace the identity of a writer on the Net, and Internet information can be downloaded by anyone (Adams et al. 328).

  An ethical writer will not fall prey to such temptation. If you haven't written it, give the other author credit. Words are like any other possession. Taking words and ideas without attributing your source through a footnote or parenthetical citation is wrong. You should respect copyright laws.

6. Strive continually to improve my professional competence. Promote a climate that encourages the exercise of professional judgment. We've combined these last two tenets from the Society for Technical Communication's Code for Communicators since together they sum up all of the preceding ethical considerations. Professional competence, for example, includes one's ability to avoid plagiarizing. Competence should also include professional courtesy, respect for another's right to confidentiality, a sense of responsibility for one's work, and the ability to write clearly and precisely. Ultimately, your competence is dependent upon professional judgment. Do you know the difference between right and wrong? Recognizing the distinction is what ethics is all about.

As a writer, you will always be confronted by a multitude of options, such as loyalty to your company, responsible citizenship, need for a salary, accountability to your client and your coworkers, and personal integrity. You must weigh the issues—ethically, legally, and practically—and then write according to your conscience.

STRATEGIES FOR MAKING ETHICAL DECISIONS

When confronted with ethical challenges, try following these writing strategies (Guy 165):

1. *Define the problem.* Is the dilemma legal, practical, ethical, or a combination of all three?

2. *Determine your audience.* Who will be affected by the problem? Clients, Coworkers, Management? What is their involvement, what are their individual needs, and what is your responsibility—either to the company or to the community?
3. *Maximize values; minimize problems.* Ethical dilemmas always involve options. Your challenge is to select the option that promotes the greatest worth for all stakeholders involved. You won't be able to avoid all problems. The best you can hope for is to minimize those problems for both your company and your readers while you maximize the benefits for the same stakeholders.
4. *Consider the big picture.* Don't just focus on short-term benefits when making your ethical decisions. Don't just consider how much money the company will make now, how easy the text will be to write now. Focus on long-term consequences as well. Will what you write please your readers so that they will be clients for years to come? Will what you write have a long-term positive impact on the economy or the environment?
5. *Write your text.* Implement the decision by writing your memo, letter, proposal, manual, or report. When you write your text, remember to
   - Use precise language and visuals.
   - Use simple words and sentences.
   - Satisfy the audience's need for information, not your own need for self-expression.
   - Take responsibility for your content, remembering that real people will follow your instructions or make decisions based on your text.
   - Respect your colleagues' confidentiality, be courteous, and abide by copyright laws.
   - Promote professionalism and good judgment.

SUMMARY

The primary goals of effective technical writing are ***clarity, conciseness, accuracy, organization,*** and ***ethics.*** Is there one technique which will help you achieve these goals? The answer is no. Clarity, conciseness, accuracy, and ethics can be achieved in numerous ways. We've suggested that you can achieve these goals if you

- Specify.
- Avoid obscure words.
- Limit and/or define your use of abbreviations, acronyms, and jargon.
- Organize.
- Use the active versus the passive voice.
- Limit paragraph, word, and sentence length.

- Proofread for accuracy.
- Consider ethics.

These suggestions do not represent a solution to all writing problems. Writing effectively is a challenge. To write well, you must also consider audience and appropriate formats for different types of technical writing. Each of these points is discussed in the following chapters.

ACTIVITIES

Specify

The following sentences are vague and imprecise. They will be interpreted differently by different readers. Revise these sentences—replace the vague, impressionistic words with more specific information.

1. We need this information as soon as possible.
2. The machinery will replace a flawed piece of equipment in our department.
3. Failure to purchase this will have a negative impact.
4. Weather problems in the area resulted in damage to the computer systems.
5. The most recent occurrences were caused by insufficient personnel.
6. Fire in the office caused substantial losses.
7. If we can't solve this problem soon, we'll lose a large percentage of our business.
8. The automobile had a smaller turning radius than last year's model.
9. Several employees commended her for her expertise.
10. Make your explanations very detailed.

Avoid Obscure Words

Obscure words make the following sentences difficult to understand. Improve the sentences by revising the difficult words and making them more easily understandable.

1. As Very Large Scale Integration (VLSI) continues to develop, a proliferation of specialized circuit simulators will be utilized.
2. As you requested at the commencement of the year, I am forwarding my regular quarterly missive.
3. Though Randolph was cognizant of his responsibility to advise you of any employment abberations, he failed to abide by this mandate.
4. Herewith is an explanation of our rationale for proferring services, pursuant to your request.
5. Please be advised that the sale constitutes a successful closure.

6. Inasmuch as we have endeavored to determine the causes of the dilemma without success, we are terminating this fact-finding operation immediately.
7. To facilitate the initiation of this activity, we have assigned the ensuing job responsibilities.
8. Can you assist us in ascertaining the causes pertaining to yesterday's mechanism malfunction?
9. I wonder if you would be so kind as to avail yourself of this opportunity to respond accordingly to our questionnaire.
10. In lieu of further discussion, we want to state in the affirmative that what transpired was due to the fact that the vehicle had insufficient braking capabilities to avoid the collision.

Use the Active Voice versus the Passive Voice

The passive voice often leads to vague, wordy sentences. Revise the following sentences by writing them in the active voice.

1. Implementation of this procedure is to be carried out by the metrology department.
2. Benefits derived by attending the conference were twofold.
3. The information was demonstrated and explained in great detail by the training supervisor.
4. Discussions were held with representatives from Allied, who supplied analytical equipment for automatic upgrades.
5. Also attended was the symposium on polymerization.
6. Process control systems for foam encapsulation were reviewed with vendors.
7. Effort should be expended to reduce overtime. Overtime in excess of eight hours should be closely monitored.
8. The reassignment of this activity was the result of changes requested by manufacturing.
9. Installation of the fiber optic networking is estimated to occur early next month.
10. Misapplication of a dry film lubricant has been the primary cause of defectiveness.

Limit Paragraph Length

You can achieve clarity and conciseness if you limit the length of your paragraphs. An excessively long paragraph (beyond eight typed lines) requires too much work for your reader. Revise the following paragraph to make it more reader friendly.

> As you know, we use electronics to process freight and documentation. We are in the process of having terminals placed in the export departments of some of our major customers around the country so they may keep track of all their shipments within our sys-

tem. I would like to propose a similar tracking mechanism for your company. We could handle all of your export traffic from your locations around the country and monitor these exports with a terminal located in your home office. This could have many advantages for you. You could generate an export invoice in your export department which could be transmitted via the computer to our office. You could trace your shipments more readily. This would allow you to determine rating fees more accurately. Finally, your accounting department would benefit. All in all, your export operations would achieve greater efficiency.

Reduce Word Length

Multisyllabic words can create long sentences. To limit sentence length, limit word length. Find shorter words to replace the following words.

1. advise
2. anticipate
3. ascertain
4. cooperate
5. determine
6. endeavor
7. inconvenience
8. indicate
9. initially
10. presently
11. prohibit
12. residence
13. subsequent
14. sufficient
15. terminate

Reduce Sentence Length

Each of the following sentences is too long. Revise them using the techniques suggested in this chapter: Use the meat cleaver approach; avoid shun words, camouflaged words, and expletives; omit redundancies; and delete wordy phrases.

1. In regard to the progress reports, they should be absolutely complete by the fifteenth of each month.
2. I wonder if you would be so kind as to answer a few questions about your proposal.
3. I am in receipt of your memo requesting an increase in pay and am of the opinion that it is not merited at this time due to the fact that you have worked here for only one month.
4. On two different occasions, I have made an investigation of your residence, and I believe that your sump pump might result in damage to your neighbor's adjacent property. I have come to the conclusion that you must take action to rectify this potential dilemma, or your neighbor might seek to sue you in a court of law.
5. In this meeting, our intention is to acquire a familiarization with this equipment so that we might standardize the replacement of obsolete machinery throughout our entire work environment.
6. It is evident that the company's request for electrical equipment to be placed in the laboratory has become rather important inasmuch as this need is prioritized in our CEO's most recent letter.
7. It is anticipated that these changes will lead to a reduction in the failure rate.

8. There is the possibility that we will implement these suggestions early next month.
9. New personnel will be assessed when brought on board and then tested on a yearly basis in order to ensure their continued successful job prowess.
10. If there are any questions that you might have, please feel free to contact me by phone.

Organize

1. *Spatial:*
   a. Using spatial organization, write a paragraph describing your classroom, your office, your work environment, your dorm room, your apartment, or any room in your house.
   b. Using spatial organization, write an advertisement describing the interior of a car, the exterior of a mechanism or tool, a piece of clothing, or a motorcycle.
2. *Chronology:* Organizing your text chronologically, write a report documenting your drive to school or work, your activities accomplished in class or at work, your discoveries at a conference or vacation, or your activities at a sporting event.
3. *Importance:* A fashion merchandizing retailer asked her buyers to purchase a new line of clothing. In her memo, she provided them the following list to help them accomplish their task. Reorganize the list by importance, and justify your decisions.

DATE:	January 15, 1996
TO:	Buyers
FROM:	Nancy Aaronson
SUBJECT:	CLOTHING PURCHASES

It's time again for our spring purchases. This year, let's consider a new line of clothing. When you go to the clothing market, focus on the following:

- Colors
- Materials
- Our customers' buying habits
- Price versus mark-up potential
- Quantity discounts
- Wholesaler delivery schedules

Good luck. Your purchases at the market are what make our annual sales successful.

4. *Comparison/Contrast:* Visit two auto dealerships, two clothing stores, two restaurants, two music shops, two prospective employers, two colleges, etc.

Based on your discoveries, write a report using comparison/contrast to make a value judgement. Which of the two cars would you buy, which of the two restaurants would you frequent, and at which of the two music shops would your purchase CDs?

5. *Problem/Solution: Case Study*

   You work for Acme Electronics as an electrical engineer. Carol Haley, your boss, informs you that your department's electronic scales are measuring tolerances inaccurately. You are asked to study the problem and determine solutions. In your study, you find that one scale (ID #1893) is measuring within 90 percent of tolerance; another scale (ID #1887) is measuring within 75 percent of tolerance; a third scale (ID #1890) is measuring within 60 percent of tolerance; a final scale (ID #1885) is measuring within 80 percent of tolerance. Standards suggest that 80 percent is acceptable. To solve this problem, the company could purchase new scales ($2,000 per scale); reduce the vibration on the scales by mounting them to the floor ($1,500 per scale); reduce the vibration around the scales by enclosing the scales in plexiglass boxes ($1,000 per scale).

   Write a memo to your boss detailing your findings (the problems) and suggesting the solutions.

Consider Ethics

Individual or Teamwork

1. The Society for Technical Communication constantly is trying to redefine their Code of Ethics. As a class, how would you define the word Ethics? Brainstorm new definitions as they apply to technical communication, and come to a class consensus. Then in small groups, based on your class's definition of Ethics,

   - List five or more examples of ethical responsibilities you believe technical writers should have when writing memos, letters, reports, proposals, and/or instructions (other than those already discussed in this chapter).
   - List five or more examples of failures to abide by ethical responsibilities you've seen either in writing or in other types of media (recordings, movies, television, newspapers, magazines, news reporting, etc.).
   - Technical writing is factual, as are newspapers, magazines, and radio and television news reports; recordings, movies, and television are art forms. Do the same ethical considerations apply for all types of media? If there are differences, explain your answer.

2. Bring to class examples of ethically flawed communication. These could include poorly written warranties (which are too difficult to understand) or dangers, warnings and cautions (which do not clearly identify the potential for harm). You might find misleading annual reports or unethical seeming advertisements. Poor examples could even include graphics which are visually misleading. Then in small groups, rewrite these types of communication or redraw the graphics to make them ethical.

3. Everyday, the Internet is presenting ethical dilemmas to lawmakers and to the populace. Congress is currently debating laws to curb unethical practices online. These unethical practices include hacking, pornography, solicitation, infringements on confidentiality, hate mail, inappropriate advertisements, unauthorized viewing of e-mail, and even the overloading of disks and servers due to an unreasonable use of bandwidth.

   To update your knowledge of ethics problems online, research any of the topics listed above. Then, present your findings as follows:

   - Write an individual or group report on your findings (we discuss reports in Unit 5).
   - Give an individual or group oral presentation on your findings (we discuss oral presentations in Chapter 16).
   - Write a summary of the article(s) you've researched (we discuss summaries in Chapter 13).

Case Study/Collaborative Writing

The Blue Valley Wastewater Treatment Plant processes water running to and from Frog Creek, a water reservoir that passes through the North Upton community. This water is usually characterized by low alkalinity (generally, <30mg/L), low hardness (generally, <40mg/L), and minimal water discoloration. Inorganic fertilizer nutrients (phosphorus and nitrogen) are also generally low with limited algae growth.

Despite the normal low readings, algae-related tastes and odors occur occasionally. Although threshold odors range from 3 to 6, they have risen to 10 in summer months. Alkalinity rises to <50mg/L, hardness to <60mg/L, and discoloration intensifies. Taste and odor problems can be controlled by powdered activated carbon (PAC); nutrient-related algae growth can be controlled by filtrated ammonia. Both options are costly.

The North Upton community is distressed. The odors and tastes are disturbing the community residents. The odors are especially bothersome to outdoor enthusiasts who use the trails bordering Frog Creek for biking and hiking. Residents also worry about the impact of increased alkalinity on fish and turtles, many of which are dying, further creating an odor nuisance. Frog Creek is a community treasure for its wildlife and recreational opportunities.

The Blue Valley Wastewater Treatment Plant is under no legal obligation to solve these problems. The alkalinity, hardness, color, and nutrient readings are all within regulated, legal ranges. However, community residents are insistent that their voices be heard and that restorative steps be taken to improve the environment around their homes.

This is an ethical and practical dilemma.

In response to this dilemma, divide the class into small groups to write the following:

- You are Blue Valley Wastewater Treatment Plant's Director of Public Relations. Write a letter to the City Commission stating your plant's point of view. (We discuss letters in Chapter 7.)

- You are North Upton Community's resident representative. Write a letter to the City Commission stating your community's point of view.
- You are an employee for the Blue Valley Wastewater Treatment Plant. Write a memo to the plant director suggesting ways in which the plant could solve this environmental and/or community-relations problem. (We discuss memos in Chapter 8.)
- You are the Blue Valley Wastewater Treatment Plant's director. Write a memo to the engineering supervisor (your subordinate) stating how to solve this environmental and/or community-relations problem.

These documents could be organized by problem/solution or comparison/contrast. Whichever method you choose, consider the strategies for making ethical decisions, discussed in this chapter.

Chapter 6

DOCUMENT DESIGN

- OBJECTIVES
- ORGANIZATION
- ORDER
- ACCESS
- VARIETY

OBJECTIVES

In technical writing, are words your only concern? The answer is an emphatic "No!"

What you say is important, but how the text looks on the page is equally important. If you give your readers excessively long paragraphs, pages full of wall-to-wall words, you've made a mistake. Ugly blocks of unreadable, unappealing text will get you and your company in trouble.

The technical writing context: Why do people read correspondence? Although individuals read poetry, short stories, novels, and drama for enjoyment, few people read memos, letters, reports, or instructions for fun. They read these types of technical writing for information about a product or service. They read this correspondence while they talk on the telephone, while they drive to work, or while they walk to meetings.

Given these contexts, your audience wants you to provide them information quickly, information they can understand at a glance. Reading word after word, paragraph after paragraph takes time and effort, which most readers can not spare. Therefore, if your technical writing is visually unappealing, your audience might not even read your words. They will either give up before they've begun or be unable to remember what they've read. You cannot assume they will labor over your text to uncover its worth. Good technical writing allows readers rapid access to information.

Damages and dangers: If your audience fails to read your text because it is visually inaccessible, imagine the possible repercussions. They could damage the equipment by not recognizing important information which you've buried in dense blocks of text. The readers could give up on the text and call your 1–800 hotline for assistance. This wastes your readers' and your coworkers' time and energy. Worse, your audience might hurt themselves and sue your company for failing to highlight potential dangers in the user manual.

Corporate identity: Your document—whether it's a memo, letter, report, instruction, newsletter, or brochure—is a visual representation of your company, graphically expressing your company's identity. It might be the only way you meet your clients. If your text is unappealing, that's the corporate image your company conveys to the customer. If your text is not reader-friendly, that's how your company will appear to your client. Visually unappealing and inaccessible correspondence can negatively affect your company's sales and reputation. In today's competitive workplace, any leverage you can provide your company is a plus. Document design is one way to appeal to a client.

To clarify how important document design is, look at the inaccessible meeting minutes in Figure 5.1.

These minutes are neither clear nor concise. You are given so much data in such an unappealing format that your first response upon seeing the correspondence probably is to say, "I'm not going to read that."

How can you make these minutes more inviting? How can you break up the wall-to-wall words and make key points jump off the page? To achieve effective document design, you'll need to provide your readers visual (a) organization, (b) order, (c) access, and (d) variety.

ORGANIZATION

The easiest way to improve your document's design is to break text into smaller chunks of information, a technique called *chunking*. When you use chunking to separate blocks of text, you help your readers understand the overall organization of your correspondence. They can see which topics go together and which are distinct (Keyes 640; Watzman ATA 49).

Chunking to organize your text is accomplished by using any of the following techniques:

- *Headings* (one to three words that summarize the content of a unit of information).
- *White space* (horizontal spacing between paragraphs, created by double or triple spacing).
- *Rules* (horizontal lines typed across the page to separate units of information).
- *Section dividers and tabs* (used in longer reports to create smaller units).

Notice how using some of these techniques improves the document design in Figure 5.2.

MINUTES

The meeting at the Carriage Club was attended by thirty members and guests. After the dinner, Roger Traver introduced the guest speaker, George Smith, university chancellor, and noted his accomplishments and experiences prior to education—U.S. Navy commander, Oak Ridge Laboratory researcher, and politician. Dr. Smith's talk, "Industry and Education Collaboration," was very interesting and included a history of special projects enjoyed by both academics and corporate heads. Dr. Smith suggested that we engineers could work with education to (1) provide training seminars, (2) help in urban development, and (3) provide intern opportunities. Recent industry-education collaborations include training seminars in computers, fiber optics, and human resource options. The chancellor's primary thrust was a request for $100,000 in financial aid for urban development. He said money had already been donated from three sources: a large realty firm, Capital Homes, had given $20,000; a philanthropic group, We Care, had donated a matching $20,000; Dr. Smith's university gave a matching $20,000. The remaining $40,000, Dr. Smith hoped, would come from industry donations. Finally, the chancellor noted that industry could help itself, as well as the community, by providing internships for university undergraduate majors. These internships could either be semester- or year-long arrangements, whereby students worked for minimum wage to learn more about the day-to-day aspects of their chosen fields. The chancellor said that these internships not only would increase the students' theoretical knowledge of engineering by giving them hands-on experience, but also that the knowledge they acquired would make them better future employees for the host engineering companies. Everyone would benefit. Dr. Smith noted that the students would receive a grade and credit for their work. After the speech, our VP introduced new business, calling for nominations for next year's officers, gave us the agenda for our next meeting, and adjourned the meeting.

Figure 5.1 Inaccessible Meeting Minutes

MINUTES

The meeting at the Carriage Club was attended by 30 members and guests. After the dinner, Roger Traver introduced the guest speaker, George Smith, university chancellor, and noted his accomplishments and experiences prior to education—U.S. Navy commander, Oak Ridge Laboratory researcher, and politician. Dr. Smith's talk, "Industry and Education Collaboration" was very interesting and included a history of special projects enjoyed by both academics and corporate heads. Dr. Smith suggested that we engineers could work with education to accomplish three goals.

Training Seminars

Recent industry-education collaborations include training seminars in computers, fiber optics, and human resource options.

Urban Development

The chancellor's primary thrust was a request for $100,000 in financial aid for urban development. He said money had already been donated from three sources: a large realty firm, Capital Homes, had given $20,000; a philanthropic group, We Care, had donated a matching $20,000; Dr. Smith's university gave a matching $20,000. The remaining $40,000, Dr. Smith hoped, would come from industry donations.

Internships

The chancellor noted that industry could help itself, as well as the community, by providing internships for university undergraduate majors. These internships could either be semester- or year-long arrangements, whereby students worked for minimum wage to learn more about the day-to-day aspects of their chosen fields. The chancellor said that these internships not only would increase the students' theoretical knowledge of engineering by giving them hands-on experience, but also that the knowledge they acquired would make them better future employees for the host engineering companies. Everyone would benefit. Dr. Smith noted that the students would receive a grade and credit for their work.

Conclusion

After the speech, our VP introduced new business, calling for nominations for next year's officers, gave us the agenda for our next meeting, and adjourned the meeting.

Figure 5.2 Document Design Using Chunking to Organize the Information

ORDER

Once a wall of unbroken words has been separated through chunking to help the reader understand the text's organization, the next thing a reader wants from your text is a sense of order. What's most important on the page? What's less important? What's least important? You can help your audience prioritize information by ordering—or *queuing*—ideas (Keyes 640–41; Watzman ATA 49). The primary way to accomplish this goal is through a hierarchy of headings set apart from each other through various techniques:

- *Typeface:* There are many different *typefaces* (or *fonts*). These include Courier, Prestige, Helvetica, Arial, Bosanova, Future, LCD, Key, and Chicago. Whichever typeface you choose, it will either be a *serif* or *sans-serif* typeface. Serif type has feet or decorative strokes at the edges of each letter. This typeface is commonly used in text because it is easy to read, allowing the reader's eyes to glide across the page (Benson 36–37).

  SERIF ← decorative feet

  Sans-serif (as seen in this parenthetical comment) is a block typeface which omits the feet or decorative lines. This typeface is best used for headings.

  SANS-SERIF ← no decorative feet

- *Typesize:* Another way of queuing for your readers, or helping them see the hierarchy of topics, is through the *size* of your type. A primary, first-level heading should be larger than subsequent, less important headings: second level, third level, and so forth. For example, a first-level heading could be typeset in 18-point type. The second-level heading would then be set in 16-point type, the third-level heading in 14-point type, and the fourth-level heading in 12-point type (Keyes 641).

  The following page shows examples of different typefaces and typesizes.

- *Density:* In addition to type size and typeface, the weight of the type prioritizes your text. Type *density* is created by boldfacing or double-striking words (Keyes 641; Benson 37).
- *Spacing:* Another queuing technique to help your readers order their thoughts is the *amount of horizontal space* used after each heading. The first-level heading should have more space following it than the second-level heading, and so forth.
- *Position:* Your headings can be centered, aligned with the left margin, indented, or outdented (*hung heads*). No one approach is more valuable or more correct than another. The key is consistency. If you center your first-level heading, for example, and then place subsequent heads at the left margin, this should be your model for all chapters or sections of that report (Keyes 641; Watzman VC 86).

Sans-Serif Typefaces

Avant Garde 12 point

Avant Garde 14 point

Avant Garde 18 point

Futura 12 point

Futura 14 point

Futura 18 point

Helvetica 12 point

Helvetica 14 point

Helvetica 18 point

Serif Typefaces

Courier 12 point

Courier 14 point

Courier 18 point

Book Antiqua 12 point

Book Antiqua 14 point

Book Antiqua 18 point

Bookman 12 point

Bookman 14 point

Bookman 18 point

Figure 5.3 shows an *outdented* first-level heading with *indented* subsequent headings. Figure 5.4 shows a *centered* heading with subsequent headings aligned with the *left margin.*

Figure 5.5 reformats the meeting minutes seen in Figure 5.2 and uses queuing to order the hierarchy of ideas.

The outdented first-level heading is set in an 18-point, bold, sans-serif typeface, all caps. The second-level heading is set in a 16-point, bold, serif typeface and is sep-

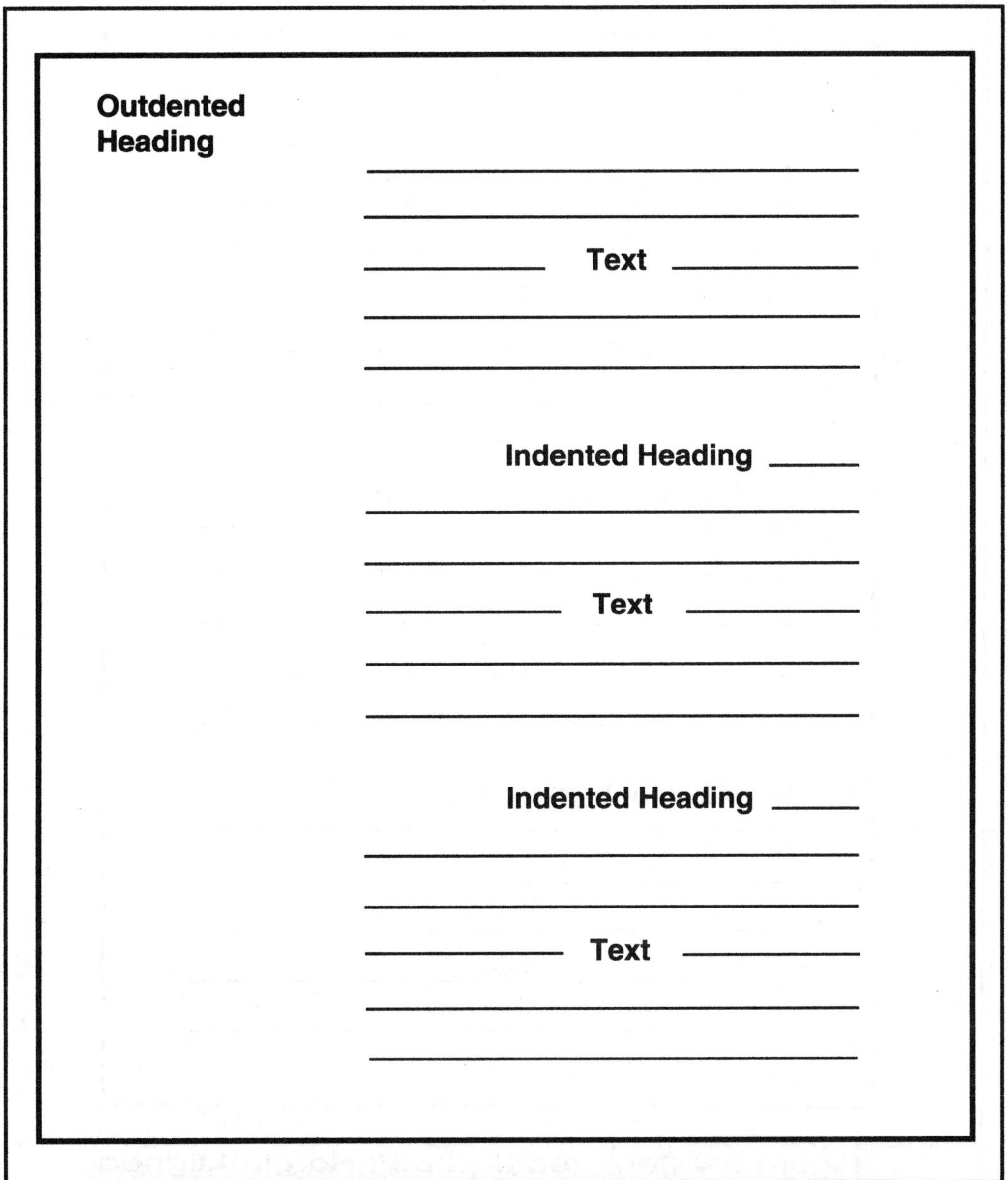

Figure 5.3 Outdented and Indented Headings

arated from the preceding text by horizontal white space. The third-level heading is set in a 14-point, bold, serif typeface and is separated from the preceding text by double spacing. It is also set on the same line as the following text.

Hierarchical heading levels allow the readers to visualize the order of information, to see clearly how the writer has prioritized text.

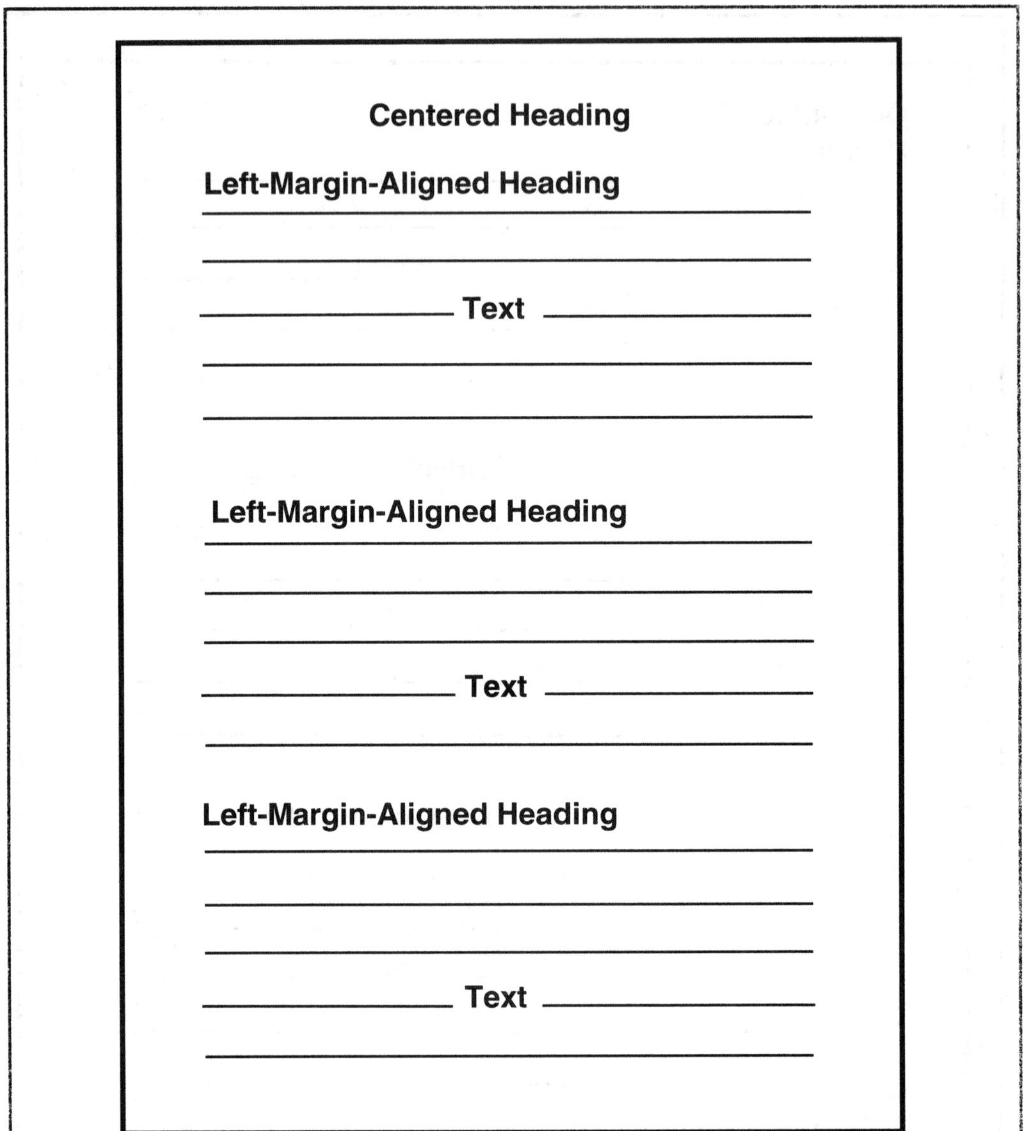

Figure 5.4 Centered and Left-Margin-Aligned Headings

ACCESS

Chunking helps the reader see which ideas go together, and a hierarchy of headings helps the reader understand the relative importance of each unit of information. Nonetheless, the document design in Figure 5.5 still needs improvement. The reader still must read every word carefully to see the key points within each chunk of text.

MINUTES The meeting at the Carriage Club was attended by 30 members and guests. After the dinner, Roger Traver introduced the guest speaker, George Smith, university chancellor, and noted his accomplishments and experiences prior to education—U.S. Navy commander, Oak Ridge Laboratory researcher, and politician. Dr. Smith's talk, "Industry and Education Collaboration," was very interesting and included a history of special projects enjoyed by both academics and corporate heads. Dr. Smith suggested that we engineers could work with education to accomplish three goals.

Urban Development

The chancellor's primary thrust was a request for $100,000 in financial aid for urban development. He said money had already been donated from three sources: a large realty firm, Capital Homes, had given $20,000; a philanthropic group, We Care, had donated a matching $20,000; Dr. Smith's university gave a matching $20,000. The remaining $40,000, Dr. Smith hoped, would come from industry donations.

Internships

The chancellor noted that industry could help itself, as well as the community, by providing internships for university undergraduate majors. These internships could either be semester- or year-long arrangements, whereby students worked for minimum wage to learn more about the day-to-day aspects of their chosen fields. The chancellor said that these internships not only would increase the students' theoretical knowledge of engineering by giving them hands-on experience, but also that the knowledge they acquired would make them better future employees for the host engineering companies. Everyone would benefit. Dr. Smith noted that the students would receive a grade and credit for their work.

Training Seminars. Recent industry-education collaborations include training seminars in computers, fiber optics, and human resource options.

Conclusion

After the speech, our VP introduced new business, calling for nominations for next year's officers, gave us the agenda for our next meeting, and adjourned the meeting.

Figure 5.5 Document Design Using a Hierarchy of Heading Levels to Order the Information by Importance

Readers are not that generous with their time. As writer, you should make your reader's task easier.

A third way to assist your audience is by helping them *access* information rapidly—at a glance. You can use any of the following highlighting techniques to help the readers filter out extraneous or tangential information and focus on key ideas (Keyes 641; Watzman ATA 49):

- *White space:* In addition to horizontal space, created by double or triple spacing, you also can create *vertical space* by indenting. This vertical white space breaks up the monotony of wall-to-wall words and gives your readers breathing room. White space invites your readers into the text and helps the audience focus on the indented points you want to emphasize.
- *Bullets: Bullets,* used to emphasize items within an indented list, are created by using asterisks (*), hyphens (-), a lower case "o", or degree signs (°), or any number of typographic symbols (■, ❑, ●, or ◆), or iconic *dingbats* (☞, ✏, or ✓).
- *Numbering: Enumeration* creates itemized lists that can show sequence or importance and that allow for easy reference.
- *Boldface:* Created on a computer or typewriter by double striking, ***boldface text*** emphasizes a key word or phrase.
- *All caps:* The technique of *capitalizing* text is an excellent way to help your reader access a WARNING, DANGER, CAUTION, or NOTE. However, capitalizing other types of information is not suggested, since reading lowercase words is easier for your audience. Reading all caps hinders the audience, since such text creates a block of letters in which individual letters aren't easily distinguished from each other.
- *Underlining: Underlining* and all caps are similar in that you should use both cautiously. If you underline too frequently or use all caps too often, none of your information will be emphatic. One underlined word or phrase will call attention to itself and achieve reader access. Several underlined words or phrases will overwhelm your readers.
- *Italics:* The use of italics and underlining are similar highlighting techniques. Notice how all subheadings in this bulleted list are italicized.
- *Windowing:* If you indent your key points and enclose them in a box, you're *windowing.* Here's an example:

> **NOTE:** Be sure to *hand-tighten* the nuts at this point. Once you've completed the installation, then go back and securely tighten all nuts.

  Windowing draws your reader's attention to an idea, thus making it more emphatic. You can also italicize, boldface, and use all caps within the windowed box, as we have in the preceding example.

- *Fills:* You can further highlight windowed text through fills (lines, patterns, waves, bricks, gradients, and shadings in a text box).

- *Color:* Another way to make key words and phrases leap off the page is to color them. *Danger* would be red, for example; *Warning* orange, and *Caution* yellow. You can also use color to help a reader access the first-level heading, a header, or a footer. (*Headers* contain information placed along the top margin of text; *footers* contain information placed along the bottom margin of text.)

  All colors are not equal in visual value. Generally, darker colors provide the most contrast with surrounding text. Therefore, they help your readers access information more than lighter colors.
- *Inverse type:* You can also help readers access information by using *inverse type*—printing white on black, versus the usual black on white.

Here's a very important consideration! When it comes to using highlighting techniques, *more is not better.* A few highlighting techniques help your readers filter out background data and focus on key points. Too many highlighting techniques are a distraction and clutter the document design. Be careful not to overdo a good thing. Figure 5.6 gives examples of several highlighting methods. And, notice how Figure 5.7 uses highlighting techniques to help the readers access information in the meeting minutes.

VARIETY

Each of the document designs you've seen so far (Figures 5.1–5.7) use one column and is printed vertically on a traditional 8 1/2 × 11 page (a type of printing called *portrait*). This is not your only option. Your reader might profit from more *variety* (Watzman ATA 48). For example, you might want to use a smaller or larger paper; to vary the weight of your paper, using 10-pound, 12-pound, or heavier card stock; or even to print your text on colored paper.

More importantly, you can vary the document design as follows:

- *Print horizontally:* Rather than print your text vertically—8 1/2 × 11 portrait—you could print *horizontally,* as an 11 × 8 1/2 *landscape.*
- *Use more columns:* Provide your reader two to five columns of text.
- *Vary gutter width:* Each column of text will be separated by vertical white space. This is called the *gutter.*
- *Use ragged-right margins:* Most text is full justified (both right and left margins aligned). Once this was considered professional, giving the text a clean look. Now, however, studies confirm that right-margin justified text is harder for the audience to read. It's too rigid. In contrast, *ragged-right* type (right margin not justified) is easier to read and more pleasing to the eye. You can use this method to provide your audience a varied page layout (Everson 397).

Figure 5.9 shows how you can use columns, landscape, and ragged-right margins to vary your document design.

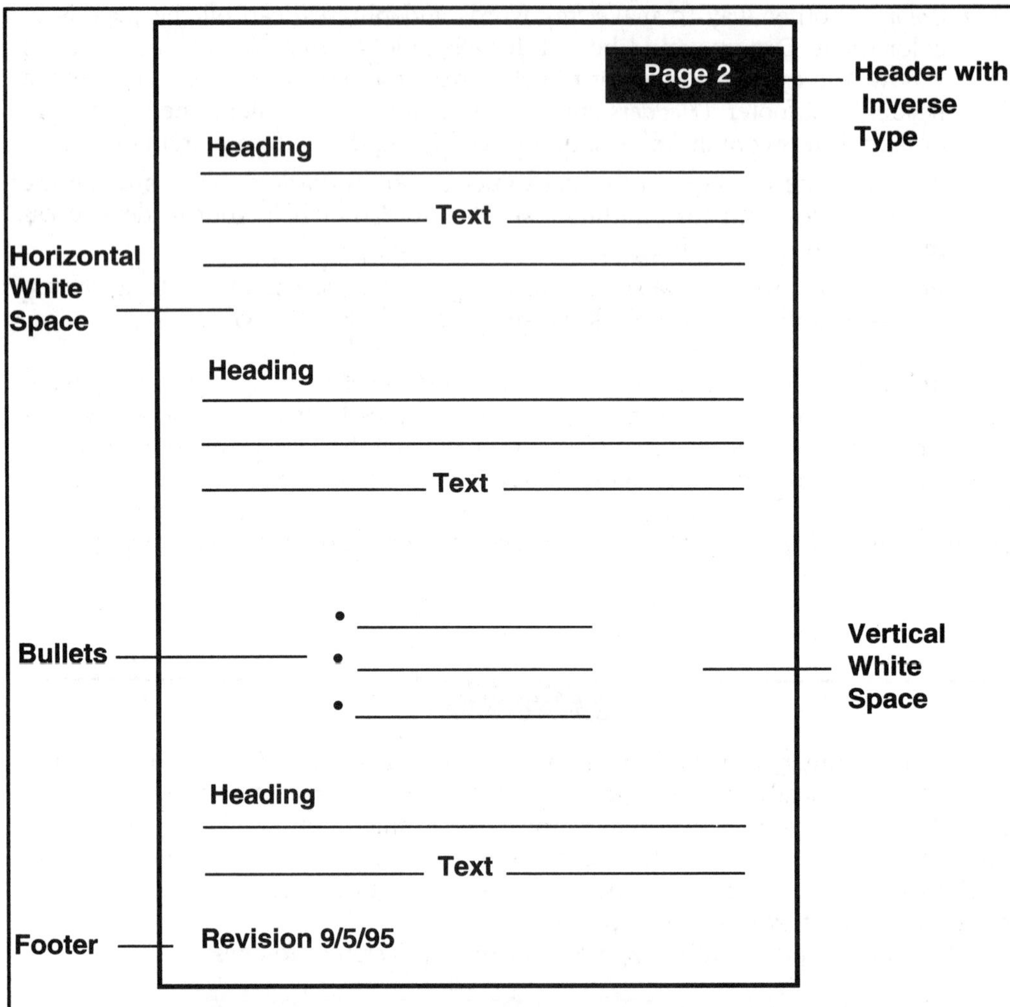

Figure 5.6 Highlighting Techniques for Access

Although you can vary your document design by printing horizontally and by using multiple columns, the audience is still confronted by words, words, and more words. The majority of readers don't want to wade through text. Luckily, words are not your only means of communication. You can reach a larger audience with different learning styles by varying your method of communication.

Graphics are an excellent alternative. Many people are more comfortable grasping information visually than verbally. Although it's a cliché, a picture is often worth a thousand words.

We discuss graphics (figures and tables) extensively in Chapter 6. However, to clarify our point about the value of variety, see Figure 5.10, which adds a graphic to the meeting minutes.

MINUTES The meeting at the Carriage Club was attended by 30 members and guests. After the dinner, Roger Traver introduced the guest speaker, George Smith, university chancellor, and noted his accomplishments and experiences prior to education:

- U.S. Navy commander
- Oak Ridge Laboratory researcher
- Politician

Dr. Smith's talk, "*Industry and Education Collaboration,*" was very interesting and included a history of special projects enjoyed by both academics and corporate heads. Dr. Smith suggested that we engineers could work with education to accomplish three goals.

Urban Development

The chancellor's primary thrust was a request for $100,000 in financial aid for urban development. He said money had already been donated from three sources:

1. A large realty firm, Capital Homes, had given $20,000.
2. A philanthropic group, We Care, had donated a matching $20,000.
3. Dr. Smith's university also gave $20,000.

The remaining $40,000, Dr. Smith hoped, would come from industry donations.

Internships

The chancellor noted that industry could help itself, as well as the community, by providing two types of internships for university undergraduate majors:

1. Semester-long internships
2. Year-long internships

Students would work for minimum wage to learn more about the day-to-day aspects of their chosen fields.

The chancellor said that these internships not only would increase the students' theoretical knowledge of engineering by giving them hands-on experience, but also that the knowledge they acquired would make them better future employees for the host engineering companies. <u>Everyone would benefit.</u> Dr. Smith noted that the students would receive a grade and credit for their work.

Training Seminars. Recent industry-education collaborations include training seminars in computers, fiber optics, and human resource options.

Conclusion

After the speech, our VP introduced new business, calling for nominations for next year's officers, gave us the agenda for our next meeting, and adjourned the meeting.

Figure 5.7 Document Design Using Highlighting Techniques to Help Readers Access Key Ideas

Figure 5.8 Portrait with One Column Full Justified

Figure 5.9.Landscape with Two Columns and Ragged-Right Margins.

MINUTES The meeting at the Carriage Club was attended by 30 members and guests. After the dinner, Roger Traver introduced the guest speaker, George Smith, university chancellor, and noted his accomplishments and experiences prior to education:

- U.S. Navy commander
- Oak Ridge Laboratory researcher
- Politician

Dr. Smith's talk, "*Industry and Education Collaboration,*" was very interesting and included a history of special projects enjoyed by both academics and corporate heads. Dr. Smith suggested that we engineers could work with education to accomplish three goals.

Urban Development

The chancellor's primary thrust was a request for $100,000 in financial aid for urban development. He said money had already been donated from three sources, but business and industry can still help significantly.

The following pie chart clarifies what money has been encumbered and how industry donations are still needed.

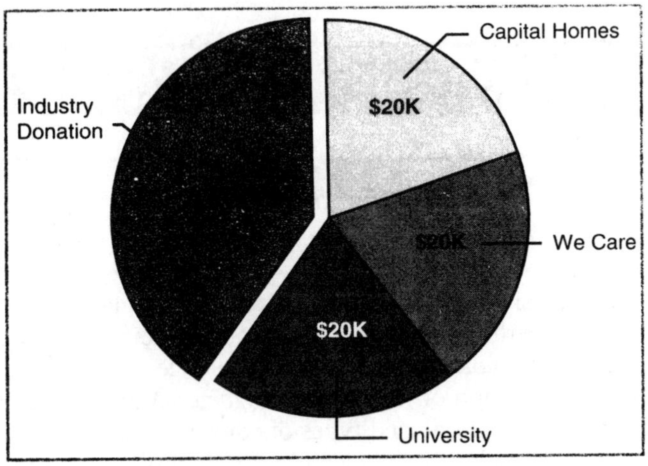

Figure 1 Donations

Internships

The chancellor noted that industry could help itself, as well as the community, by providing two types of internships for university undergraduate majors:

Figure 5.10 Document Design Using a Pie Chart to Vary the Communication

1. Semester-long internships
2. Year-long internships

Students would work for minimum wage to learn more about the day-to-day aspects of their chosen fields.

The chancellor said that these internships not only would increase the students' theoretical knowledge of engineering by giving them hands-on experience, but also that the knowledge they acquired would make them better future employees for the host engineering companies. Everyone would benefit. Dr. Smith noted that the students would receive a grade and credit for their work.

Training Seminars. Recent industry-education collaborations include training seminars in computers, fiber optics, and human resource options.

Conclusion

After the speech, our VP introduced new business, calling for nominations for next year's officers, gave us the agenda for our next meeting, and adjourned the meeting.

Figure 5.10 Document Design Using a Pie Chart to Vary the Communication (Cont.)

SUMMARY

Creating effective document design is time consuming and creatively demanding. It's easier just to write the old-fashioned way—word after word, paragraph after paragraph, blocks of inaccessible text. Although it's easier, it's also less effective.

Your job isn't just to dump data and hope your readers can figure it out. Instead, a successful technical writer works to involve the audience. Your goal is to help the readers understand the organization of your text, recognize its order, and access information at a glance. You also want to use varied types of communication, including graphics, for readers who absorb information better visually, for example, rather than logically.

What's the payoff? Studies tell us that effective document design saves money and time.

One international customs department, after revising the design of its lost-baggage forms, reduced its error rate by over 50 percent. When a utilities company changed the look of its billing statements, customers asked fewer questions, saving the company approximately $250,000 per year. In the early 1980s, the IRS redesigned the 1040A form. The new form helped taxpayers compute their income averaging more accurately. The U.S. Department of Commerce, Office of Consumer Affairs, reported that when several companies improved their documents' visual appeal, the companies increased business and reduced customer complaints (Schriver 250–51).

Document design isn't a costly frill. Effective document design is good for your company's business.

ACTIVITIES

TEAM PROJECTS

1. Bring samples of technical writing to class. These could include letters, brochures, newsletters, instructions, reports, or advertisements from magazines or newspapers.

   In groups of three to five class members, assess the document design of each sample. Determine which samples have successful document designs and which samples have poor document designs. Base your decisions on the criteria provided in this chapter: organization, order, access, and variety.

   Either orally or in writing, share your findings with other teams in the class.

2. In teams of three to five class members, take one of the less successful samples from the above activity and reformat it to improve its document design. Focus on improving the sample's organization, order, access, and variety.

   Once your team has completed reformatting the text, make photocopies or transparencies of your work. Then review the various team projects, determining which team created the best document design. Select a winner, and explain why this text now has a successful document design.

3. In teams of three to five class members, reformat the following memo to improve its document design.

```
DATE:     November 30, 1996
TO:       Jan Hunt
FROM:     Tom Langford
SUBJECT:  CLEANING PROCEDURES FOR MANUFACTURING WALK-IN
          OVENS #98731, #98732, AND #98733

The above-mentioned ovens need extensive cleaning. To do
so, vacuum and wipe all doors, walls, roofs, and floors.
All vents/dampers need to be removed, and a tack cloth
must be used to remove all loose dust and dirt. Also, all
filters need to be replaced.

I am requesting this because loose particles of dust/dirt
are blown onto wet parts when placed in the air-circulating
ovens to dry. This causes extensive rework. Please perform
this procedure twice per week to ensure clean production.
```

4. In teams of three to five class members, reformat the following executive summary to improve its document design.

EXECUTIVE SUMMARY

The City of Waluska wants to provide its community a safe and reliable water treatment facility. The goal is to protect Waluska's environmental resources and to ensure community values.

To achieve these goals, the City has issued a Request for Proposal to update the Loon Lake Water Treatment Plant (LLWTP). The City recognizes that meeting its community's water treatment needs requires overcoming numerous challenges. These challenges include managing the changing regulations and protection standards, developing financially responsible treatment services, planning land use for community expansion, and upholding community values.

For all of the above reasons, Hardtack and Sons (H & S) engineering is your best choice. We understand the project scope and recognize your community's needs.

We have worked successfully with your community for a decade, creating feasibility studies for Loon Lake toxic control, developing odor-abatement procedures for your streams and creeks, and assessing your water treatment plant's ability to meet regulatory standards.

H & S personnel are not just engineering experts. We are members of your community. Our dynamic project team has a close working relationship with your community's regulatory agencies. Our Partner in Charge, Julie Schopper, has experience with similar projects worldwide, demonstrated leadership, and the ability to communicate effectively with clients.

H & S offers the City of Waluska an integrated program that addresses all your community's needs. We believe that H & S is your best choice to ensure that your community receives a water treatment plant ready to meet the challenges of the twenty-first century.

Chapter 7

LETTERS

- OBJECTIVES
- LETTER COMPONENTS
- LETTER FORMATS
- CRITERIA FOR DIFFERENT TYPES OF LETTERS
- PROCESS
- PROCESS LOG

OBJECTIVES

Letters are external correspondence that you send from your company to a colleague working at another company, to a vendor, to a prospective client, to an agency, or to a friend who lives around the corner or across the continent. Letters leave your work site (as opposed to memos, which stay within the company).

Because letters are sent offsite to readers in other locations, you must write them effectively. Your letters not only reflect your communication abilities but also are a reflection of your company. If your letter is sloppy, marred with grammatical errors, or creates a negative tone, you will look bad and so will your company. Even worse, if your letter communicates incorrect information regarding prices, guarantees, due-date promises, or equipment and labor commitments, your company will be held legally responsible. When you write on your company's letterhead stationery and sign it, your letter constitutes a legally binding contract. Therefore, no matter what type of letter you're writing, take care to follow accepted letter formats, maintain the proper tone, and avoid errors.

This chapter helps you write the following kinds of letters: (a) inquiry, (b) cover (transmittal), (c) good news, (d) bad news, (e) complaint, (f) adjustment and (g) sales.

To write these letters effectively, we provide you with letter components and formats, criteria for writing different types of letters, process (and a process log) to follow for writing letters, and examples.

LETTER COMPONENTS

ESSENTIAL COMPONENTS

Your letter should by typed on 8-1/2" × 11" unlined paper or printed on 8-1/2" × 11" word processing paper. Leave 1" to 1-1/2" margins at the top and on both sides.

Your letter should contain the following components (see Figure 7.1).

1. Writer's Address

This section contains either your personal address or your company's address (you may be writing on printed, letterhead stationery).

If the heading consists of your address, you will include (a) your street address (do not abbreviate the words *street, avenue, road, drive,* etc.), and (b) the city, state, and zip code. Do not include your name. The state may be abbreviated with the appropriate two-letter abbreviation (see Chapter 18).

If the heading consists of your company's address, you will include (a) the company's name; (b) the street address; and (c) the city, state, and zip code.

2. Date

Document the month, day, and year in which you have written your letter. You can set up your date in one of two ways: May 31, 1996, or 31 May 1996.

Place the date two spaces below the writer's address (if the letter is long) or three to eight spaces below the writer's address (for shorter letters). For a short letter, leave more space so the spacing on the letter is balanced.

3. Inside Address

This is the address of the person or people to whom you are writing. The inside address contains, in the following order,

- Your reader's name (If you do not know the name of this person, begin the reader's address with a job title or the name of the department.)
- Your reader's title (optional if you include the name)
- The company name
- The company street address
- The company city, state, and zip code

Place this information two lines below the date.

UNITED SPECTOGRAPH

① *Writer's address*
19015 Lakeview Avenue
Columbus, OH 43212

② *Date*
June 10, 1996

③ *Inside address*
Andrea Snower
Corporate Communications, Inc.
1245 Grant
Chicago, IL 60611

④ *Salutation*
Dear Ms. Snower:

⑤ *Letter body*
Here is the schedule for your presentation during our Basic Information Training for Supervisors (BITS) seminar. You will hold your sessions in our Training Center at 19015 Lakeview Avenue.

The schedule and important information regarding your two 8-hour seminars is as follows. Group 1, which will consist of 15 employees, will meet Monday, July 6, 1996, from 8:00 a.m. to 5:00 p.m. Group 2, which will consist of 18 employees, will meet Tuesday, July 7, 1996, from 8:00 a.m. to 5:00 p.m.

As you requested, the training room will have an overhead projector, screen, flip chart, and pad. During the morning sessions, coffee, juices, and rolls will be served. In the afternoon, seminar participants will be offered cold drinks and cookies. We look forward to working with you again. If I can answer any questions, please let me know.

⑥ *Complimentary close*
Sincerely,

⑦ *Signed name*
Martha Lee

⑧ *Typed name*
Martha Lee

Figure 7.1 Essential Letter Components

4. Salutation

The traditional salutation, placed two spaces beneath the inside address, is your reader's last name, preceded by *Dear* and followed by a colon.

Dear Mr. Smith:

You can also address your reader by his or her first name if you are on a first-name basis with this person.

Dear John:

If you are writing to a woman and are unfamiliar with her marital status, address the letter as follows:

Dear Ms. Jones:

However, if you know the woman's marital status, you can address the letter accordingly:

Dear Miss Jones:
or
Dear Mrs. Jones:

Occasionally, you will write to someone whom you do not know and who has a non-gender-specific first name, such as Pat, Kim, Kelly, Stacy, or Chris. In this case, avoid either Mr., Miss, Mrs., or Ms., and write as follows:

Dear Chris Evans:

Often, when writing to another company, you will not know your reader's name. In this instance, you have limited options. You could address the reader by his or her title (Dear Vice President of Operations:) or address the letter to the reader's department (Accounting Department:). If you address the letter to the department, *Dear* would be inappropriate and should be omitted.

Each of the above salutations is acceptable. However, several common salutations are no longer valid. For example, as discussed in Chapter 4, sexist salutations such as *Dear Sir* and *Gentlemen* cannot be used (unless you know beyond all doubt that each of your readers is a man; however, we suggest that you eliminate the problem by avoiding the sexist salutation).

Other awkward salutations include *Good morning* (since mail is delivered twice daily at many corporations), *To whom it may concern* (which is trite, insensitive, and imprecise), and *Greetings* (which either has a seasonal ring to it or a military connotation). *Dear Sir/Madam* is also ineffective and should be avoided.

To avoid these pitfalls in salutations, you might want to call the company to which you're writing and ask them for the name of your intended reader (and the correct spelling of the name).

5. Letter Body

Begin the body of the letter two spaces below the salutation. The body includes your introductory paragraph, discussion paragraph(s), and concluding paragraph. The body should be single spaced with double spacings between paragraphs. Whether you indent the beginnings of each paragraph or leave them flush with the left margin is determined by the letter format you employ. We discuss this issue later in this chapter.

6. Complimentary Close

Place the complimentary close, followed by a comma, two spaces below the concluding paragraph. Although several different complimentary closes are acceptable, such as *Yours truly* and *Sincerely yours,* we suggest that you limit your close to *Sincerely.*

7. Signed Name

Sign your name legibly beneath the complimentary close.

8. Typed Name

Type your name four spaces below the complimentary close. If you wish, you may type your title one space beneath your typed name.

> Sincerely,
>
> *Henry Marshall*
>
> Henry Marshall
> Comptroller

OPTIONAL LETTER COMPONENTS

In addition to the letter essentials, you can include the following options.

Subject Line

A subject line, which is mandatory in memos (see Chapter 8), is applicable in letters. You can type the subject line in all capital letters two spaces below the inside address and two spaces above the salutation.

> Dr. Ron Schaefer
> Linguistics Department
> Southern Illinois University
> Edwardsville, IL 66205
>
> Subject: LINGUISTICS CONFERENCE REGISTRATION PAYMENT
>
> Dear Dr. Schaefer:

You also could use a subject line instead of a salutation.

Linguistics Department
Southern Illinois University
Edwardsville, IL 66205

Subject: LINGUISTICS CONFERENCE REGISTRATION PAYMENT

A subject line not only helps readers understand the letter's intent, but also (if you are uncertain of your reader's name) helps you avoid such flawed salutations as *To whom it may concern, Dear Sirs,* and *Ladies and Gentlemen.*

In the simplified letter, both the salutation and the complimentary close are omitted, and a subject line is included.

New-Page Notations

If your letter is longer than one page, you'll need to cite your name, the page number, and the date on all pages after page one. Place this notation either flush with the left margin at the top of subsequent pages or across the top of subsequent pages. (You must have at least two lines of text on the next page to justify another page.)

MARGIN LEFT SUBSEQUENT PAGE NOTATION

```
Mabel Tinjaca
Page 2
May 31, 1996
```

SECOND PAGE NOTATION ACROSS THE TOP

```
Mabel Tinjaca    2      May 31, 1996
```

Writer and Typist Initials

If the letter has been typed by someone other than the writer, include both the writer's and the typist's initials two spaces below the typed signature. The writer's initials are capitalized, the typist's initials are typed in lowercase, and the two sets of initials are separated by a colon. If both the typist and the writer are the same person, this notation is not necessary.

Sincerely,

W. T. Winnery

W. T. Winnery

WTW:mm

Enclosure Notation

If your letter prefaces enclosed information, such as an invoice, a report, or graphics, mention this enclosure in the letter and then type an enclosure notation two spaces below the typed signature (or two spaces below the writer and typist initials). The enclosure notation can be abbreviated *Enc.;* written out—*Enclosure;* show the number of enclosures, such as *Enclosures (2);* or specify what has been enclosed—*Enclosure: January Invoice.*

Copy Notation

If you have made a carbon copy or a photocopy of your letter, show this in a copy notation. A carbon copy is designated by a double lowercase *c (cc);* a photocopy is designated by lowercase *pc.* Type the copy notation two spaces below the typed signature or two spaces below either the writer and typist initials or the enclosure notation.

> Sincerely,
>
> *Brian Altman*
>
> Brian Altman
>
> Enclosure: August Status Report
>
> pc

If you are sending copies of the letter to other readers, list these readers' names following the copy notation.

> Sincerely,
>
> *Brian Altman*
>
> Brian Altman
>
> Enclosure: August Status Report
>
> pc: Andrew Dubrov
> Erica Nochlin

LETTER FORMATS

Type your letter using any of the formats shown in Figures 7.2 through 7.5.

CRITERIA FOR DIFFERENT TYPES OF LETTERS

LETTERS OF INQUIRY

If you want information about degree requirements, equipment costs, performance records, turnaround time, employee credentials, or any subject matter of interest to you, you write a letter requesting that data. Letters of inquiry require that you be spe-

1119 South Bend
Chico, CA 95926
November 1, 1996

Dr. Robert Cottrell
7806 Northway
Austin, TX 78752

Dear Dr. Cottrell:

Introduction

Discussion

Conclusion

Sincerely,

Sue Timmons

Sue Timmons

ST:sg

cc: Jeremy Isaacs

Figure 7.2 Full Block Format

7501 Carriage
Coconut Grove, FL 33133
September 7, 1996

Mr. Robin Massin
7926 Candle Lane
Pittsburgh, PA 15237

Subject: MARKETING OF ROBOTICS APPLICATIONS

Dear Mr. Massin:

Introduction

Discussion

Conclusion

Sincerely,

Ruth Schneider

Ruth Schneider

RS:sl

Figure 7.3 Full Block Format with Subject Line

3628 East Vista Road
Chamblee, GA 30341
August 13, 1996

Mr. Kenny Frankel
7810 Warrensburg
Hackensack, NJ 07649

Dear Mr. Frankel:

Introduction

Discussion

Conclusion

Sincerely,

Sylvia Light

Figure 7.4 Modified Block Format

935 West Hermosa
Oakland, CA 94610
September 5, 1996

Edie Kreisler
1126 Ranleigh Way
San Antonio, TX 78213

Subject: PURCHASE OF BEACHFRONT PROPERTY

Introduction

Discussion

Conclusion

Walt McDonald

Walt McDonald

Enclosures (3)

Figure 7.5 Simplified Format

cific and precise. For example, if you write, "Please send me any information you have on the XYZ transformer," you're in trouble. You'll either receive any information the reader chooses to dispose of or none at all. Look at the following letter of request.

> Dear Mr. Jernigan:
>
> Please send us information about the following filter pools:
>
> 1. East Lime Pool
> 2. West Sulphate Pool
> 3. East Aggregate Pool
>
> Thank you.

The disgruntled worker replied as follows:

> Dear Mr. Scholl:
>
> I would be happy to provide you with any information you would like. However, you need to tell me *what* information you require about the pools.
>
> I look forward to your response.

To receive the information you need, write an effective letter of inquiry. Successful letters of inquiry contain all the letter essentials, maintain an effective technical writing style, achieve audience involvement through pronoun usage, and avoid grammatical and mechanical errors.

In addition, you must accomplish the following:

Introduction

1. *Clarify your intent in the introduction.* Until you tell your readers why you are writing, they do not know. It's your responsibility to clarify your intent and explain your rationale for writing. Also tell your reader immediately what you are writing about (the subject matter of your inquiry). You can state your intent and subject matter in one to three sentences, as follows:

> My company is planning to purchase 30 new tractors by the end of the year. Your 1995 tractor with the on-board computer might be the answer to our problems. In addition to sending us a picture brochure of the CP95 tractor, could you also answer the following questions about your vehicle?

In this example, the first two sentences explain why you are writing. The last sentence explains what you want.

Discussion

2. *Specify your needs in the discussion.* To ensure that you get the response you want and need, ask precise questions or list specific topics of inquiry. You must quantify. For example, rather than vaguely asking about machinery specifications, you should ask more precisely about "specifications for the 12R403B Copier." Rather than asking, "Will the roofing material cover a large surface," you need to quantify—"Will the roofing material cover 150' × 180'?"

Conclusion

3. *Conclude precisely.* First, explain when you need a response (because until you tell the reader, he or she does not know). Don't write, "Please respond as soon as possible." Provide dated action—tell the reader exactly when you need your answers. Dated action doesn't mean you'll get the answers when you want them, but your chances are better. Second, to sell your readers on the importance of this date, explain why you need answers by the date given.

> Please send the above information by August 15. This will allow my shop supervisor to study the manuals and arrange for a test drive prior to our Board of Director's meeting on September 1.

Figure 7.6 will help you understand the requirements for effective letters of inquiry.

COVER LETTERS

In business, you are often required to send information to a client, vendor, or colleague. You might send multipaged copies of reports, invoices, drawings, maps, letters, memos, specifications, instructions, questionnaires, or proposals. The reader may have requested this information. Maybe you're sending the data on your own accord. Whatever the situation, if you merely submit the multipaged data without a cover letter, your readers will be overwhelmed with information that they must wade through.

A cover letter accomplishes two goals. First, it lets you tell readers up front what they are receiving. Second, it helps you focus your readers' attention on key points within the enclosures. Thus, the cover letter is a reader-friendly gesture geared toward assisting your audience.

As with the previously discussed letters, successful cover letters include the letter essentials, maintain an effective technical writing style, avoid grammatical and mechanical errors, and achieve audience recognition and involvement. In addition, a well-written cover letter contains an introduction, discussion, and conclusion.

R I Z
O Enterprises O
H 1020 Sunshine Road N
Jamaica Plain, MA 02130

July 23, 1996

Mr. Jack Halligan
Director of Marketing
Johnson Motor Company
4718 West 91st Street
Tacoma, WA 81492

Dear Mr. Halligan:

Thank you for your recent sales letter regarding the Model CP95 tractor with fuel-saving devices. My company plans to purchase 30 new tractors by the end of the year, and your tractors may be what we're looking for.

Before we make our decision, however, we need more information. Along with a picture brochure of the CP95, please answer the following questions:

1. What is the cost per tractor?
2. Do you offer financing options for quantity purchases?
3. Does your instructional manual discuss the on-board computer and the eight-gear system?
4. What are your tractor's comfort features?
5. When can you deliver 30 tractors?

Please send this information by August 15 so my shop supervisor and I can study the materials and arrange for a test drive. I plan to present a proposal for purchase to our Board of Directors on September 1. I look forward to your response.

Sincerely,

Kathy Brewington

Kathy Brewington

Figure 7.6 Letter of Inquiry

Introduction

In the introductory paragraph, tell your reader *why* you are writing and *what* you are writing about. An appropriate introduction providing your reader a rationale for your writing might read as follows: "To help you prepare for next week's audit, we have enclosed the following necessary forms."

What if the reader has asked you to send the documentation? Do you still need to explain why you're writing? The answer is yes. Although the reader requested the data, time has passed, other correspondence has been written, and your reader might have forgotten the initial request. Your job is to remind him or her. Write something like, "In response to your request, enclosed are the completed questionnaires from our engineers." These introductory sentences provide the reader information about why you are writing and what you are sending. Note that neither exceeds one sentence. Clarity of intent can be provided *concisely.*

Discussion

In the body of the letter, you want to accomplish two things. First, you either want to tell your reader *exactly what you've enclosed* or *exactly what of value is within the enclosures.* In both instances, you should provide an itemized list. For example, you can itemize enclosures as follows:

> To help you prepare for next week's audit, we have enclosed the following necessary forms:
>
> - Year-to-date sales figures
> - Fiscal year sales figures
> - Year-to-date expenditures
> - Fiscal year expenditures

Similarly, you can itemize the important facts within the enclosures as follows:

> In response to your request, enclosed are the completed questionnaires from our engineers.
>
> Of special interest to you within the questionnaires are their answers to questions regarding the following:
>
> - Easement dimensions . . . . page 1
> - Sewer construction materials . . . . page 3
> - Residential/commercial ratios . . . . page 5

This example shows where important information can be found within the enclosure. Page numbers are a friendly gesture toward your audience. Instead of just dumping the data on your reader and saying, "best of luck—hope you find what you want," you're helping the reader locate the important information. In so doing, you're achieving audience recognition and involvement.

However, including page numbers has a greater benefit than audience involvement. These page numbers also allow you to focus your reader's attention on what you want him or her to see. In other words, if you merely provide the enclosure without a cover letter, then you leave it up to readers to sift through the information and decide on their own what's important. In contrast, by providing an itemized list with page numbers, you direct the reader's attention. You can emphasize, for your benefit, the points in the enclosure which you consider to be important.

Conclusion

Your conclusion should tell your readers *what* you want to happen next, *when* you want this to happen, and *why* this data is important. Without such a conclusion, your reader will review the documentation and say, "OK, so what? What do you want me to do with the data?" or "OK, but what are your future plans?"

The *what* clarifies your intentions. The *when* specifies the date. The *why* either sells the importance of this date, possibly hinting at the urgency, or suggests your conscientiousness.

Here are examples of cover letters, complete with conclusions.

```
To help you prepare for next week's audit, we have
enclosed the following necessary forms:

  • Year-to-date sales figures
  • Fiscal year sales figures
  • Year-to-date expenditures
  • Fiscal year expenditures

Please fill out these forms before our Wednesday
arrival. Doing so will facilitate the audit, thereby
allowing you and your colleagues to return to your reg-
ular work activities more rapidly.
```

```
In response to your request, enclosed are the com-
pleted questionnaires from our engineers.

Of special interest to you within the questionnaires
are their answers to questions regarding the following:
```

```
• Easement dimensions . . . . . . . . . . . . . page 1
• Sewer construction materials. . . . . . . . . page 3
• Residential/commercial ratios . . . . . . . . page 5

We would be happy to meet with you at your convenience
to discuss this issue in greater detail. After you have
had a chance to review these enclosures, please call
my office at 469-8500 to set up a meeting. We want to
answer your questions regarding our construction plan-
ning.
```

The cover letter seen in Figure 7.7 contains letter essentials.

GOOD-NEWS LETTERS

You'll often have the opportunity to write good-news letters. For example, you might write a letter promoting an employee or offering an individual a job at your corporation. You might write to commend a colleague for a job well done. Maybe you'll write to tell a customer that his or her request for a refund was justified.

Introduction

As in other letters discussed in this chapter, the introduction should explain immediately *why* you're writing and tell *what* you're writing about. The point of these letters is good news.

Furthermore, since your goal is to convey good news, you should begin with positive word usage, as in the following examples:

Example 1
Commending a colleague (Introduction)
Judy, you've proven to be indispensable again. Your work for the textbook committee has made all of our jobs easier.

Example 2
Promoting an employee (Introduction)
Congratulations! We're proud to offer you early promotion, Jan.

Discussion

Once you've explained why you're writing and what you're writing about, the next step is to provide the detail—to show *exactly what* has justified the commendation or the promotion.

A•M•E•R•I•C•A•N

HEALTHCARE
1401 Laurel Drive
Denton, TX 76201

November 11, 1996

Jean Marks
Director of Outpatient Care
St. Michael's Hospital
Westlake Village, CA 91362

Dear Ms. Marks:

Thank you for your recent request for information regarding our line of specialized outpatient care equipment. *American Healthcare* has manufactured stairway lifts, bathlifts, and vertical wheelchair lifts for over 40 years.

To give you a better idea of how we can serve you and your patients, we've enclosed a brochure including the following information:

1. An *American Healthcare* credit application form.
2. Price lists for all our products.
3. Maintenance, warranty, and guarantee information.
4. Our 24-hour Hotline for immediate service.
5. Technical specifications for our products, including sizes, weight limitations, colors, and installation instructions.

Please look over the enclosed material. Early next month, I'll call you to set up an appointment at your convenience. I'm looking forward to explaining how *American Healthcare* can provide exceptional outpatient care for your community.

Sincerely,

Toby Sommers

Toby Sommers

Enclosure

Figure 7.7 Cover Letter

Example 1
Commending a colleague
(Introduction and discussion)
Judy, you've proven to be indispensable again. Your work for the textbook committee has made all of our jobs easier.

Thank you for performing the following services:

- Meeting with all the sales reps to convey our departmental requirements
- Reviewing those texts with computer-aided design components
- Screening the textbook options and selecting the three most suited to our needs

Example 2
Promoting an employee
(Introduction and discussion)
Congratulations! We're proud to offer you early promotion, Jan.

You've earned a grade raise to E30 for the following reasons:

1. *Productivity:* Your line personnel produced 2,000 units per month throughout this quarter.
2. *Efficiency:* You maintained a 95 percent manufacturing efficiency rating.
3. *Supervisory skills:* You received only four grievances; your annual performance appraisals showed that your subordinates appreciated your motivational management techniques.

Conclusion

Once you've clarified exactly what has resulted in the good news, your last paragraph should state *what* you plan next (or expect from your reader next), *when* this action will occur, and *why* the date is important. The following good-news letters are complete with introductions, discussions, and conclusions.

Judy, you've proven to be indispensable again. Your work for the textbook committee has made all of our jobs easier.

Thank you for performing the following services:

- Meeting with all the sales reps to convey our departmental requirements
- Reviewing those texts with computer aided design components
- Screening the textbook options and selecting the three most suited to our needs.

Due to your assistance, we have decided on the Wilkes text and plan to place our orders this April. That will allow us to stock the bookstore for the fall semester. Your work has made a difference, and we appreciate your efforts--another job well done!

Congratulations! We're proud to offer you early promotion, Jan.

You've earned a grade raise to E30 for the following reasons:

1. *Productivity*	Your line personnel produced 2,000 units per month throughout this quarter.
2. *Efficiency*	You maintained a 95 percent manufacturing efficiency rating.
3. *Supervisory Skills*	You received only four grievances; your annual performance appraisals showed that your subordinates appreciated your motivational management techniques.

Due to your excellent work, you will receive your pay increase the first of next month. Good work, Jan. You deserve it.

BAD-NEWS LETTERS

Unfortunately, you occasionally will be required to write bad-news letters. These letters might reject a job applicant, deny an employee a raise, tell a vendor that his or her company's proposal has not been accepted, or reject a customer's request for a refund. Maybe you'll have to write to a corporation to tell them that their manufacturing is not meeting your company's specifications. Maybe you'll need to write a letter to a union documenting a grievance. You might even have to write a bad-news letter to fire employees.

In any of these instances, tact is required. You can't berate a customer or client. You shouldn't reject a job applicant offensively. Even your grievance must be worded carefully to avoid future problems.

Since the point of a bad-news letter is bad news, you'll need to structure your correspondence carefully to avoid offending your reader.

Introduction

We've suggested throughout this chapter that your introduction should explain why you're writing and what you're writing about. However, such conciseness and clarity in a bad-news letter would be harsh and abrupt. Therefore, to avoid these lapses in diplomacy, begin your bad-news letter with a buffer. Start your letter with information that your reader can accept as valid but that will sway your reader to accept the bad news to come.

Example 1
Rejecting a job applicant (Introduction)
Thank you for your recent letter of application. As you can imagine, we received many letters from highly qualified applicants and appreciate your interest in Acme.

Example 2
Terminating a client/vendor relationship (Introduction)
John, as you know, our business demands exact tolerances and precise workmanship. Due to these requirements and the reputation your company has for quality production, we were happy to pursue a long-term contract with you.

Discussion

Once you've provided the buffer, swaying your audience to your point of view, you can no longer delay the inevitable. The discussion paragraph states the bad news. However, to ensure that the reader accepts the bad news, preface your assertions with quantifiable proof.

Example 1
Rejecting a job applicant
(Introduction and discussion)
Thank you for your recent letter of application. As you can imagine, we received many letters from highly qualified applicants and appreciate your interest in Acme.

The advertisement specifically required that all applicants have an M.S. in computer science and at least five years experience in telecommunications. We also suggested that a knowledge of fiber optics would be preferred. Your degree met our criteria successfully. However, your years of experience fell below our requirements, and your resume did not mention fiber optics expertise. Therefore, we must reject your application.

Example 2
Terminating a client/vendor relationship
(Introduction and discussion)
John, as you know, our business demands exact tolerances and precise workmanship. Because of these requirements and the reputation your company has for quality production, we were happy to pursue a long-term contract with you.

However, your last two shipments contained flawed goods. In fact, we found these problems:

- 37 percent of your shipped components were off tolerance by .025 mm.
- Your O-rings suffered stress fractures when under 2,000 lbs. of pressure.

Because of these failures, we are returning the products.

Conclusion

If you end your bad-news letter with the bad news, then you leave your reader feeling defeated and without hope. In contrast, you want to maintain a good customer-client, supervisor-subordinate, or employer-employee relationship. Therefore, you need to conclude your letter by giving your readers an opportunity for future success. Provide your readers options which will allow them to get back in your good graces, seek employment in the future, or reapply for the refund you've denied. Then, to leave your readers feeling as happy as possible, given the circumstances, end upbeat and positively.

The following examples are complete with introductions, discussions, and conclusions.

> Thank you for your recent letter of application. As you can imagine, we received many letters from highly qualified applicants and appreciate your interest in Acme.
>
> The advertisement specifically required that all applicants have an M.S. in computer science and at least five years experience in telecommunications. We also suggested that a knowledge of fiber optics would be preferred. Your degree met our criteria successfully. However, your years of experience fell below our requirements, and your resume did not mention fiber optics expertise. Therefore, we must reject your application.
>
> If you have fiber optics knowledge or have acquired additional work experiences which pertain to our work requirements, we would be happy to reconsider your application. In any case, we will keep your letter on file. When new positions open up, your letter will be reassessed. Good luck in your job search.

> John, as you know, our business demands exact tolerances and precise workmanship. Due to these requirements and the reputation your company has for quality production, we were happy to pursue a long-term contract with you.

```
However, your last two shipments contained flawed
goods. In fact, we found these problems:

• 37 percent of your shipped components were off tol-
  erance by .025 mm.
• Your O-rings suffered stress fractures when under
  2,000 lbs. of pressure.

Because of these failures, we are returning the products.

If you can correct these problems and document to our
satisfaction that the errors have been eliminated, we
would be willing to reconsider our stance. We have
enjoyed working with you, John, and look forward to the
possibility of future contracts.
```

Although the preceding two letters convey bad news, they couch the negatives in positive terms. For example, although the first letter rejects a job applicant, the writer uses words and phrases such as *thank you, appreciate, successfully, happy,* and *good luck.* The second letter does the same: *quality, happy, enjoyed,* and *look forward to.* As the writer of the bad-news letter, you're in charge of the tone. Why not make it positive?

The example in Figure 7.8, which is from a CEO informing an employee that he will be laid off, clarifies how a bad-news letter should be constructed.

COMPLAINT LETTERS

You are purchasing director at an electronics firm. Although you ordinarily receive excellent products and support from a local manufacturing firm, two of your recent orders have been incorrectly filled and included defective merchandise. You don't want to have to hunt for a new supplier.

How can you improve your relations with the company and receive the service you want? Write a letter of complaint.

Introduction

In the introduction, *politely* state the problem. Although you might be angry over the service you've received, you want to suppress that anger. Blatantly negative comments don't lead to communication; they lead to combat. Because angry readers won't necessarily go out of their way to help you, your best approach is diplomacy.

To strengthen your assertions, in the introduction, include supporting documents, such as the following:

- Serial numbers
- Dates of purchase

AAA
ELECTRONICS
11031 Bellbrook Drive
Stamford, CT 23091
(213) 333-8989

September 7, 1996

John Chavez
4249 Uvalde
Stamford, CT 23091

Dear Mr. Chavez:

For some time now, forces influencing our industry have caused us to alter the way we have conducted business. You have recognized these influences for several years. Reorganization, customer participation, repetitious rate case activity, competition, deregulation, and technical innovations are just a few of the changes affecting us.

These influences, coupled with the current recession, have created an oversupply in our work force. We have tried to limit employee levels through attrition, hiring freezes, early retirement, and reassignments. However, our staffing is still too high, and we can no longer delay the inevitable. Therefore, your job is being terminated as of this month.

We have taken great pride in the stability of our work force. I personally think of our employees as family members. Thus, to help you in this difficult time, AAA is providing you options for future employment. Our company is offering the following transitional training opportunities:

1. resume and application workshops
2. interviewing training
3. job networking sessions
4. new-skills training

We haven't given up on you. When the economy corrects itself and our company releases the new-hire freezes, we'll call you immediately. Until then, we want to help you any way we can. Thank you for your patience and your understanding.

Sincerely,

Darryl Kennedy

Darryl Kennedy

Figure 7.8 Bad-News Letter

- Invoice numbers
- Check numbers
- Names of salespeople involved in the purchase.

Also state that copies of these documents are enclosed.

> ***Example***
> On August 15, you shipped to my company 36 XYZ digital oscilloscopes (copies of invoice #3492 are enclosed). Several of our customers have since complained that the o-scopes are malfunctioning.

Discussion

In the discussion paragraph(s), explain in detail the problems experienced. This could include dates, contact names, information about shipping, breakage information, and/or an itemized listing of defects. Be specific. Generalized information won't sway your readers to accept your point of view. In a complaint letter, you suffer the burden of proof. Clearly help your audience understand the extent of the problem. After documenting your claims, state what you want done and why.

> ***Example***
> The following occurred after we delivered the o-scopes to three of our customers:
> 1. August 20—AAA Electronics stated that two of their five o-scopes were malfunctioning, giving incorrect readings.
> 2. August 27—Richards Electronics, Inc., said three of their o-scopes were incorrectly calibrated.
> 3. September 5—Five of ABC Computers' o-scopes would not interface with their computers.
>
> These ten o-scopes need to be repaired. You also should send service technicians to troubleshoot our clients' other o-scopes to avoid future problems.

Conclusion

End your letter positively. Remember, you want to ensure cooperation with the vendor, and you want to be courteous, reflecting your company's professionalism. And, in this paragraph, include your phone number and the time you can best be reached.

> ***Example***
> You can reach me at 469–8200 from 8:00 A.M. to 5:00 P.M., Monday through Friday. Thank you for your help. After working with your company for the past eight years, I have been impressed with the way you stand behind your products. I know you'll help us with these defective o-scopes.
>
> Figure 7.9 is an example of a complaint letter.

1234 18th Street
Galveston, TX 77001
May 10, 1996

Mr. Holbert Lang
Customer Service Manager
Gulfstream Auto
1101 21st Street
Galveston, TX 77001

Dear Mr. Lang:

On February 12, 1996, I purchased two shock absorbers in your automotive department. Enclosed are copies of the receipt and the warranty for that purchase. One of those shocks has since proven defective.

I attempted to exchange the defective shock at your store on May 2, 1996. The mechanic on duty, Vernon Blanton, informed me that the warranty was invalid because your service staff did not install the part. I believe that your company should honor the warranty agreement and replace the part for the following reasons:

1. The warranty states that the shock is covered for 48 months and 48,000 miles.
2. The warranty does not state that installation by someone other than the dealership will result in warranty invalidation.
3. The defective shock absorber is causing potentially expensive damage to my tire and suspension system.

I can be reached between 1 p.m. and 6 p.m. on weekdays at 763-9280 or at 763-9821 anytime on weekends. I look forward to hearing from you. Thank you for helping me with this misunderstanding.

Sincerely,
Carlos De La Torre

Carlos De La Torre

Enclosures (2)

Figure 7.9 Letter of Complaint

ADJUSTMENT LETTERS

Responses to letters of complaint, also called adjustment letters, can take three different forms:

- 100 percent Yes—You could agree 100 percent with the writer of the complaint letter.
- 100 percent No—You could disagree 100 percent with the writer of the complaint letter.
- Partial Adjustment—You could agree with some of the writer's complaints but disagree with other aspects of the complaint.

100 Percent Yes Letter

This letter is like the good-news letter discussed earlier in the chapter. Since you've got good news for the reader, there's no reason to delay the message. In the *introductory paragraph,* state that you agree with your reader's complaint and will honor his or her recommendations for adjustment.

> ***Example***
> Thank you for calling our attention to your problem. We will be happy to replace your defective oscilloscopes.

In the *discussion paragraph(s),* explain what happened, why the problem occurred, and how the problem will be avoided in the future.

> ***Example***
> I have looked into your order and discovered the cause of the problem. The o-scopes were damaged during shipment. They were stacked too high, which led to breakage while handling. I have met with the carrier who agrees that the packages were handled improperly. I assure you that none of these problems will occur again. Also, I am sending a service technician to check on your other o-scopes from this order.

In your *conclusion paragraph,* resell to maintain customer satisfaction. End the letter upbeat.

> ***Example***
> Acme has worked with your company for many years, and I look forward to continuing this business relationship. I apologize for the inconvenience. Please call me at 392–8270 if you have any other questions.

100 Percent No Letter

Unfortunately, sometimes you have to say no to a letter of complaint. If the customer is wrong, you have no alternative but to say so.

However, you still want to maintain positive customer relationships. Although you will deny the customer's request for adjustment, you want to keep that customer. To do so, follow the pattern discussed earlier in this chapter for a bad-news letter.

In the introductory paragraph, begin with a buffer. This would include a positive statement and facts that all readers can accept, regardless of the situation.

Example
Thank you for your letter regarding the XYZ oscilloscopes. We were sorry to hear about the malfunctions your customers are experiencing. Although such occurrences are rare, as you know, products occasionally are damaged in shipment.

In the discussion paragraph(s), precisely explain what happened, providing facts, figures, and incontestable detail. Then state the bad news.

Example
After researching the matter thoroughly, we found that the problem was created by the shipping company. They stacked the boxes too high, which led to damage during handling. Since the damage was caused by the carriers and was not due to our negligence during manufacturing, we can not replace the o-scopes.

In the *conclusion,* end on an upbeat note. To do so, use positive words and provide the reader an alternative.

Example
To assist you in solving this problem, we have contacted Archie Cox, the shipping manager at ABC Freight (535–2020, ext. 345). He expects to hear from you soon. If we can help you in any other ways, please call.

Partial Adjustment

Life is complex. Sometimes you can agree with part of a writer's complaint but disagree with other parts. If you're not going to agree completely or disagree completely, then you'll want to write a partial adjustment letter.

In the *introductory paragraph,* state the good news first. As always, you want to be diplomatic, winning the reader to your point of view.

Example
Thank you for your letter regarding the XYZ oscilloscopes. I was sorry to hear about the malfunctions your customers are experiencing. Since we pride ourselves on our products' quality, I am happy to replace the ten defective o-scopes.

In the *discussion paragraph(s),* precisely explain what happened, and then state the bad news.

Example
The ten o-scopes, which were damaged during shipment due to packaging problems, will be replaced within six to eight weeks. I am unable to send a service technician to troubleshoot the remaining 26 o-scopes. That service is not part of our contract with you. (Please see section 4.1 of your service contract: "On-site service will not be provided in case of malfunction.")

In the *conclusion,* resell. Your reader will not be completely happy with you. You've provided some relief but not all that was requested. The last paragraph is your opportunity to win back a bit of the reader's good faith in your company. After all, you want to keep the customer for future contracts.

Example
If any of the other o-scopes malfunction, please call us immediately. We stand by our products, as you know from having been one of our satisfied customers for over a decade. I'll be happy to help you in any way I can.

Figure 7.10 An example of a 100 Percent Yes letter

SALES LETTERS

You've just manufactured a new product (an electronic testing device, a fuel injection mechanism, a fiber optic cable, or a high-tech, state-of-the-art computer). Perhaps you've just created a new service (computer maintenance, automotive diagnosis, home repair, or telecommunications networking). Congratulations!

However, if your product just sits in your basement gathering dust or your service exists only in your imagination, what have you accomplished? To benefit from your labors, you must market your invention. Connect with your end users. Let the public know that you exist. The question is, how? If you have unlimited time, money, and personnel, you can try telemarketing or door-to-door cold calls. However, a more time-efficient and cost-effective way to market your product or service is to write a sales letter. You write a sales letter once (which saves money) and mass mail it (which saves time).

To write your sales letter, you'll have to include the letter essentials discussed earlier in this chapter, maintain an effective technical writing style with a low fog index, and avoid grammatical and mechanical errors. You will also have to accomplish the following:

Arouse Reader Interest

The introductory paragraph of your sales letter tells your readers *why* you are writing (you want to increase their happiness or reduce their anxieties). You also tell your readers *what* you are writing about (the product or service you are marketing). However, studies tell us that you have only about 30 seconds to grab your readers' attention, after which they will lose interest and toss out your letter. To lure readers into your correspondence, you must arouse their interest imaginatively in the first few sentences. Try any of the following lead-ins:

GULFSTREAM AUTO
1101 21st
Galveston, TX 77001
(712) 451-1010

May 31, 1996

Mr. Carlos De La Torre
1234 18th Street
Galveston, TX 77001

Dear Mr. De La Torre:

Thank you for your recent letter. I am pleased to inform you that Gulfstream will happily replace your defective shock absorber according to the warranty agreement.

The Trailhandler Performance XT shock absorbers that you purchased were discontinued in October 1995. Mr. Blanton, the mechanic to whom you spoke, incorrectly assumed that Gulfstream was no longer honoring the warranty on that product. Because we no longer carry that product, we either will replace it with a comparable model or refund the purchase price—you make the decision. Just ask to see Mrs. Brandsgard at the automotive desk on your next visit to our store. She is expecting you and will handle the exchange.

We appreciate your business, Mr. De La Torre. I'm glad you brought this problem to my attention. If I can help you in the future, please contact me.

Sincerely,

Holbert Lang

Holbert Lang

Figure 7.10 100% Yes Adjustment Letter

- *An anecdote*—a brief, dramatic story.

It's late at night, the service stations are closed, and you've just had a blowout on Highway 35. Don't worry. Our new Tire-Right will solve your problems!

- *A question*—to make your readers read on for an answer.

"Where will I get the money for my kid's college education?" "How am I going to afford to retire?" "Will my insurance cover all the medical bills?" You've asked yourself these questions. Our estate planning video has the answers.

- *A quotation*—to give your letter the credibility of authority.

"Omit needless words," technical writers say. If you can't, let us help you. *Write Now,* our new office communications service, can help you write your inhouse newsletters—clearly and concisely.

- *Data*—researched information, again ensuring your credibility.

You're not alone. In fact, if you're at least 25 years old, you're in the majority. Today, 51 percent of our students are older than 25. So why not enroll now? Our college offers the nontraditional student many benefits.

Develop Your Assertions

In the discussion paragraph(s), specify exactly what you offer to benefit your audience or how you'll solve your readers' problems. You can do this in a traditional paragraph. In contrast, you might want to itemize your suggestions in a numerical or bulletized list. Whichever option you choose, the discussion should accomplish any of the following:

- *Provide data* to document your assertions.

Eighty-five percent of the homeowners contend that ...

or

Seven out of ten buyers said they would ...

or

Ten thousand retired metal workers can't be wrong!

- *Give testimony* from satisfied customers.

The Job Corps of Blue Valley, Titan Co., Amex Inc., and the Southwestern Parish swear by our product.

- *Document your credentials*—years in business, certification of employees, number of items sold, and/or satisfied customers (this last point overlaps with our suggestions regarding data).

In business since 1889.

or

Each of our mechanics is ASE certified.

or

We've sold over two billion widgets.

or

Over 3,000 corporate managers and supervisors have benefited from our training services.

Make Your Readers Act

If your conclusion says, "We hope to hear from you soon," you've made a mistake. Such a weak conclusion forces you to stare at the phone, twiddle your thumbs, and hope for a customer response. The concluding paragraph of a sales letter can't let the reader off the hook. Do something to make the reader act. Here are some suggestions:

- Give directions (with a map) to your business location.
- Provide a tear-out to send back for further information.
- Supply a self-addressed, stamped envelope for customer response.
- Offer a discount if the customer responds within a given period of time.
- Give your name or a customer-contact name and a phone number (toll free if possible).

Style

Your sales letter should not only convey the necessary information, but also it should present an appealing style. Consider the following requirements:

- Use verbs: Verb usage, or power writing, will give your letter punch.
- Format for reader-friendly ease of access: Highlight through white space, underlining, boldface, bullets, numbers, and so on.
- Achieve audience recognition and involvement through *You* orientation.
- Show ease of use: Sprinkle the words *easy* and/or *simple* throughout your correspondence.
- Imply urgency: Use the words *now, today, soon,* or *don't delay* to force the reader to immediate action.

Figure 7.11 is an example of a successful sales letter.

IMAGE
GRAPHICS

2629 Westport   Osweego, ND 55290   (402) 555-2121

October 9, 1996

Dave Moore
Media Publishing
10901 College Blvd.
Mountainview, ND 55292

Dear Mr. Moore:

"You *don't* have the software I use?" "You *can't* print my PC job?" Have you ever found yourself asking these questions at the neighborhood printing company? At Image Graphics, you won't hear words like *can't* and *don't.*

Image Graphics has the printing technology, accessibility, and knowledge that you're looking for.

- ✓ Image Graphics is the most technologically advanced graphic design firm in the Midwest, according to *Printer's Wheel Weekly.*
- ✓ We are the only design firm in your area with an in-house, 24-hour service bureau.
- ✓ Our service bureau can print any job to any media with no color or resolution limitations.
- ✓ We support all brands of software.
- ✓ Each member of our support staff has a master's degree in graphic technology.

I'm glad I could introduce you to Image Graphics, Mr. Moore. Look at the enclosed brochure and pricing sheet. Then call me personally (ext. 2055) this week for a 50 percent discount on your first output job.

Sincerely,

Macy Hart

Macy Hart

Enclosure

Figure 7.11 Sales Letter

[illegible]

Now that you know what letters of inquiry, cover letters, good-news letters, bad-news letters, and sales letters entail, the next question is, "How do I write these letters?" If you merely get out a blank piece of paper, or turn on your computer screen, and then fill it with words, assuming that they'll be good enough, you're making a mistake. No one can write a successful letter the first time through. In contrast, you need to approach writing more systematically. As we discussed in Chapter 2, to construct effective correspondence, approach writing as a step-by-step, sequential process.

You should do the following:

- Prewrite (to gather your data and to determine your objectives).
- Write a draft (to organize and format your text).
- Rewrite (to revise your correspondence, making it as perfect as it can be).

PREWRITING

To overcome the blank-page syndrome or writer's block, spend some time *before* writing your letter gathering as much information as you can about your subject matter. After all, how can you expect to write an effective letter if you aren't sure what you want to say? In addition, determine your objectives. Ask yourself why you're writing the letter and what you want to achieve.

No single way of prewriting is more effective than another. In fact, a primary focus of this text is to introduce you to numerous prewriting techniques. Our goal is to teach you various ways to gather data and determine objectives so you'll have options to choose from.

One prewriting technique that lends itself to letters is reporters' questions. By providing answers to *who, what, when, why, where,* and *how,* you can help yourself write more effective letters. Answers to these questions provide you content for your correspondence as well as focus in your writing objectives.

Following is a *reporters' questions checklist* for a letter of inquiry.

Letter of Inquiry—Reporters' Questions Checklist

1. *Who* is your audience?
   —High-tech peer
   —Low-tech peer
   —Lay reader
   —Management
   —Subordinate
   —Multiple audiences
2. *Why* are you writing?

3. *What* is the general topic of your request?
4. *What exactly* do you want to know (the specifics itemized in the discussion paragraph of your letter)?
5. *What* do you want the reader to do next?
6. *When* do you want the reader to act (dated action)?
7. *Why* is this date important?

WRITING

Once you've gathered your data and determined your objectives, the next step in the process is to begin your rough draft. Doing so requires the following:

1. *Study the letter criteria.* By studying the specific criteria for the type of letter you'll write, you can remind yourself of what information should be included in each paragraph.

2. *Review your prewriting.* Now that you have reminded yourself of what each paragraph should include, reviewing the prewriting will help you determine if, in fact, you have provided the correct details. Have you omitted any significant information? If so, now's the time to add missing content. Have you included unnecessary information? If so, now's the time to delete these irrelevancies.

3. *Organize the data for your discussion paragraph.* One organizational pattern especially effective for most letters is *importance.* When you organize by importance, you place the most important information first and lesser important ideas later. To do so, you can use the inverted journalist's pyramid shown in Figure 7.12.

This method works well for itemizing the discussion paragraph in your sales letters, letters of inquiry, and cover letters. You also can use importance to organize the body paragraph in your good-news letter.

However, since a bad-news letter leads up to the bad news rather than begins with it, importance would not be an effective organizational pattern. Instead, you'll want to organize your ideas inductively (indirectly)—specifics to general result. For instance, in a bad-news letter, you'll begin with the specific causes leading to bad news (recession, depression, changes in the market, unfavorable work habits, etc.). Then, after setting the stage with these specifics, you'll relate the general conclusion reached—the bad news (layoffs, refunds denied, promotions rejected, etc.). The bad-news letter examples in this chapter reveal this inductive organizational pattern.

4. *Draft your correspondence.* Finally, after you've organized your information, the last step is to write your rough draft. Throughout this text, we suggest that you write a rough draft using a technique called *sufficing.* Once you know what you want to say, you should just say it—and let it suffice for the moment. Write a rapid rough draft, focusing on content and organization, not on grammar, mechanics, or style. Your primary goal in a rough draft is to get words on the paper or screen. The time for fine tuning comes later in rewriting. During rewriting, you'll be able to check your spelling,

Inverted Journalist's Pyramid

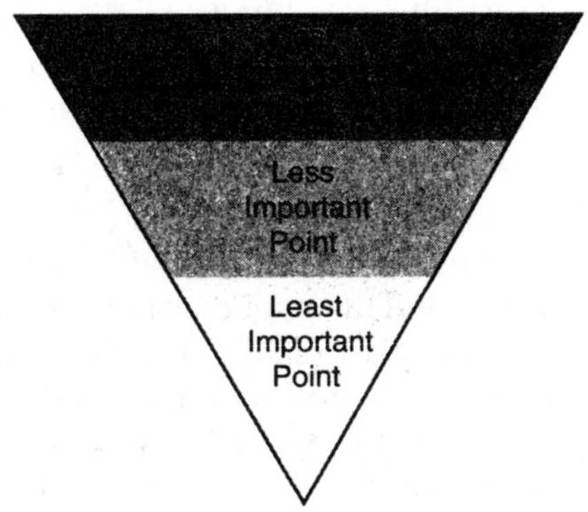

Figure 7.12

consider your punctuation, and perfect your tone. Drafting, in contrast, should be a stage in the writing process still free of those fears caused by grammar anxiety. After all, if you're worrying about the correctness of every word while you write it, you'll never complete a sentence.

REWRITING

After you've drafted your correspondence, the final step in the writing process and, in many people's opinion, the most important step, is to revise your rough copy. Rewriting is the step that most mediocre writers omit. Poor writers merely let the rough draft suffice as their finished version. They assume that their draft is sufficient. It isn't. Successful writers, in contrast, realize that an effective letter must be as perfect as it can be. To achieve this level of expertise, good writers revise their rough drafts—fine tuning, honing, sculpting, molding, and polishing so what leaves their hands is something they can be proud of.

To revise your letters, consider the following revision criteria:

1. *Add for clarity and correctness.* Look back over your rough draft. In doing so, ask yourself what you might need to add for clarity. This might entail reviewing the reporters' questions. For example, has your letter clarified *who* will do the work (personnel), act as a contact person (liaison), manage the system (management), etc.? If not, then you need to provide further information by answering the reporters' ques-

tion *who*. Have you correctly stated *when* you'll follow up, when you need the information, or when the bad news will occur? If not, add these dates. The same applies for all the reporters' questions. Add any missing information regarding *what, why, where,* or *how.*

In addition to adding answers to the reporters' questions, review your draft and add any missing letter essentials: letterhead address, date, inside address, salutation, complimentary close, typed and/or signed signature, and optional inclusions such as enclosure or copy notations.

2. *Delete for conciseness.* Deleting relates to style and content. Review your rough draft to delete any dead words and phrases which will raise your fog index (discussed in Chapter 3). Delete irrelevant content. This might include background sentences in the introductory paragraph which delay your main point. Writers often feel compelled to lead in to their thesis. This is a mistaken notion in technical writing. All the reader really wants to know is why you are writing and what you are writing about. Get to your point immediately; delete the unneeded background data.

3. *Simplify to aid easy understanding.* Chapter 3 stated that you should avoid old-fashioned words and phrases, such as *pursuant, accede, supersede,* and *in lieu of.* Rather than using such pompous words, simplify. Just write naturally. Why not say *after, accept, replace,* and *instead of?* This simplified style not only affects your fog index positively but also helps your readers understand your content, and that's the goal of good writing.

4. *Move information for emphasis.* This involves cutting and pasting—moving information within your letter. For example, let's say you've read your rough draft and realized that the itemized discussion paragraph is not organized according to importance. In fact, you have buried a key point deep in the body where readers might miss it. To focus your reader's attention on this idea, you should move it from the bottom of the list to the top. Doing so makes the idea more emphatic.

5. *Reformat for reader-friendly ease of access.* Review your letter's format. How does the letter look on the page? The letter's appearance affects your readers before they read one word. If the letter is open and appealing, then you're off to a good start. If the letter is blocky and inaccessible, then you've already done yourself a disservice.

Before you type your final copy, answer the following questions.

- Have you used enough (or too much) white space?
- Should you underline a key word or phrase?
- Are bullets appropriate in your discussion paragraph, or should you use numbers instead?
- Could you use a colored highlighter to emphasize a sentence?
- Would boldfacing help you draw attention to a key concern?

6. *Enhance the letter's tone.* Letters aren't the inanimate objects they appear to be. They don't just dump data. Your letter is a reflection of your interpersonal com-

munication skills and your company's attitudes. Reread your rough draft; is it revealing the personality or attitude that you want it to reveal? If the letter is stuffy, impersonal, high-handed, abrupt, offensive, or mean-spirited, then you must alter the tone.

To do so, add more pronouns, especially *you*-oriented ones; add verbs for punch; use contractions for a conversational tone; and/or add positive words and phrases to give your letter an upbeat tone. Using such personalization techniques (as discussed in Chapter 4) ensures customer and client cooperation.

7. *Correct errors.* Finally, before your letter leaves your office, correct any errors you've committed. The most important step of rewriting may be proofreading. Check and double-check your grammar; check and double-check your mathematical computations and scientific notations. Your letter is a legal document. A mistake can cost your company money and you your job. Proofreading is boring, but sitting at home, reading the want ads, and looking for a new job is worse. We presented several proofreading tips in Chapter 3. Save yourself future problems by proofing your letters now.

PROCESS LOG

To give you a better idea of how this three-step process approach to letter writing works, we provide the following student-written process log. It includes the student's answers to the reporters' questions (prewriting), her rough draft (writing), her revisions (rewriting), and her finished copy.

PREWRITING

First, the student filled in a letter of inquiry reporters' questions checklist (Figure 7.13).

WRITING

After the student gathered her data, she wrote a rough draft (Figure 7.14).

REWRITING

Next, with the assistance of a peer review group consisting of two other students, the writer revised the letter (Figure 7.15).

Once the student made the suggested revisions, she submitted the finished copy (Figure 7.16).

1. *Who* is your audience?
   - High-tech peer Vendor
   - Low-tech peer
   - Lay reader
   - Management
   - Subordinate
   - Multiple audiences
2. *Why* are you writing? In response to sales letter- to request information
3. *What* is the general topic of your request? Information about the personal shipping service
4. *What exactly* do you want to know (the specifics itemized in the discussion paragraph of your letter)?
   - cost of services
   - number of employees needed
   - commission?
   - what department to work with
   -
5. *What* do you want the reader to do next? Respond to questions
6. *When* do you want the reader to act (dated action)? March 15, e
7. *Why* is this date important? for meeting with management

Figure 7.13 Letter of Inquiry Reporters' Questions Checklist

Barney Allis Stores
5000 Main
Omaha, NE 32001

February 15, 1996

Fashion Pace
100 Eby
New York, NY 01034

Dear Ms. Pace:

Thank you for the information about your Personal Shopping service. I am interested in Fashion Pace, and would like to receive the following information:

1. Sales figures.
2. Customers serviced.
3. Requirements and costs to start service.

I would appreciate your response by March 1, 1996. Since I will be attending a meeting of the board on March 10, 1996 your early response will allow me to present your service at this time.

Sincerely,

Shirley Chandley

Shirley Chandley, Manager

Figure 7.14 Letter of Inquiry
Rough Draft

Barney Allis Stores
5000 Main
Omaha, NE 32001

February 15, 1996

Fashion Pace *add name of contact*
100 Eby
New York, NY 01034

Dear Ms. Pace:

Thank you *capitalize?* for the information about your Personal Shopping service. I am interested in Fashion Pace, and would like to receive the following information:

Do you need the periods?

1. Sales figures. *too vague - which ones?*
2. Customers serviced. *Awk! A list of satisfied customers*
3. Requirements and costs to start service. *too vague*

*Please... * Add more questions*

I would appreciate your response by March 1, 1996. Since I will be attending a meeting of the board on March 10, 1996, your early response will allow me to present your service at this time.

Sincerely,

Shirley Chandley, Manager *move under name*

** office space needed*
** required training*
** # of employees needed*

Figure 7.15 Letter of Inquiry Revision

BAS

Barney Allis Stores
5000 Main
Omaha, NE 32001

February 15, 1996

Ms. Jackie Pace
Fashion Pace
100 Eby
New York, NY 01034

Dear Ms. Pace:

Thank you for the information about your Personal Shopping Service.

I am interested in Fashion Pace and would like to receive answers to the following questions:

1. What are your sales figures for the last two years?
2. Would you send me a satisfied customer list?
3. How much office space will your consultants need?
4. How many employees will you need to run your service?
5. What training is required for these employees?
6. What will you charge customers for your service?

Please send answers to these questions by March 1, 1996. Your early response will allow me to present your proposal at our March 10 sales meeting. I look forward to hearing from you.

Sincerely,

Shirley Chandley

Shirley Chandley
Manager

Figure 7.16 Letter of Inquiry Final Copy

ACTIVITIES

Writing Letters

1. Write a sales letter. To do so, imagine what product or service you could provide to a potential client. Select one from your area of expertise or academic major. Write your letter according to the criteria for sales letters and the writing process techniques discussed in this chapter.
2. Write a letter of inquiry. You might want to write to a college or university requesting information about a degree program, or to a manufacturer for information about a product or service. Whatever the subject matter, be specific in your request. Follow the criteria for writing letters of inquiry and the writing process techniques.
3. Write a cover letter. Perhaps your cover letter will preface a lab report you're working on in school, a report you're writing at work, or documentation you'll need to send to a client. Use the criteria for writing cover letters and the writing process techniques.
4. Write a good-news letter. Commend a coworker for a job well done. Congratulate a subordinate for his or her promotion. Better yet, write a thank-you letter to a teacher showing your appreciation for his or her professionalism and dedication. Follow the criteria for writing a good-news letter and the writing process techniques.
5. Write a bad-news letter. Inform a job candidate that he or she has not been offered the job, tell a customer that his or her request for a refund is denied, or explain to employees why they are to be laid off from their work. Use the criteria for writing bad-news letters and the writing process techniques.
6. Write a complaint letter. Perhaps you've purchased a product which has malfunctioned, received poor service from a salesperson, ordered one item but received another, failed to have a warranty honored, or received damaged or broken equipment in shipment. You want to write a letter of complaint to solve these problems. To do so, write your letter by following the suggestions provided in this chapter.
7. Write an adjustment letter. Envision that a client has written a complaint letter about a problem he or she has encountered with your product or service. Write a letter in response to their complaint. This could either be a 100 percent Yes letter, a 100 percent No letter, or a partial adjustment letter. Follow the suggestions provided in this chapter when writing your letter.

Team Projects

1. Find letters from your home and/or work environment and bring them to class. In small groups of three to five students, categorize these letters as either sales letters, letters of inquiry, cover letters, good-news letters, bad-news letters, complaint letters, or adjustment letters. Then, in your groups, decide whether the letters are successful or unsuccessful, based on the criteria pro-

vided in this chapter. If the letters are good, be prepared to explain why, either in writing or orally. If the letters fail, discuss how they could be improved.

2. In small groups of three to five students, select any of the flawed letters from activity 1 above (Team Projects) and rewrite them. Use the revision techniques discussed in this chapter.

Case Studies

After reading the following case studies, write the appropriate letters required for each assignment.

1. Vivian Davis, who lives at 2939 Cactus, in Santa Clara, CA 95054, has invented a new product, VAST (a Voice-Activated Speaker Telephone). This telephone can be "dialed" without the use of one's hands, simply by saying names or numbers into the system's speaker. Vivian believes that such a machine could benefit the handicapped, the elderly, the infirm, homemakers, and businesspeople. She can sell this phone for $25 to electronic stores, hobby shops, general-purpose retailers, etc., who then can market it for $50. Write a sales letter for Ms. Davis based on the preceding information.
2. Mark Shabbot works for Apex, Inc., 1919 W. 23rd Street, Denver, CO 80204. Apex, a retailer of electronic equipment, wants to purchase 125 new oscilloscopes from a vendor, Omnico, located at 30467 Sheraton, Phoenix, AZ 85023. The oscilloscopes will be sold to a Vo-Tech college in Denver (Northwest Hills Vocational-Technical College). However, before Apex purchases these oscilloscopes, Mark needs information regarding bulk rates, shipping schedules, maintenance agreements, equipment specifications, and machinery capabilities. Northwest Hills needs this equipment before the new term (August 15). Write a letter of inquiry for Mr. Shabbot based on the preceding information.
3. Sharon Baker works as a technical writer for Prismatic Consulting Engineering, 123 Park, Boston, MA 01755. In response to an RFP (Request for Proposal), she has written a proposal to the Oceanview City Council, 457 E. Cypress Street, Oceanview, MA 01759. The proposal suggests ways in which Oceanview can improve its flood control. Now Sharon needs to write a cover letter prefacing her proposal. In this cover letter, she wants to call her readers' attention to key concerns within the proposal: suggested costs, time frames, potential problems which could occur if the proposed suggestions are not implemented, ways in which the proposal will solve these problems, and Prismatic's credentials. Once the Oceanview City Council receives the proposal, Prismatic representatives will contact them for follow-up discussions. Write Ms. Baker's cover letter based on the preceding information.
4. Bob Ward, a lineworker at HomeCare Health Equipment, 8025 Industrial Parkway, Ashley, NC 27709, deserves a letter of commendation for his excellent job record. He has not missed a day of work in five years. In addition, his production line has achieved a 5 percent error reading (7 percent considered acceptable). He has also trained new hires. Most importantly, he made six suggestions for improvements, three of which saved the company money. The

company president, Peter Tsui, based at HomeCare's home office at 4791 Research Avenue, Wasa, MN 55900, wants to award Bob with a plaque at the annual awards dinner, September 7, 1996. Write Mr. Tsui's good-news letter based on the preceding information.

5. Craig Salvay works as a service technician for EEE Electronic Servicing, 11201 Blanco, Santa Fe, NM 88004. Yesterday, he went to Schoss-McGraw Associates, 1628 W. 18th Street, Taos, NM 88003, to service their computer systems. He billed them $75 for his time, but he did not bill them for parts since the machinery was supposedly under warranty. However, when he returned to EEE, Craig's manager, Marilyn Hoover, informed Craig that the machinery was not under warranty and that Schoss-McGraw would have to be billed an additional $45.87 for parts. Schoss-McGraw is an excellent client, so Marilyn wants Craig to be especially tactful in requesting the additional money. Based on the preceding information, write Craig's bad-news letter.
6. Diane Waisner (who lives at 1439 87th, Monroe, LA 67054) purchased a VCR on August 13 from Smiley's TV Town (8201 Magnolia, Monroe, LA 67056). The VCR came with a "ninety-day warranty against all defects" and a guarantee for "in-home free repairs and labor." On October 30, Diane's VCR showed a horizontal line across the screen when she replayed tapes. She called the store manager, Jill Miller, and explained the problem. Jill said the horizontal lines were caused by a dirty head and told Diane to bring the VCR in for cleaning. Jill also told Diane that she would be charged for this service since dirty VCR heads were basic wear and, therefore, not covered by the warranty. Diane was angered by this response from the store manager and decided to write a letter of complaint. Based on the information provided, write Diane's letter of complaint.
7. Gregory Peña (121 Mockingbird Lane, San Marcos, NV 87900) has written a letter of complaint to Donya Kahlili, the manager of CompuRam (4236 Silicon Dr., Reno, NV 87601). Mr. Peña purchased a 486 computer from a CompuRam outlet in San Marcos. San Marcos' newspaper, *The Tattler,* advertised that the computer "came loaded with all the software you'll need to write effective letters and perform basic accounting functions." (Mr. Peña has a copy of this advertisement.) When Mr. Peña booted up his computer, he expected to access word production software, multiple fonts, a graphics package, a grammar check, and a spreadsheet. All he got was a word processing package and a spreadsheet. Mr. Peña wants Ms. Kahlili to upgrade his software to include fonts, graphics, and a grammar check; wants a computer technician from CompuRam to load the software on his computer; and wants CompuRam to reimburse him $400 (the full price of the software) for his trouble.

   Ms. Kahlili agrees that the advertisement is misleading and will provide Mr. Peña software including the fonts, graphics, and grammar check (complete with instructions for loading the software). However, she refuses Mr. Peña's other two requests.

   Write Ms. Kahlili partial adjustment to Mr. Peña based on the information provided.

Chapter 8

TECHNICAL DESCRIPTION

- OBJECTIVES
- CRITERIA FOR WRITING TECHNICAL DESCRIPTIONS
- PROCESS
- PROCESS LOG

OBJECTIVES

Technical descriptions are a part-by-part depiction of the components of a mechanism, tool, or piece of equipment. Technical descriptions are important features in several types of correspondence.

OPERATIONS MANUALS

Whenever a company manufactures a product, it encloses an *operations manual* in the packaging of the mechanism, tool, or piece of equipment. This manual helps the end user construct, install, operate, and service the equipment. These operations manuals often include technical descriptions.

Technical descriptions provide the end user with information about the mechanism's features or capabilities. For example, this information may tell the user which components are enclosed in the shipping package, clarify the quality of these components, specify what function these components serve in the mechanism, or allow the user to reorder any missing or flawed components. Here's a brief example of a technical description found in an operations manual:

The Modern Electronics Tone Test Tracer, Model 77A, is housed in a yellow, high-impact plastic case that measures 1-1/4" × 2" × 2-1/4", weighs 4 ounces, and is powered by a 1604 battery. Red and black test leads are provided. The 77A has a standard four-conductor cord, a three-position toggle switch, and an LED for line polarity testing. A tone selector switch located inside the test set provides either solid tone or dual alternating tone. The Tracer is compatible with the EXX, SetUp, and Crossbow models.

PRODUCT DEMAND SPECIFICATIONS

Sometimes a company needs a piece of equipment that does not currently exist. To acquire this equipment, the company writes a *product demand* specifying its exact needs, as in the following example:

Subject: Requested Pricing for EDM Microdrills

Please provide us with pricing information for the construction of 50 EDM Microdrills capable of meeting the following specifications:

- Designed for high-speed, deep-hole drilling
- Capable of drilling to depths of 100 times the diameter using .012-inch to .030-inch diameter electrodes
- Able to produce a hole through a 1.000-inch thick piece of AISI D2 or A6 tool steel in 1.5 minutes, using a .020-inch diameter electrode

We need your response by January 13, 1996.

STUDY REPORTS PROVIDED BY CONSULTING FIRMS

Companies hire a consulting engineering firm to study a problem and provide a descriptive analysis. The resulting *study report* is used as the basis for a product demand specification requesting a solution to the problem.

One firm, when requested to study crumbling cement walkways, provided the following technical description in its study report:

The slab construction consists of a wearing slab over a 1/2"-thick waterproofing membrane. The wearing slab ranges in thickness from 3-1/2" to 8-1/2", and several sections have been patched and replaced repeatedly in the past. The structural slab varies in thickness from 5-1/2" to 9" with as little as 2" over the top of the steel beams. The removable slab section, which has been replaced since original construction, is badly deteriorated and should be replaced. Refer to Appendix A, Photo 9, and Appendix C for shoring installed to support the framing prior to replacement.

SALES LITERATURE AND PROPOSALS

Not all technical writing is photographic and quantifiable information. Some descriptions are impressionistic. Note that the following sales piece uses impressionistic adjectives and adverbs (italicized), allowing your imagination to depict the product's components:

> Inside the *elegant* Zephyr you'll find *comfortably designed* seats done in *rich, tailored* cloths. The *special* suspension system surrounds you with a driving experience quieter than Zephyr's past. Outside you'll find a *new bright* grille, sport mirrors, and a *smart* dual pinstripe. Finally, underneath all this *comfort* and *luxury* beats the road-hugging heart of an American classic.

Whatever your purpose in writing a technical description, the following will help you write more effectively:

- Criteria
- Process (with sample Process Log)
- Technical description examples

CRITERIA FOR WRITING TECHNICAL DESCRIPTIONS

As with any type of technical writing, there are certain criteria for writing technical descriptions.

TITLE

Preface your text with a title stating precisely the topic of your description. This could be the name of the mechanism, tool, or piece of equipment you're writing about.

OVERALL ORGANIZATION

In the *introduction* you specify what *topic* you are describing, explain the mechanism's *functions or capabilities,* and list the *major components* of this topic.

Example 1
The Apex Latch (#12004), used to secure core sample containers, is composed of three parts: the hinge, the swing arm, and the fastener.

Example 2
The DX 56 DME (Distance Measuring Equipment) is a vital piece of aeronautical equipment. Designed for use at altitudes up to 30,000 feet, the DX 56 electronically converts elapsed time to distance by measuring the length of time between your transmission and the reply signal. The DX 56 DME contains the transmitter, receiver, power supply, and range and speed circuitry.

In the *discussion,* you use highlighting techniques (itemization, headings, underlining, white space) to describe each of the mechanism's components.

Your *conclusion* depends on your purpose in describing the topic. Some options are as follows:

- *Sales:* "Implementation of this product will provide you and your company..."
- *Uses:* "After implementation, you will be able to use this XYZ to..."
- *Guarantees:* "The XYZ carries a 15-year warranty against parts and labor."
- *Testimony:* "Parishioners swear by the XYZ. Our satisfied customers include...."
- *Comparison/contrast:* "Compared to our largest competitor, the XYZ has sold three times more...."
- *Reiteration of introductory comments:* "Thus, the XYZ is composed of the aforementioned interchangeable parts."

Use *graphics* in your technical descriptions. Today, many companies use the *super comic book look*—large, easy-to-follow graphics that complement the text. You can use line drawings, photographs, clip art, exploded views, or sectional cutaway views of your topic, each accompanied by *call-outs* (labels identifying key components of the mechanism). These types of graphics are discussed in Chapter 6. When using graphics, try one of the techniques shown in Figures 10.1, 10.2, and 10.3.

INTERNAL ORGANIZATION

When describing your topic in the discussion portion of the technical description, itemize the topic's components in some logical sequence. Components of a piece of equipment, tool, or product can be organized by importance (discussed in Chapter 3).

However, *spatial* organization is better for technical descriptions. When a topic is spatially organized, you literally lay out the components as they are seen, as they exist in space. You describe the components either as they are seen from left to right, from right to left, from top to bottom, from bottom to top, from inside to outside, or from outside to inside.

DEVELOPMENT

To describe your topic clearly and accurately, detail the following:

Weight	Materials (composition)
Size (dimensions)	Identifying numbers

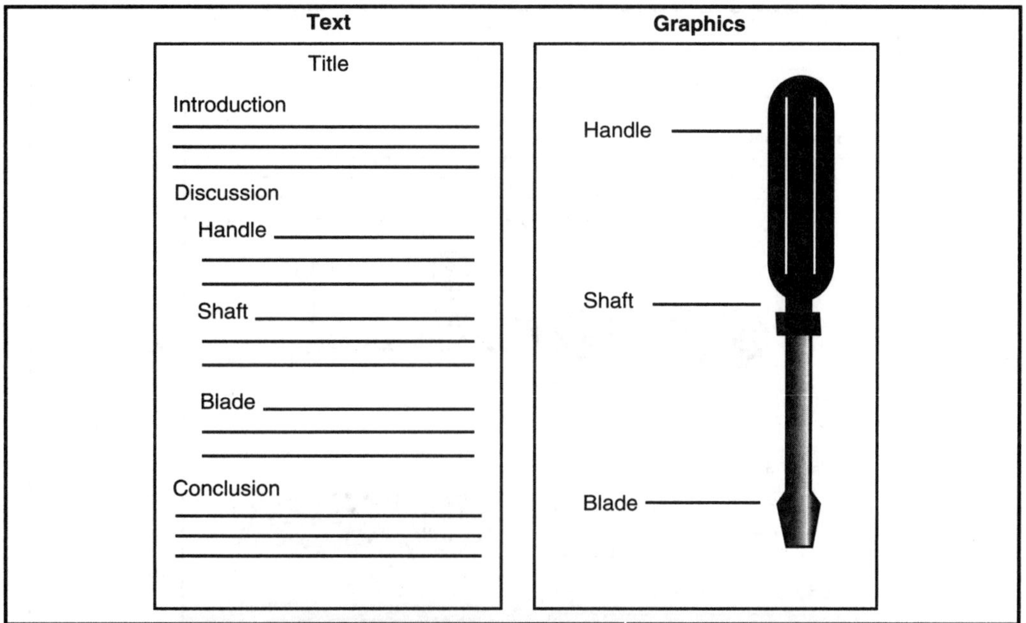

Figure 10.1 Text and Graphics Separate

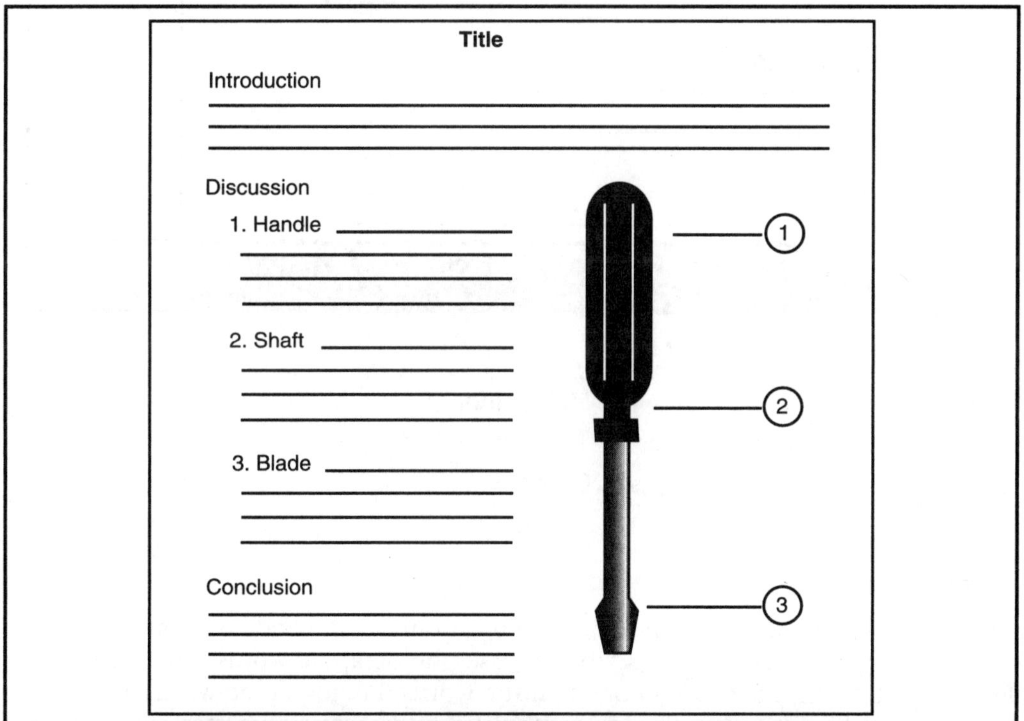

Figure 10.2 Text and Graphics Merged

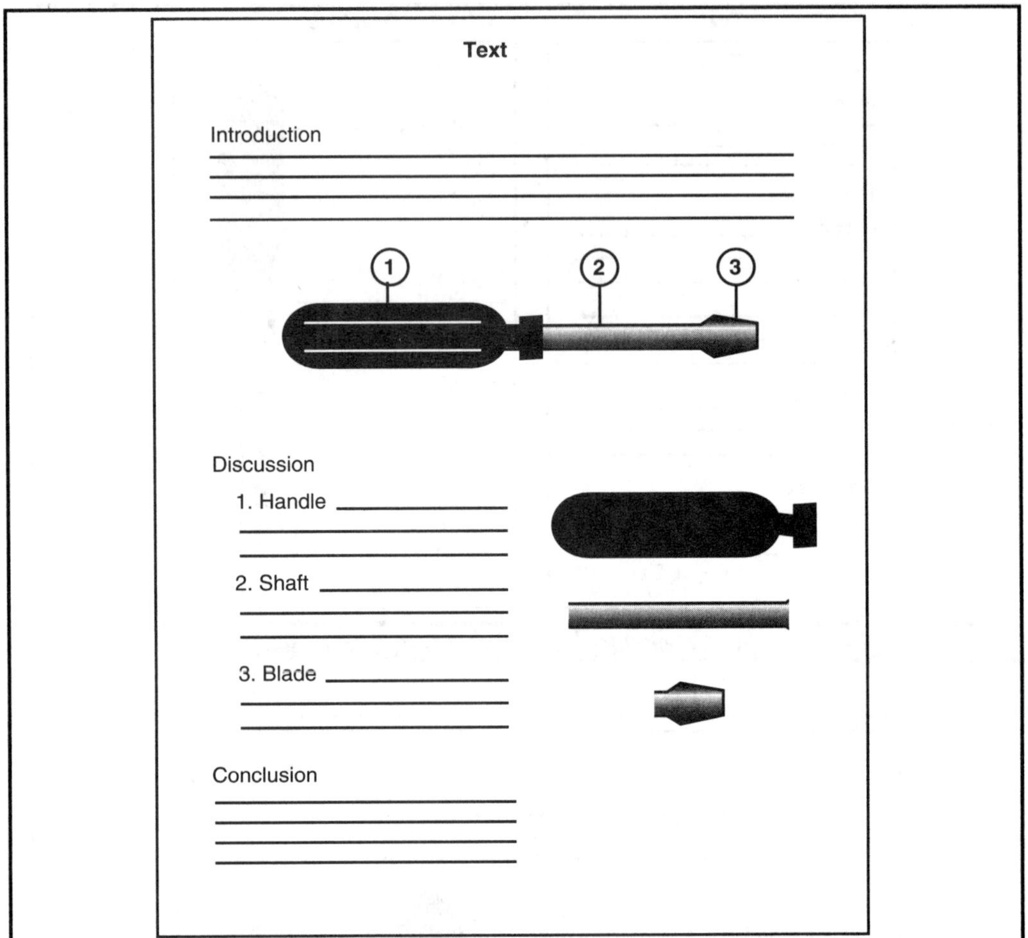

Figure 10.3 Text and Graphics Merged with Exploded View

Color	Make/model
Shape	Texture
Density	Capacity

WORD USAGE

Your word usage, either photographic or impressionistic, depends on your purpose. For factual, objective technical descriptions, use photographic words. For subjective, sales-oriented descriptions, use impressionistic words. Photographic words are denotative, quantifiable, and specific. Impressionistic words are vague and connotative. Table 10.1 shows the difference.

Table 10.1

Photographic versus Impressionistic Word Usage

PHOTOGRAPHIC	IMPRESSIONISTIC
6'9"	tall
350 lb.	fat
gold	precious metal
6,000 shares of United Can	major holdings
700 lumens	bright
.030 mm	thin
1966 XKE Jaguar	impressive car

Another way to note the difference between impressionistic words and photographic detail is through the ladder of abstraction, shown in Figure 10.4.

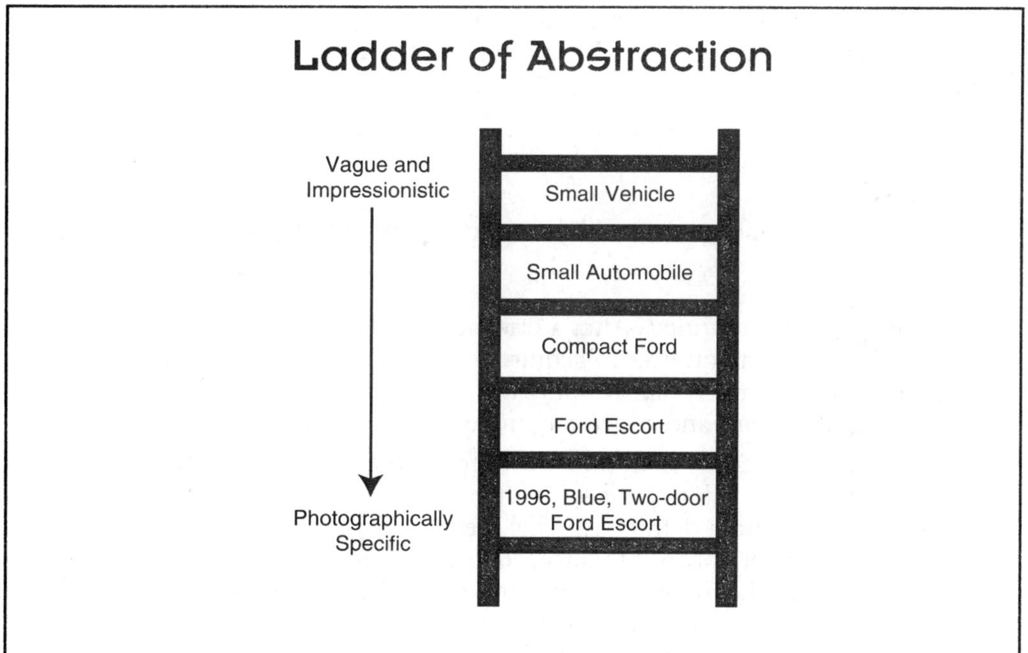

Figure 10.4

PROCESS

Now that you know what should be included in a technical description, your next question is, "How do I go about writing this type of correspondence?" As always, effective writing follows a systematic, step-by-step process. To write your technical description, (a) *prewrite* to gather data and determine objectives; (b) *write* a draft of the description; and (c) *rewrite* by revising the draft, thereby making it as perfect as possible.

PREWRITING

So far we've discussed reporters' questions (Chapter 7) and clustering/mind mapping (Chapter 8) as techniques for gathering data and determining objectives. Either of these two prewriting tools can be used for your technical description. However, another prewriting technique can be helpful: *brainstorming/listing*.

Brainstorming/listing, either individually or as a group activity, is a good, quick way to sketch out ideas for your description. To brainstorm/list, do the following:

1. *Title your activity,* at the top of your page, to help you maintain your focus. For example, *Description: XYZ (model 2267) Light Pen.*
2. *List any and all ideas* you might have on the topic. Don't editorialize. Avoid criticizing ideas at this point. Just randomly jot down as many aspects of the topic as possible, without making value judgments.
3. *Edit your list.* Reread the list and evaluate it. To do so, (a) select the most promising features, (b) cross out any that don't fit, and (c) add any obvious omissions.

WRITING

Once you've gathered your data and determined your objectives, the next step is writing your description.

1. *Review your prewriting.* After a brief gestation period (an hour, a half-day, or a day) in which you wait to acquire a more objective view of your prewriting, go back to your brainstorming/listing and reread it. Have you omitted all unneeded items and added any important omissions? If not, do so.
2. *Organize your list.* Make sure the items in the list are organized effectively. To communicate information to your readers, organize the data so readers can follow your train of thought. This is especially important in technical descriptions. You not only want your readers to understand the information, but also to visualize the mechanism or component. This visualization can be achieved by organizing your data spatially.
3. *Title your draft.* At the top of the page, write the name of your piece of equipment, tool, or mechanism.

4. *Write a focus statement.* In one sentence, write (a) the name of your topic (plus any identifying numbers), (b) the possible functions of your topic or your reason for writing the description, and (c) the number of parts composing your topic. This will eventually act as the introduction. For now, however, it can help you organize your draft and maintain your focus.
5. *Draft the text.* Use the sufficing technique discussed in earlier chapters. Write quickly without too much concern for grammatical or textual accuracy, and let what you write suffice for now. Just get the information on the page, focusing on overall organization and a few highlighting techniques (headings, perhaps). The time to edit is later.
6. *Sketch a rough graphic of your equipment, component, or mechanism.*

REWRITING

Rewriting is the most important part of the process. This is the stage during which you fine tune and polish your technical description, making it as perfect as it can be. A perfected description ensures your credibility. An imperfect description makes you and your company look bad.

Revise your draft as follows:

1. *Add any detail required to communicate more effectively.* This can involve brand names, model numbers, and/or specificity of detail (size, material, density, dimensions, color, weight, etc.).
2. *Delete dead words and phrases for conciseness.* (Refer to our discussion of effective technical writing style in Chapter 3.)
3. *Simplify long-winded, old-fashioned words and phrases for easier understanding.* Chapter 3 will help you with this important aspect of your writing.
4. *Move (cut and paste) information to ensure spatial organization.* You don't want to give your reader a distorted view of your mechanism. To avoid doing so, the technical description must maintain a spatial order—left to right, right to left, and so on. For example, let's say you are describing a pencil, graphically depicted horizontally so the eraser end is to the left and the graphite tip is to the right. This pencil consists of the eraser, metal ferrule, wooden body, and sharpened point (that's the correct spatial order). If you describe the eraser first, then the tip, then the body, and then the ferrule, you've distorted the spatial order.
5. *Reformat your text for ease of access through highlighting techniques—headings, boldface type, font size and style, itemization, and so forth.* Rewriting is also the time to perfect your graphics. When revising your description, make sure that your graphics are effective. To do so,

   - Add a figure number and title. Place these beneath the graphic. For example, "Figure 10.5. Exhalation Valve with Labeled Call-Outs."
   - Draw or reproduce graphics neatly.

Exhalation Valve with Labeled Call-Outs

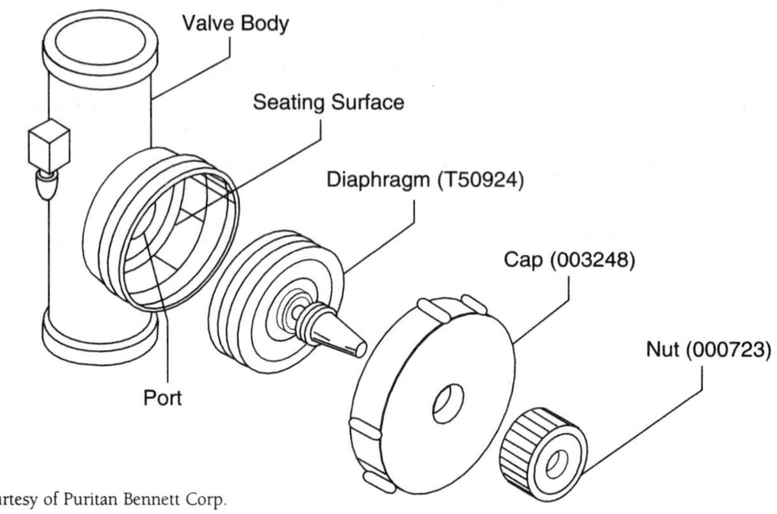

Source: Courtesy of Puritan Bennett Corp.

Figure 10.5

- Place the graphics in an appropriate location, near where you first mention them in the text.
- Make sure that the graphics are an effective size. You don't want the graphics to be so small that your reader must squint to read them, nor do you want them to be so large that they overwhelm the text.
- Label the components. Use call-outs to name each part, as in Figure 10.5.

6. *Enhance the style of your text.* Make sure that you've avoided impressionistic words. Instead, use photographic words, which are precise and specific. In addition, strive for a personalized tone. Pronoun usage is rare and difficult to achieve in technical descriptions. However, even when writing about a piece of equipment, remember that "people write to people." Although you're describing an inanimate object, you're writing to another human being. Therefore, use pronouns to personalize the text. (Examples later in this chapter clarify how you can accomplish this.)
7. *Correct your draft.* Proofread to correct grammar errors as well as errors in content: measurements, shapes, textures, materials, colors, and so on.
8. *Avoid sexist language.*

TECHNICAL DESCRIPTION CRITERIA CHECKLIST

The following checklist will help you in writing technical descriptions.

1. Does the technical description have a title noting your topic's name (and any identifying numbers)?
2. Does the technical description's introduction (a) state the topic, (b) mention its functions or the purpose of the mechanism, and (c) list the components?
3. Does the technical description's discussion use headings to itemize the components for reader-friendly ease of access?
4. Is the detail within the technical description's discussion photographically precise? That is, does the discussion portion of the description specify the following?

Colors	Capacities
Sizes	Textures
Materials	Identifying numbers
Shapes	Weight
Density	Make/model

5. Are all of the calculations and measurements correct?
6. Do you sum up your discussion using any of the optional conclusions discussed in this chapter?
7. Does your technical description provide graphics which are correctly labeled, appropriately placed, neatly drawn or reproduced, and appropriately sized?
8. Do you write using an effective technical style (low fog index) and a personalized tone?
9. Have you avoided sexist language and multicultural biases?
10. Have you avoided grammatical and mechanical errors?

PROCESS LOG

The following student-written process log clarifies the way process is used in writing technical descriptions.

PREWRITING

We asked students to describe a piece of equipment, tool, or mechanism of their choice. One student chose to describe a cash register pole display. To do so, he first had to gather data using listing/brainstorming. He provided the following list:

1. Three parts
2. Pole printed circuit board (PCB)
3. Case assembly
4. Filter
5. Plastic materials

Next, we asked students to go back to their initial lists and edit them. Since this student's list was so sketchy, he didn't need to omit any information. Instead, he had to add omissions and missing detail, as in Figure 10.6.

WRITING

After the prewriting activity, we asked students to draft a technical description. Focusing only on overall organization, highlighting, detail, and a sketchy graphic, the aforementioned student wrote a rough draft (Figure 10.7).

REWRITING

Once students completed their rough drafts, we used peer review groups (PRGs) to help each student revise his or her paper. In the following revision, students (a) added new detail for clarity, (b) corrected any errors, and (c) perfected graphics.

The preceding rough draft, complete with student comments, is shown in Figure 10.8.

The student incorporated these suggestions and prepared the finished copy (Figure 10.9).

Pole PCB

- length—15 mm
- width—5.1mm
- tube length—10.8 mm
- face plate width—2.3 mm
- thick—1.7 mm
- PCB thickness—0.2 mm
- 10" stranded wire with female connectors
- fiberglass and copper construction

Pole Case Assembly

- long—15.5 mm
- bottom width—2.5 mm
- top width—0.9 mm
- mounting pole—5 mm high × 3.2 mm diameter
- tounge for mounting—3.1 mm
- lower mounting tounge—1.5 mm
- side mounting tounge—0.8 mm high
- high—6.1 mm
- almond-colored plastic

Filter

- long—15.6 mm
- high—6.2 mm
- thick—0.7 mm
- plastic, blue

Figure 10.6 Student's Listing/Brainstorming

The QL 169 Customer Pole Display provides the viewing of all transaction data for the customer. The display consist of a printed circuit board, a case assembly, and a filter display.

Display Circuit Board

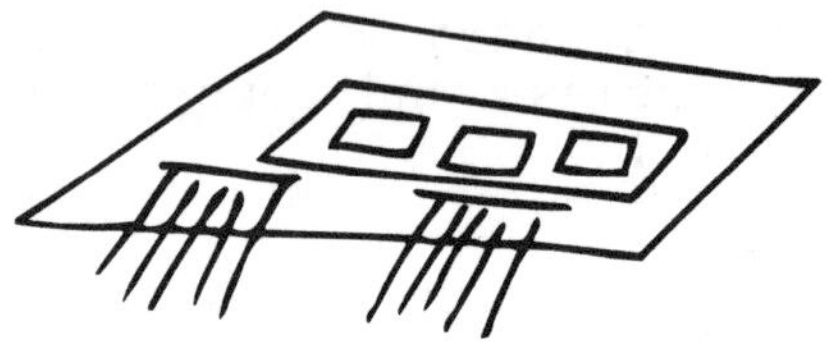

- length—15 mm
- width—5.1 mm
- tube length—10.8 mm
- face plate width—2.3 mm
- thick—1.7 mm
- PCB thickness—0.2 mm
- 10" stranded wire with female connectors
- fiberglass and copper construction

Display Case Assembly

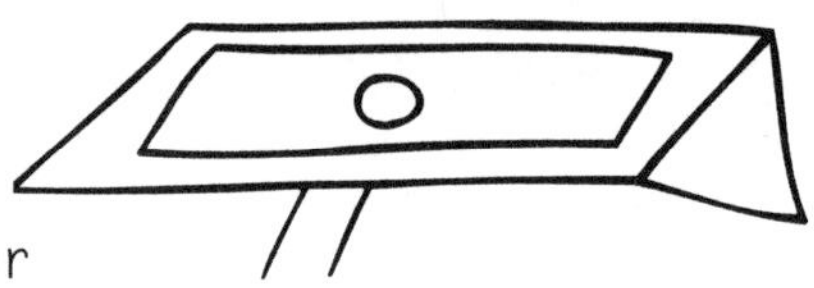

- long—15.5 mm
- bottom width—2.5 mm
- top width—0.9 mm
- mounting pole—
  5 mm high × 3.2 mm diameter
- tounge for mounting—3.1 mm
- lower mounting tounge—1.5 mm wide
- side mounting tounge—0.8 mm high
- high—6.1 mm
- almond-colored plastic

Display Filter

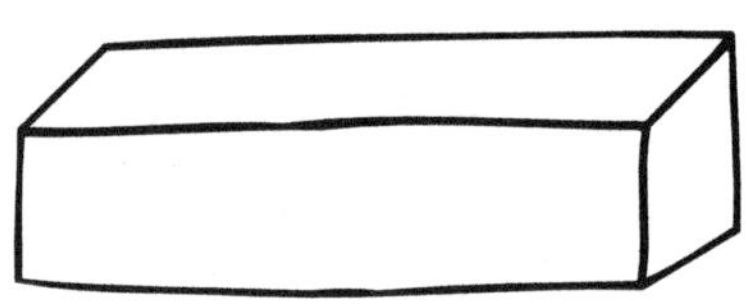

- long—15.6 mm
- high—6.2 mm
- thick—0.7 mm
- plastic, blue

Figure 10.7 Student's Rough Draft

No Title

The QL 169 Customer Pole Display provides the viewing of ~~all transaction data~~ for the customer. The display consist of a printed circuit board, a case assembly, and a filter display. *awkward* *SP*

Display Circuit Board *Make All Caps*

- length—15 mm
- width—5.1 mm
- tube length—10.8 mm
- face plate width—2.3 mm
- thick—1.7 mm *thickness*
- PCB thickness—0.2 mm
- 10" stranded wire with female connectors
- fiberglass and copper construction

number your components

To vague (specify)

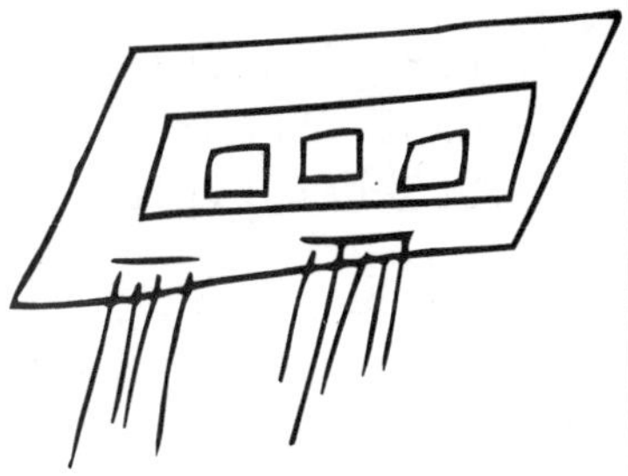

Display Case Assembly *Make All Caps*

Number Components

- long—15.5 mm *length*
- bottom width—2.5 mm
- top width—0.9 mm
- mounting pole—5 mm high × 3.2 mm diameter
- tounge for mounting—3.1 mm
- lower mounting tounge—1.5 mm wide
- side mounting tounge—0.8 mm high
- high—6.1 mm *height*
- almond-colored plastic *vague*

SP

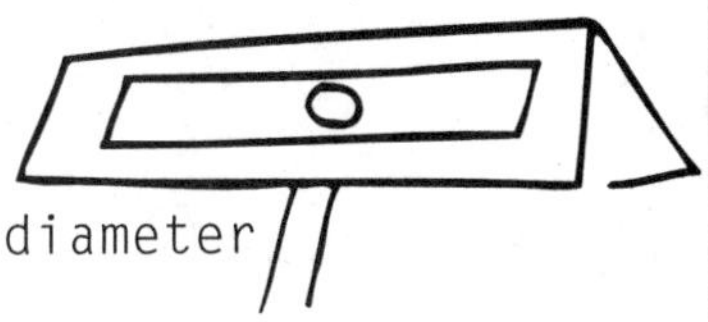

Display Filter

- long—15.6 mm *length*
- high—6.2 mm *height*
- thick—0.7 mm *thickness*
- plastic, blue *what*

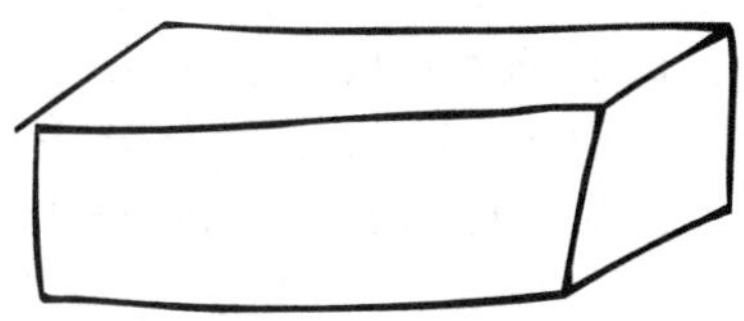

add a conclusion

Figure 10.8 Student's Suggested Revisions

QL169 Pole Display

The QL169 pole display provides an alphanumeric display for customer viewing of cash register sales. The display consists of a printed circuit board (PCB) assembly, a case assembly, and a display filter.

Item Description

1. PCB ASSEMBLY
2. CASE ASSEMBLY
3. DISPLAY FILTER

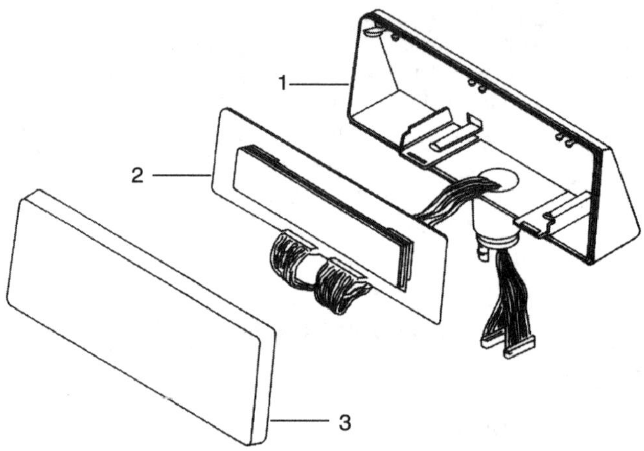

Figure 1 QL169

1.0 PCB Assembly

The printed circuit board, containing the display's electrical circuitry, is constructed of fiberglass with copper etchings.

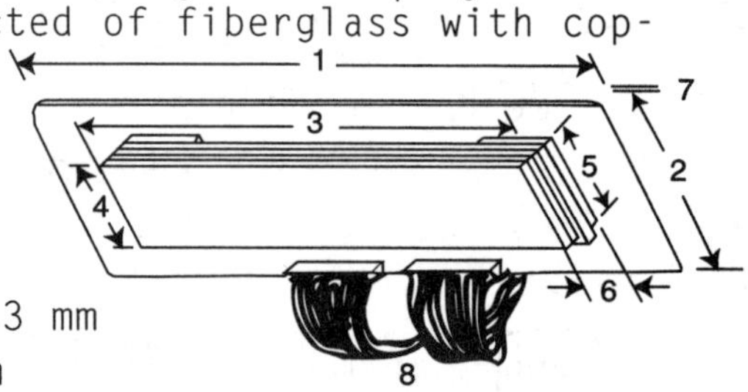

Figure 2 PCB

- 1.1 Length–15 mm
- 1.2 Width–5.1 mm
- 1.3 Tube length–10.8 mm
- 1.4 Tube faceplate width–2.3 mm
- 1.5 Tube total width–2.8 mm
- 1.6 Tube thickness–1.7 mm
- 1.7 PCB thickness–0.2 mm
- 1.8 20 conductor 10" 22 gauge stranded wire with 2 AECC female connectors (AECC part #7214-001)
- 1.9 American Display Company blue phosphor display tube (ADC part #1172177)

Figure 10.9 Student's Finished Copy

2.0 Case Assembly

Almond-colored ABS plastic, used to construct the case assembly, protects the PCB.

2.1 Length—15.5 mm
2.2 Bottom width—2.5 mm
2.3 Top width—0.9 mm
2.4 Mounting pole—5 mm high and 3.2 mm in diameter
2.5 Mounting tongue inside width—3.1 mm from side of assembly
2.6 Lower mounting tongue—1.5 mm wide
2.7 Side mounting tongue—0.8 mm high
2.8 Tongue thickness—0.2 mm
2.9 Height—6.1 mm

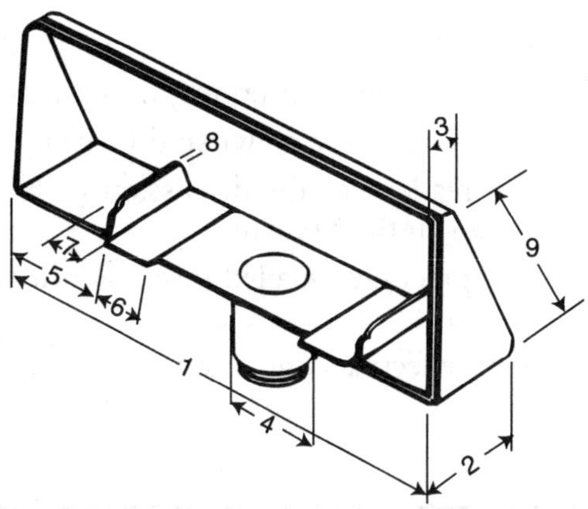

Figure 3 Case Assembly

3.0 Display Filter

3.1 Length—15.6 mm
3.2 Height—6.2 mm
3.3 Thickness—0.7 mm

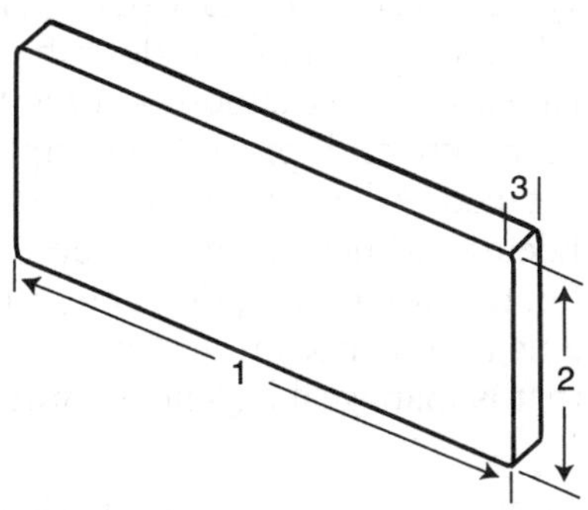

Figure 4 Display Filter

Transparent blue plastic, used to construct the display filter, allows the customer to view the readings.
The QL169 display provides easy viewing of clerk transactions and ensures cashier accuracy.

Figure 10.9 Student's Finished Copy (Cont.)

SAMPLE TECHNICAL DESCRIPTION

Following is a professionally written technical description merging graphic and text (Figure 10.10).

This is a highly effective technical description. It has

- A title
- An excellent introduction that lists topic, function, and components
- An effectively drawn and placed graphic
- A reader-friendly discussion with headings exactly corresponding to the callouts in the drawing
- A precisely detailed discussion focusing on materials, color, dimensions, and so on
- An effective conclusion

ACTIVITIES

INDIVIDUAL OR TEAM PROJECTS

1. Write a technical description, either individually or as a team. To do so, first select a topic. You can describe any tool, mechanism, or piece of equipment. However, don't choose a topic too large to describe accurately. To provide a thorough and precise description, you'll need to be exact and minutely detailed. A large topic, such as a computer, an oscilloscope, a respirator, or a Boeing airliner, would be too demanding for a two-to-four-page description. On the other hand, don't choose a topic that is too small, such as a paperclip, a nail, or a shoestring. Choose a topic that provides you with a challenge but that is manageable. These could include any of the following topics:

hammer	computer disk	VCR remote control
wrench	computer mouse	Xacto knife
screwdriver	light bulb	ballpoint pen
plier	calculator	pencil
wall outlet	automobile tire	credit card

   Once you or your team has chosen a topic, prewrite (listing the topic's components), write a draft (abiding by the criteria provided in this chapter), and rewrite (revising your draft).

2. Find examples of professionally written technical descriptions in technical books and textbooks and professional magazines and journals. Bring these examples to class and discuss whether they are successful according to the cri-

Electronic A1 Feed Switch

The Electronic A1 Feed Switch provides an automatic solid-state closure (normally open type) after sensing the lack of presence of food. Figure 1 shows the three principal parts of the feed switch.

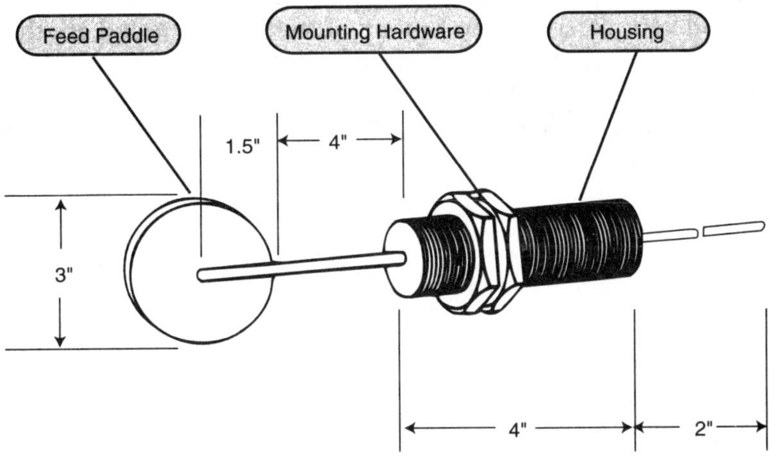

Figure 1. Electronic A1 Feed Switch

- HOUSING: The housing consists of a blue molded polycarbonate cylinder, 4" in length and 1" in diameter. Encircling the complete length of the housing are 1"-18 threads. At the middle of one end of the housing is a 2' Belden 6906 cable. Attached to the middle of the other end of the housing is a feed paddle.
- MOUNTING HARDWARE: The mounting hardware consists of two, white, flat, hexagonal, plastic Delryn locking nuts, Grade 2, 1" ID, 1 1/4" OD, 1/8" thick, and 1"-18 EF threads per inch.
- FEED PADDLE: The feed paddle consists of a 3" diameter, 16 Gauge (.060") No. 304 galvanized steel, Finish 2D or better, welded to a No. 101 Finish 3D or better galvanized steel shaft 5 1/2" in length and 1/4" in diameter. Exposed threads 1/4"-20 and 1/2" in length protrude from the free end of the shaft. Welded on three sides to the middle of the 3" diameter steel is the 1 1/2" of the unthreaded shaft end. The feed paddle is white teflon coated to a thickness of 1/64".

The Electronic Feed Switch, with its five-year warranty, is reliable in dusty and dirty environments. The easy-to-install, short-circuit-protected switch is internally protected for transient voltage peaks to a maximum of 5 KV, for up to 10 msec duration. Our feed switch can detect dry concentrate, meal, rolled barley, fine and coarse feeds, as well as special feeds such as soybean meal and high-moisture corn.

Figure 10.10 Professionally Written Technical Description

teria presented in this chapter. If the descriptions are good, specify how and why. If they are flawed, state where and suggest ways to improve them. You might even want to rewrite the flawed descriptions.

3. Select a simple topic for description, such as a pencil, coffee cup, toothbrush, or textbook (you can use brainstorming/listing to come up with additional topics). Describe this item without mentioning what it is or providing any graphics. Then, read your description to a group of students/peers and ask them to draw what you've described. If your verbal description is good, their drawings will resemble your topic. If their drawings are off base, you haven't succeeded in providing an effective description. This is a good test of your writing abilities.

Chapter 9

INSTRUCTIONS AND USER'S MANUALS

- OBJECTIVES
- CRITERIA FOR WRITING INSTRUCTIONS
- PROCESS
- PROCESS LOG
- CRITERIA FOR WRITING A USER'S MANUAL

OBJECTIVES

Instructions and User's Manuals are the heartbeat of technical writing. Every manufactured product comes complete with either a short (one- to four-page) instruction or with a more detailed user's manual (user's manuals can be anywhere from four pages to a book-length text).

You can receive short instructions for baking brownies; making pancakes; putting together children's toys; or changing a tire, the oil in your car, or the coolant in your engine. Longer user's manuals help you set up your stereo systems, construct electronic equipment, maintain computers, and operate fighter planes.

There are even instructions for making chicken noodle soup. One major soup manufacturer recently stopped printing instructions for soup preparation on its cans of soup. Executives assumed that such information was unnecessary. They were mistaken. The company received thousands of calls from consumers asking how to prepare the soup. Responding to befuddled customers, the company reverted to printing these instructions. "Pour soup in pan. Slowly stir in one can of water. Heat to simmer, stirring occasionally."

Even pop-top cans of soda include instructions: "1. Lift up. 2. Pull back. 3. Push down." When such simple items as soup and soda need instructions, you can imagine how necessary instructions are for complex products and procedures. Include instructions or user's manuals whenever your audience needs to know how to

Operate a mechanism	Restore a product
Install equipment	Correct a problem
Manufacture a product	Service equipment
Package a product	Troubleshoot a system
Unpack equipment	Plant
Test components	Harvest
Maintain equipment	Set up a product
Clean a product	Implement a procedure
Monitor a system	Construct anything
Repair a system	Assemble a product

Whatever your objectives are, this chapter will help you write your short instructions or help you construct a longer user's manual.

CRITERIA FOR WRITING INSTRUCTIONS

Follow these criteria for writing an effective instruction.

TITLE

Preface your text with a title that explains two things: *what* you're writing about (the name of your product or service) and *why* you're writing (the purpose of the instruction). For example, to merely title your instruction "Overhead Projector" would be uninformative. This title names the product, but it doesn't explain why the instruction is being written. Will the text discuss maintenance, setup, packing, or operating instructions? A better title would be "Operating Instructions for the XYZ Overhead Projector."

ORGANIZATION

As the writer of the instruction, you know what your objectives are. You know why you're writing and what you want to accomplish. However, your readers, upon picking up the instruction, are unaware of your intentions. Whereas you know where you're going, they must patiently await further information regarding the destination. To help your readers follow your train of thought, provide them with a road map. One way to do this is through organization. A neatly organized instruction can orient your readers, thereby helping them follow your directions. To organize your instruction effectively, include an *introduction,* a *discussion,* and a *conclusion.*

Introduction

In the first paragraph of your instruction, tell your readers three things: what *topic* you'll be discussing, your *reasons* for writing, and the *number of steps* involved in the instruction. The topic names the product or service. Your reason for writing either explains the purpose of the instruction ("maintaining the machine will increase its longevity") or comments about the product's capabilities or ease of use. Stating the number of steps allows your readers to plan ahead and organize their thoughts and their time. Look at the following examples:

> ***Good***
> The following seven steps will help you operate the Udell PQ 4454 Overhead projector.
>
> ***Better***
> The Udell PQ 4454 is an overhead projector for business and school. It's easy to use and requires little maintenance. Follow these eight steps for operating the machine.
>
> ***Best***
> The Udell PQ 4454 Overhead Project is used to project written or graphic material onto a screen or wall. Because of its capability to enlarge and project, it is ideal for use in schools or businesses. Six simple steps will help you operate the projector.

The first of the preceding examples includes product plus steps; the second adds ease of use. The third example, however, is best because it mentions product, steps, ease of use, plus capabilities.

In addition to this introductory overview focusing on the topic and steps to be performed, you also might want to tell your readers what tools or equipment they'll need to perform the procedures. You can provide this through a simple list, or perhaps you'll want to add graphics (the type of tool needed plus a picture of that tool). This depends on whether your readers are high tech, low tech, or lay.

> ***Example 1***
> ***List of Required Tools***
> *Tools Required*
> 1—2 mm hex wrench
> 1—pliers

Example 2
List of Required Tools
plus Graphic Depiction
Tools Required
1—2 mm hex wrench

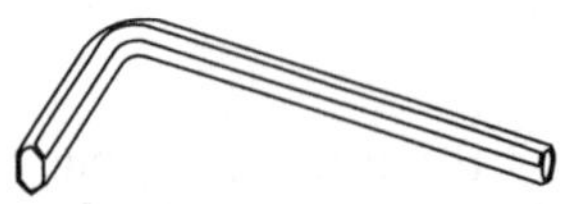

1—pliers

Finally, decide if you should preface your instructions by either stating Dangers, Warnings, Cautions, or Notes. This is an essential consideration to avoid costly lawsuits and to avoid potentially harming an individual or damaging equipment.

When including hazard alert messages, you need to consider the following:

- *Placement:* Where should the Caution or Warning go? Do you place the information before or after the appropriate text? If you place the information after the text, *after the reader has already performed the task,* the damage is done. Your readers already will have hurt themselves or harmed the equipment. The hazard alert is placed before the step. In fact, you might want to state your Warnings or Cautions in the introduction, before the audience even begins to perform a task.
- *Access:* If your hazard alert is printed before the appropriate step, but you haven't used any highlighting techniques to make it obvious, your readers won't see the danger. You need to make the Warning or Caution obvious. To do so, vary your typeface and type size, use white space to separate the Warning or Caution from surrounding text, and/or box in the Warning or Caution.
- *Definitions:* What does *Caution* mean? How does it differ from *Warning, Danger,* or *Note?* Unfortunately, these terms are not defined consistently.

  Three primary institutions that seek to provide a standardized definition of terms are ANSI (The American National Standards Institute), the U.S. Military (MILSPEC), and OSHA (Occupational Safety and Health Administration). However, these institutions often define terms differently. For example, both ANSI and MILSPEC define *Note* similarly as essential operating information. OSHA defines *Notice* as general instructions relative to safety measures. ANSI defines *Caution* as a hazardous situation that might cause minor or moderate injury, whereas MILSPEC defines *Caution* as something that could result in damage or destruction to equipment. OSHA uses *Caution* to designate potential hazards regarding unsafe practices. Personal injury, damage to equipment, and hazardous unsafe practices should be distinguished more clearly. Both ANSI and MILSPEC define both *Warning* and *Danger* as an activity possessing the potential for serious injury or death. OSHA defines *Danger* as immediate danger. The words overlap and don't distinguish between death and serious harm.

To avoid confusion, we suggest the following hierarchy of definitions, which clarifies the degree of hazard:

1. *Note:* Important information, necessary to perform a task effectively or to avoid loss of data or inconvenience.
2. *Caution:* The potential for damage or destruction of equipment.
3. *Warning:* The potential for serious personal injury.
4. *Danger:* The potential for death.

Our goal is to avoid confusion, which can occur if one writes, "Cautionary Warning Notice!"

- *Colors:* Another way to emphasize your hazard message is through a colored window (box) around the word. Usually, *Note* is printed in blue or black, *Caution* in yellow, *Warning* in orange, and *Danger* in red.
- *Text:* To further clarify your terminology, provide the readers text to accompany your hazard alert. Your text should have the following three parts:

1. *A one- or two-word identification alerting the reader. High Voltage, Hot Equipment, Sharp Objects,* or *Magnetic Parts,* for example, will warn your reader of potential dangers, warnings, or cautions.
2. *The consequences of the hazards, in three to five words.* "Electrocution can kill," "Can cause burns," "Cuts can occur," or "Can lead to data loss," for example, will tell your readers the results stemming from the dangers, warnings, or cautions.
3. *Avoidance steps.* In three to five words, tell the readers how to avoid the consequences noted above: "Wear rubber shoes," "Don't touch until cool," "Wear protective gloves," or "Keep disks away."

- *Icons:* Equipment is manufactured and sold globally; people speak different languages. Your hazard alert should contain an *icon*—a picture of the potential consequence—to help everyone understand the caution, warning, or danger. (Icons are discussed in Chapter 6.)

Figure 11.1 shows an effective page layout and the necessary information to communicate hazard alerts.

Hazard Alert

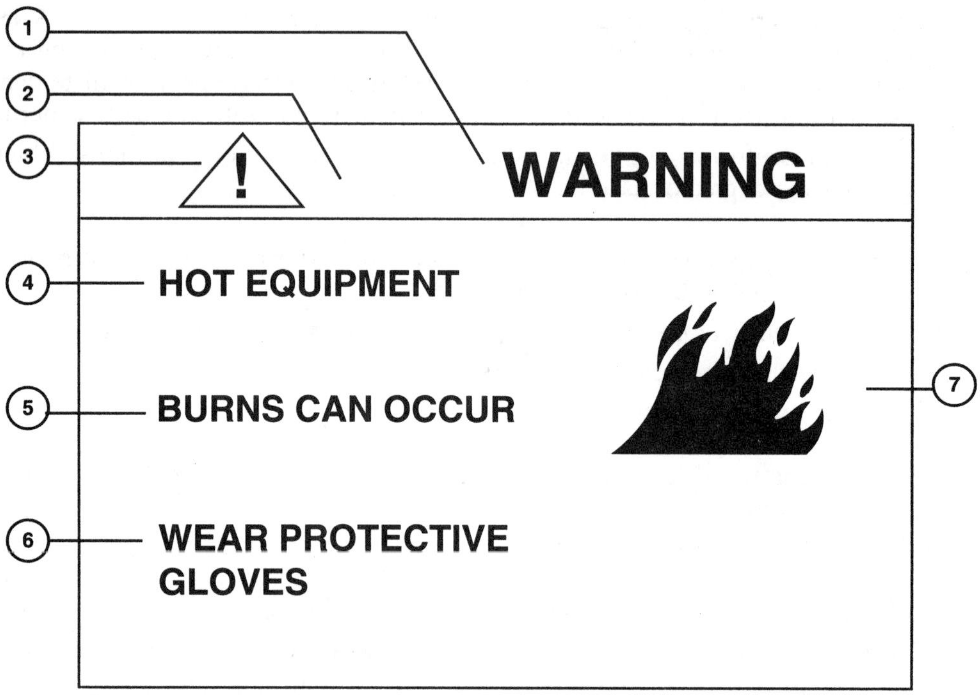

1	Hazard Alert Word
2	Hazard Alert Color
3	Alert Symbol
4	Identification–What is the specific hazard?
5	Consequence–What are the potential results?
6	Avoidance Steps–What should you do?
7	Hazard Icon

Figure 11.1

Discussion

Itemize and thoroughly discuss the steps in your instruction. Organize them *chronologically*—a step-by-step sequence. Obviously, you cannot tell your readers to do step six, then go back to step two, then accomplish step twelve, then do step four. Such a distorted sequence would fail to accomplish your goals. To operate machinery, monitor a system, or construct equipment, your readers must follow a chronological sequence. Be sure that your instruction is chronologically accurate.

Conclusion

As with a technical description, you can conclude your instruction in various ways. You can end your instruction with a (a) comment about warranties, (b) sales pitch highlighting the product's ease of use, (c) reiteration of the product's applications, or (d) summary of the company's credentials. (For examples, see the discussion on conclusions in Chapter 10.)

Another valid way to conclude, however, is to focus on *disclaimers,* as in the following example:

> This operating guide to the Udell PQ 4454 Overhead Projector is included primarily for ease of customer use. Service and application for anything other than normal use or replacement parts must be performed by a trained and qualified technician.

AUDIENCE RECOGNITION

How many times have you read an instruction and been left totally confused? You were told to "place the belt on the motor pulley," but you didn't know how. Or you were told to "discard the used liquid in a safe container," but you didn't know what was safe for this specific type of liquid. You were told to "size the cutting according to regular use," but you had never regularly performed this activity.

Here's a typical instruction, written without considering audience.

> To overhaul the manual starter, proceed as follows: Remove the engine's top cover. Untie starter rope at anchor and allow starter rope to slowly wind onto pulley. Tie a knot on the end of starter rope to prevent it from being pulled into housing. Remove pivot bolt and lift manual starter assembly from power head.

Although many high-tech readers might be able to follow these instructions, many more readers will be confused. How do you remove the engine's top cover? Where's the anchor? Where's the pivot bolt and how do you remove it? What's the power head?

The problem is caused by writers who assume that their readers have high-tech knowledge. This is a mistake for several reasons. First, even high-tech readers often need detailed information because technology changes daily. You can't assume that every high-tech reader is up-to-date on these technical changes. Thus, you must clarify. Second, low-tech and lay readers—and that's most of us—carefully read each and every step, desperate for clear and thorough assistance.

As writer, you should provide your readers with the clarity and thoroughness they require. To do this, recognize accurately who your readers are and give them what they want, whether that amounts to technical updates for high-tech readers or precise, even simple information for low-tech or lay readers. The key to success as a writer of instructions is, "Don't assume anything. Spell it all out—clearly and thoroughly!"

GRAPHICS

As with technical descriptions, clarify your points graphically using the super comic book look. Use drawings and/or photographs which are big, simple, clear, keyed to the text, and labeled accurately. Not only do these graphics make your instructions more visually appealing, but also they help your readers and you. What the reader has difficulty understanding, or you have difficulty writing clearly, your graphic can help explain pictorially.

A company's use of graphics often depends on audience. With a high-tech reader, the graphic might not be needed. However, with a low-tech reader, the graphic is used to help clarify. Look at the following examples of instructions for the same procedure. Figure 11.2 uses text with the super comic book look; Table 11.1 uses text without graphics.

Note that Figure 11.2 uses large, bold graphics to supplement the text, clearly depicting what action must be taken. This is appropriate for a low-tech end user. On the other hand, Table 11.1, written for a manufacturer's technician (high tech), assumes greater knowledge and, therefore, deletes the graphic.

STYLE

1. Number your steps. Don't use bullets or the alphabet. Numbers, which you can never run out of, help your readers refer to the correct step. In contrast, if you used bullets, your readers would have to count to locate steps—seven bullets for step seven, and so on. If you used the alphabet, you'd be in trouble when you reached step twenty-seven.

Text with Super Comic Book Graphics

Presetting Ventilation Controls and Alarms

Begin by setting ventilator controls and alarms as follows, prior to connecting patient to ventilator.

(1) Set Mode Selector Switch at the "Power Off" position.

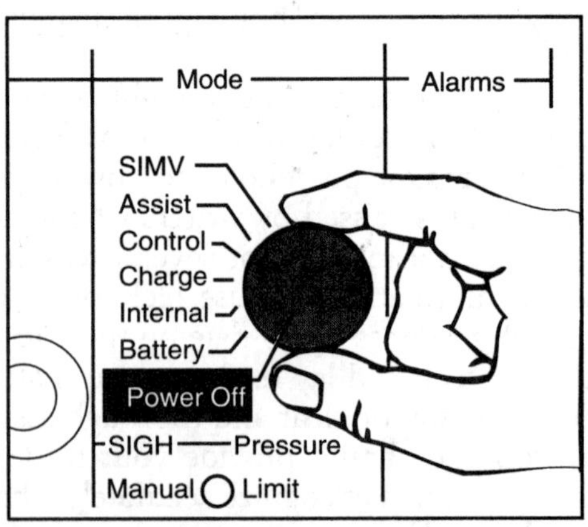

(Courtesy of Puritan Bennett Corp.)

Figure 11.2

Table 11.1

Text without Graphics for High-Tech Readers

LOCATION ITEM	ACTION	REMARKS
	NOTE For additional operating instructions, refer to Companion 2800 operator's manual.	
1. MODE switch	Set to POWER OFF.	
2. Rear panel	Ensure that instructions on all labels are observed.	
3. Patient tubing circuit	Assemble and connect to unit.	See Table 2, step 3.
4. Power Cord	Connect to 120/220 V ac grounded outlet.	If power source is external battery, connect external battery cable to unit per Table 2, step 4.
5. Cascade 1 humidifier	Connect to unit.	See Table 2, step 2.

(Courtesy of Puritan Bennett Corp.)

2. *Use highlighting techniques.* Boldface, different size and style font, emphatic warning words, color, italicization, and so on call attention to special concerns. A danger, caution, warning, or specially required technique must be evident to your reader. If this special concern is buried in a block of unappealing text, it will not be read. This could be dangerous to your reader or costly to you and your company. To avoid lawsuits and/or to help your readers see what is important, call it out through formatting.

3. *Limit the information within each step.* Don't overload your reader by writing lengthy steps, as in Example 1.

EXAMPLE 1 OVERLOADED STEPS

1. Start the engine and run it to idling speed while opening the radiator cap and inserting the measuring gauge until the red ball within the glass tube floats either to the acceptable green range or to the dangerous red line.

Instead, separate distinct steps, as in Example 2.

EXAMPLE 2 SEPARATED STEPS

1. Start the engine and run it to idling speed.
2. Open the radiator cap and insert the measuring gauge.
3. Note whether the red ball within the glass tube floats to the acceptable green range or up to the dangerous red line.

4. *Develop your points thoroughly.* Don't say, "After rotating the discs correctly, grease each with an approved lubricant." Instead, clarify what you mean by correct rotating and specify the approved lubricant, as in Example 3. Unless you tell your readers what you mean, they won't know.

EXAMPLE 3 WELL-DEVELOPED STEPS

1. Rotate the disks clockwise so that the tabs on the outside edges align.
2. Lubricate the discs with 2 oz. of XYZ grease.

5. *Use short words and phrases.* Remember the fog index. (See Chapter 3.)

6. *Begin your steps with verbs—the imperative mood.* Note that each of the numbered steps in the following example begins with a verb:

EXAMPLE 4 VERBS BEGIN STEPS

1. *Number* your steps.
2. *Use* highlighting techniques.
3. *Limit* the information within each step.
4. *Develop* your points thoroughly.
5. *Use* short words and phrases.
6. *Begin* your steps with verbs.

7. *Personalize your text.* Remember, people write to people. Involve your readers in the instruction by using pronouns. (See Chapter 4.)

8. *Do not omit articles. Articles—a, an,* and *the*—are part of our language. Although you might see an instruction omit these articles, please don't. Articles do not take up much room in your text, but they do make your sentences read more fluidly.

PROCESS

Now that you know what should be included in an instruction, it's time to write. But how do you start? Where do you begin?

As in other technical writing activities, follow a step-by-step process: *prewriting* to gather data and determine objectives, *writing* to draft your correspondence, and *rewriting* to revise and perfect.

PREWRITING

You've already been introduced to three prewriting techniques: reporters' questions, clustering/mind mapping, and brainstorming/listing. For writing an instruction, reporters' questions would be a good place to start gathering data and determining objectives. Ask yourself:

- *Who* is my reader?
  - —High tech?
  - —Low tech?
  - —Lay?
- *What* detailed information is needed for my audience? For example, a low-tech or lay reader will be content with "inflate sufficiently" whereas an instruction geared toward high-tech readers will require "inflate to 25 psi."
- *How* must this instruction be organized?
  - —Chronologically
- *When* should the procedure occur?
  - —Daily, weekly, monthly, quarterly, biannually, or annually?
  - —As needed?
- *Why* should the instruction be carried out?
  - —To repair, maintain, install, operate, and so on. (See the list of reasons for using an instruction at the beginning of this chapter.)

Once you've gathered this information, you can use brainstorming to sketch out a rough list of the steps required in the instruction and the detail needed for clarity. After that, your major responsibility is to sequence your steps chronologically. To accomplish this goal, use a prewriting technique called *flowcharting*.

Flowcharts chronologically trace the stages of an instruction, visually revealing the flow of action, decision, authority, responsibility, input/output, preparation, and termination of process. Flowcharting is not just a graphic way to help you gather data and sequence your instruction, however. It is two-dimensional writing. It provides your reader content as well as a panoramic view of an entire sequence. Rather than just reading an instruction step by step, having little idea what's around the corner, with a flowchart your reader can figuratively stand above the instruction and see where it's going. With a flowchart, readers can anticipate cautions, dangers, and warnings, since they can see at a glance where the steps lead.

To create a flowchart, use the International Standardization Organization (ISO) flowchart symbols shown in Figure 11.3.

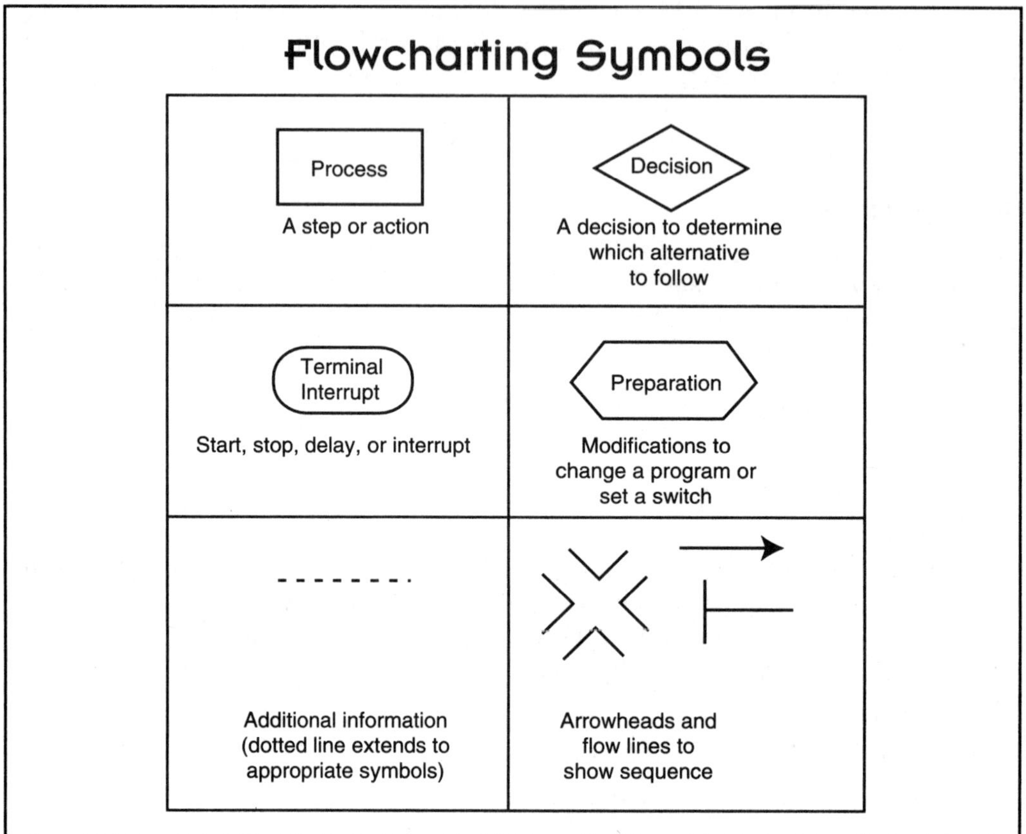

Figure 11.3

Figure 11.4 shows an excellent example of a flowchart, visually depicting an instruction's sequence.

WRITING

Once you've graphically depicted your instruction sequence using a flowchart, the next step is to write a rough draft of the instruction.

1. *Review your prewriting.* In doing so, you will accomplish the following:

- *Clarify your audience:* Now is a good time to review your reporters' questions and to determine if your initial assumptions regarding audience are still correct. If your attitude toward your audience has changed, redefine your readers and their needs.
- *Determine your focus:* In your prewriting, you answered the question *why.* Are you still certain of your objectives for writing the instruction? If so, write a one-sentence thesis or statement of objectives to summarize this purpose. For

Flowchart of Handling Service Problems

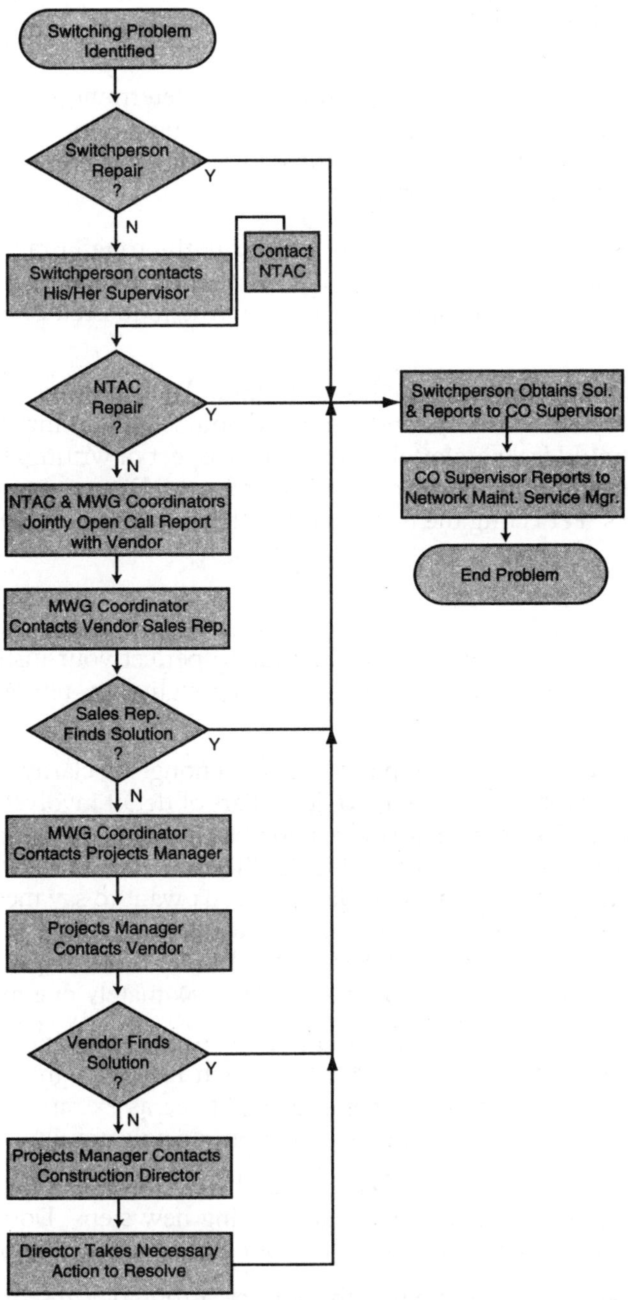

Figure 11.4

example, you could write, "This instruction should be followed so that glitches in the system can be discovered and corrected." This thesis or topic sentence will help you maintain your focus throughout the instruction. If you are uncertain about your purpose for writing the instruction, however, rethink the situation. You will not be able to write an effective instruction until your objectives are clearly stated.

- *Organize your steps:* Review your flowchart to determine if any steps in the instruction have been omitted or misplaced. If the chronological sequence is incorrect, reorganize your detail. If the chronology is correct, you're ready to move on to the next step in drafting.

2. *Review the instruction criteria:* Before you write the rough draft, remind yourself what the instruction will consist of. You'll need an introduction, a discussion with itemized steps, graphics to help your reader perform the requested procedures, and a conclusion.

3. *Write the draft:* You've gathered your data and determined your objectives. You've correctly sequenced the steps and reminded yourself of the instruction criteria. At this point, you should feel comfortable with the prospect of writing. Follow the sufficing technique again, roughly drafting your instruction. Don't worry about perfect grammar or graphics. Perfecting the text comes in the next step, rewriting.

REWRITING

Rewriting, the last stage in the process, is the time to perfect your instruction. To do so, reread your instruction and improve it using the eight-step rewriting procedure that follows.

1. *Add detail for clarity:* Don't hope you've said enough to clarify your steps. Tell your readers *exactly* how to do it or why to do it. Part of detail involves warnings and cautions, for example. Make sure that you've added all necessary dangers or concerns. In addition, assess each step. Have you added sufficient detail to clarify your intent? For instance, if you are writing to a lay reader, you don't want to say merely "insert the guide posts." You must say, "Before inserting the guide post, dig a 2-ft. deep by 2-ft. wide hole. Pour the ready-mixed concrete into the hole. Insert the post into the hole and hold it steady until the concrete starts to set (approximately one minute)."

2. *Delete:* Omit unnecessary words and phrases to achieve conciseness. In addition, delete extraneous information which a high-tech reader might not find useful. This, however, could be dangerous. What you might see as extraneous, your reader might see as necessary. If you delete any information, do so carefully.

3. *Simplify.* Don't overload your steps. If you have too much information in any one stage, divide this detail into smaller units, adding new steps. Doing so will help your readers follow your instructions. Simplify your word usage; refer to the fog index.

4. *Move information.* Make sure that the correct chronological sequence has been achieved.

5. Reformat using highlighting techniques. If you include dangers, cautions, warnings, or additional information for clarity, set these off (make them emphatic) through formatting. Use color, windowing, font size and style, emphatic words, graphics, etc.

6. Enhance your text. Use the imperative mood for each step in your instruction. Whenever an action is required, begin with a verb to emphasize the action. In addition, you can enhance your text through personalization. Remember, people write to people. To achieve this person-to-person touch, add pronouns to your instruction.

7. Correct your instruction for accuracy. Proof your text for grammatical correctness as well as for contextual accuracy.

8. Avoid sexist language.

To make sure that your instruction is effectively written, refer to the effective instruction checklist.

EFFECTIVE INSTRUCTION CHECKLIST

1. *Does the instruction have an effective title?*
   - Is the topic mentioned?
   - Is the reason for performing the instruction mentioned?
2. *Does the instruction have an effective introduction?*
   - Is the topic mentioned?
   - Is the reason for performing the instruction mentioned?
   - Is the ease of use or capabilities mentioned?
   - Have the number of steps been listed?
   - Has a list of required tools or equipment been provided?
3. *Are hazard alert messages used effectively?*
   - Are the hazard alert messages placed correctly?
   - Is the correct term used (Danger, Warning, Caution, or Note)?
   - Is the correct color used with the appropriate term?
   - Does the hazard alert text identify the hazard, provide the consequences, and suggest avoidance steps?
   - Is an effective icon used to depict the hazard?
4. *Is the instruction's discussion effective?*
   - Is the instruction organized chronologically?
   - Does each step avoid overloading by presenting one clearly defined action?
   - Does each step begin with a verb?
   - Does the instruction's discussion contain the same number of steps mentioned in the introduction?
5. *Is the instruction well developed?*

- Does the instruction avoid assuming that readers will understand and, instead, clearly explain each point?

6. *Does the instruction recognize audience effectively?*
   - Is the instruction written for a high-tech, low-tech, or lay audience?
   - Has sexist language been avoided?
   - Does the text include language appropriate for a multicultural audience?
   - Is the text personalized using pronouns?
7. *Is the conclusion effective?*
   - Have warranties been mentioned?
   - Is a sales pitch provided showing ease of use?
   - Has the conclusion reiterated a reason for performing these steps?
   - Are disclaimers provided?
8. *Is the instruction's document design effective?*
   - Are highlighting techniques effectively used? These include graphics (such as comic-book-look photographs or line drawings), varied typefaces and type sizes, color, and white space.
9. *Is correct technical writing style used, abiding by the fog index?*
10. *Have grammatical and textual errors been avoided?*

PROCESS LOG

Following is an example of an instruction collaboratively written by a group of students. To write this instruction, the students gathered data, determined objectives and sequenced their instruction through prewriting, drafted an instruction in writing, and finally revised their draft in rewriting.

Their assignment was to write an instruction on how to use an overhead projector, an item readily available in most classrooms.

PREWRITING

Figure 11.5 illustrates reporters' questions and students' flowcharting.

WRITING

After completing the prewriting, the students composed a draft, complete with sketchy graphics (Figure 11.6).

REWRITING

The students revised the rough draft, considering all the postwriting techniques discussed in this text. The revision is shown in Figure 11.7. The students then prepared their finished copy (Figure 11.8).

Reporters' Questions/Listing

- Who is the reader?

  Lay Reader - End User

- What detail is needed?
  - Turn on
  - Turn off
  - Focus
  - Warnings
  - Use of transparencies
  - Cautions
  - Size of viewed image

- How must the detail be organized?

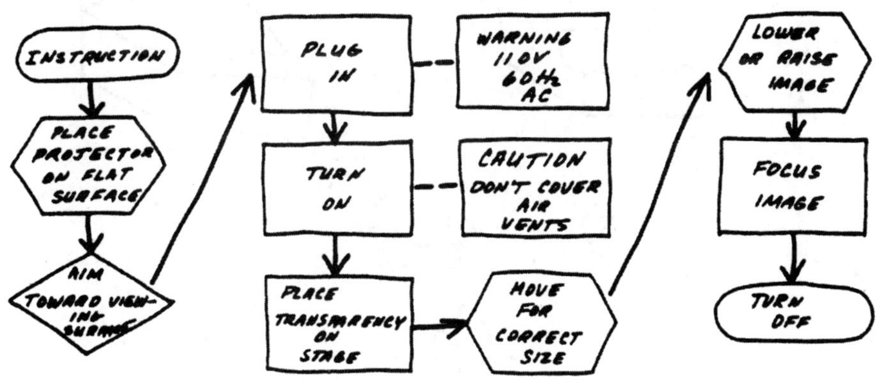

Figure 11.5 Students' Prewriting

The Udell Overhead Projector projects material on a flat surface. Follow these five steps to do so.

1. Place the machine on a flat surface within viewing range of the screen.
2. Plug power plug into a wall outlet and turn the machine on.
3. Put the transparency on the projectors horizontal viewing surface.
4. Move the image up or down for better viewing and focus image by adjusting the focus knob.
5. Turn machine off when completed and umplug.

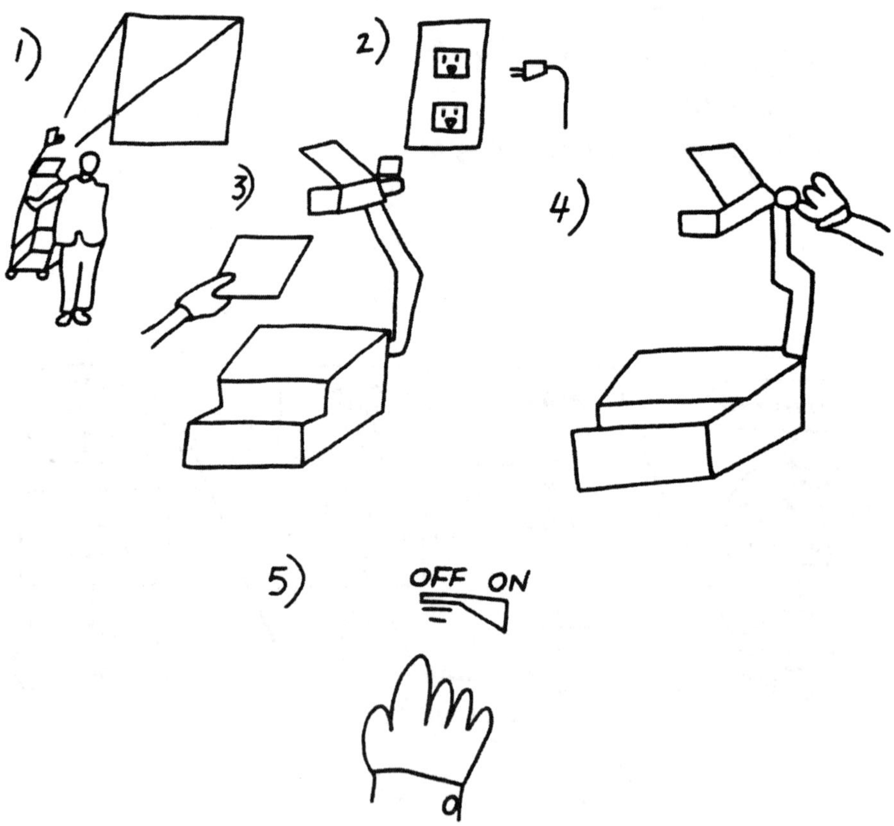

Figure 11.6 Students' Rough Draft

Title?

ID# SP vague - such as?

The Udell Overhead Projector projescts material on a ~~flat surface~~. Follow these ~~five~~ 8 steps to do so.

wall or screen

1. Place the machine on a ~~flat~~ level surface within ~~viewing range~~ 6-10' of the screen.

2. Plug power plug into a 110V 60Hz wall outlet. ~~and~~ 3. turn the machine on. (Repetitious)

4 ~~3~~. ~~But~~ Place the transparency on the projector's horizontal viewing surface.

5 ~~4~~. Move the image up or down for better viewing. ~~and~~ 6. Rotate the focus image by adjusting the focus knob to adjust the image.

7 ~~5~~. Turn machine off when completed ~~and~~ 8. Unplug the machine. ◯lug. proofread

Any cautions/warnings?

Figure 11.7 Students' Suggested Revisions

THE UDELL 4454 OVERHEAD PROJECTOR

The Udell 4454 Overhead Projector is used to project written or graphic material onto a screen or wall. Because of its capability to enlarge and project, the Udell is ideal for use in school and business.

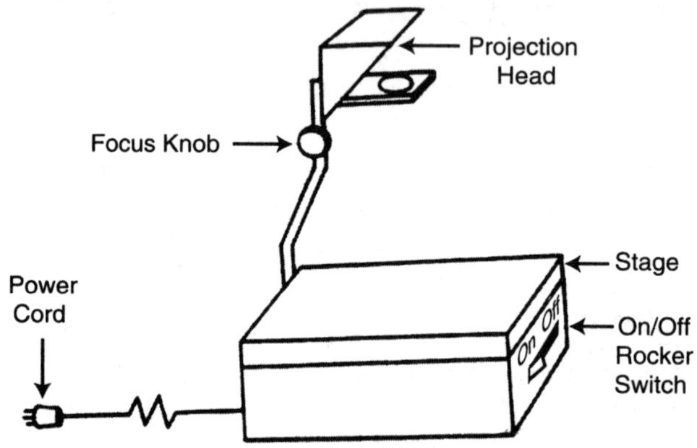

WARNING

The projector bulb heats up during operation. DO NOT TOUCH.

CAUTION

Keep air vents uncovered to allow for proper cooling.

To operate the Udell, follow these eight simple steps.

1. Place the projector on a level surface, approximately 6-10 feet from a projection screen or blank wall.

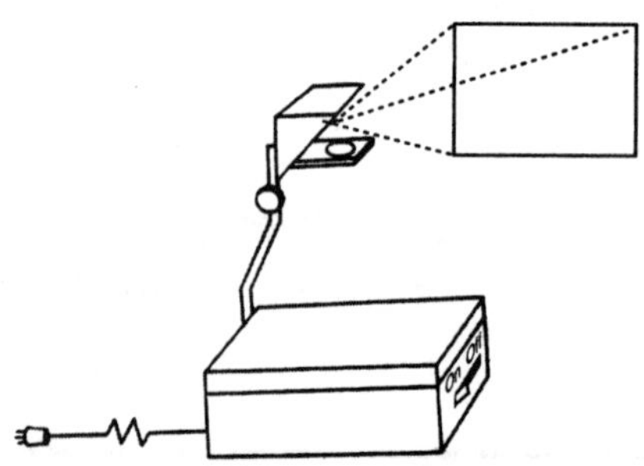

Figure 11.8 Students' Finished Copy

2. Plug the power supply cord into a 110 v 60 hz AC wall outlet.

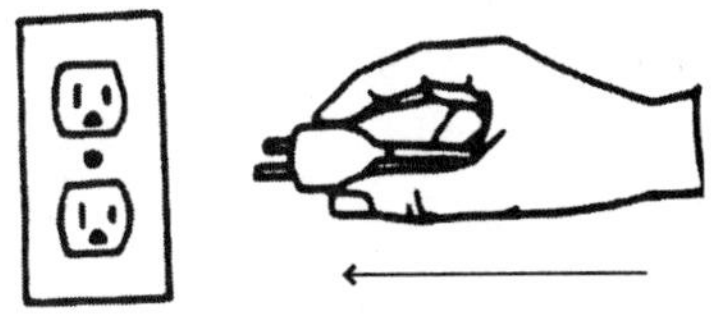

3. Push the rocker switch to the "on" position.

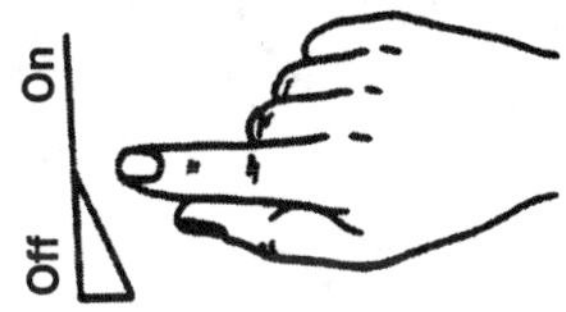

CAUTION

Keep air vents uncovered to allow for proper cooling.

4. Place the material to be viewed squarely on the projector's stage.

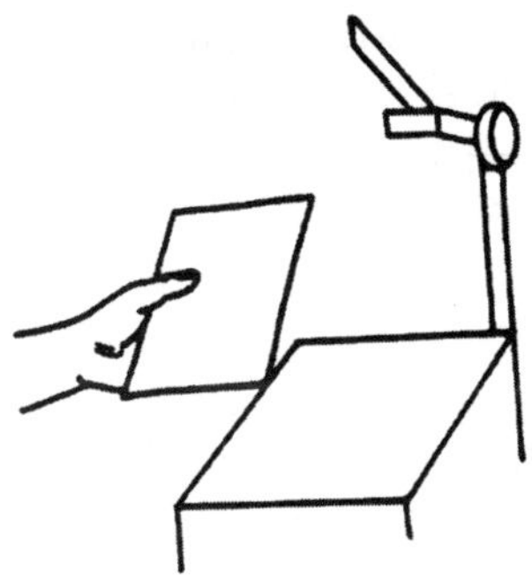

5. Adjust the height of the projected image by lowering or raising the projector's lens head.

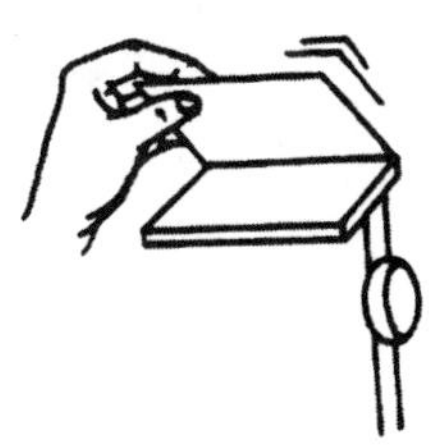

Figure 11.8 Students' Finished Copy (Cont.)

6. Rotate the focus knob for clear viewing of the projected image.

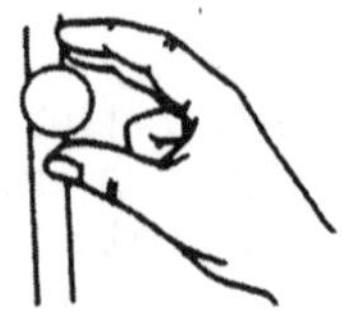

7. Push the rocker switch to the "off" position when you are through viewing your material.

8. Unplug the unit's power cord.

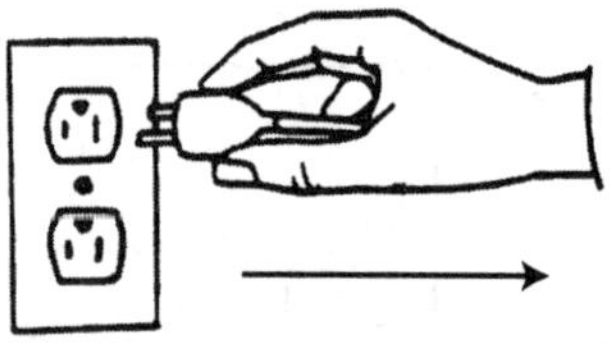

Following these eight simple steps will help you use the Udell overhead projector.

Figure 11.8 Students' Finished Copy (Cont.)

SAMPLE INSTRUCTION

Figure 11.9 is an excellent student-written instruction.

INSTRUCTIONS FOR DRY MOUNTING PHOTOGRAPHS

Dry mounting photographs keeps them safe for your family and generations to come. To successfully dry mount your photographs, follow the seven steps we've provided.

Dry mounting requires the following materials:

Materials

1. Press
2. Tacking iron
3. Mat knife
4. Mat board
5. Dry-mount tissue
6. Ruler
7. Print (photographed image)

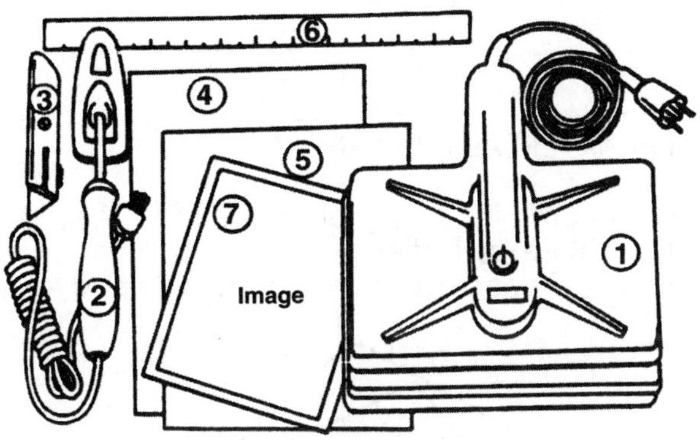

Figure 1 Materials

WARNING

Hot Equipment
Burns may occur.
Use the tacking iron handle.
Keep fingers outside the press.

Figure 11.9 Dry Mounting Instruction

1.0 DRYING THE MATERIAL

1.1 Plug in the press and turn it on. Wait to see the red light.
1.2 Heat the press to 250 degrees by adjusting the dial on the lid.
1.3 Predry the mount board and the print.
1.4 Place them in the press and hold the lid down for 30 seconds.

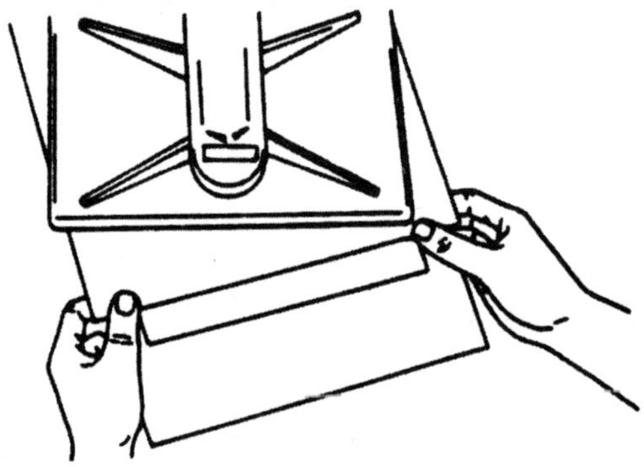

Figure 2

2.0 WIPING THE MATERIALS CLEAN

2.1 After the materials have been baked, let them cool for two to three minutes.
2.2 Wipe away any loose dust or dirt with a clean cloth.

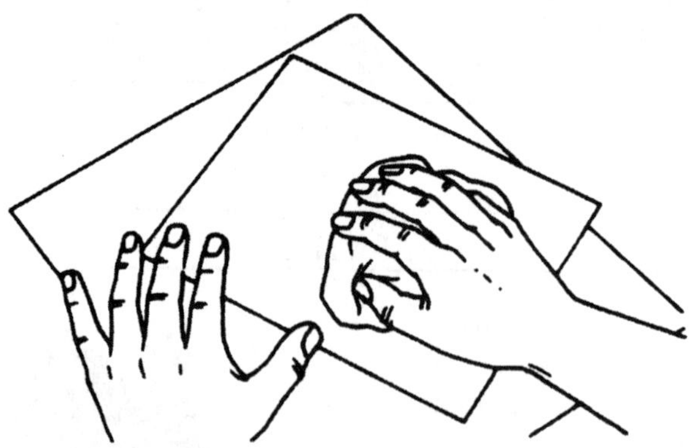

Figure 3

Figure 11.9 Dry Mounting Instruction (Cont.)

3.0 TACKING THE MOUNTING TISSUE TO THE PRINT

3.1 Plug in the tacking iron and turn it on.
3.2 With the print face down and the mounting tissue on top, tack the tissue to the center of the print.

Figure 4

4.0 TRIMMING THE MOUNTING TISSUE

4.1 Place a piece of smooth cardboard under the print so that you won't cut your table.
4.2 Trim off excess mounting tissue using the ruler.

CAUTION

Press firmly on the ruler to prevent slipping!
Don't cut into the image area of the print!

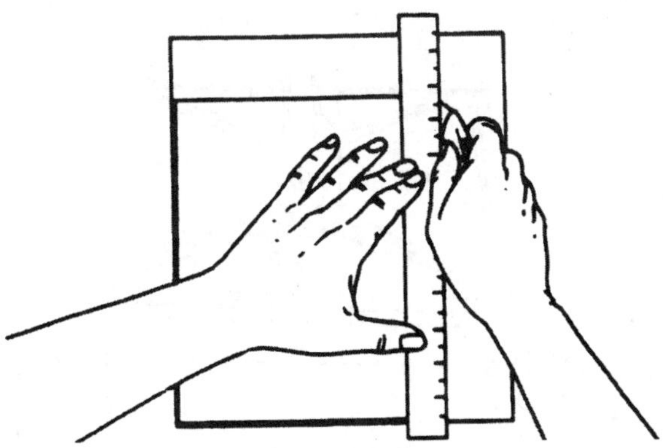

Figure 5

Figure 11.9 Dry Mounting Instruction (Cont.)

5.0 ATTACHING THE MOUNTING TISSUE AND PRINT TO THE BOARD

CAUTION

The tissue must lie completely flat on the board to prevent wrinkles under the print!

5.1 Position the print and the tissue, face up, on the top of the mount board.
5.2 Slightly raise one corner of the print and touch the tacking iron to the tissue on top of the board.
5.3 Tack each corner down in this manner.

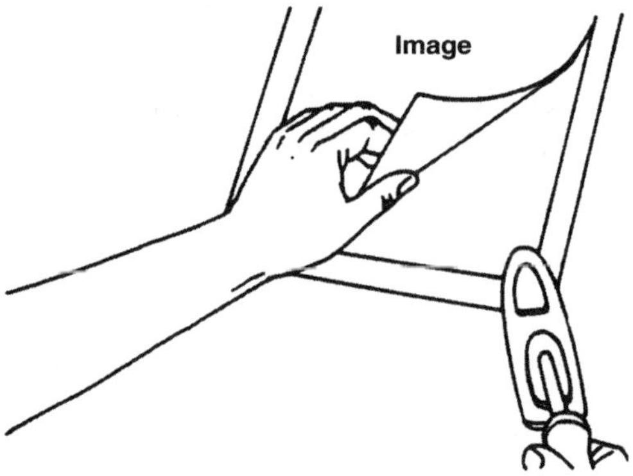

Figure 6

6.0 MOUNTING THE PRINT

6.1 Put the board, tissue, and print (with cover sheet on top) into the press.
6.2 Hold down the press lid firmly for 30 seconds.

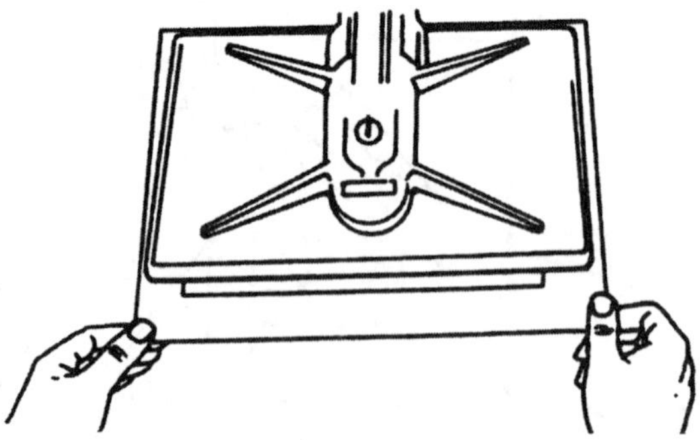

Figure 7

Figure 11.9 Dry Mounting Instruction (Cont.)

7.0 TRIMMING THE MOUNTED PRINT

7.1 Pressing down firmly on the ruler to avoid slipping, trim the edges of the mounted print with a sharp mat knife.

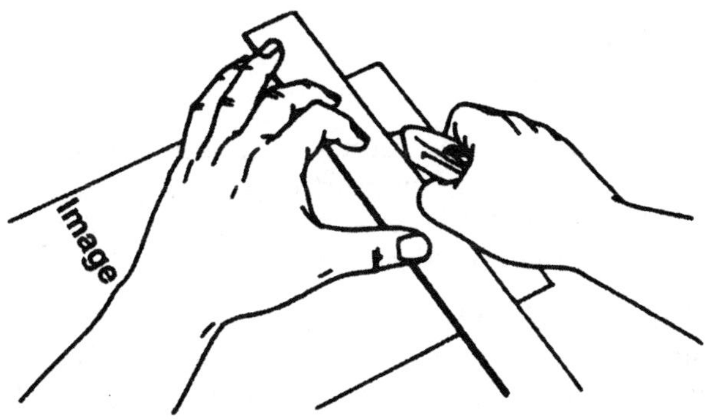

Figure 8

By carefully dry mounting your photographs, they will look beautiful and last longer. Enjoy your artistry.

Figure 11.9 Dry Mounting Instruction (Cont.)

CRITERIA FOR WRITING A USER'S MANUAL

Your user's manual might focus on installation, operation, maintenance, or troubleshooting. It might be packed with the product or produced separately to be sold at a later date. The user's manual might be sized to fit in your car's glove compartment, or it might be as large as an encyclopedia. Whatever the size, shape, or purpose of your user's manual, it will include an instruction or several instructions, abiding by the criteria already provided in this chapter.

However, in contrast to a short instruction, user's manuals contain additional information, including *any* or *all* of the following components (the order of these components will vary):

1. Cover page. The cover page accomplishes at least two goals. First, the cover page will name the product or service being discussed *and* explain the purpose of the manual.

Example 1
All CALLS Cordless Telephone
Instruction Manual

Example 2
Direct Line Cordless Telephone
Owner's Manual
for
Installation and Operation

Example 3
AutoCall Cordless Telephone
Use and Care Guide

Second, in addition to naming the product or service and stating the purpose of the manual, a cover page might also graphically depict the product or service. This could be accomplished either through a photograph or a line drawing. Doing so allows the readers to identify the product or service more readily.

2. *Hazard alerts.* Usually, when readers turn the cover page to open the manual, they see hazard alerts or safety guidelines. Companies want to protect their customers from harm, minimize potential damage to equipment, and avoid costly lawsuits.

These hazard alerts could be a list of safety tips, such as the following guidelines from a roofing user's manual:

- Please read all instructions.
- Use care with ladders.
  —Rest ladders on steady ground
  —Lean ladders against a wall
  —Allow only one person on a ladder
- Do not touch electric lines.
- Stay off your roof during strong winds.
- Use a scaffolding system for steep roofs.

Better than a list, however, would be a hazard alert like those already discussed in this chapter. A more effective hazard alert would include the appropriate word (Danger, Warning, Caution, or Note), color, hazard identification, consequence, avoidance steps, and icon depicting the hazard.

3. *Table of contents.* Your user's manual will have several sections. As already noted, you'll include numerous instructions (setup, installation, maintenance, operation, troubleshooting, for example). In addition, you might include specifications, warranties, guarantees, and customer service contact numbers.

However, readers might only want to access one of these sections. An effective table of contents will allow your readers to find the one or two items they specifically want. (We discuss successful tables of content in Chapter 15, "Long Reports and Proposals.")

4. *Introduction.* Companies need customers. A user's manual might be the only contact a company has with its customer. Therefore, user's manuals often are reader-

friendly and seek to achieve audience recognition and audience involvement. The manuals try to reach out and touch the customer.

Look at these introductions from three user's manuals:

Example 1
Thank you for purchasing our Drip Coffeemaker. Before your first use, please take a few minutes to read our Use and Care manual. Then find a safe place to keep it for future reference.

Example 2
Installation and operating procedures are contained in this booklet about your new color TV. The minutes you spend reading this book will contribute to hours of viewing pleasure.

Example 3
Welcome to the world of modern electronics. The cordless phone you have purchased is the product of advanced technology. This manual will help you install your new phone easily.

Each of the above introductions uses pronouns ("you," "your," and "our") to personalize the manual. The introductions also use positive words, such as "Welcome," "Thank you," and "pleasure" to achieve a positive customer contact. This is important because companies know that without customers, they're out of business. An effective introduction promotes good customer-company relationships.

5. *Definitions of terminology.* If your manual uses the abbreviations BDC, CCW, or CPR, will the readers know that you are referring to "Bottom Dead Center" (BDC), "Counter Clockwise" (CCW), or "Continuing Property Records" (CPR)? Probably not.

If the readers aren't familiar with your terminology, they might miss important information and perform an operation incorrectly.

To avoid this problem, define your abbreviations, acronyms, and/or symbols. Since "Danger," "Warning," "Caution," and "Note" are rarely defined the same way in different manuals, an effective manual defines what it means by these hazard alerts. You can either give your definitions early in the user's manual or in a glossary located at the end of your manual (we discuss glossaries in Chapter 15). The following example defines terms alphabetically:

Example 1

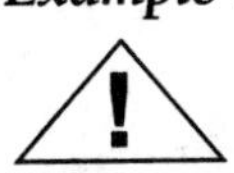	This symbol designates an important operating or maintenance step.
BDC	Bottom Dead Center
CCW	Counter Clockwise
Danger	This hazard alert designates the possibility of death. Be extremely careful when performing an operation.
RMS	Root Mean Square

6. Technical descriptions. In addition to instructions, many user's manuals contain technical descriptions of the product or system. These descriptions could be a part-by-part explanation or labeling of a product or system's components. Such a description helps readers recognize parts when they are referred to in the instruction. For example, if the user's manual tells the reader to lay shingles with the tabs pointing up, but a reader doesn't know what a "tab" is, the step cannot be performed. In contrast, if a description with appropriate call-outs is provided, then the reader's job has been simplified.

Perhaps the user's manual will contain a list of the product's specifications, such as its size, shape, capacity, capability, and materials of construction. Table 11.2 is an example of a specification from a cordless telephone user's manual. Such a specification allows the user to decide if the product meets his or her needs. Does it state the desired frequency? Is it the preferred weight and size? The specification answers these questions.

Finally, a user's manual might include a schematic, depicting the product or system's electrical layout. This would help the readers troubleshoot the mechanism. (Chapter 6 provides a sample schematic.)

Table 11.2

Cordless Telephone Specifications

BASE UNIT	SPECIFICATIONS
Transmit Frequency	46.6 to 46.9 MHz
Receive Frequency	49.6 to 49.9 MHz
Power Requirements	117V, 60Hz, 6W
Size	84mm(W) × 60m(H) × 246mm(D)
Weight	755g
HANDSET	**SPECIFICATIONS**
Transmit Frequency	49.6 to 49.9 MHz
Receive Frequency	46.6 to 46.9 MHz
Power Requirements	Rechargeable nickel cadmium batteries
Size	60mm(W) × 210mm(H) × 44mm(D)
Weight	345g

7. *Warranties.* Warranties protect the customer and the manufacturer. Many warranties tell the customer, "This warranty gives you specific legal rights, and you may also have other rights which vary from state to state." A warranty protects the customer if a product malfunctions sooner than the manufacturer suggests it might: "This warrants your product against defects due to faulty material or workmanship." In such a case, the customer usually has a right to free repairs or a replacement of the product.

However, the warranty also protects the manufacturer. No product lasts forever, under all conditions. If the product malfunctions after a period of time designated by the manufacturer, then the customer is responsible for the cost of repairs or a replacement product. The designated period of time differs from product to product. Furthermore, many warranties tell the customers that "This warranty does not include damage to the product resulting from normal wear, accident, or misuse."

Disclaimers are another common part of warranties which protect the manufacturer. For example, some warranties include the following disclaimers:

Example 1
Note: Any changes or modifications to this system not expressly approved in this manual could void your warranty.

Example 2
Proof of purchase by way of a receipt clearly noting that this unit is under warranty must be presented.

Example 3
The warranty is only valid if the serial number appears on the product.

Example 4
The manufacturer of this product will not be liable for damages caused by failure to comply with the installation instructions enclosed within this manual.

8. *Accessories.* A company always tries to increase its income. One way to do so is by selling the customer additional equipment. A user's manual promotes such equipment in an accessories list. This equipment isn't mandatory, required for the product's operation. Instead, accessories lists offer customers extra-long cables or cords, carrying cases, long-life rechargeable batteries, extendable antennas, a modem, CD-ROM capabilities, and video instruction packages. Often the specifications are also provided for these accessories.

9. *Corporate contact information.* Finally, the user's manual helps customers purchase accessories, answer customer questions, and solve customer complaints. Therefore, most user's manuals conclude by giving telephone numbers and/or addresses for local and regional service locations, twenty-four-hour service hotlines, and consumer information bureaus.

Figure 11.10 is a sample user's manual.

INSTALLATION GUIDE

TO YOUR

FOREVER

ASPHALT ROOF

Figure 11.10 Installation Guide

IMPORTANT SAFETY TIPS

Please read the entire manual before starting installation of *FOREVER* Asphalt Shingles.

1. DO NOT touch electric lines above your house.

2. Use care in climbing your ladder.
   - Rest ladders on steady ground.
   - Lean ladders against a wall.
   - Allow only one person on a ladder.

3. On steep roofs, use a scaffolding system.

4. Stay off your roof during strong winds or thunder-storms.

2

Figure 11.10 Installation Guide (Cont.)

TABLE OF CONTENTS

3

Figure 11.10 Installation Guide (Cont.)

TOOLS REQUIRED FOR INSTALLATION AND SPECIFICATIONS

TOOLS	SPECIFICATIONS
Ladder	Appropriate size
Hammer	Claw-type, smooth face
Utility Knife	6" retractable safety blade
Tape Measure	10' minimum
Chalk Line	Light-colored chalk
Shovel	Flat-end, long-handled, tear-off shovel
Underlayment	#15 asphalt saturated roofing felt One roll covers 400 sq. ft. of roof.
Three-tab *FOREVER* Asphalt Shingles	One sq. of shingles covers 100 sq. feet of roof. Add 10% for capping, borders, and waste.
Nails	2 1/2 lbs., 11 or 12 guage, 3/8" diameter, hot-galvanized nails will cover 1 sq. of shingles.

4

Figure 11.10 Installation Guide (Cont.)

DEFINITION OF TERMS

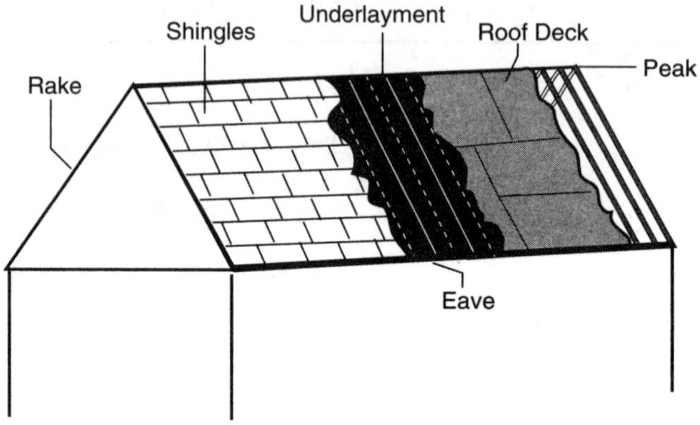

Figure 1 Parts of the Roof

- Rake—The vertical edge or side of the roof
- Shingles—Asphalt coverings for your roof
- Underlayment—Saturated felt to protect your roof deck from rot and mildew
- Peak—The upper horizontal edge of the roof
- Roof Deck—The plywood base that covers your rafters
- Eave—The lower horizontal edge of the roof
- Tab—The cut-out side of the shingle

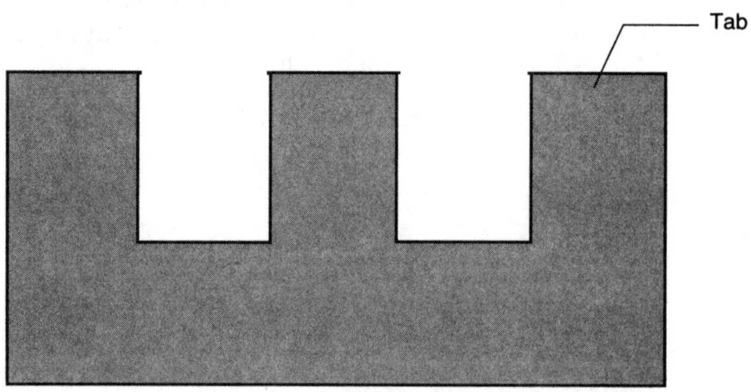

Figure 2 Shingle

5

Figure 11.10 Installation Guide (Cont.)

INTRODUCTION:
Benefits of Choosing *FOREVER* Asphalt Shingles

Congratulations! You have made an outstanding decision by choosing to install *FOREVER* Asphalt Shingles. Our shingles are superior to other types of roofing materials for the following reasons:

Table 1 Benefits of Asphalt Shingles

ITEM	Asphalt	Wood	Slate	Ceramic
INEXPENSIVE	X	X		
BEAUTIFUL	X	X	X	X
DURABLE	X		X	
EASY TO INSTALL	X			

Figure 11.10 Installation Guide (Cont.)

PREPARING YOUR ROOF DECK

Before you can install your new *FOREVER* Asphalt Shingles, you need to prepare your roof deck. To do so, follow these steps.

TOOLS REQUIRED:

Hammer
Shovel

1. Use the hammer to pry up old shingles, the old underlayment, and old nails.
2. Scoop up and remove the roof debris with the shovel.
3. After removing the old roofing material, check the roof deck for sagging, rotting wood.

NOTE: If you find any sagging or rotting wood, you will need to replace those sections with new plywood. Please call 1-800-FOREVER for information about our quality plywood products.

7

Figure 11.10 Installation Guide (Cont.)

LAYING AND MARKING THE UNDERLAYMENT

Once you have prepared the roof deck, next you need to install the underlayment. To do so, follow these steps:

TOOLS/EQUIPMENT REQUIRED

Underlayment
Chalk Lines

> NOTE: Underlayment roofing felt comes in rolls 4' wide X 50' long. Each roll covers 200 sq. ft. You will need half as many rolls as squares of shingles.

1. Install the underlayment by rolling it out perpendicular to the peak and the eave.

> NOTE: Be sure to overlap each piece of underlayment by 2" to provide weatherproofing coverage.

2. Use the chalk line to put horizontal guidelines on the underlayment.

2.1 Make the first line 12" from the eave and parallel to it.

2.2 Mark subsequent lines 5" to the roof peak (see Figure 3, "Marking the Underlayment").

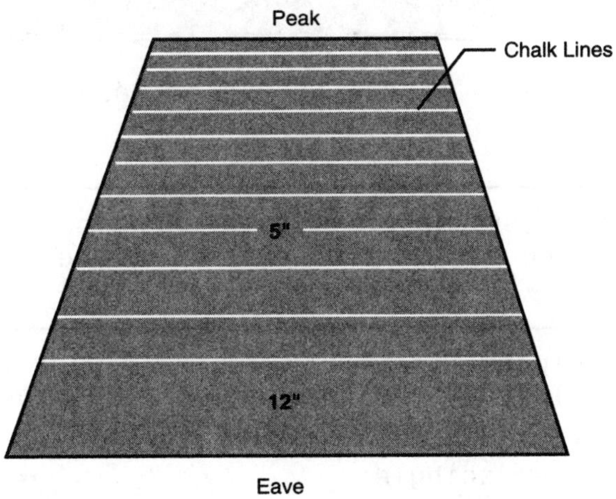

Figure 3 Marking the Underlayment

8

Figure 11.10 Installation Guide (Cont.)

INSTALLING YOUR *FOREVER* ASPHALT SHINGLES

Starter Course
The starter course is the first row of shingles installed. This row is closest to the eave. To lay this starter course, follow these steps:

EQUIPMENT/TOOLS REQUIRED

Hammer
Nails
Shingles

1. Starting at the left rake, lay the shingles side by side on the roof with the tabs pointing up to the roof peak.
2. Nail the shingles to the roof using three nails per shingle (see Figure 4, "Starter Course," for nail placement).

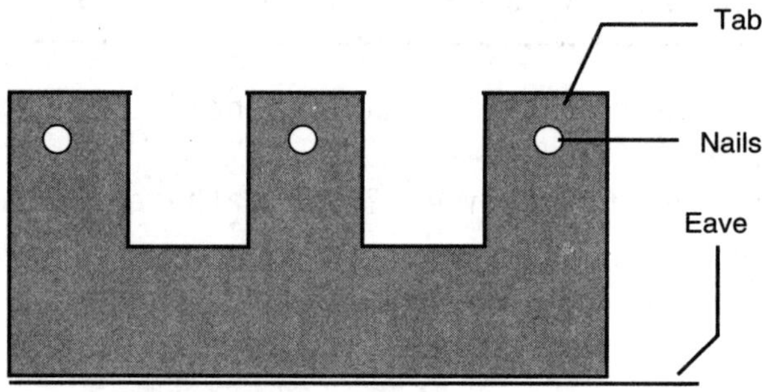

Figure 4 Starter Course

First Course

NOTE: This course and all subsequent courses will be laid with the tabs pointing down to the eave, not up to the peak.

1. Beginning at the left rake eave, lay a full shingle directly over the starter course shingle.
2. Nail this shingle to the starter course using three nails per shingle.
3. Continue to the right two to three full shingles.

9

Figure 11.10 Installation Guide (Cont.)

Second and Other Courses

1. Cut off a tab on the left side of a shingle.
2. Overlapping the starter course halfway, place this shingle over the first shingle in the first course.
3. Nail the shingle to the first course using two nails per shingle.
4. Alternating full shingles with shingles missing a tab, install all subsequent courses as noted above. (See Figure 5, "Shingle Placement for Second and Other Courses.")

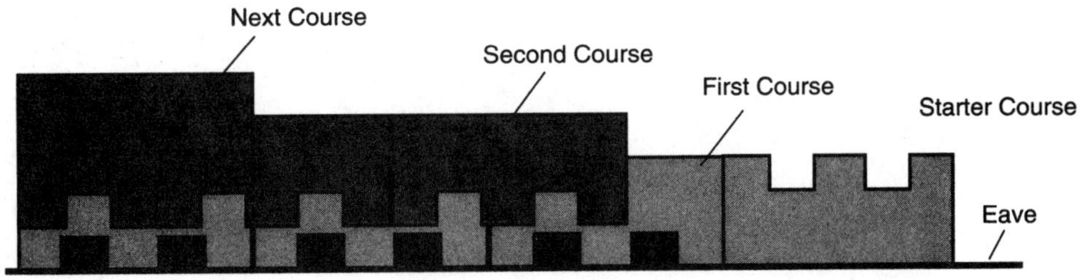

Figure 5 Shingle Placement for Second and Other Courses

Figure 11.10 Installation Guide (Cont.)

WARRANTY

FOREVER Asphalt Shingles are warranted to give normal service for 20 years or as long as you own your home. We will replace any shingle which cracks, chips, flakes, or peels under normal conditions. As with all roofing material, some non warranted damage may occur in severe hail or windstorms, or if the roof is not properly installed. To receive warranty service, save your dated sales receipt and proofs of purchase from each square of shingles you purchase.

For tips on installation, call our 24-hour service hotline at 1-800-FOREVER

FOREVER Ashpalt Shingles
8942 Hancock Center
Clearwater, FL 40043

11

Figure 11.10 Installation Guide (Cont.)

ACTIVITIES

Individual or Team Projects

1. Write an instruction. To do so, first select a topic. You can write an instruction telling how to monitor, repair, test, package, plant, clean, operate, manage, open, shut, set up, maintain, troubleshoot, install, and so on. Choose a topic from within your field of expertise or one that interests you. Follow the writing process techniques to complete your instruction. Prewrite (using a flowchart), write a draft (abiding by the criteria for instructions presented in this chapter), and rewrite to perfect your text.
2. Write a user's manual. To do so, first select a topic. For example, you could write a user's manual which explains how to operate a portable CD player, a cassette tape player, or a combination radio–alarm clock. The user's manual could focus on the installation and operation of any one of the following computer accessories: printer, modem, CD-ROM unit, or software package. In addition, TV sets, VCRs, ceiling fans, wall telephone units, or classroom overhead projectors could serve as the topic of a user's manual that explains installation and operation. Finally, a user's manual could explain the installation, operation, and maintenance for a coffee maker, kitchen blender, a stereo system with CD player, tape cassette, and VCR. Search your home, garage, or workplace for items about which you could write a user's manual.
3. Find examples of instructions or user's manuals for consumer products. These can include instructions for assembling children's toys, refinishing furniture, insulating attics or windows, setting up stereo systems, flushing out a radiator, installing ceiling fans, and so on. Try rummaging around in your kitchen pantry for examples of instructions—look at boxes and cans of food that tell you how to bake brownies or cook spaghetti. Instructions are everywhere.

   Once you find some examples, bring them to class. Then, applying the criteria for good instructions presented in this chapter, determine the success of the examples. If they are successful, explain why and how. If they fail, show where the problems are and rewrite the instructions to improve them.
4. Find examples of instructions or user's manuals written in your work environment. Bring these to class. Using the criteria for instructions presented in this chapter, decide whether the instructions are successful or unsuccessful. If the instructions are good, show how and why. If they are flawed, explain the problem(s). Then rewrite the instructions to improve them.
5. Find an example of a successful instruction or user's manual, either from your work environment or home (a consumer product). To make this instruction even more effective, construct a flowchart that will graphically enhance the writing and make the instruction easier to follow.
6. Find an example of a successful instruction or user's manual, either from your work environment or home (a consumer product). To make this instruction even more effective, draw super-comic-book pictures to accompany the text.

These drawings will graphically enhance the writing, making it easier for your reader to follow the instructions.

7. Good writing demands revision. Following is a flawed instruction. To improve it, rewrite the text, abiding by the criteria for instructions and the rewriting techniques included in this chapter.

> Date: November 30, 1996
> To: Maintenance Technicians
> From: Second Shift Supervisor
> Subject: Oven Cleaning
>
> The convection ovens in kiln room 33 need extensive cleaning. This would consist of vacuuming and wiping all walls, door, roofs, and floors. All vents and dampers need to be removed and a tack cloth used to remove loose dust and dirt. Also, all filters need replacing. I am requesting this because when wet parts are placed in the ovens to cure the paint, loose particles of dust and dirt are blown onto the parts which causes extensive rework. I would like this done twice a week to ensure cleanliness of product.

8. One of the keys to success in writing instructions is audience recognition. One reason flawed instructions fail is lack of audience recognition. For example, an instruction uses high-tech terms but is intended for low-tech readers.

   Find an example of an instruction or user's manual geared to a high-tech audience that correctly uses high-tech terms. Then find an example of an instruction geared to low-tech readers that incorrectly uses high-tech words. Next, find an instruction geared to low-tech or lay readers that has correctly defined its terms and explained its technology. Finally, find an example of an instruction that talks down to the reader, using low-tech or lay terms when high-tech words or phrases would have been better.

9. Find examples of instructions or user's manuals that do not provide effective hazard alerts. Using the criteria for effective hazard alerts provided in this chapter, decide where the alerts are flawed. Then improve the instructions or user's manuals by creating effective hazard alerts.

Chapter 10

SHORT REPORTS

- OBJECTIVES
- CRITERIA FOR WRITING SHORT REPORTS
- TYPES OF SHORT REPORTS: CRITERIA
- PROCESS
- PROCESS LOG

OBJECTIVES

At one time or another, you'll be asked to write a report. This report will satisfy one or all of the following needs:

- Supply a record of work accomplished
- Record and clarify complex information for future reference
- Present information to a large number of people
- Record problems encountered
- Document schedules, timetables, and milestones
- Recommend future action
- Document current status
- Record procedures

The most common types of reports include the following:

1. *Accident/incident reports:* What happened, how did it happen, when did it happen, why did it happen, who was involved?

2. *Feasibility reports:* Can we do it, should we do it?
3. *Inventory reports:* What's in storage, what's been sold, what needs to be ordered?
4. *Staff utilization reports:* Is labor sufficient and efficiently used?
5. *Progress/activity reports* (weekly, monthly, quarterly, annually): What's our status?
6. *Travel reports:* Where did I go, what did I learn, who did I meet, and so on?
7. *Lab reports:* How did we do it?
8. *Performance appraisal reports:* How's an employee doing on the job?
9. *Study reports:* What's wrong?
10. *Justification reports:* Here's why we need the material (or will pursue this action) on this date.

Although there are many different types of reports and individual companies have unique demands and requirements, certain traits are basic to all report writing.

CRITERIA FOR WRITING SHORT REPORTS

All reports share certain generic similarities in format, development, and style.

FORMAT

Every short report should contain four basic units: heading, introduction, discussion, and conclusion/recommendations.

Heading

The heading includes the date on which the report is written, the name(s) of the people to whom the report is written, the name(s) of the people from whom the report is sent, and the subject of the report (as discussed in Chapters 7 and 8, the subject line should contain a *topic* and a *focus*).

SAMPLE REPORT HEADING

DATE:	August 13, 1996
TO:	Shelley Stine
FROM:	Julie Jones J.J.
SUBJECT:	REPORT ON TRIP TO SOUTHWEST REGIONAL CONFERENCE ON ENGLISH (FORT WORTH, TX)

Introduction

The introduction supplies an overview of the report. It can include three optional subdivisions:

- Purpose—a topic sentence(s) explaining why you are submitting the report (rationale, justification, objectives) and exactly what the report's subject matter is.
- Personnel—names of others involved in the reporting activity.
- Dates—what period of time the report covers.

INTRODUCTION

Objectives: I attended the National Electronic Packaging Conference in Anaheim, CA, to review innovations in vapor phase soldering.

Dates: September 26–30, 1996

Personnel: Susan Lisk and Larry Rochelle

Some businesspeople omit the introductory comments in writing reports and begin with the discussion. They believe that introductions are unnecessary because the readers know why the reports are written and who is involved.

These assumptions are false for several reasons. First, it is false to assume that readers will know why you're writing the report, when the activities occurred, and who was involved. Perhaps if you are writing only to your immediate supervisor, there's no reason for introductory overviews. However, even in this situation you might have an unanticipated reader because

- Immediate supervisors change—they are promoted, fired, retired, or go to work for another company.
- Immediate supervisors aren't always available—they're sick for the day, on vacation, or off site for some reason.

Second, avoiding introductory overviews assumes that your readers will remember the report's subject matter. This is false because reports are written not just for the present, when the topic is current, but for the future, when the topic is past history. Reports go on file—and return at a later date. At that later date,

- You won't remember the particulars of the reported subject matter.
- Your colleagues, many of whom weren't present when the report was originally written, won't be familiar with the subject.
- You might have outside, lay readers who need additional detail to understand the report.

An introduction—which seemingly states the obvious—is needed to satisfy multiple readers, readers other than those initially familiar with the subject matter, and future readers who are unaware of the original report.

Discussion

The discussion of the report summarizes your activities and the problems you encountered. This is the largest section of the report and involves development, organization, and style (more on these later).

Conclusion/Recommendations

The conclusion allows you to sum up, to relate what you've learned, or to state what decisions you have made regarding the activities reported. The recommendations allow you to suggest future action, to state what you believe you and/or your company should do next.

CONCLUSION/RECOMMENDATIONS:

The conference was beneficial. It not only taught me how the computer can save us time and money, but also I received hands-on training. Because the computer can assist our billing and inventory control, let's buy and install three terminals in bookkeeping before our next quarter.

DEVELOPMENT

Now that you know what subdivisions are traditional in reports, your next question is, "What do I say in each section? How do I develop my ideas?"

First, answer the reporters' questions.

1. *Who* did you meet or contact, who was your liaison, who was involved in the accident, who comprised your technical team, etc.?
2. *When* did the activities documented occur (dates of travel, milestones, incidents, etc.)?
3. *Why* are you writing the report and/or why were you involved in the activity (rationale, justification, objectives)? Or, for a lab report, for example, why did the electrode, compound, equipment, or material act as it did?
4. *Where* did the activity take place?
5. *What* were the steps in the procedure, what conclusions have you reached, or what are your recommendations?

Second, when providing the foregoing information, *quantify!* Don't hedge or be vague or imprecise. Specify to the best of your abilities with photographic detail.

The following justification is an example of vague, imprecise writing.

> Installation of the machinery is needed to replace a piece of equipment deemed unsatisfactory by an Equipment Engineering review.

Which machine are we purchasing? Which piece of equipment will it replace? Why is the equipment unsatisfactory (too old, too expensive, too slow)? When does it need to be replaced? Where does it need to be installed? Why is the installation important?

A department supervisor will not be happy with the preceding report. Instead, supervisors need information *quantified,* as follows:

> The exposure table needs to be installed by 9/96 so that we can manufacture printed wiring products with fine line paths and spacing (down to .0005 inches). The table will replace the outdated printer in Dept. 76. Failure to install the table will slow the production schedule by 27%.

Note that the underlined words and phrases provide detail by quantifying.

STYLE

Style includes conciseness, simplicity, and highlighting techniques. As already discussed, you achieve conciseness by eliminating wordy phrases. Say *consider* rather than *take into consideration*; say *now* rather than *at this present time.* You achieve simplicity by avoiding old-fashioned words: *utilize* becomes *use, initiate* becomes *begin, supersedes* becomes *replaces.*

The value of highlighting has already been shown in this chapter. The parts of reports reviewed earlier use headings (Introduction, Discussion, Conclusion/Recommendation). Graphics can also be used to help communicate content, as evident in the following example. A recent demographic study of Kansas City predicted growth patterns for Johnson County (a large county south of Kansas City):

> Johnson County is expected to add 157,605 persons to its 1980 population of 270,269 by the year 2010. That population jump would be accompanied by a near doubling of the 96,925 households the county had in 1980. The addition of 131,026 jobs also is forecast for Johnson County by 2010, more than doubling its employment opportunity.

This report is difficult to access readily. We are overloaded with too much data. Luckily, the report provided a table (Table 14.1) for easier access to the data. Through highlighting techniques (tables, white space, headings), the demographic forecast is made accessible at a glance.

TYPES OF SHORT REPORTS: CRITERIA

All short reports include a heading (date, to, from, subject), an introduction, a discussion, and conclusion/recommendations. However, different types of short reports customize these generic components to meet specific needs. Let's look at the criteria

Table 14.1

Johnson County Predicted Growth by 2010

	POPULATION	HOUSEHOLDS	EMPLOYMENT
1980	270,269	96,925	127,836
2010	427,874	192,123	258,862
%change	+58.3%	+98.2%	+102%

for five common types of short reports: trip reports, progress reports, lab reports, feasibility reports, and incident reports.

TRIP REPORTS

When you leave your work site to go to a conference, analyze problems in another work environment, give presentations, or make sales calls, you must report on these work-related travels. Your supervisors not only require that you document your expenses and time while off site, but they also want to be kept up to date on your work activities. Following is an overview of what you'll include in an effective trip report.

1. **Heading**

   Date

   To

   From

   Subject (topic + focus)

2. **Introduction (overview, background)**

   Purpose: In the purpose section, document the date(s) and destination of your travel. Then comment on your objectives or rationale. What motivated the trip, what did you plan to achieve, what were your goals, why were you involved in job-related travel?

   You might also want to include these following optional subheadings:

   Personnel: With whom did you travel?

   Authorization: Who recommended or suggested that you leave your work site for job-related travel?

3. **Discussion (body, findings, agenda)**

   Using subheadings, document your activities. This can include a review of your observations, contacts, seminars attended, or difficulties encountered.

4. **Conclusion/recommendations**

Conclusion: What did you accomplish—what did you learn, who did you meet, what sales did you make, what of benefit to yourself, colleagues, and/or your company occurred?

Recommendations: What do you suggest next? Should the company continue on the present course (status quo) or should changes be made in personnel or in the approach to a particular situation? Would you suggest that other colleagues attend this conference in the future, or was the job-related travel not effective? In your opinion, what action should the company take?

Figure 14.1 presents an example of a trip report.

PROGRESS REPORTS

Your supervisors want to know what you're doing at work. They want to know what progress you're making on a project, whether you're on schedule, what difficulties you might have encountered, and/or what your plans are for the next reporting period. Because of this, supervisors ask you to write progress (or activity or status) reports—daily, weekly, monthly, quarterly, or annually. The following are components of an effective progress report.

1. Heading

Date

To

From

Subject: Include the topic about which you are reporting and the reporting interval (date).

Date:	May 31, 1996
To:	Joanna Freeman
From:	Lupe Salinas
Subject:	JANUARY PROGRESS REPORT ON SALES CALLS

2. Introduction (overview, background)

Objectives: These can include the following:

- Why are you working on this project (what's the rationale)?
- What problems motivated the project?
- What do you hope to achieve?
- Who initiated the activity?

Personnel: With whom are you working on this project (i.e., work team, liaison, contacts)?

DATE: February 26, 1996
TO: Pat Berry
FROM: Debbie Rulo DR
SUBJECT: TRIP REPORT—RENTON WEST SEMINAR ON ELECTRONIC PACKAGING

INTRODUCTION

On Tuesday, February 23, 1996, I attended the Renton West National Electronic Packaging Seminar, held in Ruidoso, NM. My goal was to acquire hands-on training and to learn new techniques for electronic packaging for our Telemetry Department. Also in attendance from our department were Richard DiBono and Bill Cole.

DISCUSSION

Richard, Bill, and I attended the following seminars:

- *Production Automation*
  This two-hour workshop was presented by Dr. Wang Ng, a noted scientist from Southwest Texas State University. During Dr. Ng's presentation, we reviewed four foam-encapsulation automated techniques for electronic packaging and received hands-on training. Dr. Ng worked individually with each seminar participant.

- *Vapor Phase Soldering*
  The hour-long presentation was facilitated by Garth Nelson, a manufacturing supervisor from Spark Welding and Soldering, Inc. (Colorado Springs, CO). Mr. Nelson showed a slide presentation on techniques for processing double-sided chip components.

- *Electronics for Extreme Temperatures*
  This hour-long presentation was led by Randy Towner and Leanna Wilson, professors at the University of Nevada, Las Vegas. Their scientific data on packaging under temperature extremes was accompanied by a workbook and a multimedia presentation.

- *Robotics and You*
  Denise Pakula, Canyon Electronics, Tempe, AR, spoke about her company's robotics packaging equipment. This

Figure 14.1 Trip Report

Page 2
Debbie Rulo
February 26, 1996

half-hour presentation focused on the various machines Canyon manufactures and their diverse capabilities.

CONCLUSION/RECOMMENDATION

Every presentation we attended was beneficial. However, the following information will clarify which workshop(s) would profit our company the most:

1. Dr. Ng's program was the most useful and informative. His interactive presentation skills were superb, including hands-on activities, small-group discussions, and individual instruction. Richard, Bill, and I suggest that you invite Dr. Ng to our site for further consultation and training.

2. Vapor phase soldering is costly. We could not pay back our investment within this quarter. In addition, Garth Nelson's training techniques are outdated—training videos are not as interactive as our personnel request in their annual training evaluations.

3. The Towner/Wilson scientific data on packaging under temperature extremes would benefit our supervisors, who are interested in up-to-date information. However, our new hires would be overwhelmed by the data. If we considered inviting these professors in for consultation, we would have to assess audience carefully.

4. Canyon Electronics' half-hour presentation was geared more to sales than to instruction. Ms. Pakula's focus was on new models of robotics equipment. Our current equipment is satisfactory. If the Purchasing Department is looking for new vendors, we could suggest that they contact Canyon.

Figure 14.1 Trip Report (Cont.)

Previous activity: If this is the second, third, fourth, etc. report in a series, remind your readers what work has already been accomplished. Bring them up-to-date with background data or a reference to previous reports.

3. **Discussion (findings, body, agenda)**

   Work accomplished: Using subheadings, itemize your work accomplished either through a chronological list or a discussion organized by importance.

   Work Remaining: Tell your reader what work you plan to accomplish next. List these activities, if possible, for easy access.

   A visual aid, such as a Gantt chart or a pie chart, fits well after these two sections. The chart will graphically depict both work accomplished and work remaining. (See Chapter 6 for discussions of Gantt and pie charts.)

   Problems encountered: Inform your reader(s) of any difficulties encountered (late shipments, delays, poor weather, labor shortages) not only to justify your possibly being behind schedule but also to show the readers where you'll need help to complete the project.

4. **Conclusion/Recommendations**

   Conclusion: Sum up what you've achieved during this reporting period and provide your target completion date.

   Recommendations: If problems were presented in the discussion, you can recommend changes in scheduling, personnel, budget, or materials which will help you meet your deadlines.

Figure 14.2 presents an example of a progress report.

LAB REPORTS

Professionals in electronics, engineering, medical fields, the computer industry, and other technologies often rank the ability to communicate as highly as they do technical skills. Conclusions derived from a technical procedure are worthless if they reside in a vacuum. The knowledge you acquire from a lab experiment *must* be communicated to your colleagues and supervisors so they can benefit from your discoveries. That's the purpose of a lab report—to document your findings. You write a lab report after you've performed a laboratory test to share with your readers

- Why the test was performed
- How the test was performed
- What the test results were
- What follow-up action (if any) is required

The following are components of a successful lab report.

DATE: April 2, 1996
TO: Buddy Ramos
FROM: Pat Smith *Pat*
SUBJECT: FIRST QUARTERLY REPORT—PROJECT 80 CONSTRUCTION

INTRODUCTION

In response to your December 10, 1995, request, following is our first quarterly report on Project 80 Construction (Downtown Airport). Department 93 is in the start-up phase of our company's FY1997 build plans for the downtown airport and surrounding site enhancements. These construction plans include the following:

1. Airport construction—terminals, runways, feeder roads, observation tower, parking lots, maintenance facilities.

2. Site enhancements—northwest and southeast collecting ponds, landscaping, berms, and signage.

DISCUSSION

Work Accomplished
In this first quarter, we've completed the following:

1. *Subcontractors:* Toby Summers and Karen Kuykendahl worked with our primary subcontractors (Apex Engineering and Knoblauch and Sons Architects). Toby and Karen arranged site visitations and confirmed construction schedules. This work was completed January 12, 1996.

2. *Permits:* Once site visitations were held and work schedules agreed upon, Karen and Toby acquired building permits from the city. They accomplished this task on January 20, 1996.

3. *Core Samples:* Core sample screening has been completed by Department 86 with a pass/fail ratio of 76.4 percent pass to 23.6 percent fail. This meets our goal of 75 percent. Sample screening was completed January 30, 1996.

Figure 14.2 Progress Report

Page 2
Pat Smith
April 2, 1996

4. *Shipments:* Timely concrete, asphalt, and steel beam shipments this quarter have provided us a 30-day lead on scheduled parts provisions. Materials arrived February 8, 1996.

5. *EPA Approval:* EPA agents have approved our construction plans. We are within guide-lines for emission controls, pollution, and habitat endangerment concerns. Sand cranes and pelicans nest near our building site. We have agreed to leave the north plat (40 acres) untouched as a wildlife sanctuary. This will cut into our parking plans. However, since the community will profit, we are pleased to make this concession. EPA approval occurred on February 15, 1996.

<u>Work Remaining</u>
To complete our project, we need to accomplish the following:

1. *Advertising:* Our advertising department is working on brochures, radio and television spots, and highway signs. Advertising's goal is to make the construction of a downtown airport a community point of pride and civic celebration.

2. *Signage:* With new roads being constructed for entrance and exit, our transportation department is working on street signage to help the public navigate our new roads.

   In addition, transportation is working with advertising on signage designs for the downtown airport's two entrances. These signs will juxtapose the city's symbol (a flying pelican) with an airplane taking off. The goal is to create a logo that simultaneously promotes the preservation of wildlife and suggests progress and community growth.

Figure 14.2 Progress Report (Cont.)

Page 3
Pat Smith
April 2, 1996

3. *Landscaping:* We are working with Anderson Brothers Turf and Surf to landscape the airport, roads, and two ponds. Our architectural design team, led by Fredelle Schneider, is selecting and ordering plants, as well as directing a planting schedule. Anderson Brothers also is in charge of the berms and pond dredging. Fredelle will be our contact person for this project.

4. *Construction:* The entire airport must be built. Thus, construction comprises the largest remaining task.

The Gantt Chart in Figure 1 clarifies our status at this time.

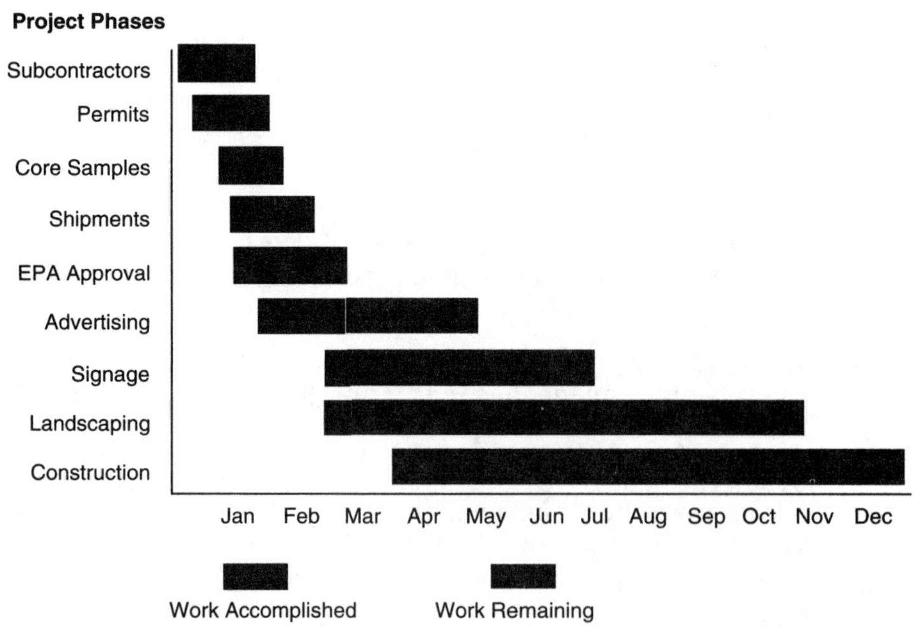

Figure 14.2 Progress Report (Cont.)

Page 4
Pat Smith
April 2, 1996

Problems Encountered

Core samples are acceptable throughout most of our construction site. However, the area set aside for the northwest pond had a heavy rock concentration. We believed this would cause no problem. Unfortunately, when Anderson Brothers began dredging, they hit rock which had to be removed with explosives. Since this northwest pond is near the sand crane and pelican nesting sites, EPA requested that we wait until the birds were resettled. The extensive rock removal and wait for wildlife resettlement has slowed our progress. We are behind schedule on this phase. This schedule delay and increased rock removal will affect our budget.

CONCLUSION/RECOMMENDATION

Though we have just begun this project, we still are approximately 15 percent of the way toward our goal. We anticipate a successful completion, especially since deliveries have been timely.

Only the delays at the northwest pond site present a problem. We are behind schedule and over cost. With additional personnel to speed the rock removal and increased funds, we can meet our target dates. Darlene Laughlin, our city council liaison, is the person to see about corporate investors, city funds, and big-ticket endowments. With your help, and Darlene's cooperation, we should meet our build schedules.

Figure 14.2 Progress Report (Cont.)

1. **Heading**

   Date

   To

   From

   Subject (topic + focus)

2. **Introduction (overview, background, purpose)**

   Why is this report being written? To answer this question, provide any or all of the following:

   - The rationale (What problem motivated this report?)
   - The objectives (What does this report hope to prove?)
   - Authorization (Under whose authority is this report being written?)

3. **Discussion (body, methodology)**

   How was the test performed? To answer this question, provide the following:

   - Apparatus (What equipment, approach, or theory have you used to perform your test?)
   - Procedure (What steps—chronologically organized—did you follow in performing the test?)

4. **Conclusion/recommendations**

   Conclusion: The conclusion of a lab report presents your findings. Now that you've performed the laboratory experiment, what have you learned or discovered or uncovered? How do you interpret your findings? What are the implications?

   Recommendations: What follow-up action (if any) should be taken?

You might want to use graphics to supplement your lab report. Schematics and wiring diagrams are important in a lab report to clarify your activities, as shown in Figure 14.3.

FEASIBILITY REPORTS (RECOMMENDATION REPORTS)

Occasionally, your company plans a project but is uncertain whether the project is feasible. For example, your company might be considering the purchase of equipment but is concerned that the machinery will be too expensive, the wrong size for your facilities, or incapable of performing the desired tasks. Perhaps your company wants to expand and is considering new locations. The decision makers, however, are uncertain which locations would be best for the expansion. Maybe your company wants to introduce a new product to the marketplace, but your CEO wants to be sure that a customer base exists before funds are allocated.

One way a company determines the viability of a project is to perform a feasibility study and then write a feasibility report documenting the findings. The following are components of an effective feasibility report.

Date: July 18, 1996
To: Dr. Jones
From: Sam Ascendio, Lab Technician *Sam*
Subject: LAB REPORT ON THE ACCURACY OF DECIBEL VOLTAGE GAIN (A) MEASUREMENTS

INTRODUCTION

Purpose
Technical Services has noted inaccuracies in recent measurements. In response to their request, this report will present results of tested A (gain in decibels) of our ABC voltage divider circuit. Measured A will be compared to calculated A. This will determine the accuracy of the measuring device.

DISCUSSION

Apparatus
- Audio generator
- Decade resistance box
- 1/2 W resistor: four 470 ohm, two 1 kilohm, 100 kilohm
- AC millivoltmeter

Procedure
1. Figure A shows a voltage divider. For each value of R (resistances) in Table 1, voltage gain was calculated (table attached).
2. An audio generator was adjusted to give a reading of 0 dB for input voltage.
3. Output voltage was measured on the dB scale. This reading is the measured A and is recorded in Table 1.
4. Step 3 was repeated for each value of R listed in Table 1.
5. Figure B shows three cascaded voltage dividers. A1 = v2/v1, A2 = v3/v2, and A3 = v4/v3. These voltage gains added together give the total voltage, as recorded in Table 2.
6. The circuit in Figure B was connected.
7. Input voltage was set at 0 dB on the 1-V range of the AC millivoltmeter.
8. Values V2, V3, and V4 were read and recorded in Table 3.

Figure 14.3 Lab Report

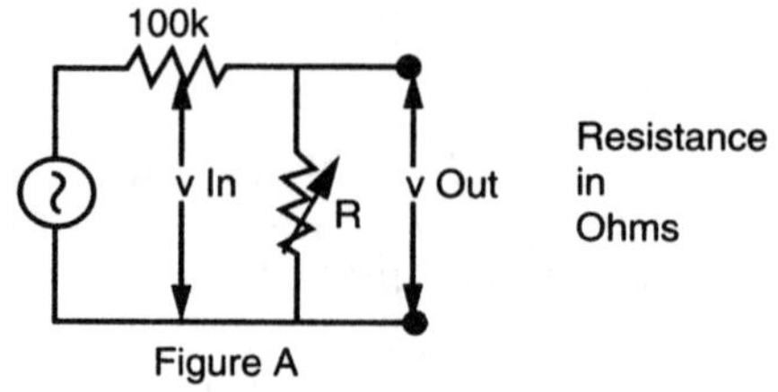

Figure A

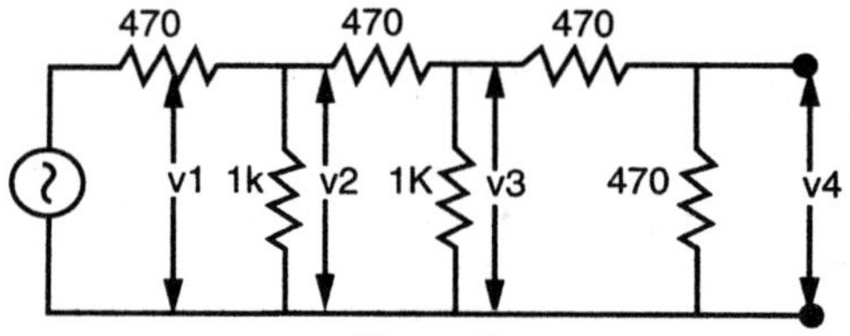

Figure B

TABLE 1

R	Calculated A	Measured A
240 kilohm	-3.02 dB	-3.21 dB
100 kilohm	-6.02 dB	-6.13 dB
46 kilohm	-10.00 dB	-9.71 dB
11 kilohm	-20.00 dB	-20.00 dB
1 kilohm	-40.00 dB	-40.00 dB

TABLE 2

A1	.500
A2	.500
A3	.500
A	.125

TABLE 3

V1	0 dB
V2	-5.97 dB
V3	-11.97 dB
V4	-18.06 dB

CONCLUSION/RECOMMENDATIONS

Accuracy between measured and calculated A in Table 1 was between .01 and .1 dB. This is acceptable. Accuracy between measured A in Table 3 and calculated voltage gain in Table 2 was between .01 and .1 dB—also very accurate. These tests show minimal error. No further action should be taken.

Figure 14.3 Lab Report (Cont.)

1. **Heading**
   Date
   To
   From
   Subject (topic + focus)

Subject: FEASIBILITY REPORT ON XYZ PROJECT
(focus) (topic)

2. **Introduction (overview, background)**

   Objectives: Under this subheading, you can answer any of the following questions:

   - What is the purpose of this feasibility report? Until you answer this question, your reader doesn't know. As mentioned earlier in this chapter, it's false to assume prior knowledge on the part of your audience. One of your responsibilities is to provide background data. To answer the question regarding the report's purpose, you should provide a clear and concise statement of intent.
   - What problems motivated this study? To clarify for your readers the purposes behind the study, *briefly* explain either

     —what problems cause doubt about the feasibility of the project (i.e., is there a market, is there a piece of equipment available which would meet the company's needs, is land available for expansion?)

     —what problems led to the proposed project (i.e., current equipment is too costly or time consuming, current facilities are too limited for expansion, current net income is limited by an insufficient market)
   - Who initiated the feasibility study? List the name(s) of the manager(s) or supervisor(s) who requested this report.

   Personnel: Document the names of your project team members, your liaison between your company and other companies involved, and/or your contacts at these other companies.

3. **Discussion (body, findings)**

   Under this subheading, provide accessible and objective documentation.

   Criteria: State the criteria upon which your recommendation will be based. Criteria are established so you have a logical foundation for comparison of personnel, products, vendors, costs, options, schedules, and so on.

   Analysis: In this section, compare your findings against the criteria. You might want to use a visual such as a table to organize the criteria and to provide easy access.

4. **Conclusion/recommendations**

   Conclusion: In this section, you go beyond the mere facts as evident in the discussion section: You state the significance of your findings. Draw a conclusion from what you've found in your study. For example, state that "Tim is the best candidate for Director of Personnel" or "Site 3 is the superior choice for our new location."

Recommendations: Once you've drawn your conclusions, the next step is to recommend a course of action. What do you suggest that your company do next? Which piece of equipment should be purchased, where should the company locate its expansion, or is there a sufficient market for the product?

Figure 14.4 presents an example of a feasibility report.

INCIDENT REPORTS

If a problem occurs within your work environment that requires investigation and suggested solutions, you might be asked to prepare an *incident report* (also called a *trouble report* or *accident report*).

Engineering environments requiring maintenance reports rarely provide employees with easy-to-fill-in forms. To write an incident report when you have not been given a printed form, include the following components.

1. **Heading**

   Date

   To

   From

   Subject (topic + focus)

Subject: REPORT ON CHILLED WATER LEAKS IN D/823
(focus) (topic)

2. **Introduction**

   Purpose: In this section, document when, where, and why you were called to perform maintenance. What motivated your visit to the scene of the problem?

3. **Discussion (body, findings, agenda, work accomplished)**

   Using subheadings or itemization, quantify what you saw (the problems motivating the activity) and what you did to solve the problem.

4. **Conclusion**

   Explain what caused the problem.

5. **Recommendations**

   Relate what could be done in the future to avoid similar problems.

Figure 14.5 presents an example of an incident report.

DATE: August 13, 1996
TO: Pat Hobby
FROM: Nick Adams NA
SUBJECT: RECOMMENDED PURCHASE OF THREE AAA VIDEO CASSETTE RECORDERS (VCRs)

INTRODUCTION

Purpose

The purpose of this report is to recommend the purchase of three new VCRs.

Problem

We need these VCRs in the Management Development Training Department for the following reasons:

1. Currently, our two ABC VCRs (purchased in 1990) break down approximately twice per week. When this occurs, they are unusable for ten hours per week and cost the department $150 each for weekly repairs.
2. Our department has acquired four new trainers. We offer 25 percent more management development courses this year than we did last year. Enrollment has increased 115 percent. These factors, coupled with the increased use of video presentations, require working VCRs.

Personnel

Our vendor contacts are as follows:

ABC Electeck	XYZ Inc.	AAA Electronic
Steve Ross	Jay Rochlin	Karen Allen
415-628-9704	415-489-7286	415-459-3872

DISCUSSION

Criteria

The following criteria were considered when I compared the three top-selling VCRs:

1. Maintenance—We need to purchase a VCR which comes with a frequent (either quarterly or biannual) service agreement (at no extra charge).

Figure 14.4 Feasibility Report

Page 2
Nick Adams
August 13, 1996

2. Service Personnel—The service people should be trained by the company that sells the VCR.
3. Warranty—The warranty should be for at least one year.
4. Cost—The VCR should cost no more than $1,000.

Analysis of Three VCRs

The following table compares the top three VCRs we researched:

Table 1 Criteria Comparison

CRITERIA	AAA	ABC	XYZ
Maintenance Package	Quarterly	Biannual	No Options
Service Personnel	AAA Certified	Subcontracted	No Options
Warranties	1 Year Parts and Labor	90 Days Parts and Labor	1 Year Parts and Labor
Cost	$950.00	$899.99	$1,500.00

CONCLUSION

Although The ABC and XYZ VCRs are good pieces of equipment, neither meets all our criteria. In particular, their service personnel are not trained by the VCR manufacturers. Also, the XYZ VCR, our current model, is the most expensive and offers the fewest service options.

RECOMMENDATION

Given the combination of cost, service contracts, and warranties, AAA is our best choice for purchase. With three, new AAA VCRs, we will be able to offer more efficient and effective seminars to a greater number of company personnel.

Figure 14.4 Feasibility Report (Cont.)

Date: October 16, 1996
To: Tom Warner
From: Carlos Sandia CS
Subject: REPORT ON CHILLED WATER LEAKS IN D/823

INTRODUCTION

On October 15, 1996, a flood was reported in D/823. I was called in to repair this leak. Following is a report on my findings and maintenance activities.

DISCUSSION

Agenda

8:15 p.m.	The flood was reported.
8:25 p.m.	I arrived at D/823 and discovered that the water level in the expansion tank at HVAC unit #253R-01 was 4 feet above normal and the tank valve was open.
8:30 p.m.	A second flood was reported at HVAC unit #937-01 in the same department.
8:35 p.m.	I shut off the open tank valves.
9:00 p.m.	The expansion tank levels and pressure returned to normal.
9:30 p.m.	All leaks were secure.

CONCLUSION

The chilled water leaks were caused by a malfunctioning level switch on the chilled water expansion tanks in the west boiler rooms. This caused the water level in the tanks to rise, which increased the system pressure to 150 lb.

RECOMMENDATIONS

The level control switch will be repaired. An alarm system will be installed by November 1, 1996.

Figure 14.5 Incident Report

PROCESS

Now that you know the criteria for short reports in general and for specific types of short reports (trip reports, progress reports, lab reports, feasibility reports, and incident reports), the next step is to construct these reports. How do you begin? As always, *prewrite, write,* and *rewrite.*

PREWRITING

We've presented several techniques for prewriting—reporters' questions, clustering/mind mapping, flowcharting, and brainstorming/listing. An additional technique is called *branching.*

As with flowcharting and mind mapping, branching allows you to depict information graphically so you can not only gather data but also visualize it. This type of prewriting benefits both left-brain and right-brain people—those who are linear (outline oriented) as well as those who are more graphically attuned. Figure 14.6 shows an example of branching.

Branching is ideally suited for short reports. You can focus on whether the primary subject is a trip report, progress report, lab report, feasibility report, or incident report in the *main idea.* In addition, the *subordinate points* easily correspond to the introduction, discussion, and conclusion/recommendations. Finally, you can develop your ideas more specifically in the *subheadings.* Figure 14.7 shows an example of branching for a trip report.

You can see in Figure 14.7 how branching meshes with reporters' questions. Branching allows you to sketch out your organization and visualize your content. The reporters' questions help you make that content factual, precise, specific, and quantified.

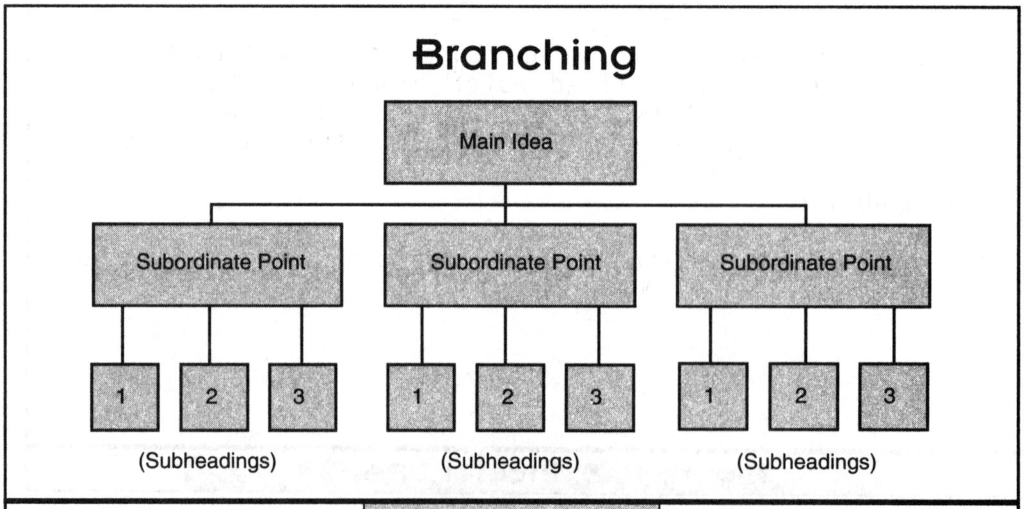

Figure 14.6

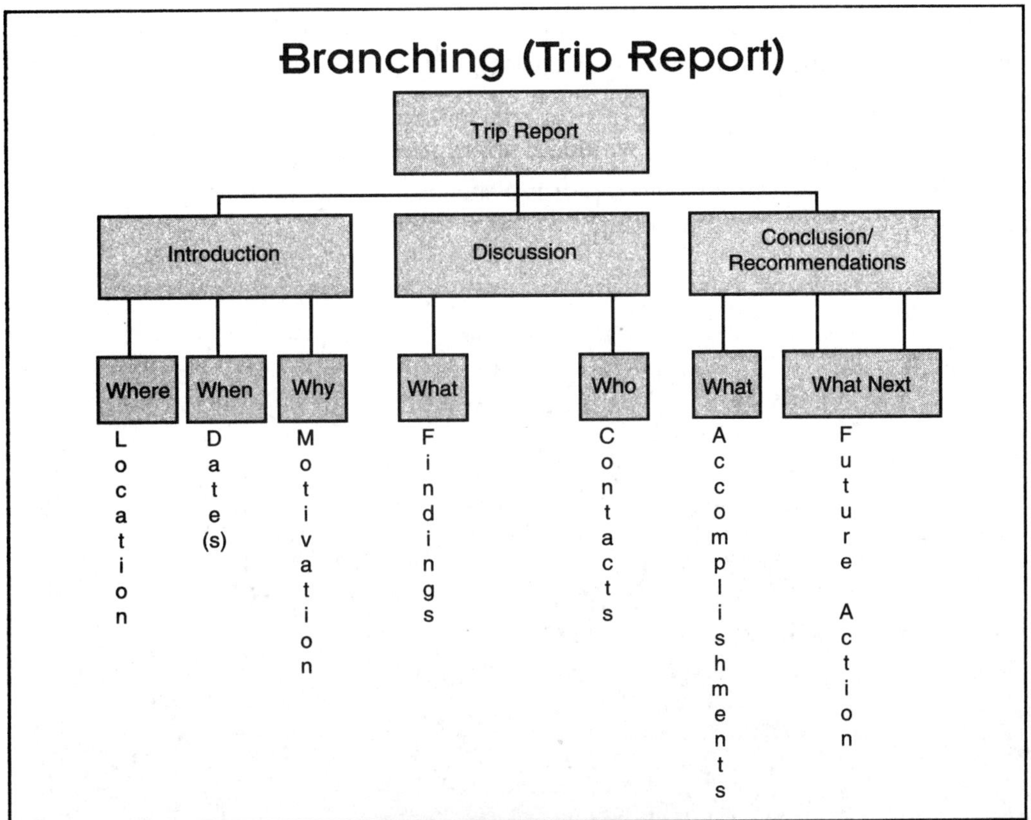

Figure 14.7

WRITING

Once you've sketched an outline for your report using branching, the next step is to write the text. To write your report, do the following:

1. *Reread your prewriting.* Review what you've sketched in branching. Determine whether you've covered all important information. If you believe you've omitted any significant points, add them for clarity. If you've included any irrelevant ideas, omit them for conciseness.

2. *Assess your audience.* Your decisions regarding points to omit or include will depend on your audience. If your audience is familiar with your subject, you might be able to omit background data. However, if you have multiple audiences or an audience new to the situation, you'll have to include more data than you might have assumed necessary in your prewriting.

3. *Draft the text.* Focusing on your major headings (introduction, discussion, conclusion/recommendations), use the sufficing technique mentioned in earlier chapters. Just get your ideas down on paper in a rough draft without worrying about grammar.

4. Organize your content. You can organize the discussion portion of your report using any one of these four modes: *chronology, importance, comparison/contrast,* and *problem/solution.* Which of these modes you use depends on your subject matter.

For example, if the subject of your trip report is a price check of sales items at two stores, comparison/contrast would be appropriate, as in Figure 14.8.

If the subject of your incident report is a site evaluation, chronology might work in the report's discussion, as in the following example:

DISCUSSION

8:00 A.M.	I arrived at the site and met with the supervisor to discuss procedures.
9:00 A.M.	We checked the water tower for possible storm damage. Only 10 shingles were missing.
10:00 A.M.	We checked the irrigation channel. It was severely damaged, the wall cracked in six places and water seeping through its barriers. Surrounding orchards will be flooded.
11:00 A.M.	We checked fruit bins. No water had entered.
1:00 P.M.	We checked the freezer units. The storm had disrupted electricity for four hours. All contents were destroyed.
2:00 P.M.	The supervisor and I returned to his office to evaluate our findings.

As discussed in earlier chapters, chronology is an easy method of organization to use and to follow. However, it is not always your most successful choice. Chronology inadvertently buries key data. For instance, in the preceding report findings, the most important discoveries occur at 10:00 A.M. and at 1:00 P.M., hidden in the middle of the list. To avoid making your readers guess where the important information is, use the third method of organization—importance—in which you list the most important point first, lesser points later, as in the following example:

DISCUSSION

1. Freezer units: Electricity was out for four hours. All contents were destroyed.
2. Irrigation channel: The wall was cracked in six places. Seepage was significant and sure to affect the orchards.
3. Water tower: Minor damage to shingles.
4. Fruit bins: No damage.

To: Meagan Clem
From: Mary Jane Post *Mary Jane*
Date: January 12, 1996
Subject: PRICE CHECK REPORT—HANDY SANDY HARDWARE

INTRODUCTION

On Thursday, January 8, 1996, I compared our sales prices on plumbing items with those on sale at Handy Sandy Hardware, 1000 W. 29th St., Newtown, WI.

DISCUSSION

Item	Hughes's Sale Price	Handy Sandy's Sale Price
1/2" copper tubing	$4.89 (10')	$4.99 (10')
3/4" copper tubing	10.50 (10')	9.99 (10')
1/2" CPVC pipe	2.39 (10')	2.99 (10')
3/4" CPVC pipe	3.49 (10')	5.99 (10')
1 1/2" PVC pipe	3.99 (10')	4.99 (10')
Acme 800 faucet	40.95	39.95
Acme 700 faucet	22.95	25.95

CONCLUSION

On five of the seven items (71.4%), Hughes's had the lower price.

RECOMMENDATIONS

We should continue to compare our prices to Handy Sandy's. We should also try to lower our prices which exceed theirs.

Figure 14.8 Trip Report Organized by Comparison/Contrast

If you're writing a progress report to document a problem and suggest a solution, use problem/solution to organize your data, as follows:

DISCUSSION

Problem—Production schedules on our M23 and B19 are behind three weeks due to machinery failures. Our numerical control device no longer maintains tolerance. This is forcing us to rework equipment, which is costing us $200 per reworked piece.

Solution—We must purchase a new numerical control device. The best option is an Xrox 1234. This machine is guaranteed for five years. Any problems with tolerance during this period are covered. Xrox either will correct the errors on site or provide us a loaner until the equipment is fixed. To avoid further production delays, we must purchase this machine by 1/18/96.

REWRITING

After a gestation period in which you let the report sit so you can become more objective about your writing, retrieve the report and rewrite. Perfect your text by using the following rewriting techniques:

1. *Add detail for clarity.* Have you answered the reporters' questions as thoroughly as needed? Don't assume your readers will know the why's and wherefore's. Spell it all out, exactly. You often have multiple readers, many of whom do not know your motivations or objectives. They need clarity.

2. *Delete dead words and phrases for conciseness.* For example, in your recommendations, don't say, "Acme's opinion is that apparently the proposed ideas will not successfully supersede those already implemented." Instead, simply write, "Recommendations: No further action is required."

3. *Simplify old-fashioned words and phrases.* What does *pursuant* mean? And how about *issuance of this report?* The ultimate goal of technical writing is to communicate, not to confuse.

4. *Move information within your discussion for emphasis.* Make sure that you've either maintained chronology (if you're documenting an agenda) or used importance to focus on your main point. If you've confused the two, cut and paste—move information around to achieve your desired goals.

5. *Reformat your text for accessibility.* Highlight your key points with underlining or boldface. Use graphics to assist your readers. Don't overload your readers with massive blocks of impenetrable text.

6. *Enhance your text for style.* Be sure to quantify when needed, personalize with pronouns for audience involvement, and be positive. Stress words like *benefit, success-*

ful, achieved, and *value* rather than bowing to negative words like *can't, failed, confused,* or *mistaken.*

7. *Proofread and correct the report for grammatical and contextual accuracy.*

8. *Avoid sexist language. Foreman* should be *supervisor, chairman* should be *chairperson* or *chair,* and *Mr. Swarth, Mr. James, and Sue* must be *Mr. Swarth, Mr. James, and Ms. Aarons.*

Use the following short-report criteria checklist to help you in writing your short report.

SHORT REPORT CRITERIA CHECKLIST

1. *Does your subject line contain a topic and a focus?* If you write only "Subject: TRIP REPORT" or "Subject: FEASIBILITY REPORT," you have not communicated thoroughly to your reader. Such a subject line merely presents the focus of your correspondence. But what's the topic? To provide both topic and focus, you need to write "Subject: TRIP REPORT ON SOLVENT TRAINING COURSE, ARCO CORPORATION—3/15/96" or "Subject: FEASIBILITY REPORT ON COMPANY EXPANSION TO BOLKER BLVD."
2. *Does the introduction explain the purpose of the report, document the personnel involved, and/or state when and where the activities occurred?*
3. *When you write the discussion section of the report, do you quantify what occurred?* In this section, you must clarify precisely. Supply accurate dates, times, calculations, and problems encountered.
4. *Is the discussion accessible?* To create reader-friendly ease of access, use highlighting techniques, such as headings, boldface, underlining, and itemization. You also might want to use graphics, such as pie charts, bar charts, or tables.
5. *Have you selected an appropriate method of organization in your discussion?* You can use chronology, importance, comparison/contrast, and/or problem/solution to document your findings.
6. *Does your conclusion present a value judgment regarding the findings presented in the discussion?* The discussion states the facts; the conclusion decides what these facts mean.
7. *In your recommendations, do you tell your reader(s) what to do next or what you consider to be the appropriate course of action?*
8. *Have you maintained a low fog index for readability?*
9. *Have you effectively recognized your audience's level of understanding (high tech, low tech, lay, management, subordinate, colleague) and written accordingly?*
10. *Is your report accurate?* Correct grammar and calculations make a difference. If you've made errors in spelling, punctuation, grammar, or mathematics, you will look unprofessional.

PROCESS LOG

Let's look at how one student used the writing process (prewriting, writing, and rewriting) to construct her progress report.

PREWRITING

First, the student used branching so she could visually gather data and determine objectives (Figure 14.9).

WRITING

Next, the student wrote a quick draft without worrying about correctness. She focused on the main units of the information she discovered in prewriting (Figure 14.10).

REWRITING

After drafting this report, the student submitted her copy to a peer review group, which helped her revise her text (Figure 14.11).

After discussing the suggested changes with her peer review group, the student revised her draft and submitted her finished copy (Figure 14.12).

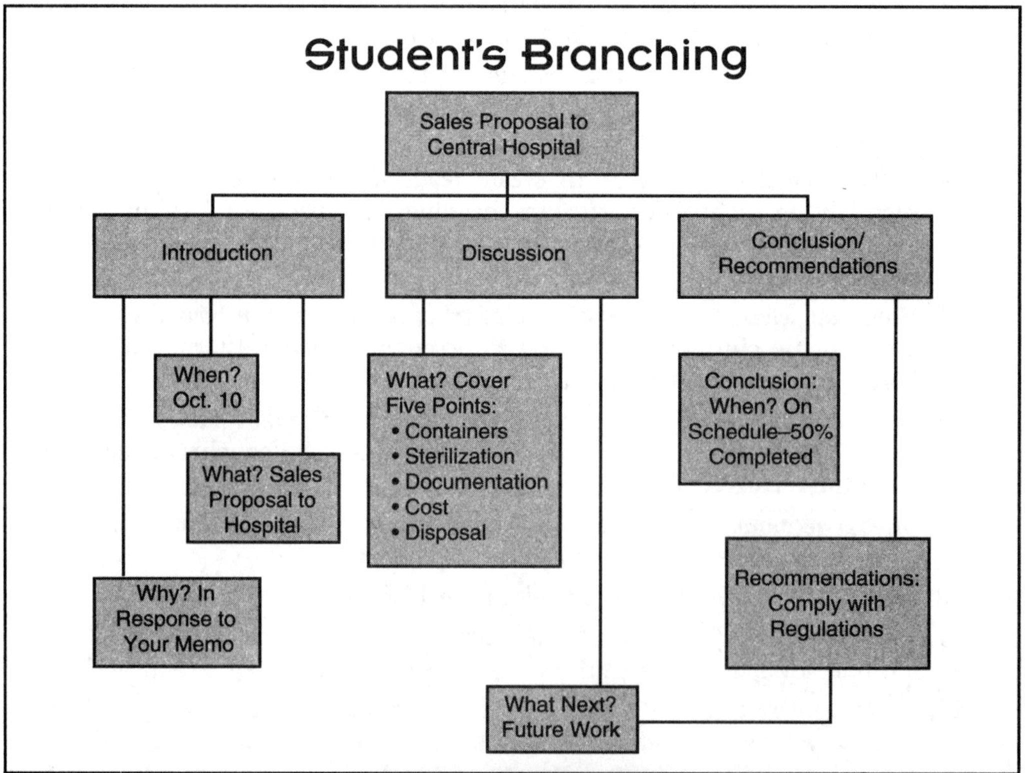

Figure 14.9

November 6, 1996

To: Carolyn Jensen
From: Shuan Wang.
Subject: PROGRESS REPORT.

Purpose: This is a progress report on the status of a sales proposal you requested in your memo of October 10, 1996. The objective of this proposal is the sale of a total program for infectious waste control and disposal to a Central Hospital. The proposal will cover the following five areas.

1. Containers
2. Steam sterilization
3. Cost savings
4. Landfill operating
5. Computerized documentation

Work Completed: The following is a list of items that are finished on the project.

Containers
I have finished a description of the specially designed containers with disposable biohazard bag.

Steam sterilization
I have set a instructions for using the Biological Detector, model BD 12130 as a reliable indicator of sterilization of infectious wastes.

Cost savings
Central Hospital sent me some information on installing a pathological incinerator as well as the constant manpower and maintenance costs to operate them. I ran this information through our computer program “Save-Save”. The results show that a substantial savings will be realized by the use of our services.

Future Work: I have an appointment to visit Central Hospital on November 7, 1996. At that time I will make on-site evaluations of present waste handling practices at Central Hospital. After carefully studying this evaluations, I will report to you on needed changes to comply with governmental guidelines.

Conclusion: The project is proceeding on schedule. Approximately 50 percent of work is done (see graph). I don’t see any problem at this time and should be able to meet the target date.

Figure 14.10 Student's Rough Draft

November 6, 1996

To: Carolyn Jensen

From: Shuan Wang X

Subject: PROGRESS REPORT X

Needs topic & focus

Reformat underline & use all CAPS

Purpose: This is a progress report on the status of a sales proposal you requested in your memo of October 10, 1996. The objective of this proposal is the sale of a total program for infectious waste control and disposal to a Central Hospital. The proposal will cover the following five areas. *weak word*

Redundant *wordy?*

1. Containers
2. Steam sterilization
3. Cost savings
4. Landfill operating *–Needs new title*
5. Computerized documentation

Reformat

Work Completed: The following is a list of items that are finished on the project. *wordy*

Containers
I have finished a description of the specially designed containers with disposable biohazard bag. *when?*

Steam sterilization *Huh?*
I have set a instructions for using the Biological Detector, model BD 12130 as a reliable indicator of sterilization of infectious wastes. *wordy* *when*

Cost savings
Central Hospital sent me some information on installing a pathological incinerator as well as the constant manpower and maintenance costs to operate them. I ran this information through our computer program "Save-Save". The results show that a substantial savings will be realized by the use of our services. *vague* *vague*

Figure 14.11 Peer Group Revisions

Reformat

Future Work: I have an appointment to visit Central Hospital on November 7, 1996. At that time I will make on-site evaluations of present waste handling practices at Central Hospital. After carefully studing this evaluations, I will report to you on needed changes to comply with governmental guidelines. SP

Reformat

Conclusion: The project is proceeding on schedule. Approximately 50 percent of work is done (see graph). I don't see any problem at this time and should be able to meet the target date.

Figure 14.11 Peer Group Revisions (Cont.)

INTEROFFICE CORRESPONDENCE

DATE: November 6, 1996
TO: Carolyn Jensen
FROM: Shuan Wang SW
SUBJECT: PROGRESS REPORT ON CENTRAL HOSPITAL SALES PROPOSAL

INTRODUCTION

Purpose
In response to your October 10, 1996, request, following is a report on the status of our Central Hospital sales proposal. This proposal will present Central Hospital our total program for infectious waste control and disposal. The proposal will cover these five topics:

- Containers
- Steam sterilization
- Cost savings
- On-site evaluations
- Landfill disposal

DISCUSSION

Work Completed

1. *Containers*—On October 5, I finished a description of the specially designed containers with biohazard bags.
2. *Steam sterilization*—On November 4, I wrote instructions for using our Biological Detector, model BG 12130. This detector measures infectious waste sterilization levels.
3. *Cost savings*—Central Hospital sent me their cost charts for pathological incinerator expenses and maintenance costs. I used our computer program "Save-Save" to evaluate these costs. The program results show that our services can save Central Hospital $15,000 per year on annual incinerator costs, after a two-year break-even period.

Figure 14.12 Final Copy

Page 2
Shuan Wang
November 6,1996

Central Hospital $15,000 per year on annual incinerator costs, after a two-year break-even period.

Work Remaining

1. *On-site evaluations*—When I visit Central Hospital on November 11, 1996, I will evaluate their present waste handling system. After studying these evaluations, I will report changes necessary for government compliance.
2. *Landfill disposal*—I will contact the Environmental Protection Agency on November 13, 1996, to receive authorization for disposing sterilized waste at our sanitary landfill.

CONCLUSION

The project is proceeding on schedule. Approximately 55 percent of our work is completed. I see no problems at this time. We should meet our December 31, 1996, target date.

Figure 14.12 Final Copy (Cont.)

ACTIVITIES

Writing and Analyzing Reports

1. Write a progress report. The subject of this report can involve a project or activity at work. Or, if you haven't been involved in job-related projects, write about the progress you're making in this class or another course you're taking. Write about the progress you're making on a home improvement project (refinishing a basement, constructing a deck, painting and papering a room). Write about the progress you're making on a hobby (rebuilding an antique car, constructing a computer, or making model trains, etc.). Whatever your topic, first prewrite (using branching), then write a draft, and, finally, postwrite, revising the text. Abide by all the criteria presented in this chapter regarding progress reports.
2. Write a lab report. The subject of this report can involve a test you're running at work or in one of your classes. Whatever topic you select, follow the three stages in the writing process to construct your report: Prewrite (using branching), write a draft, and then revise the draft in postwriting. Use the criteria regarding lab reports presented in this chapter to help you write the report.
3. Write a feasibility report. You can draw your topic either from your work environment or home. For example, if you and your colleagues are considering the purchase of new equipment, the implementation of a new procedure, expansion to a new location, or the marketing of a new product, you could study this idea and then write a feasibility report on your findings. If nothing at work lends itself to this topic, then consider plans at home. For example, are you and your family planning a vacation, the purchase of a new home or car, the renovation of your basement, or a new business venture? If so, study this situation. Research car and home options, study the market for a new business, and/or get bids for the renovation. Then write a feasibility report to your family documenting your findings. Whether your topic comes from business or home, gather your data in prewriting (using branching), draft your text in writing, and then revise in rewriting. Follow the criteria for feasibility reports provided in this chapter to help you write the report.
4. Write an incident report. You can select a topic either from work or home. If you have encountered a problem at work, write an incident report documenting the problem and providing your solutions to the incident. If nothing has happened at work lending itself to this topic, then look at home. Has your car broken down, did the water heater break, did you or any members of your family have an accident of any sort, did your dog or cat knock over the vase your mother-in-law gave you for Christmas? Consider such possibilities, and then write an incident report documenting the incident. Follow the criteria for incident reports provided in this chapter, and use writing process techniques (prewriting, writing, and rewriting).

Team Projects

1. Find examples of lab reports, trip reports, progress reports, feasibility reports, and/or incident reports. You can find these at your company or visit another job site. Bring these reports to class. Then, using the criteria presented in this chapter, form small groups and discuss whether the reports are successful or unsuccessful. If they are good, specify how and why. If they are flawed, discuss what's wrong, prescribe solutions, and rewrite the reports to improve them.
2. Look around your company or visit another job site and find examples of short reports not discussed in this chapter. Bring these reports to class. Then, using the criteria for short reports presented in this chapter, form small groups and discuss how these unique reports differ from or abide by the criteria we've presented. Also discuss whether the reports you've found are successful or unsuccessful. If they are good, discuss why and how. If they are flawed, talk about how they could be improved and rewrite them.
3. Interview an employee and a supervisor in your profession or the field of your choice. Ask these people why they write reports, what their reports are supposed to accomplish, who their audiences are, what length reports are preferred in their company, how many reports they write in a week or month, and so on. Use your imagination regarding the questions you ask. Then, once you've received your answers, form small groups and convey your findings to your classmates. To do so, either present an oral presentation or—better yet—write a group report!
4. As a class, take a field trip. Visit a publishing firm, see a play, go to a museum, hear a guest speaker on campus, or interview a professional technical writer, for example. Then, in small groups, write a trip report about your observations. Once the reports are written, compare and contrast the writing. Which group of students (or which student) has written the best report? To make this judgment, specify why the report is successful. Doing so will provide for the class a model of good writing, as agreed on by class consensus. Class members can replicate this report for future success. In addition, discuss how less successful reports fell short of the desired objectives. This will help show students what to avoid in future report-writing activities.
5. Revision is the key to good writing. An example of a seriously flawed progress report that needs revising is shown in Figure 14.13. To improve this report, form small groups and first decide what's missing according to this chapter's criteria for good progress reports. Then, use the rewriting techniques presented in this chapter to rewrite and revise the report.

Case Studies

In small groups, read the following case studies and write a feasibility report.

1. You manage an engineering department at Acme Aerospace. Your current department supervisor is retiring. Thus, you must recommend the promotion

DT1234 Test Equipment Project

Date: February 17, 1996 SL
Software Engineer: Sylvia Light
Section Supervisor: Sam Tintereto

Responsibilities:
- Test Executives
- Test Routines
- Calibration
- Enhancements
- Troubleshooting Software

Test Executives:	Complete	Incomplete
Entry	X	
Troubleshooting		X
Calibration		X
Enhancements		X

Test Routines:	Complete	Incomplete
ProLog		X
PreSet		X
Flight		X
Switch		X
Contact		X
Clear		X

Peripherals:	Complete	Incomplete
6000		X
5335		X
1001		X
4250		X

Note: All calibrations, enhancements, and troubleshooting software are incomplete.

Figure 14.13 Flawed Report

of a new supervisor to the company's executive officer, Kelly Adams. You know that Acme seeks to promote individuals who have the following traits:

- Familiarity with modern management techniques and concerns, such as TQM (Total Quality Management), teamwork, global economics, and the management of hazardous materials.
- An ability to work well with colleagues (subordinates, lateral peers, and management).
- Thorough knowledge of one's areas of expertise.

You have the following candidates for promotion. Using the information provided about each and the criteria for feasibility reports discussed in this chapter, write your report recommending your choice for a new supervisor.

A. *Pat Jefferson:* Pat has worked for Acme for 12 years. Pat, in fact, has worked up to his or her position as a lead engineer by having started as an assembler, then working in test equipment, quality control, and environmental safety and health (ESH). As an engineer in ESH, Pat was primarily in charge of hazardous waste disposal. Pat's experience is lengthy, although he or she has only taken two years of college coursework and one class in management techniques. Pat is well liked by all colleagues and is considered to be a team player.

B. *Kim Kennedy:* Kim is a relatively new employee at Acme, having worked for the company for two years. Kim was hired directly out of college where Kim earned an M.B.A. degree from the Mountaintop College School of Management. As such, Kim is extremely familiar with today's management climate and modern management techniques. Kim's undergraduate degree was a B.S. in business with a minor in engineering. Currently, Kim works in the engineering department as a departmental liaison, communicating the engineering department's concerns to Acme's other departments. Kim has developed a reputation as an excellent coworker who is well liked by all levels of employees.

C. *Chris Clinton:* Chris has a B.S. degree in engineering from Poloma College and an M.B.A. degree from Weatherford University. Prior to working for Acme, Chris served on the IEEE (Institute of Electrical and Electronic Engineering) Commission for Management Innovation, specializing in global concerns and Total Quality Management. In 1991, Chris was hired by Acme; since being hired, he or she has worked in various capacities. Chris is now lead engineer in the engineering Department. Chris has earned high scores on every yearly evaluation, especially regarding his or her knowledge of engineering. Whenever you have needed assistance with new management techniques, Chris has been a valued resource. Chris's only negative points on evaluations have resulted from difficulties with colleagues, some of whom regard Chris as haughty.

Who will you recommend for supervisor? Write your feasibility report stating your decision.

2. You are the accountant at AAA Computing, a retail store specializing in computer hardware. Your boss states that all new computers sold should be accompanied by an optional service contract. This service will be held by an outside vendor. Your job is to research several vendors and write a feasibility report recommending the best choice for your company. To do so, you know your boss will emphasize the following criteria:

   - Years in business/expertise—to be sure that customers receive quality service, the vendor should have a good track record and be familiar with computer hardware innovations.
   - Quick response/turnaround—since many of your customers depend on their computers for daily business operations, the vendor should provide on-site service for minor repairs and 24-hour turnaround service on major repairs.
   - Cost-effective pricing—the less the vendor charges, the more you can mark up the service cost. Thus, AAA can receive more profit.

   The following vendors have proposed their services. Using the information provided about each company and the criteria for feasibility reports provided in this chapter, write your report recommending a vendor for AAA's service contracts.

   A. *QuickBit:* This company has 16 months experience in computer hardware service. QuickBit, although without a lengthy track record, is co-owned by three graduates of the Silicon Valley Institute of Technology's renowned B.A. program in computer information services. The three individuals are very knowledgeable about computers, having received superior instruction and hands-on training using today's most up-to-date technology. Because QuickBit is small, it can provide immediate, 24-hour on-call service. Furthermore, QuickBit owns a twelve-wheeler truck fully stocked with parts. Therefore, all service can be handled on site. QuickBit charges $50 per hour plus parts.
   B. *ROM on the Run:* This company has been in business for ten years. They employ 50 servicepeople, have a lengthy track record, and have provided service for ARC Telecommunications, Capital Bank, Helping Hand Hospital, and the State Penitentiary at Round Rock. Because of their years in business and the fact that all their employees have at least two-year certificates from vocational colleges, they charge $85.50 per hour plus parts. ROM on the Run promises on-site service within 24 hours of all service requests.
   C. *You Bet Your Bytes (YBYB):* YBYB has been in business for four years, employs ten servicepeople (all of whom have at least a B.S. degree in com-

puter systems), and specializes in retail outlets. YBYB charges $70 per hour plus parts. They advertise that they respond within thirty minutes for on-site service calls. Furthermore, they advertise that most parts are carried on their service trucks. Any repairs requiring unavailable parts can be made within 24 hours if the service call is received by 3:30 P.M. Calls after that time require two working days.

Which company do you recommend? Write the feasibility report stating your choice.

3. Your company, Telecommunication R Us (TRU), has experienced a 45 percent increase in business, a 37 percent increase in warehoused stock, and a 23 percent increase in employees. You need more room. Your executive officer, Polina Gertsberg, has asked you to research existing options. To do so, you know you must consider these criteria:

- *Ample space for further expansion:* Gertsberg suggests that TRU could experience further growth upwards of 150 percent. You need to consider room for parking, warehouse space, additional offices, and a cafeteria—approximately 20,000 sq. ft. total.
- *Cost:* Twenty million dollars should be the top figure, with a preferred payback of five years at 10 percent.
- *Location:* Most of your employees and customers live within 15 miles of your current location. This has worked well for deliveries and employee satisfaction. A new location within this 15-mile radius is preferred.
- *Aesthetics:* Ergonomics suggest that a beautiful site improves employee morale and increase productivity.

After research, you've found three possible sites. Based on the following information and on the criteria for feasibility reports discussed in this chapter, write your report recommending a new office site.

A. *Site 1 (11717 Grandview):* This four-story site, located 12 miles from your current site, offers three floors of finished space equaling 18,000 sq. ft. The fourth floor is an unfinished shell equaling an additional 3,000 sq. ft. As is, the building will sell for $19 million. If the current owner finishes the fourth floor, the addition would cost $4 million more. For the building as is, the owner asks for payment in five years at 12 percent interest. If the fourth floor is finished by the owner, payment is requested in seven years at 10 percent. The building has ample parking space but no cafeteria, although a building next door has available food services. Site 1 is nestled in a beautifully wooded area with hiking trails and picnic facilities.

B. *Site 2 (808 W. Blue Valley):* This one-story building offers 21,000 sq. ft. that includes 100 existing offices, a warehouse capable of holding eighty storage bins that measure 20-ft. tall × 60 yds. long × 8 ft. wide, and a full-service cafeteria. Because the complex is one story, it takes up 90 percent of the lot, leaving only 10 percent for parking. Additional parking is located across an eight-lane highway which can be crossed via a foot bridge. The building, located 18 miles from your current site, has an asking price of $22 million at 8.75 percent interest for five years. Site 2 has a corn field to its east, the highway to its west, a small lake to its north where flocks of geese nest, and a strip mall to its south.

C. *Site 3 (1202 Red Bridge Avenue):* This site is 27 miles from your current location. It has three stories offering 23,000 sq. ft., a large warehouse with four-bay loading dock, and a cafeteria with ample seating and vending machines for food and drink. Because this site is located near a heavily industrialized area, the asking price is $15 million at 7.5 percent interest for five years.

Which site do you recommend? Write your feasibility report stating your choice.

Chapter 11

ORAL PRESENTATIONS

- OBJECTIVES
- TYPES OF ORAL PRESENTATIONS
- CRITERIA FOR EFFECTIVE ORAL PRESENTATIONS
- PROCESS
- POST SPEECH ACTIVITIES

OBJECTIVES

Many confident and successful people are frightened by the idea of giving an oral presentation. This chapter suggests ways to prepare and to present information verbally so the experience will be rewarding rather than frightening.

Too often college students fail to realize the importance of speech classes, or they may be in a curriculum which does not require oral communication classes. However, after they graduate and begin their careers, they quickly realize that oral communication skills are important.

You may be called on to make oral presentations at work for any number of reasons.

- Your boss needs help preparing his or her presentation. To do so, you conduct research, interview appropriate sources, and prepare reports. When you've concluded your research, you might be asked to present your findings orally.
- Your company is making numerous cuts in its work force. As a supervisor, you have to present an oral briefing justifying the preservation of your staff.
- A customer needs work done; you and several coworkers have studied the problem and have prepared an oral presentation proposing alternate solutions.

- Your company asks you to represent it at a conference by giving a speech.
- At a departmental meeting, you are asked to report orally on the work you and subordinates have completed and to explain future activities.
- You are asked to give a sales speech promoting, explaining, and selling a service or product to a potential customer.
- Your company asks you to represent it at a city council meeting. You will give an oral presentation explaining your company's desired course of action or justifying activities already performed.
- Your company asks you to visit a civic club meeting and to provide an oral presentation to maintain good corporate/community relations.

In addition to the aforementioned instances, you must communicate daily with your peers, your supervisors, your subordinates, and the public.

Think about the number of times you have spoken to someone today or this week. Each time you communicated orally, you reflected something about yourself and your company. The goal of effective oral communication, of course, is to ensure that your verbal skills reflect positively.

TYPES OF ORAL PRESENTATIONS

Four types of oral presentations include the following:

1. The impromptu speech
2. The memorized speech
3. The manuscript speech
4. The extemporaneous speech

THE IMPROMPTU SPEECH

You are asked a question in a meeting. In this instance, you will have to organize your thoughts and answer the question quickly. You will have no time to prepare. For example, you might be asked to explain the progress of a project, your company's stand on a civic issue, how your business will meet revised construction schedules, or how your club will finance a proposed activity. To answer these questions, you must give an *impromptu speech.*

THE MEMORIZED SPEECH

The least effective type of oral presentation for technical communication is the *memorized speech.* This is a well-prepared speech which has been committed to memory. Although such preparation might make you feel less anxious, too often these speeches sound mechanical and impersonal. They are stiff, formal, and allow no speaker-audience interaction. Moreover, technical data, statistics, and definitions do not lend themselves easily to memorization. You might think you've memorized your technical information, but odds are against it.

THE MANUSCRIPT SPEECH

In a *manuscript speech,* you read from a carefully prepared manuscript. The entire speech is written on paper. This may lessen your speaker anxiety and help you accurately communicate your technical data, but such a speech can become monotonous, wooden, and boring to your audience. Imagine what college would be like if all your professors read their lectures without writing on the board, creating short class projects, asking and answering questions, using the overhead projector, or ever making eye contact. Your audience will not be able to maintain interest in a speech read from a manuscript. However, if you are presenting purely statistical information, you will need to read from a manuscript.

THE EXTEMPORANEOUS SPEECH

Extemporaneous speeches are probably the best and most widely used method of oral communication. You carefully prepare your speech by conducting necessary research, and then you create a detailed outline. However, you do not write the speech in a complete manuscript form. Instead, you study your outline and present the speech from it or from 3" × 5" cards on which you have written important points. This type of speech helps you avoid dull and mechanical presentations, allows you to interact with your audience, and still ensures that you correctly present complex technical data.

CRITERIA FOR EFFECTIVE ORAL PRESENTATIONS

Several criteria for a successful oral presentation include the following:

OVERALL ORGANIZATION

As with any well-written communication, a speech consists of an introduction, discussion, and conclusion.

Introduction

The introduction should arouse and capture your audience's interest. This is the point in the speech where you are drawing in your listener, hoping to create enthusiasm and a positive impression.

To create a positive impression, you should address the audience politely by saying, "Good Morning" or "Good Afternoon." You can welcome them to the conference or seminar; you can thank them for inviting you to speak.

To arouse audience interest, you can begin with

- An anecdote (a short, appropriate story)
- Facts and figures
- A suitable joke
- A question
- A quotation
- A startling comment

The important factor is to stimulate your audience's interest. Once you have grasped their interest, then state the subject of your speech, just as you would provide a thesis statement for an essay or topic sentence for a paragraph.

Discussion

In the discussion section of your speech, provide details to support your thesis statement. These can be presented in any order, but there are several traditional ways in which you can organize your data: (a) comparison/contrast, (b) problem/solution, (c) argument/refutation/persuasion, (d) least to most important, and (e) chronological.

You also want to maintain coherence throughout your speech. To do so,

- Restate your topic often. Constant restating of the topic is required because listeners have difficulty retaining spoken ideas. Whereas a reader can refer to a previously discussed point simply by turning back a page or two, listeners do not have this option. Furthermore, a listener is easily distracted from your speech by external noises, room temperature, uncomfortable chairs, or movement inside and outside the meeting site. Restating your topic helps your reader maintain focus.
- Use transitional words and phrases to help your listener follow your train of thought. Some appropriate transitional terms are *first, second, next, therefore, furthermore, another reason for,* and so on.
- Use clear topic sentences to state each new point.

Conclusion

Conclude your speech by (a) reiterating the main points discussed and (b) recommending a future course of action.

DEVELOPMENT

To maintain credibility, develop your discussion with thorough and accurate research (discussed further in the process section of this chapter).

STYLE

As with good writing, effective oral communication demands clarity, conciseness, and audience recognition. To achieve clarity, stick to your point. Don't allow yourself to digress about side issues or irrelevancies. Maintain your focus. Concise oral presentations depend on the same skills evident in concise writing—word and sentence length. Trim your sentences of excess words (fifteen words per sentence is still your average, preferred length). Stick to monosyllabic words versus multisyllabic ones. Finally, speak to your audience's level of understanding. Either avoid highly technical terms or define them.

DELIVERY

Effective oral communicators interact with and establish a dynamic relationship with their audiences. The most thorough research will be wasted if you are unable to create rapport and sustain your audience's interest.

Eye Contact

Don't keep your eyes glued to your notes. Look into your listeners' eyes (or at least glance over the heads of those sitting in the back row). Your audience probably has been in your position at one time and feels more sympathy for you than you might guess. They're not out to "get" you. They're in the audience to listen and to learn.

Rate

Since your audience wants to listen and learn, you must speak at a rate geared toward those two goals. Determine your normal rate of speech, and cut it in half. *Slow down.* Do not speak in a monotone, however. To keep your audience alert, vary your rate of speech. Speed up your delivery when discussing less interesting facts. Slow down for more interesting points. Match your rate of speaking to the content of your speech, just as actors vary their speech rate to reflect emotion and changes in content.

Enunciation

Don't mumble. Speak each syllable of every word clearly and distinctly. No one will ask you to repeat yourself, so speak more clearly than you might in a more conversational setting. Slowing down your delivery will help you enunciate clearly.

Pitch

When we speak, our voices create high and low sounds. In your presentation, capitalize on this fact. Vary your pitch by using even more high and low sounds than you do in your normal, day-to-day conversations. Modulate to stress certain key words or major points in your oral presentation.

Pauses

As mentioned earlier, you want to speak slowly. One way to achieve a successful pace is to pause within the oral presentation. Pause to ask for and to answer questions, to allow ideas to sink in, and to use visual aids or give the audience handouts. These pauses won't lengthen your speech; they'll only improve it. In fact, a well-prepared speech will allow for pauses and will have budgeted time effectively. Know in advance if your speech is to be five minutes, ten minutes, or an hour long. Then plan your speech according to the time restraints, building pauses into your presentation.

Practicing the speech beforehand will help you determine where and how many pauses are appropriate.

Emphasis

You can't underline or boldface comments made in oral presentations. However, just as in written communication, you will want to emphasize key ideas. Your body language, pitch, gestures, and enunciation will enable you to highlight words, phrases, or even entire sentences.

APPEARANCE

When you speak in front of people, they see you as well as hear you. Therefore, you don't want the way you look to interfere with what you're saying. With this in mind, avoid wearing clothes or jewelry which might distract the audience. Studies show that dark clothes are best to wear when making oral presentations. You might be representing your company or trying to make a good impression for yourself when you speak, so dress appropriately.

BODY LANGUAGE AND GESTURES

During an oral presentation, nonverbal communication can be as important as verbal communication. Your appearance is important, but in addition, the way you present your speech through your movements and tone of voice will affect your listeners. If you are enthusiastic about your topic, your listeners will respond enthusiastically. If you are bored or ambivalent, your tone and mannerisms will reflect your attitude. This will be communicated to your audience. To communicate effectively, then, be aware of your body language and your gestures.

One aspect of body language already discussed is eye contact. In addition, you must be concerned with how you stand and how you control your hands and arms. If, for example, you spend the entire speech standing in one place as if rooted to the spot, your audience will get bored. On the other hand, if you jump around the room like an atom whirling through a superconductor, you'll make your listeners dizzy. Find a happy medium. Move around the dais casually, speaking to different sides of the room.

Furthermore, watch your hands. If you're nervous and your hands shake, hold onto a chair, table, or lectern (something immobile), or place your hands in your pockets. Again, however, don't just maintain one posture. Vary your hand placements. The same applies to your arms. You don't want to wave them wildly and frighten your audience, but neither do you want to fold them stiffly across your chest. This body language communicates a negative attitude.

Many aspects of body language overlap with gestures (hand and arm movements, for example). One additional point relates to effective hand movements. As mentioned earlier, you need to help your listeners follow your train of thought. Through hand motions, you can emphasize ideas and provide transitions. For instance, you could put one finger up for a first point, two fingers up for a second point, and so forth. Be inventive but controlled.

VISUAL AIDS

Most speakers find that illustrations help them communicate more effectively. You must be the judge of whether visual aids will enhance your speech. Avoid using them if you think they'll distract from your presentation or if you lack confidence in your ability to create them and integrate them effectively.

Table 16.1 lists the advantages, disadvantages, and helpful hints for using visual aids. For all types of visual aids, practice using them *before* you give your speech.

Table 16.1

Visual Aids: Advantages and Disadvantages

TYPE	ADVANTAGES	DISADVANTAGES	HELPFUL HINTS
Chalkboards	Are inexpensive Help audiences take notes Allow you to emphasize a point Allow audiences to focus on a statement Help you be spontaneous Break up monotonous speeches	Make a mess Can be noisy Make you turn your back to the audience Can be hard to see Can be hard to read if your hand-writing is poor	Clean the board well. Have extra chalk. Stand to the side as you write. Print largely. Write slowly. Avoid talking with your back to the audience. Don't erase too soon.
Chalkless Boards	Same as above except for expense	Are expensive Require unique, erasable pens Can stain your clothes Can be hard to erase if left on the board too long	Use blue or red ink. Cap your pens to avoid drying out. Use pens made especially for these boards. Erase soon after use.
Flip Charts	Can be prepared in advance Are neat and clean Can be reused Are inexpensive Are portable Help you avoid a nonstop presentation Allow for spontaneity Help audiences take notes Allow you to emphasize ideas Encourage audience participation Allow easy reference by turning back to prior pages Allow highlighting through different color	Are limited by small size Require an easel Require neat hand-writing Won't work well with large groups Can run out of paper Markers can run out of ink	Have two pads of paper. Have numerous markers. Use different colors. Print largely and neatly. Turn pages when through with an idea so audiences won't be distracted. Don't write on the back of pages.

Table 16.1 (Cont.)

Visual Aids: Advantages and Disadvantages

TYPE	ADVANTAGES	DISADVANTAGES	HELPFUL HINTS
Overhead Transparencies	Are inexpensive Can be used with lights on Can be prepared in advance Can be reused Can be used for large audiences Allow you to return to a prior point Allow you to face audiences	Require an overhead projector Can be hard to focus Require an electrical outlet Can become scratched and smudged Can be too small for viewing Can malfunction (bulbs burn out)	Use larger print. Protect the transparencies with separating sheets of paper. Frame the transparencies for better handling. Turn the overhead off to avoid distractions. Focus the overhead before your speech. Keep spare bulbs. Don't write on transparencies. Face audience.
Slides	Are portable Are easy to protect Can be used for large groups Can be prepared in advance Are entertaining and colorful Allow for later reference	Are immobile Require dark rooms Deny speaker/audience interaction (eye contact) Are somewhat expensive Are challenging to create Require screen, machinery, and electrical outlets Can get out of order Don't allow audience to take notes Machinery can malfunction	Use a pointer. Use remote control. Check order of presentation. Check working condition of machinery.
Videotapes	Allow instant replay Can be freeze-framed for emphasis Can be economically duplicated Can be rented or leased inexpensively Are entertaining	Require costly equipment (monitor and recorder) Are difficult to move Can malfunction Require dark rooms Require compatible equipment (VHS or Beta) Deny easy notetaking Deny speaker/audience interaction	Practice operating the equipment. Avoid long tapes.

Table 16.1 (Cont.)

Visual Aids: Advantages and Disadvantages

TYPE	ADVANTAGES	DISADVANTAGES	HELPFUL HINTS
Films	Are easy to use Are entertaining Have many to choose from Can be used for large groups	Require dark rooms Require equipment and outlets Don't allow notetaking Deny speaker/audience interaction Malfunction Become dated	Use up-to-date films. Avoid long films. Provide discussion time. Use to supplement the speech, not replace it. Practice with the equipment.
Computerized Presentations	Are entertaining Offer flexibility, allowing you to move from topic to topic randomly Can be customized and updated Can be used for large groups Allow speaker/audience interaction	Require equipment and outlets Require dark rooms Malfunction	Practice with the equipment. Bring spare cables. Be prepared with a backup plan if the system crashes.

PROCESS

As with writing memos, letters, and reports, approach your oral presentation systematically. Follow the three-part, step-by-step process to organize your speech effectively:

- Prewrite
- Write, and
- Make your presentation

PREWRITING

Prewriting is the work you do to get started on your speech. Similar to prewriting for written communication, when you prewrite a speech, you (a) consider audience, (b) determine objectives, and (c) gather data.

Consider Audience

Before giving your speech, ask yourself the following questions:

- Are you speaking laterally to peers?
- Are you speaking to supervisors?
- Are you speaking to subordinates?
- Are you speaking to lay customers?
- Is your audience high tech or low tech?
- Is your audience composed of multiple levels of expertise and authority?
- Does your audience know you?
- Is your audience interested in the subject matter?
- Will your audience be receptive to the topic, or will they be hostile?

Answering these questions will help you decide how technical you can be, when you need to define terms, and what tone you should take. You won't communicate effectively if your audience fails to understand your terminology or if your tone is offensive. Your only reason for speaking is to communicate to your audience. Tailor your content and style accordingly.

Determine Objectives

Determining your reason for speaking is as important as recognizing your audience. Is the purpose of your speech to *inform?* Or do you hope to *persuade, explain procedures,* or *motivate?*

Inform

If your speech is to inform, all you want to do is update your listeners. Such a speech could be about new taxation laws affecting listeners' pay, new management hirings, or budget restraints affecting capital equipment purchases. Speeches which inform don't require any action on the part of your audience. Your listeners won't change the tax laws, alter hiring practices, or increase the budget. The informative speech merely keeps the audience up to date on business changes.

In such a speech, you'll want to clarify *when* changes will occur, *who* will be affected, and *how* the changes will affect your audience. Leave time for questions and answers to clarify any confusing points. However, in an informative speech, little audience involvement is necessary.

Persuade, Explain Procedures, and/or Motivate

In contrast, speeches that persuade, explain procedures, and/or motivate demand audience involvement. You're not just informing; you're asking your listeners to act. For instance, you might be speaking about the need to hold more regular and constructive quality circle meetings (persuasion). You might be telling your audience how to perform a series of steps for computer operation (explaining procedures). You might be telling your audience that they can achieve a higher level of productivity through mutual trust and cooperation (motivation). In each instance, you want your audience to leave the speech ready to implement your suggestions.

Gather Data

The best delivery by the most polished professional will lack credibility if the speaker has nothing to say. Therefore, you must study and research your topic thoroughly before you write about it.

Chapter 12 discusses how to collect information in a library. Businesspeople also rely on numerous other sources for data, including

- Interviews
- Questionnaires and surveys
- Conversations in meetings
- Company monthly, quarterly, and year-end reports

Gathering data from company reports requires that you read and document your information (discussed in Chapter 12). Gathering data through interviews, questionnaires, or conversations, however, requires assistance from other people. To do so,

- Ask politely for their assistance.
- Explain your reasons for seeking the interview and information.
- Set up convenient interview dates.
- Come prepared.
  —Research the subject matter so you'll be prepared to ask appropriate questions.
  —Write your interview questions before the meeting to save time.
  —Be sure you have whatever paper, writing utensils, or recording devices you'll need for the interview.
- Thank them politely for their help, and/or make another date for follow-up discussions.

WRITING

Once you obtain information, your next step is to write a draft for your speech. As mentioned earlier in this chapter, avoid committing the entire speech to paper. Instead, organize your data and then outline the details.

You can begin writing by using either a presentation plan, an outline, and/or note cards.

Presentation Plan

Figure 16.1 is an example of a presentation plan.

Outline

You may want to write a more detailed outline focusing on your speech's major units of discussion and supporting documentation. The following *skeleton speech outline* (Figure 16.2) and *student-written outline* (Figure 16.3) provide you with templates for your speech presentation.

Directions: Use this plan to help you clarify your thinking about the topic.

Topic: ____

Objectives: What do you want your audience to believe or do as a result of your presentation?

Development: What main points are you going to develop in your presentation?

1.

2.

3.

Organization Will this presentation lend itself to a particular organizational format, such as comparison/contrast, chronology, or analysis?

Visuals: What visuals will be used?

Figure 16.1 Presentation Plan

Title:______________________________

Purpose:______________________________

I. Introduction______________________________

- A. Attention getter: ______________________________
- B. Focus statement: ______________________________

II. Body______________________________

- A. First main point: ______________________________
  - 1. Documentation/subpoint: ______________________________
    - a. Documentation/subpoint: ______________________________
    - b. Documentation/subpoint: ______________________________
  - 2. Documentation/subpoint: ______________________________
  - 3. Documentation/subpoint: ______________________________
- B. Second main point: ______________________________
  - 1. Documentation/subpoint: ______________________________
  - 2. Documentation/subpoint: ______________________________
    - a. Documentation/subpoint: ______________________________
    - b. Documentation/subpoint: ______________________________
  - 3. Documentation/subpoint: ______________________________
- C. Third main point: ______________________________
  - 1. Documentation/subpoint: ______________________________
  - 2. Documentation/subpoint: ______________________________
  - 3. Documentation/subpoint: ______________________________
    - a. Documentation/subpoint: ______________________________
    - b. Documentation/subpoint: ______________________________

III. Conclusion

- A. Summary of main points: ______________________________
- B. Recommended future course of action: ______________________________

Figure 16.2 Skeleton Outline

Title: How Leather Is Made
Purpose: To Explain Procedure

I. Introduction
   A. Attention getter: How many of you own leather products? How many of you know how leather is made? Working at Houston's Leathery, I am often asked to explain the procedure for making leather.
   B. Focus statement: Leather comes from animal skin preserved by a process called tanning. Tanning requires the application of chromium salt, a chemical solution. The process of leather tanning is divided into three phases: pretanning, tanning, and dyeing and finishing.

II. Body
   A. Phase one: Pretanning requires six steps.
      1. The skin is cured so it will not decompose. Curing can be accomplished in either of two ways.
         a. Salt can be spread on the underside of the skin and kept in packs for approximately a week.
         b. The skin can be soaked in a lime solution for several days.
      2. The cured skins are sent to a tannery where they are trimmed and the best parts are kept for leather.
      3. The excess salt from the skins is removed by soaking them in water.
      4. The skins are run through a machine where revolving blades remove excess fat.
      5. The skins are placed in vats of lime solution for several days.
      6. Pretanning is complete when the skins are pickled by placing them in salt and chemical solutions.
   B. Phase two: The tanning stage requires three steps.
      1. The tanning process begins by soaking the skins in revolving drums containing tanning agents.
      2. The skins are put through a ringer to remove excess moisture and chemicals.
      3. The skins are split to proper thickness and measured by a leather gauge.
   C. Phase three: Dyeing and finishing are the last phase of making leather.
      1. Dyeing requires four steps.
         a. A machine smooths and stretches the skin while further removing any remaining moisture.
         b. The skin is dried in an oven.

Figure 16.3 Student-Written Sentence Outline

c. The leather is buffed and sanded to achieve a smooth-grained texture.
d. Color is added by drum dyeing or spray dyeing.
  i. Drum dyeing penetrates both sides of the leather.
  ii. Spray dyeing covers only one side and small blemishes.
2. There are five basic types of finishes.
  a. Finished leather is created by spraying a pigment onto the outer surface of the leather. This finish is the most durable because it resists water, soil, and stains.
  b. Aniline finish is achieved by soaking the leather in aniline dye. This type of finish lets you see the actual grain of the leather, but it leaves the leather unprotected.
  c. Semi-aniline finish is a combination of the above two finishes. An aniline dye is applied and an opaque pigment is sprayed to achieve an even color.
  d. Suede finish is achieved when the leather is split and buffed to a silky nap.
  e. Shearling finish is derived from sheep's wool. The wool is left on the skin when tanned and then used as the lining for the garment.

III. Conclusion
  A. Summation: I now have explained the three phases of the tanning process and the five types of finishes.
  B. Recommendations: You not only should have a better understanding of how leather is made, but also you will be able to select the finish that will best suit your needs.

Figure 16.3 Student-Written Sentence Outline (Cont.)

Note Cards

If you decide that presenting the speech from the outline will not work for you, then you can write highlights of the speech on 3" × 5" cards. One caution—avoid writing complete sentences or filling the cards side to side. Just write short notes (phrases or key words) which will aid your memory.

Once your speech is outlined and note cards are prepared, practice, incorporating all your visual aids. If you were told to present a twenty-minute speech, that is how long you should talk. To speak longer than requested will infringe on another speaker's time, on question-and-answer time, or on coffee-break time. Practicing will help you meet any time constraints.

PRESENTATION

Use the following speaker's checklist to determine if your presentation will be successful.

SPEAKER'S CHECKLIST

1. Is my choice of topic relevant and appropriate?
2. Is my beginning polite and upbeat?
3. Have I used an attention-getting device?
4. Is my focus statement clear?
5. Do I have an effective overall organization?
6. Are my major points evident?
7. Do I remind my audience of my topic at the beginning of the speech, in the middle, and at the end?
8. Do I move smoothly from point to point using transitional words and phrases?
9. Have I documented my findings using effective research?
10. Do I define any unfamiliar terms?
11. Do I use my note cards or outline well?
12. Are my visual aids presented effectively?
13. Is my conclusion effective?
14. Do I enunciate clearly?
15. Is my grammar correct?
16. Is my body language effective?
17. Do I maintain eye contact?
18. Are my volume, tone, and pitch good?
19. Is my pace effective (not too slow or too fast)?
20. Am I confident and sincere?

POST SPEECH ACTIVITIES

After your speech, be prepared for a question-and-answer session. Politely invite your audience to participate by saying, "If you have any questions, I am happy to answer them."

When an audience member asks a question, make sure everyone hears it. If not, you can repeat the question. If you don't understand the question, ask the audience member to repeat it and clarify.

If you have no answer, tell the audience. You will only mar the effect of your presentation if you stumble over an answer and appear to be unsure of yourself. Credibility is essential to your success; faking an answer will not ensure credibility.

If a member of the audience is rude or has disliked your speech, you can say that you will be happy to discuss the matter after the presentation. Don't let a successful speech be marred by one disgruntled listener.

ACTIVITIES

1. Go to a library, research a topic that interests you, and take notes on the topic from a journal or magazine article. In class, present a three- to five-minute speech briefing your classmates about the article's content.
2. In groups of three to five students, read an article about a technical concept or mechanism. Prepare a list of questions about the subject matter. Then select one member of the group who will answer questions while the rest of the group members ask them. Do this several times so each group member has an opportunity to answer and ask questions.
3. Prepare an extemporaneous speech of about ten to fifteen minutes. Include an outline, note cards, and visual aids. For your subject matter, focus on a problem at work or school. In your speech, explain how the problem arose, offer alternative solutions, and persuade your audience to pursue a future course of action solving the problem.
4. Prepare a three- to five-minute extemporaneous speech informing your audience of the status of an activity on which you are working. This could be a school project or a work-related activity. Provide visual aids to supplement your presentation.
5. Interview a professional in the career of your choice to determine whether the field will provide you with the challenges, opportunities, and financial remuneration you desire. To perform this interview, set up an interview date, be prepared with questions, and take notes. Then return to class and present a three- to five-minute extemporaneous speech about your interview.
6. Attend a lecture. Assess the speaker's presentation according to the criteria checklist presented in this chapter. Then provide an oral presentation reporting on your findings.

Chapter 12

GRAMMAR, PUNCTUATION, MECHANICS, AND SPELLING

- GRAMMAR RULES
- PUNCTUATION
- MECHANICS
- SPELLING

Correctly organizing and developing your memo, letter, or report are essential. However, no one will be impressed with the quality of your work, or with you, if your writing is riddled with errors in sentence construction or punctuation. Your written correspondence is often your first contact with business associates. Many people mistakenly believe that only English teachers notice grammatical errors and wield red pens, but businesspeople as well take note of such errors and may see the writer as less competent.

We were working recently with a young executive who is employed by a branch of the federal government. This executive told us that whenever his supervisor found a spelling error in a subordinate's report, this report was paraded around the office. Everyone was shown the mistake, had a good laugh over it, and the report was then returned to the writer for correction. Our acquaintance assured us that all of this was in good-natured fun. However, he also said that employees quickly learned to edit and proof their work to avoid such public displays of their errors. He went on to say that his dictionary was well thumbed and always on his desk.

Your writing at work may not be exposed to such scrutiny by coworkers. Instead, your writing may go directly to another firm, and those readers will see your mistakes. To avoid this problem, you must evaluate your writing for grammar, punctuation, and spelling errors. If you don't, your customers and colleagues will.

This chapter focuses on (a) grammar rules, (b) punctuation, (c) rules for effective mechanics, (d) spelling, and (e) proofreader's marks. In addition, the chapter also provides hands-on experience with grammar, punctuation, and spelling in the form of memos and letters needing correction.

GRAMMAR RULES

To understand the fundamentals of grammar, you must first understand the basic components of a sentence.

A correctly constructed sentence consists of a subject and a predicate (some sentences also include a phrase or phrases).

The *meeting*	*began*	*at 4:00 a.m.*
subject	predicate	phrase

Subject: The *doer* of the action; the subject usually precedes the predicate.

Predicate: The *action* in the sentence

He	*ran*	to the office to avoid being late.
doer	action	phrases

If the subject and the predicate (a) express a complete thought, and (b) can stand alone, you have an *independent clause.*

The meeting began	at 4:00 p.m.
independent clause	phrase

A *phrase* is a group of related words that does not contain a subject and a predicate and cannot stand alone or be punctuated as a sentence. The following are examples of phrases:

at the house
in the box
on the job
during the interview

If a clause is dependent, it cannot stand alone.

Although he tried to hurry, he was late for the meeting.

dependent clause independent clause

He was late for the meeting although he tried to hurry.

independent clause dependent clause

Note: When a dependent clause begins a sentence, use a comma before the independent clause. However, when an independent clause begins a sentence, do not place a comma before the dependent clause.

PRONOUN AND ANTECEDENT (REFERENT) AGREEMENT

A pronoun has to agree in gender and number with its referent.

Susan went on *her* vacation yesterday.
The *people* who quit said that *they* deserved raises.

Problems often arise when a singular indefinite pronoun is the referent. The following require singular pronouns: *anybody, each, everybody, everyone, somebody,* and *someone.*

Incorrect
Anyone can pick up *their* applications at the job placement center.

Correct
Anyone can pick up *his or her* applications at the job placement center.

Problems also arise when the referent is separated from the pronoun by numerous words.

Incorrect
Even when the best *employee* is considered for a raise, *they* often do not receive it.

Correct
Even when the best *employee* is considered for a raise, *she* often does not receive it.

SUBJECT AND VERB AGREEMENT

Writers sometimes create disagreement between subjects and verbs, especially if other words separate the subject from the verb. To ensure agreement, ignore the words that come between the subject and verb.

Incorrect
Her *boss* undoubtedly *think* that all the employees want promotions.

Correct
Her *boss* undoubtedly *thinks* that all the employees want promotions.

Incorrect
The *employees* who sell the most equipment *is* going to Hawaii for a week.

Correct
The *employees* who sell the most equipment *are* going to Hawaii for a week.

If a sentence contains two subjects (a compound subject) connected by *and,* use a plural verb.

Incorrect
Joe and Becky *was* both selected employee of the year.

Correct
Joe and Becky *were* both selected employee of the year.

Incorrect
The bench workers and their supervisor *is* going to work closely to complete this project.

Correct
The bench workers and their supervisor *are* going to work closely to complete this project.

Add a final *s* or *es* to create most plural subjects or singular verbs, as follows:

Plural Subjects	**Singular Verbs**
boss*es* hire	a boss hire*s*
employee*s* demand	an employee demand*s*
experiment*s* work	an experiment work*s*
attitude*s* change	the attitude chang*es*

If a sentence has two subjects connected by *either … or, neither … nor,* or *not only … but also,* the verb should agree with the closest subject.

Either the salespeople or the warehouse worker deserv*es* raises.

Not only the warehouse worker but also the salespeople deserv*e* raises.

Neither the salespeople nor the warehouse worker deserv*es* raises.

Singular verbs are used after most indefinite pronouns, such as the following:

another	everything
anybody	neither
anyone	nobody
anything	no one
each	nothing
either	somebody
everybody	someone
everyone	something

Anyone who works here *is* guaranteed maternity leave.
Everybody wants the company to declare a profit this quarter.

Singular verbs often follow collective nouns, such as the following:

class	organization
corporation	platoon
department	staff
group	team

The *staff* is sending the boss a bouquet of roses.

COMMA SPLICE

A *comma splice* occurs when two independent clauses are joined by a comma rather than a period or semicolon.

Incorrect
Sue was an excellent employee, she got a promotion.

Several remedies will correct this error.

1. Separate the two independent clauses with a semicolon.

Correct
Sue was an excellent employee; she got a promotion.

2. Separate the two independent clauses with a period.

Correct
Sue was an excellent employee. She got a promotion.

3. Separate the two independent clauses with a comma and a *coordinate conjunction (and, but, or, for, so, yet).*

Correct
Sue was an excellent employee, *so* she got a promotion.

4. Separate the two independent clauses with a semicolon, a conjunctive adverb, and a comma. *Conjunctive adverbs* include *also, additionally, consequently, furthermore, however, instead, moreover, nevertheless, therefore,* and *thus.*

Correct
Sue was an excellent employee; *therefore,* she got a promotion.

5. Use a *subordinate conjunction* to make one of the independent clauses into a dependent clause. Subordinate conjunctions include *after, although, as, because, before, even though, if, once, since, so that, though, unless, until, when, where,* and *whether.*

Correct
Because Sue was an excellent employee, she got a promotion.

FAULTY OR VAGUE PRONOUN REFERENCE

A pronoun must refer to a specific noun (its referent). Problems arise when (a) there is an excessive number of pronouns (causing vague pronoun reference), and (b) there is no specific noun as a referent.

Notice that there seems to be an excessive number of pronouns in the following passage, and the referents are unclear:

> Although Bob had been hired over two years ago, *he* found that his boss did not approve his raise. In fact, *he* was also passed over for *his* promotion. The boss appears to have concluded that *he* had not exhibited zeal in *his* endeavors for their business. Instead of being a highly valued employee, *he* was not viewed with pleasure by those in authority. Perhaps it would be best if *he* considered *his* options and moved to some other company where *he* might be considered in a new light.

The excessive and vague use of *he* and *his* causes problems. Do they refer to Bob or to his boss? You're never completely sure. To avoid this problem, limit pronoun usage, as in the following revision:

> Although Bob had been hired over two years ago, he found that his boss, Joe, did not approve his raise. In fact, Bob was also passed over for promotion. Joe appears to have concluded that Bob had not exhibited zeal in his endeavors for their busi-

ness. Instead of being a highly valued employee, Bob was not viewed with pleasure by those in authority. Perhaps it would be best if Bob considered his options and moved to some other company where he might be considered in a new light.

To make the preceding paragraph more precise, we've replaced vague pronouns (*he* and *his*) with exact names (*Bob* and *Joe*).

FRAGMENTS

A *fragment* occurs when a group of words is incorrectly used as an independent clause. Often the group of words begins with a capital letter and has end punctuation but is missing either a subject or a predicate.

Incorrect
Working with computers.
(lacks a predicate and does not express a complete thought)

The group of words may have a subject and a predicate but be a dependent clause.

Incorrect
Although he enjoyed working with computers.
(has a subject, *he,* and a predicate, *enjoyed,* but is a dependent clause because it is introduced by the subordinate conjunction *although*)

It is easy to remedy a fragment by doing one of the following:

- Add a subject.
- Add a predicate.
- Add both a subject and a predicate.
- Add an independent clause to a dependent clause.

Correct
Joe found that working with computers used his training.
(subject, *Joe,* and predicate, *found,* have been added)

Correct
Although he enjoyed working with computers, he could not find a job in a computer-related field.
(independent clause, *he could not find a job,* added to the dependent clause, *Although he enjoyed working with computers*)

FUSED SENTENCE

A *fused sentence* occurs when two independent clauses are connected with no punctuation.

Incorrect
The company performed well last quarter its stock rose several points.

There are several ways to correct this error.

1. Write two sentences separated by a period.

Correct
The company performed well last quarter. Its stock rose several points.

2. Use a comma and a coordinate conjunction to separate the two independent clauses.

Correct
The company performed well last quarter, *so* its stock rose several points.

3. Use a subordinate conjunction to create a dependent clause.

Correct
Because the company performed well last quarter, its stock rose several points.

4. Use a semicolon to separate the two independent clauses.

Correct
The company performed well last quarter; its stock rose several points.

5. Separate the two independent clauses with a semicolon, a conjunctive adverb or a transitional word or phrase, and a comma.

Correct
The company performed well last quarter; *therefore,* its stock rose several points.

Correct
The company performed well last quarter; *for example,* its stock rose several points.

The following are transitional words and phrases, listed according to their use:

To Add

again
also
besides
first
furthermore
in addition
moreover
next
second
still

To Compare/Contrast

also
but
conversely
in contrast
nevertheless
on the contrary
still

To Provide Examples

for example
for instance
in fact
of course
put another way
to illustrate

To Show Place

above
adjacent to
below
elsewhere
further on
here
nearby
on the other side
there

To Reveal Time

afterward
first
meanwhile
presently
second
shortly
subsequently
thereafter

To Summarize

all in all
finally
in conclusion
in summary
last
on the whole
therefore
thus

MODIFICATION

A *modifier* is a word, phrase, or clause that explains or adds details about other words, phrases, or clauses.

Misplaced Modifiers

A *misplaced modifier* occurs when the modifier is not placed next to the word it modifies.

Incorrect
He had a heart attack *almost* every time he was reviewed by his supervisor.

Correct
He almost had a heart attack every time he was reviewed by his supervisor.

Incorrect
The worker had to *frequently* miss work.

Correct
The worker frequently had to miss work.

Dangling Modifiers

To avoid *dangling modifiers,* place the modifying word or phrase next to the modified word (that is, do not imply a modified word).

Incorrect
While working, tiredness overcame them.
(Who was working? Who was overcome by tiredness?)

Correct
While working, the staff became tired.

Incorrect
After soldering for two hours, the equipment was ready for shipping.
(Who had been soldering for two hours? Not the equipment!)

Correct
After soldering for two hours, the technicians prepared the equipment for shipping.

PARALLELISM

When listing items, all parts of this list should be parallel in grammatical form.

Incorrect
We will discuss the following at the departmental meeting:

1. Entering mileage in logs
2. All employees have to enroll in a training seminar.
3. Purpose of quarterly reviews
4. Some data processors will travel to job sites.

Correct
We will discuss the following at the departmental meeting:

1. Entering mileage in logs
2. Enrolling in training seminars
3. Reviewing employee performance quarterly
4. Traveling to job sites

Correct
At the departmental meeting, you will learn how to

1. Enter mileage in logs
2. Enroll in training seminars
3. Review employee performance quarterly
4. Travel to job sites

APOSTROPHE (')

Place an *apostrophe* before the final *s* in a singular word to indicate possession.

Jim's tool chest is next to the furnace.

Place the apostrophe after the final *s* if the word is plural.

The employees' reception will be held next week.

Don't use an apostrophe to make singular abbreviations plural.

Incorrect
The EXT's will be shipped today.

Correct
The EXTs will be shipped today.

COLON (:)

Use a *colon* after a salutation.

Dear Mr. Sandhaus:

In addition, use a colon after an emphatic or cautionary word if explanations follow.

Note: Hand-tighten the nuts.

Caution: Wash thoroughly if any mixture touches your skin.

Finally, use a colon after an independent clause to precede a quotation, list, or example.

She said the following: "No comment."

These supplies for the experiment are on order: plastic hose, two batteries, and several chemicals.

The problem has two possible solutions: hire four more workers or simply give everyone a raise.

Note: In the preceding examples, the colon follows an independent clause.

A common mistake is to place a colon after an incomplete sentence. Except for salutations and cautionary notes, whatever precedes a colon *must* be an independent clause.

Incorrect
The two keys to success are: earning money and spending wisely.

Correct
The two keys to success are earning money and spending wisely.

or

The two keys to success are as follows: earning money and spending wisely.

or

The two keys to success are as follows:

1. earning money
2. spending wisely

COMMA (,)

Writers often get in trouble with *commas* when they employ one of two common "words of wisdom":

- When in doubt, leave it out.
- Use a comma when there is a pause.

Both rules are inexact. Writers use the first rule to justify the complete avoidance of commas; they use the second rule to sprinkle commas randomly throughout their writing. On the contrary, commas have several specific conventions which determine usage.

1. Place a comma before a coordinate conjunction (*and, but, or, for, so, yet*) linking two independent clauses.

You are the best person for the job, *so* I will hire you.

We spent several hours discussing solutions to the problem, *but* we failed to decide on a course of action.

2. Use commas to set off introductory comments.

First, she soldered the components.

In business, people often have to work long hours.

To work well, you need to get along with your coworkers.

If you want to test equipment, do so by 5:25 P.M.

3. Use commas to set off sentence interrupters.

The company, started by my father, did not survive the last recession.

Mrs. Mittleman, the proprietor of the store, purchased a wide array of merchandise.

4. Set off parenthetical expressions with commas.

A worker, it seems, should be willing to try new techniques.

The highway, by the way, needs repairs.

5. Use commas between items in a series.

Fred, Helene, and Ron were chosen as Employees of the Year.

We found the following problems: corrosion, excessive machinery breakdowns, and power failures.

6. Use commas to set off sections of dates, addresses, and long numbers.

On January 9, 1996, the company opened its new offices.

We live at 11517 Grant, Overland Park, Kansas.

Our business netted over $2,500,000 in 1996.

7. Use commas to set off the day and year when they are part of a sentence.

The company hired her on September 7, 1996, to be its bookkeeper.

Note: If the year is used as an adjective, do not follow it with a comma.

The 1995 Corporate Report came out today.

8. Use commas to set off the city from the state and the state from the rest of the sentence.

The new warehouse in Austin, Texas, will promote increased revenues.

Note: If you omit either the city or the state, you do not need commas.

The new warehouse in Austin will promote increased revenues.

DASH (—)

A *dash,* typed as two consecutive hyphens with no spaces before or after, is a versatile punctuation mark used in the following ways:

1. After a heading and before an explanation.

Forecasting—Joe and Joan will be in charge of researching fourth quarter production quotas.

2. To indicate an emphatic pause.

You will be fired—unless you obey company rules.

3. To highlight a new idea.

Here's what we can do to improve production quality—provide on-the-job training, salary incentives, and quality controls.

4. Before and after an explanatory or appositive series.

Three people—Sue, Luci, and Tom—are essential to the smooth functioning of our office.

ELLIPSES (. . .)

Ellipses (three spaced periods) indicate omission of words within quoted materials.

> "Six years ago, prior to incorporating, the company had to pay extremely high federal taxes."
>
> "Six years ago, . . . the company had to pay extremely high federal taxes."

EXCLAMATION POINT (!)

Use an *exclamation point* after strong statements, commands, or interjections.

> You must work harder!
>
> Do not use the machine!
>
> Danger!

HYPHEN (-)

A *hyphen* is used in the following ways:

1. To indicate the division of a word at the end of a typed line. Remember, this division must occur between syllables.
2. To create a compound adjective.

> He is a well-known engineer.
>
> Until her death in 1996, she was a world-renowned chemist.
>
> Tom is a 24-hour-a-day student.

3. To join the numerator and denominator of fractions.

> Four-fifths of the company want to initiate profit sharing.

4. To write out two-word numbers.

> Twenty-six people attended the conference.

PARENTHESES ( )

Parentheses enclose abbreviations, numbers, words, or sentences for the following reasons:

1. To define a term or provide an abbreviation for later use.

We belong to STC (the Society for Technical Communication).

2. To clarify preceding information in a sentence.

The people in attendance (all regional sales managers) were proud of their accomplishments.

3. To number items in a series.

The company should initiate (1) new personnel practices, (2) a probationary review board, and (3) biannual raises.

PERIOD (.)

A *period* must end sentences (independent clauses).

I found the business trip rewarding.

Periods are often used with abbreviations.

D.C.	e.g.	A.M. or a.m.
M.D.	Mr.	P.M. or p.m.
Ph.D.	Mrs.	
B.A.	Ms.	

It is incorrect to use periods with abbreviations for organizations and associations.

Incorrect
S.T.C. (Society for Technical Communication)

Correct
STC (Society for Technical Communication)

State abbreviations no longer use periods.

Incorrect

KS. (Kansas)
MO. (Missouri)
TX. (Texas)

Correct
KS
MO
TX

QUESTION MARK (?)

Use a *question mark* after direct questions.

Do the lab results support your theory?
Will you work at the main office or at the branch?

QUOTATION MARKS (" ")

Quotation marks are used in the following ways:

1. When citing direct quotes.

He said, "Your division sold the most compressors last year."

Note: When you are citing a quote within a quote, use double quotation marks (" ") and single quotation marks (' ').

Kim's supervisor, quoting the CEO, said the following to explain the new policy regarding raises: "'Only employees who deserve them will receive merit raises.'"

2. To note the title of an article or a subdivision of a report.

The article "Robotics in Industry Today" was an excellent choice as the basis of your speech.
Section III, "Waste Water in District 9," is pertinent to our discussion.

When using quotation marks, abide by the following punctuation conventions:

- Commas and periods always go *inside* quotation marks.

She said, "Our percentages are fixed."

- Colons and semicolons always go *outside* quotation marks.

He said, "The supervisor hasn't decided yet"; however, he added that the decision would be made soon.

- Exclamation points and question marks go inside the quotation marks if the quoted material is either exclamatory or a question. However, if the quoted material is not exclamatory or a question, then these punctuation marks go outside the quotation marks.

John said, "Don't touch that liquid. It's boiling!"

(Although the sentence isn't exclamatory, the quote is. Thus, the exclamation point goes inside the quotation marks.)

How could she say, "We haven't purchased the equipment yet"?

(Although the quote isn't a question, the sentence is. Thus, the question mark goes outside the quotation marks.)

SEMICOLON (;)

Semicolons are used in the following instances:

1. Between two independent clauses *not* joined by a coordinate conjunction.

The light source was unusual; it emanated from a crack in the plastic surrounding the cathode.

2. To separate items in a series containing internal commas.

When the meeting was called to order, all members were present, including Susan Bailey, the president; Ruth Schneider, the vice president; Harold Holbert, the treasurer; and Linda Hamilton, the secretary.

MECHANICS

ABBREVIATIONS

Never use an abbreviation which your reader will not understand. A key to clear technical writing is to write on a level appropriate to your reader. You may use the following familiar abbreviations without explanation: *Mrs., Dr., Mr., Ms., Ph.D.,* and *Jr.*

A common mistake is to abbreviate inappropriately. For example, some writers abbreviate *and* as follows:

I quit my job & planned to retire young.

This is too colloquial for professional technical writing. Spell out *and* when you write.

The majority of abbreviation errors occur when writers incorrectly abbreviate states and technical terms.

States

Writers often abbreviate states incorrectly. For example, if you write, "I was transferred from Tex. to Kans.," your abbreviations are incorrect. Instead, you must abide by the following conventions regarding the abbreviations of states.

Abbreviations for States

AL	Alabama	MT	Montana
AK	Alaska	NC	North Carolina
AZ	Arizona	ND	North Dakota
AR	Arkansas	NE	Nebraska
CA	California	NV	Nevada
CO	Colorado	NH	New Hampshire
CT	Connecticut	NJ	New Jersey
DE	Delaware	NM	New Mexico
FL	Florida	NY	New York
GA	Georgia	OH	Ohio
HI	Hawaii	OK	Oklahoma
IN	Indiana	OR	Oregon
IA	Iowa	PA	Pennsylvania
ID	Idaho	RI	Rhode Island
IL	Illinois	SC	South Carolina
KS	Kansas	SD	South Dakota
KY	Kentucky	TN	Tennessee
LA	Louisiana	TX	Texas
ME	Maine	UT	Utah
MD	Maryland	VT	Vermont
MA	Massachusetts	VA	Virginia
MI	Michigan	WA	Washington
MN	Minnesota	WV	West Virginia
MS	Mississippi	WI	Wisconsin
MO	Missouri	WY	Wyoming

Technical Terms

Units of measurement and scientific terms must be abbreviated accurately to ensure international reader understanding. Writers often incorrectly use such abbreviations. For example, "The unit measured 7.9 cent." is inaccurate. The correct abbreviation for centimeter is *cm*, not *cent*. Use the following abbreviation conventions:

Technical Abbreviations for Units of Measurement and Scientific Terms

absolute	abs
alternating current	ac
(adjective form)	a-c
American wire gauge	AWG
ampere	amp
ampere-hour	amp-hr
amplitude modulation	AM
Angstrom unit	A
atmosphere	atm
atomic weight	at wt
audio frequency	AF
azimuth	az
barometer	bar.
barrels	bbl
billion electron volts	bev
biochemical oxygen demand	bod
board feet	bd-ft
Brinell hardness number	Bhn
British thermal unit	Btu
bushel	bu
calorie	cal
candela	cd
Celsius	C
center of gravity	cg
centimeter	cm
circumference	circum
cologarithm	colog
continuous wave	cw
cosine	cos
cotangent	cot
cubic centimeter	cc
cubic feet	cu ft
cubic feet per second	cfs
cubic inch	cu in.
cubic meter	cu m

cubic yard	cu yd
current	I
cycles per second	cps
decibels	dB
decigrams	dg
deciliters	dl
decimeters	dm
degree	deg
dekagrams	dkg
dekaliters	dkl
dekameters	dkm
dewpoint	dp
diameter	dia
direct current	dc
(adjective form)	d-c
dozen	doz or dz.
drams	dr
electromagnetic force	emf
electron volts	ev
elevation	el
equivalent	equiv
Fahrenheit	F
farads	f
feet	ft
feet per second	ft/sec
fluid ounce	fl oz
foot board measure	fbm
foot-candle	ft-c
foot-pound	ft-lb
frequency modulation	FM
gallons	gal
gallons per day	gpd
gallons per minute	gpm
grains	gr
grams	gm
gravitational acceleration	g

hectare	ha
hectoliter	hl
hectometer	hm
henries	h
hertz	Hz
high frequency	hf
horsepower	hp
horsepower-hours	hp-hr
hours	hr
hundredweight	cwt
inch	in.
inch-pounds	in.-lb
infrared	IF
inside diameter	ID
intermediate frequency	i.f.
international unit	iu
joules	j
kelvin	K
kilocalories	kcal
kilocycles	kc
kilocycles per second	kc/sec
kilograms	kg
kilohertz	khz
kilojoules	kj
kiloliters	kl
kilometers	km
kilovolts	kv
kilovolt-amperes	kva
kilowatt-hours	kw-hr
lambert	L
latitude	lat
length	l
linear	lin
linear foot	lin ft
liter	l
logarithm	log.

longitude	long.
low frequency	l.f.
lumen	lm
lumen-hour	lm-hr
maximum	max
megacycles	mc
megahertz	MHz
megawatts	mw
meter	m
microamperes	muamp
microinches	muin.
microseconds	musec
microwatts	muw
miles per gallon	mpg
milliamperes	ma
millibars	mb
millifarads	mf
milligrams	mg
milliliters	ml
millimeters	mm
millivolts	mv
milliwatts	mw
minutes	min
nautical miles	NM
negative	neg or -
number	no.
octance	oct
ounce	oz
outside diameter	od
parts per billion	ppb
parts per million	ppm
pascal	pas
positive	pos or +
pounds	lb
pounds per square inch	psi

pounds per square inch absolute	psia
pounds per square inch gauge	psig
quart	qt
radio frequency	RF
radian	rad
radium	r
resistance	R
revolution	rev
revolutions per minute	rpm
second or secant	sec
specific gravity	sp gr
square foot	ft^2
square inch	$in.^2$
square meter	m^2
square mile	mi^2
tablespoon	tbsp
tangent	tan.
teaspoon	tsp
temperature	temp
tensile strength	ts
thousand	M
tons	t
ultra high frequency	UHF
vacuum	vac
very high frequency	VHF
volt-amperes	va
volts	v
volts per meter	v/m
volume	vol
watt-hour	whr
watts	w
wavelength	wl
weight	wt
yards	yd
years	yr

CAPITAL LETTERS

Capitalize the following:

1. Proper nouns.

people	cities	countries	companies	schools	buildings
↓	↓	↓	↓	↓	↓
Susan	Houston	Italy	Bendix	Harvard	Oak Park Mall

2. People's titles (only when they *precede* the name).

Governor Sally Renfro
or
Sally Renfro, governor

Technical Supervisor Pat Berry
or
Steve Simon, the technical supervisor

3. Titles of books, magazines, plays, movies, television programs, and record albums (excluding the prepositions and all articles after the first article in the title).

The Catcher in the Rye
The New Yorker
The Taming of the Shrew
Top Gun
All in the Family
Abbey Road

4. Names of organizations.

Girl Scouts
Kansas City Regional Home Care Association
Kansas City Regional Council for Higher Education
Programs for Technical and Scientific Communication
The American Civil Liberties Union
Students for Democratic Society

5. Days of the week, months, and holidays.

Monday
December
Thanksgiving

6. Races, religions, and nationalities.

American Indian
Jewish
Polish

7. Events or eras in history.

the Vietnam War
the Depression

8. North, South, East, and West (when used to indicate geographic locations).

They moved from the North.
People are moving to the Southwest.

Note: Don't capitalize these words when giving directions.

We were told to drive south three blocks and then to turn west.

9. The first word of a sentence.

10. Don't capitalize any of the following:

Seasons—spring, fall, summer, winter
Names of classes—freshman, senior
General groups—middle management, infielders, surgeons

NUMBERS

Write out *numbers* one through nine.
Use numerals for numbers 10 and above.

10	12
104	2,093
536	5,550,286

Although the preceding rules cover most situations, there are exceptions.

1. Use numerals for all percentages.

2 percent 18 percent 25 percent

2. Use numerals for addresses.

12 Elm 935 W. Harding

3. Use numerals for miles per hour.

45 mph 225 mph

4. Use numerals for time.

3:15 A.M.

5. Use numerals for dates.

May 31, 1948

6. Use numerals for monetary values.

$45 $.95

7. Use numerals for units of measurement.

14' 6 3/4" 16 mm 10 v

8. Do not use numerals to begin sentences.

Incorrect
568 people were fired last August.

Correct
Five hundred and sixty-eight people were fired last August.

9. Do not mix numerals and words when writing a series of numbers. The larger number determines the form.

We attended 4 meetings over a 16-day period.

10. Use numerals and words in a compound number adjective to avoid confusion.

The worker needed six 2-inch nails.

SPELLING

The following is a list of commonly misspelled, misused words. You can avoid many common spelling errors if you familiarize yourself with these words.

accept, except
addition, edition
access, excess
advise, advice
affect, effect
all ready, already
assistants, assistance
bare, bear
brake, break
coarse, course
cite, site, sight
council, counsel
desert, dessert
disburse, disperse
fiscal, physical
forth, fourth
incite, insight
its, it's
loose, lose
miner, minor
passed, past
patients, patience
personal, personnel
principal, principle
quiet, quite
rite, right, write
stationery, stationary
their, there, they're
to, too, two
whose, who's
your, you're

PROOFREADER'S MARKS

Figure 18.1 illustrates proofreader's marks and how to use them.

ACTIVITIES

SPELLING

In the following sentences, circle the correctly spelled words.

1. Each of the employees attended the meeting (accept except) the line supervisor, who was out of town for job-related travel.
2. The (advise advice) he gave will help us all do a better job.
3. Management must (affect effect) a change in its employees' attitudes toward absenteeism.
4. Let me (site cite sight) this most recent case as an example.

PROOFREADER'S MARKS			
Proofreading Symbol	Meaning	Mark on Copy	Revision
ℓ	delete	hire better peoplesℓ	hire better people
(tr) or ∩	transpose	computer systme	computer system
⁀‿	close space	we ne ed 40	we need 40
#	insert space	threemistakes	three mistakes
¶	begin paragraph	¶ The first year	The first year
(RUN IN)	no paragraph	financial. We earned twelve dollars.	financial. We earned twelve dollars.
[	move left	[Next year	Next year
]	move right	] Next year	Next year
^.	insert period	happy employee	happy employee.
^,	insert comma	For two years	For two years,
^;	insert semicolon	We need you come to work.	We need you; come to work.
^:	insert colon	dogs brown, black, and white.	dogs: brown, black, and white.
^-	insert hyphen	first rate	first-rate
∨'	insert apostrophe	Marys car	Mary's car
∨" / ∨"	insert quotation marks	Like a Rolling Stone	"Like a Rolling Stone"
(sp)	spell out	(4) chips	four chips
(cap) or ≡	capitalize	the meeting	The meeting
(lc)	lower case	the Boss	the boss
^	insert	the left margin	the left margin

Figure 18-1

5. (Its It's) too early to tell if our personnel changes will help create a better office environment.
6. If we (lose loose) another good employee to our competitor, our production capabilities will suffer.
7. I'm not (quite quiet) sure what she meant by that comment.
8. (Their There They're) budget has gotten too large to ensure a successful profit margin.
9. We had wanted to attend the conference (to too two), but our tight schedule prevented us from doing so.
10. (You're Your) best chance for landing this contract is to manufacture a better product.

In the letter on page 458, correct the misspelled words.

Fragments and Comma Splices

In the following sentences, correct the fragments and comma splices by inserting the appropriate punctuation or adding any necessary words.

1. She kept her appointment with the salesperson, however, the rest of her staff came late.
2. When the CEO presented his fiscal year projections, he tried to motivate his employees, many were not excited about the proposed cuts.
3. Even though the company's sales were up 25 percent.
4. The supervisor wanted the staff members to make suggestions for improving their work environment, the employees, however, felt that any grievances should be taken directly to their union representatives.
5. Which he decided was an excellent idea.
6. Because their machinery was prone to malfunctions and often caused hazards to the workers.
7. They needed the equipment to complete their job responsibilities, further delays would cause production slowdowns.
8. Their client who was a major distributor of high-tech machinery.
9. Robotics should help us maintain schedules, we'll need to avoid equipment malfunctions, though.
10. The company, careful not to make false promises, advertising their product in media releases.

In the letter on page 459, correct the fragments and comma splices.

March 5, 1996

Joanna Freeman
Personel Director
United Teletype
1111 E. Street
Kansas City, MO 68114

Dear Ms. Freeman:

Your advertizmemt in the Febuary 18, 1996, Kansas City Star is just the opening I have been looking for. I would like to submit my quallifications.

As you will note in the inclosed resum, I recieved an Enginneering degree from the Missouri Institute of Technology in 1979 and have worked in the electronic engin-neering department of General Accounts for two years. I have worked a great deal in design electronics for micro-procesors, controll systems, ect.

Because your company has invented many extrordinary design projects, working at your company would give me more chances to use my knowlege aquired in school and through my expirences. If you are interested in my quallifications, I would be happy to discuss them futher with you. I look foreward to hearing from you.

Sincerly,

Bob Cottrell

Bob Cottrell

May 12, 1996

Maurene Pierce
Dean of Residence Life
Mann College
Mannsville, NY 10012

Subject: Report on Dormitory Damage Systems

Here is the report you authorized on April 5 for an analysis of the current dormitory damage system used in this college.

The purpose of the report was to determine the effectiveness of the system. And to offer any concrete recommendations for improvement. To do this, I analyzed in detail the damage cost figures for the past three years, I also did an extensive study of dormitory conditions. Although I had limited manpower. I gathered information on all seven dormitories, focusing specifically on the men's athletic dorm, located at 1201 Chester. In this dorm, bathroom facilities, carpeting, and air conditioning are most susceptible to damage. Along with closet doors.

Nonetheless, my immediate findings indicate that the system is functioning well, however, improvements in the physical characteristics of the dormitories, such as new carpeting and paint, would make the system even more efficient.

I have enjoyed conducting this study, I hope my findings help you make your final decision. Please contact me. If I can be of further assistance.

Edie Kreisler

Edie Kreisler

PUNCTUATION

In the following sentences, circle the correct punctuation marks. If no punctuation is needed, draw a slash mark through both options.

1. John took an hour for lunch (, ;) but Joan stayed at her desk to eat so she could complete the project.
2. Sally wrote the specifications (, ;) Randy was responsible for adding any needed graphics.
3. Manufacturing maintained a 93.5 percent production rating in July (, ;) therefore, they earned the Golden Circle Award at the quarterly meeting.
4. In their year-end requests to management (, ;) supervisors asked for new office equipment (, ;) and a 10 percent budget increase for staffing.
5. The following employees attended the training session on stress management (, :) Steve Janasz, purchasing agent (, ;) Jeremy Kreisler, personnel director (, ;) and Karen Rochlin, staff supervisor.
6. The promotions were given to all sales personnel (, ;) secretaries, however, received only cost of living raises.
7. The technicians voted for better work benefits (, ;) as an incentive to improve morale.
8. Although the salespeople were happy with their salary increases (, ;) the technicians felt slighted.
9. First (, ;) let's remember that meeting schedules should be a priority (, ;) and not an afterthought.
10. The employee (, ;) who achieves the highest rating this month (, ;) will earn 10 bonus points (, ;) therefore (, ;) competition should be intense.

In the letter on page 461, no punctuation has been added. Instead, there are blanks where punctuation might be inserted. First, decide if any punctuation is needed (not every blank requires punctuation). Then, insert the correct punctuation—a comma, colon, period, semicolon, or question mark.

AGREEMENT (SUBJECT/VERB AND PRONOUN/ANTECEDENT)

In the following sentences, circle the correct choice to achieve agreement between subject and verb or pronoun and antecedent.

1. The employees, though encouraged by the possibility of increased overtime, (was were) still dissatisfied with their current salaries.
2. The supervisor wants to manufacture better products, but (they he) doesn't know how to motivate the technicians to improve their work habits.
3. The staff (was were) happy when the new manager cancelled the proposed meeting.
4. Anyone who wants (his or her their) vote recorded must attend the annual board meeting.

January 8_ 1996

Mr_ Ron Schaefer
1324 Homes
Carbondale_ IL_ 34198

Dear Mr_ Schaefer_

Yesterday_ my partners_ and I read about your invention in the *Herald Tribune*_ and we want to congratulate you on this new idea_ and ask you to work with us on a similar project_

We cannot wait to begin our project_ however_ before we can do so_ I would like you to answer the following questions_

- Has your invention been tested in salt water_
- What is the cost of replacement parts_
- What is your fee for consulting_

Once_ I receive your answers to these questions_ my partners and I will contact you regarding a schedule for operations_ We appreciate your design concept_ and know it will help our business tremendously_ We look forward to hearing from you_

Sincerely_

Ron Sandhaus

Ron Sandhaus

5. According to the printed work schedule, Susan and Tom (work works) today on the manufacturing line.
6. According to the printed work schedule, either Susan or Tom (work works) today on the manufacturing line.
7. Although Larry is responsible for distributing all monthly activity reports, (he they) failed to mail them.
8. Every one of the engineers asked if (he or she they) could be assigned to the project.
9. Either the supervisor or the technicians (is are) at fault.
10. The CEO, known for her generosity to employees and their families, (has have) been nominated for the humanitarian award.

In the following memo, find and correct the errors in agreement.

MEMO

Date: October 30, 1996
To: Tammy West
From: Susan Lisk SL
Subject: Report on Air Handling Unit

There has been several incidents involving the unit which has resulted in water damage to the computer systems located below the air handler.

The occurrences yesterday was caused when a valve was closed creating condensation to be forced through a humidifier element into the supply air duct. Water then leaked from the duct into the room below causing substantial damage to four disc-drive units.

To prevent recurrence of this type of damage, the following actions has been initiated by maintenance supervision:

- Each supervisor must ensure that their subordinates remove condensation valves to avoid unauthorized operation.
- Everyone must be made aware that they are responsible for closing condensation valves.
- The supply air duct, modified to carry away harmful sediments, are to be drained monthly.

Maintenance supervision recommend that air handlers not be installed above critical equipment. This will avoid the possibility of coil failure and water damage.

CAPITALIZATION

In the following memo, nothing has been capitalized. Capitalize those words requiring capitalization.

```
date:     december 5, 1996
to:       jordan cottrell
from:     richard davis
subject:  self-contained breathing apparatus (scba) and
          negative pressure respirator evaluation and fit-
          testing report

the evaluation and fit-testing have been accomplished. the
attached list identifies the following:

     • supervisors and electronic technicians who have used
       the scba successfully.
     • the negative pressure respirators used for testing in
       an isoaml acetate atmosphere.

fit-testing of waste management personnel will be accom-
plished annually, according to president chuck carlson. new
supervisors and technicians will be fit-tested when hired.

all apex corporation personnel located in the new york dis-
trict (12304 parkview lane) must submit a request form when
requesting a respirator or scba for use. any waste manage-
ment personnel in the north and south facilities not iden-
tified on the attached list will be fit-tested when use of
scba is required. if you have any questions, contact chuck
carlson or me (richard davis, district manager) at ext.
4036.
```

Chapter 13

Interpersonal Communications

Learning Objectives

After reading and studying this chapter and doing the exercises you should be able to

- Explain the basic steps in the communication process.
- Understand nonverbal communication and improve your nonverbal communication skills.
- Understand barriers to communication and know how to overcome them, including enhancing your listening skills.

"Why isn't this project ready for shipment today?" barked the manager. "I told you to get it done as soon as you could get to it." "That's why it isn't done," replied the group member. "I was too busy to get to it."

The communication problem just described took place because the phrase "as soon as you can get to it" was interpreted differently by the two people involved. The mix-up that took place illustrates that communication breakdowns are responsible for many problems that take place on the job.

Communication is the sending, receiving, and understanding of messages. It is also the basic process by which managers, customer-contact workers, and professionals accomplish their work. For example, a customer service representative cannot resolve a thorny customer problem without carefully receiving and sending information. Communication is also important because communication skills are a success factor for workers in a wide variety of jobs. Table 3-1 presents details on this topic.

The information in this chapter is aimed at reducing communication problems among people and helping you enhance your communication effectiveness. We approach these ends in two ways. First, we explain the nature of a few key facets of interpersonal communication. Second, we present guidelines for improving your effectiveness along with skill development exercises.

STEPS IN THE COMMUNICATION PROCESS

One way to understand how people communicate is to examine the steps involved in transmitting and receiving a message. The process involves the following sequence of events: ideation, encoding, transmission over a

TABLE 3-1

EMPLOYEE SKILLS COMPANIES WOULD MOST LIKE TO ENHANCE

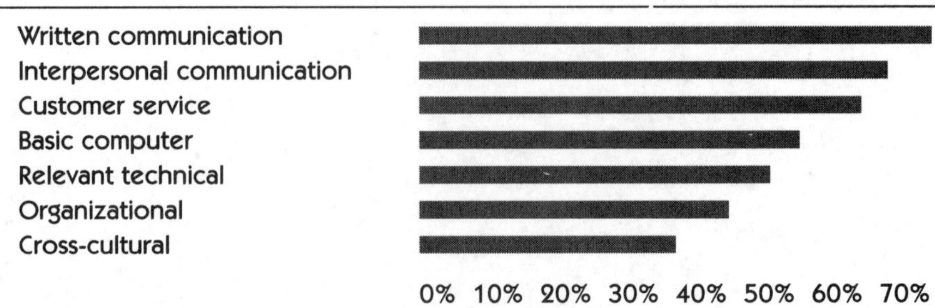

SOURCE: Based on data presented in *Human Resource Measurements,* Wonderlic Personnel Test, Inc., December 1991, and updated January 1995.

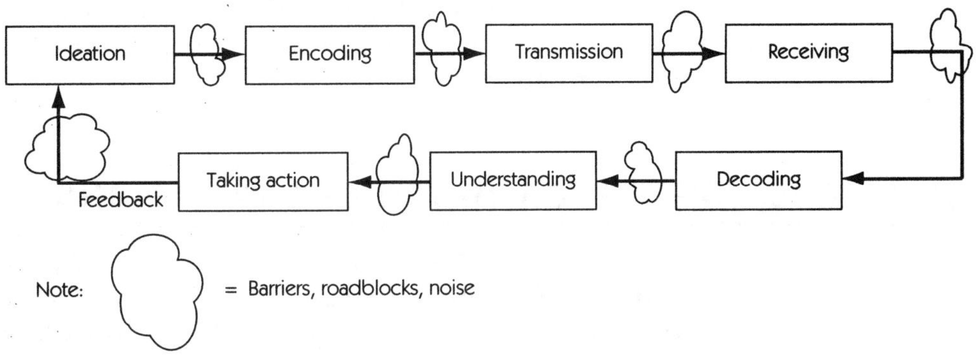

FIGURE 3-1 A Basic Model of Communication Process

medium, receiving, decoding, understanding, and taking action. The clouds in Figure 3-1 symbolize barriers that can arise at any step in communication.

The process is cyclical. Upon decoding a message, understanding it, and then taking action, the receiver sends out his or her own message. The cycle is therefore repeated at least once. Assume Conrad wishes to communicate to his boss, Barbara, that he wants a salary increase.

Step 1 is *ideation* by Conrad. He organizes his thoughts about this sensitive problem. This stage is both the origin and the framing of the idea or message in the sender's mind. Conrad says to himself, "I think I'll ask for a raise."

Step 2 is *encoding.* Here the ideas are organized into a series of symbols (words, hand gestures, body movements, drawings) designed to communicate to the intended receiver. Conrad says, "Barbara, there is something I would like to talk to you about when you have the time."

Step 3 is *transmission* of the message orally or in writing. In this situation, the sender chose the oral mode.

Step 4 is *receiving* of the message by the other party. Barbara can only receive the message if she is attentive to Conrad. Not being attentive is a barrier to communication.

Step 5 is *decoding* the symbols sent by the sender to the receiver. In this case decoding is not complete until Barbara hears the whole message. The opening comment, "Barbara, there is something I would like to talk about . . . ," is the type of statement often used by employees to broach a sensitive topic, such as discussing a resignation or salary increase. Barbara therefore listens attentively for more information.

Step 6, *understanding,* follows upon the decoding process. Barbara has no trouble understanding that Conrad wants a salary increase. When communication barriers exist (as described in the next section of this chapter), understanding may be limited.

Step 7 is *taking action.* Barbara understands Conrad's request, but does not agree. She acts by telling Conrad that he will have to wait three more months until his salary will be reviewed. Action is also a form of feedback, because it results in a message being sent back to the original sender from the receiver.

NONVERBAL COMMUNICATION IN ORGANIZATIONS

Our discussion so far has emphasized the use of words, or verbal communication. A substantial amount of communication between people, however, takes place at the nonverbal level. **Nonverbal communication** refers to the transmission of messages through means other than words. These messages accompany verbal messages or sometimes stand alone. The general purpose of nonverbal communication is to communicate the feeling behind a message. For instance, you can say no with either a clenched fist or with a smile to communicate the intensity of your negative feelings.

A classic study by Albert Mehrabian dramatizes the relevance of nonverbal communication. He calculated the relative weights of three elements of communication with their respect to conveying emotion. The words we choose account for only about 7 percent of our emotional impact on others. Our voice tone accounts for 38 percent of the impact, and our facial expressions for 55 percent. Nonverbal behavior therefore accounts for 93 percent of the emotional impact of a message.[1] Merhabian's study is often interpreted to mean that 93 percent of communication is nonverbal. In truth the study deals with the emotional impact of a message; it does not mean that the content of your message is unimportant.

We will summarize the major modes of transmission of nonverbal communication and provide guidelines for improving nonverbal communication. In Chapter 7 about cross-cultural relations, we describe cultural differences in nonverbal communication.

MODES OF TRANSMISSION OF NONVERBAL COMMUNICATION

Nonverbal communication can be transmitted in many modes, as described next. You may be surprised that certain actions, such as dress and appearance, are considered part of nonverbal communication.

Environment

The setting or environment in which you send a message can influence the receiving of that message. Assume that your manager invites you out to lunch to discuss a problem. You will think it is a more important topic under these circumstances than if the manager had lunch with you in the company cafeteria.

Other important environmental silent messages include room color, temperature, lighting, and furniture arrangement. A person who sits behind a large, uncluttered desk, for example, appears more powerful than a person who sits behind a small, messy desk.

Interpersonal Distance

The placement of one's body in relation to someone else (*proxemics*) is widely used to transmit messages. (See Figure 3-2.) In general, getting physically close to another person conveys a positive attitude toward him or her. Putting your arm around someone is generally interpreted as a friendly act. (Some people, however, recoil when touched by someone other than a close friend. Touching others on the job can also be interpreted as sexual harassment.)

Posture

Your posture communicates a variety of meanings. Standing erect usually conveys the message that the person is self-confident and experiencing positive emotion. Slumping makes a person appear to be lacking in self-confidence or down in the dumps. Another interpersonal meaning of pos-

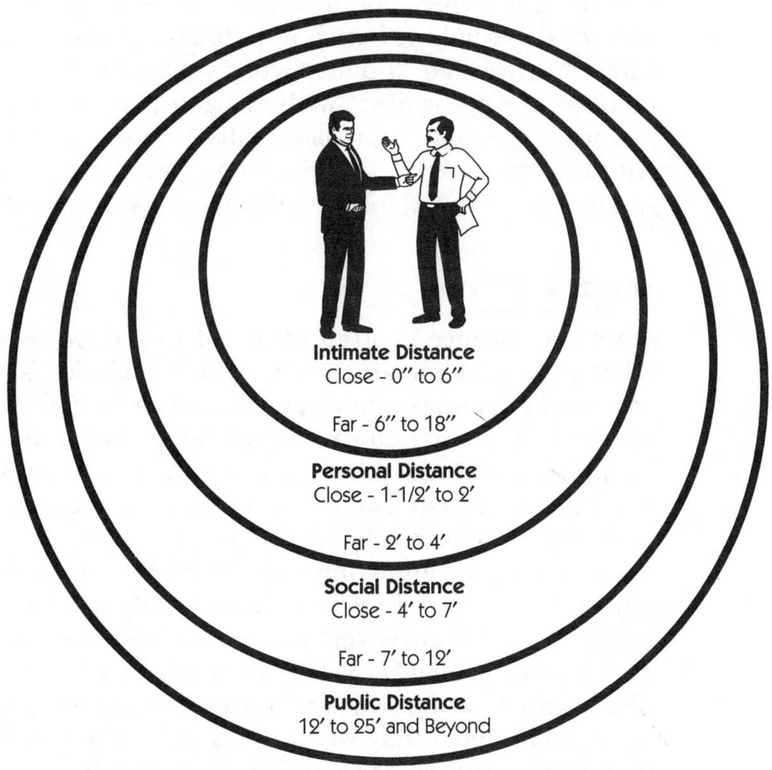

FIGURE 3-2 Four Circles of Intimacy

ture involves the direction of leaning. Leaning toward the sender suggests that you are favorably disposed toward his or her message; leaning backward communicates the opposite message. Openness of the arms or legs serves as an indicator of liking or caring. In general, people establish closed postures (arms folded and legs crossed) when speaking to people they dislike.

Gestures

Positive attitudes toward another person are shown by frequent hand movements. In contrast, dislike or disinterest usually produces few gestures. An important exception is that some people wave their hands furiously while arguing. Gestures are also said to provide clues to a person's levels of dominance and submission. The gestures of dominant people are typically directed outward toward the other person. Examples include a steady, unwavering gaze and touching one's partner. Submissive gestures are usually protective, such as touching oneself or shrugging one's shoulders.

Facial Expressions

Using your head, face, and eyes in combination provides the clearest indications of interpersonal attitudes. Looking at the ceiling—without tilting your head—combined with a serious expression almost always communicates the message, "I doubt what you're saying is true." As is well known, maintaining eye contact with another person improves communication. To maintain eye contact, it is usually necessary to move your face and eyes with the other person. Moving your face and eyes *away* from the other person is often interpreted as defensiveness or a lack of self-confidence.

Voice Quality

More significance is often attached to the *way* something is said than to *what* is said. A forceful voice, which includes a consistent tone without vocalized pauses, connotes power and control. Closely related to voice tone are volume, pitch, and rate of speaking. Anger, boredom, and joy can often be interpreted from voice quality. Anger is noted when the person speaks loudly, with a high pitch and fast rate. Boredom is indicated by a monotone. Joy is indicated by loud volume.

Avoiding an annoying voice quality can make a positive impact on others. The research of voice coach Jeffrey Jacobbi provides some useful suggestions. He surveyed a nationwide sample of 1,000 men and women, and asked, "Which irritating or unpleasant voice annoys you the most?" The most irritating was a whining, complaining, or nagging tone.

Jacobbi notes that we are judged by the way we sound. He also notes that careers can be damaged by voice problems such as those indicated in the survey. "We think about how we look and dress," says Jacobbi. "And that gets most of the attention. But people judge our intelligence much more by how we sound than how we dress."[2] Do Self-Assessment Exercise 3-1 to apply Jacobbi's findings to your development.

Personal Appearance

Your external image plays an important role in communicating messages to others. Job seekers show recognition of this aspect of nonverbal communication when they carefully groom for a job interview. People pay more respect and grant more privileges to those they perceive as being well dressed and neatly groomed. Furthermore, some research indicates that a favorable personal appearance leads to high starting salaries and later salary increases.[3]

SELF-ASSESSMENT

EXERCISE 3-1

VOICE-QUALITY CHECKUP

The voice-quality study cited in the text ranked voice quality in decreasing order of annoyance, as follows:

- Whining, complaining, or nagging tone—44.0 percent
- High-pitched, squeaky voice—15.9 percent
- Mumblers—11.1 percent
- Very fast talkers—4.9 percent
- Weak and wimpy voice—3.6 percent
- Flat, monotonous tone—3.5 percent
- A thick accent—2.4 percent

Directions: Ask yourself and two other people familiar with your voice if you have one or more of the preceding voice-quality problems. If your self-analysis and feedback from others does indicate a serious problem, get started on self-improvement. Record your voice on tape and attempt to modify the biggest problem. Another avenue of improvement is to consult with a speech coach or therapist.

GUIDELINES FOR IMPROVING NONVERBAL COMMUNICATION

Nonverbal communication, as with verbal communication, can be improved. Here are six suggestions to consider.

1. *Obtain feedback on your body language by asking others to comment upon the gestures and facial expressions that you use in conversations.* Be videotaped conferring with another individual. After studying your body language, attempt to eliminate those mannerisms and gestures that you think detract from your effectiveness. Common examples include nervous gestures, such as moving knees from side to side, cracking knuckles, rubbing the eyes or nose, head scratching, and jingling coins.

2. *Learn to relax when communicating with others.* Take a deep breath and consciously allow your body muscles to loosen. Tension-reducing techniques should be helpful here. A relaxed person makes it easier for other people to relax. You are likely to elicit more useful information from other people when you are relaxed.

3. *Use facial, hand, and body gestures to supplement your speech, but don't overdo it.* A good starting point is to use hand gestures to express enthusiasm. You can increase the potency of enthusiastic comments by shaking the other person's hand, nodding approval or smiling.

4. *Avoid using the same nonverbal gesture indiscriminately.* If you want to use nodding to convey approval, do not nod with approval when you dislike what somebody else is saying. Also, do not pat everybody on the back. Nonverbal gestures used indiscriminately lose their communication effectiveness.

5. *Use role playing to practice various forms of nonverbal communication.* A good starting point would be to practice selling your ideas about an important project or concept to another person. During your interchange, supplement your spoken messages with appropriate nonverbal cues such as posture, voice intonation, gestures, and so forth. Later, obtain the other person's perception of the effectiveness of your nonverbal communication.

6. *Use mirroring to establish rapport.* Nonverbal communication can be improved through **mirroring,** or subtly imitating someone. The most successful mirroring technique is to imitate another's breathing pattern. If you adjust your own breathing rate to match someone else's, you will soon establish rapport with that individual. You can also use mirroring by imitating a manager to win favor. Many group members have a relentless tendency to copy the boss's mannerisms, gestures, way of speaking, and dress. As a consequence, without realizing why, your manager may think more favorably of you.

Caution: Do not use mirroring to the extent that you appear to be mocking another person, thus adversely affecting rapport. To get started developing your mirroring skills, do Skill-Development Exercise 3-1.

SKILL-DEVELOPMENT

EXERCISE 3-1

THE MIRRORING TECHNIQUE

To practice mirroring, during the next ten days each class member schedules one mirroring session with an unsuspecting subject. An ideal opportunity would be an upcoming meeting on the job. Another possibility would be to ask a friend if you could practice your interviewing techniques with him or her—but do not mention the mirroring technique. A third possibility would be to sit down with a friend and conduct a social conversation.

While holding an interview or discussion with the other party, use the mirroring technique. Imitate the person's breathing pattern, hand movements, eye movements, leg movements, or any other noticeable aspect of behavior.

After the mirroring sessions have been conducted, hold a class discussion about the results. Questions to seek answers to include:

1. Did the other person notice the mirroring and comment on the behavior of the person doing the mirroring?
2. Was the rapport enhanced (or hindered) by the mirroring?
3. How many of the students intend to repeat the mirroring technique in the future?

GUIDELINES FOR OVERCOMING COMMUNICATION PROBLEMS AND BARRIERS

Communication problems in organizations are ever present. Some interference usually takes place between ideation and action, as suggested earlier by the clouds in Figure 3-1. The type of message influences the amount of interference. Routine or neutral messages are the easiest to communicate. Interference is most likely to occur when a message is complex, emotionally arousing, or clashes with a receiver's mental set.

An emotionally arousing message deals with topics such as a relationship between two people or money. A message that clashes with a receiver's mental set requires the person to change his or her typical pattern of receiving messages. Try this experiment. The next time you visit a restaurant, order dessert first and the entrée second. The server will probably not receive your dessert order because it deviates from the normal sequence.

Here we will describe strategies and tactics for overcoming some of the more frequently observed communication problems in organizations, as outlined in Table 3-2.

TABLE 3-2

OVERCOMING COMMUNICATION PROBLEMS AND BARRIERS

1. Understand the receiver.
2. Discuss differences in paradigms.
3. Minimize defensive communication.
4. Use multiple channels.
5. Use verbal and nonverbal feedback.
6. Use persuasive communication.
7. Engage in active listening.
8. Engage in complementary transactions with people.
9. Recognize gender differences in communication styles.

UNDERSTAND THE RECEIVER

Understanding the person you are trying to reach is a fundamental principle of overcoming communication barriers. The more you know about your receiver, the better able you are to effectively deliver your message. Three important aspects of understanding the receiver are (1) developing empathy, (2) recognizing his or her motivational state, and (3) understanding the other person's frame of reference.

Developing **empathy** requires placing yourself in the receiver's shoes. To accomplish this you have to imagine yourself in the other person's role and assume the viewpoints and emotions of that individual. For example, if a supervisor were trying to communicate the importance of customer service to sales associates, the supervisor might ask him- or herself. "If I were a part-time employee being paid close to the minimum wage, how receptive would I be to messages about high-quality customer service?" To empathize you have to understand another person. *Sympathy* means that you understand and agree.

The receiver's **motivational state** could include any active needs and interests operating at the time. People tend to listen attentively to messages that show promise of satisfying an active need. Management usually listens attentively to a suggestion framed in terms of cost savings or increased profits.

People perceive words and concepts differently because their vantage points and perspectives differ. Such differences in **frame of reference** create barriers to communication. To reduce this barrier, you have to understand where the receiver is "coming from." A manager attempted to chastise a team member by saying, "If you keep up your present level of performance, you'll be a repair technician all your life." The technician replied, "That's good news," because he was proud of being the first person in his family to hold a skilled job. Understanding another person's frame of reference requires empathy.

DISCUSS DIFFERENCES IN PARADIGMS

Another way of understanding differences in frames of reference is to recognize that people often have different **paradigms** that influence how they interpret events. A paradigm is a model, framework, viewpoint, or perspective. When two people look at a situation with different paradigms, a communication problem may occur. For instance, one person may say, "Let's go to Las Vegas for the computer show." The other person may respond, "A ridiculous idea. It cost too much money and takes too much time. Besides, the company would never approve."

These objections are based on certain unstated beliefs:

- Air travel is the most suitable mode of transportation.
- Traveling over 500 miles a day by auto is fatiguing and dangerous.
- Traveling over a weekend for business and using vacation days cannot be considered seriously.
- Paying for such a trip with personal money is out of the question.

The other person has a different set of unstated beliefs:

- It is possible, traveling on interstate highways and using two drivers, to cover 1,000 miles in one day.
- Traveling over a weekend and taking vacation days is sensible.
- Paying for the trip with personal money is a sound educational investment.

The solution to this communication clash is to discuss the paradigms. Both people live by different rules or guidelines (a major contributor to a paradigm). If the two people can recognize that they are operating with different paradigms, the chances for agreement are improved. Keep in mind that people can change their paradigms when the reasons are convincing.[4] For example, the first person in the preceding situation may never have thought about using personal funds for a trip as being an educational investment.

MINIMIZE DEFENSIVE COMMUNICATION

An important general communication barrier is **defensive communication**—the tendency to receive messages in such a way that our self-esteem is protected. Defensive communication is also responsible for people sending messages to make themselves look good. For example, when being criticized for low production, an investment banker might blame the advertising agency used by his or her firm.

Overcoming the barrier of defensive communication requires two steps. First, people have to recognize the existence of defensive communication. Second, they have to try not to be defensive when questioned or criticized. Such behavior is not easy because of the unconscious or semiconscious process of **denial**—the suppression of information we find uncomfortable. For example, the investment banker just cited would find it uncomfortable to think of him- or herself as being responsible for below-average performance.

USE MULTIPLE CHANNELS

Repetition enhances communication, particularly when different channels are used to convey the same message. Effective communicators at many job levels follow spoken agreements with written documentation. Since most communication is subject to at least some distortion, the chances of a message being received as intended increase when two or more channels are used. It has become standard practice in many firms for managers to use a multiple-channel approach to communicate the results of a performance appraisal. The subordinate receives an oral explanation from the superior of the results of the review. The subordinate is also required to read the form and indicate by signature that he or she has read and understands the meaning of the review.

USE VERBAL AND NONVERBAL FEEDBACK

Ask for feedback to determine if your message has been received as intended. A frequent managerial practice is to conclude a meeting with a question such as, "Okay, what have we agreed upon?" Unless feedback of this nature is obtained, you will not know if your message has been received until the receiver later carries out your request. If the request is carried out improperly, or if no action is taken, you will know that the message was received poorly.

Feedback is also important because it provides reinforcement to the sender, and few people will continue to communicate without any reinforcement. The sender is reinforced when the receiver indicates understanding of the message. When the original receiver indicates that he or she understands the message, that person becomes the sender. A nod of approval would be an appropriate type of nonverbal reinforcement for the sender to receive.

USE PERSUASIVE COMMUNICATION

An elegant tactic for overcoming communication barriers is to communicate so persuasively that obstacles disappear. Persuasiveness refers to the sender convincing the receiver to accept his or her message. Persuasion thus involves selling to others. One communication specialist defines persuasiveness as "that hard-to-pin-down quality made up of an effective mix of commitment, eloquence, honesty, enthusiasm, and humor."[5]

Hundreds of articles, books, audiotapes, and videos have been developed to help people become more persuasive. As part of the quality-improvement movement in the workplace, many organizations now offer employees training in oral and written communications. Following are some representative suggestions for becoming a more persuasive communicator, both in speaking and in writing.[6]

1. *Know exactly what you want.* Your chances of selling an idea increase to the extent that you have clarified the idea in your own mind. The clearer and more committed you are at the outset of a selling or negotiating session, the stronger you are as a persuader.

2. *Develop fallback positions.* Keep in mind what you might do if you cannot convince the other side to accept your first proposal. If plan A does not work, shift to plan B, then to plan C.

3. *Never suggest an action without telling its end benefit.* In asking for a raise, you might say, "If I get this raise, I'll be able to afford to stay with this job as long as the company likes."

4. *Phrase your proposition in terms of the receiver's interests.* The basic rule of selling is an extension of the communication strategy "understand the receiver." People are far more likely to accept your idea if it is clear how they will benefit. Almost every receiver wants to know "What's in it for me?"

5. *Explore the reasons for people's objections.* Assume a potential customer says, "I like this model but I don't want it in my living room." An effective response would be "What is it that you don't like about it?" Another would be "Which features do you like in this product?"

6. *Explain why you are asking whenever you ask a question.* The sales representative in item 5 might say, "The reason I asked you about features is that may we have another model with similar features."

7. *Get a yes response early on.* It is helpful to give the selling session a positive tone by establishing a "yes pattern" at the outset. Assume that an employee wanted to convince his or her boss to allow the employee to perform some work at home during normal working hours. The employee might begin the idea-selling questions with the question, "Is it important for the company to obtain maximum productivity from all its employees?"

8. *Use power words.* An expert tactic for being persuasive is to sprinkle your speech with power (meaning *powerful*) words. Power words stir emotion and bring forth images of exciting events. Examples of the use of power words include *decimating* the competition, *bonding* with customers, *surpassing* previous profits, *capturing* customer loyalty, and *rebounding* from a downturn.

9. *Avoid or minimize common language errors.* You will enhance your persuasiveness if you minimize common language errors, because you will appear more articulate and informed. Here are several common language errors:

a. "Just between you and I" is wrong. "Just between you and me" is correct.
b. *Irregardless* is a nonword; *regardless* is correct.
c. *Imply* means to hint or suggest, while *infer* means to assume something. It would therefore be correct to say, "I infer from your report" or "Your report implies . . ."
d. "We are customer-oriented" is correct. "We are customer-orientated" is wrong.

If you can learn to implement most of the preceding nine suggestions you are on your way toward becoming a persuasive communicator. In addition, you will need solid facts behind you and will need to make skillful use of nonverbal communication. To further think through how you are doing as a communicator, do Self-Assessment Exercise 3-2.

ENGAGE IN ACTIVE LISTENING

Persuasion deals primarily with sending messages. Improving one's receiving of messages is another part of developing better communication skills. Unless you receive messages as they are intended, you cannot perform your job properly or be a good companion. Listening has even been described as our primary communication activity. We spend about 80 percent of our waking hours communicating. And 45 percent of that time is spent listening. Listening is a particularly important skill for anybody whose job involves troubleshooting, since one needs to gather information in order to solve problems.

Another reason that improving the listening skills of employees is important is that insufficient listening is extraordinarily costly. Listening mistakes lead to reprocessing letters, rescheduling appointments, reshipping orders, and recalling defective products. Effective listening also improves interpersonal relationships because the people listened to feel understood and respected.

A major component of effective listening is to be an active listener. The active listener listens intensely, with the goal of empathizing with the speaker. As a result of listening actively, the listener can feed back to the speaker what he or she thinks the speaker meant. Feedback of this type relies on both verbal and nonverbal communication. Active listening also involves **summarization.** When you summarize, you pull together, condense, and thereby clarify the main points communicated by the other person. Here are two examples of summarization statements:

"What I heard you say during our meeting is that . . ."

"As I understand it, your position is that . . ."

SELF-ASSESSMENT

EXERCISE 3-2

A TEST OF COMMUNICATION EFFECTIVENESS

The following scale consists of opposite descriptions of communication style. Between each pair is a 7-to-1 scale. Assess your communication style in terms of each pair of descriptions and circle the appropriate number. If you are not currently working as a manager, imagine how the situation would be based on your other work or social experience with people.

I think my communication with people in the workplace:

Increases my credibility	7 6 5 4 3 2 1	Decreases my credibility
Is precise	7 6 5 4 3 2 1	Is imprecise
Is clear	7 6 5 4 3 2 1	Is unclear
Answers more questions than it raises	7 6 5 4 3 2 1	Raises more questions than it answers
Is effective	7 6 5 4 3 2 1	Is ineffective
Is competent	7 6 5 4 3 2 1	Is incompetent
Is productive	7 6 5 4 3 2 1	Is unproductive
Gets the results I want	7 6 5 4 3 2 1	Does not get the results I want
Is impressive	7 6 5 4 3 2 1	Is unimpressive
Creates a positive image of me	7 6 5 4 3 2 1	Creates a negative image of me
Is good	7 6 5 4 3 2 1	Is bad
Is skillful	7 6 5 4 3 2 1	Is unskillful
Is relaxed	7 6 5 4 3 2 1	Is strained
Is self-rewarding	7 6 5 4 3 2 1	Is not self-rewarding
Does not embarrass me	7 6 5 4 3 2 1	Does embarrass me

Total score ________ To find your total score, add the numbers you circled.

Interpretation: If your total score is 81 or above, you have analyzed yourself as a very effective communicator. If your total score is 59–80, you have analyzed yourself as an effective communicator. If your total score is 37–58, you have analyzed yourself as an ineffective communicator. If your total score is 15–46, you have analyzed yourself as a very ineffective communicator.

To increase the accuracy of your self-evaluation, ask another person to evaluate your on-the-job communication by taking this test. Many of the ideas contained in this chapter, and in books and articles about communication skills, will help you improve your communication effectiveness.

SOURCE: Adapted from Lyle Sussman and Paul D. Krivnos, *Communication for Supervisors and Managers*, 1979, pp. 10–12. Used by permission of Mayfield Publishing.

Specific suggestions for improving listening skills are summarized in Exhibit 3-1. These suggestions relate to good listening in general, and also to active listening. As with any other suggestions for developing a new skill, considerable practice (with some supervision) is needed to bring about actual changes in behavior. One of the problems a poor listener would

EXHIBIT 3-1

ELEVEN KEYS TO EFFECTIVE LISTENING

These keys are a positive guideline to better listening. In fact, they're at the heart of developing better listening habits that could last a lifetime.

Eleven keys to effective listening	The bad listener	The good listener
1. Find areas of interest	Tunes out dry subjects	Seeks opportunities; asks "What's in it for me?"
2. Judge content, not delivery	Tunes out if delivery is poor	Judges content, skips over delivery errors
3. Hold your fire	Tends to enter into argument	Doesn't judge until comprehension is complete
4. Listen for ideas	Listens for facts	Listens for central themes
5. Be flexible	Takes intensive notes using only one system	Takes fewer notes; uses four or five different systems, depending on speaker
6. Work at listening	Shows no energy output; fakes attention	Works hard, exhibits active body state
7. Resist distractions	Is distracted easily	Fights or avoids distractions, tolerates bad habits, knows how to concentrate
8. Exercise your mind	Resists difficult expository material; seeks light, recreational material	Uses heavier material as exercise for the mind
9. Keep your mind open	Reacts to emotional words	Interprets color words; does not get hung up on them
10. Capitalize on the fact that *thought* is faster than speech	Tends to daydream with slow speakers	Challenges, anticipates, mentally summarizes, weighs the evidence, listens between the lines to tone of voice
11. Restate what you hear	Reacts to what he or she hears	Clarifies what he or she hears until other person says "Yes, this is what I'm saying."

SOURCE: John W. Richter, "Listening: An Art Essential to Success," *Success*, September 1980, p. 26.

encounter is the difficulty of breaking old habits in order to acquire new ones. To practice your listening skills, do Skill-Development Exercise 3-2.

ENGAGE IN COMPLEMENTARY TRANSACTIONS WITH PEOPLE

A specific technique for improving communications with people, and thereby breaking down barriers, is to engage in **complementary transactions.** A complementary transaction is an exchange of words between two people that reduces tension and moves the two people toward a positive resolution. The complementary transaction occurs when one person gets the kind of response he or she wants from the other. The skill of using complementary transactions involves adapting your response precisely to the actions and words of the other person, just as a complementary angle completes a circle.

According to the discipline called *transactional analysis,* transactions between people are classified as complementary or noncomplementary (crossed). Complementary transactions lead to effective interaction and *positive strokes,* or ego-building statements. Noncomplementary transactions lead to ineffective interactions and *negative strokes,* or ego-tearing insults.

SKILL-DEVELOPMENT EXERCISE 3-2

LISTENING TO A COWORKER

Before conducting the following role plays, review the 11 keys to effective listening presented in Exhibit 3-1. Suggestion 11 about restating what you hear (summarization) is particularly important when listening to a person who is talking about an emotional topic.

The Elated Coworker: One student plays the role of a coworker who has just been offered a promotion to supervisor of another department. She will be receiving a 10 percent raise in pay and be able to travel overseas twice a year for the company. She is eager to describe full details of her good fortune to a coworker. Another student plays the role of the coworker to whom the first worker wants to describe her good fortune. The second worker decides to listen intently to the first worker. Other class members will rate the second student on his or her listening ability.

The Discouraged Coworker: One student plays the role of a coworker who has just been placed on probation for poor job performance. His boss thinks that his performance is below standard and that his attendance and punctuality are poor. He is afraid that if he tells his girlfriend, she will leave him. He is eager to tell his tale of woe to a coworker. Another student plays the role of a coworker he corners to discuss his problems. The second worker decides to listen intently to his problems but is pressed for time. Other class members will rate the second student on his or her listening ability.

Finding a complementary response is especially useful when attempting to keep communications running smoothly in a tense situation. You search for the type of response the person is seeking so you can keep the conversation positive. You then stand a reasonable chance of overcoming a communications barrier.

Assume that Dorothy is red in the face with anger because an important file she had been working on is erased from the personal computer she was using. Acting in a childlike manner, she goes into a tirade about how some fool must have been messing around with her computer files. By the tone of her voice, you get the impression she thinks you are the culprit.

One way you can engage in a complementary transaction is by acting in a controlling, parentlike manner in response to her childish state. You might respond, "Please calm down, Dorothy. I am good at finding lost files, and I will do my best to help you." Communication will probably continue because Dorothy is receiving the type of helping response she wants.

Another way to engage in a complementary transaction with Dorothy is to respond in a childish manner to her childish tirade. You might respond, "Holy cats, what a mess. I bet some fool did mess up your files. Some of the temps we have working in this office are irresponsible. They have no respect for other people's work." Because a person acting like a child will also welcome a childish response in return, communication is likely to continue.

A crossed transaction occurs when a person does not get the type of response he or she sought. In Dorothy's situation, she is not looking for a response that will put her in her place and suggest she take responsibility for her own problems. You would engage in a crossed transaction with Dorothy if you responded: "Hey, Dorothy, don't yell at me in those accusatory tones. It's your responsibility to manage your own computer files. If you want to blame someone, look in the mirror."

In short, if another person is communicating to you in a childish, immature manner, transactional analysis suggests you can salvage the situation two ways. First, you can exert control in a firm, controlling manner, much like a parent. Second, you can respond in an immature manner, thus communicating on the same wavelength. Both responses result in complementary transactions. In a crossed transaction the second party is troubled or irritated by the message sent by the first party. As a result, the second party responds in a way that surprises and troubles the first party.[7] Skill-Development Exercise 3-3 gives you practice in identifying complementary versus crossed transactions.

RECOGNIZE GENDER DIFFERENCES IN COMMUNICATION STYLES

A trend in organizations since the early 1970s has been to move toward equality of the sexes. Despite this trend, substantial interest has arisen in identifying differences in communication styles between men and women. A book by linguist Deborah Tannen, *Talking from 9 to 5,* focuses especially

SKILL-DEVELOPMENT

EXERCISE 3-3

COMPLEMENTARY VERSUS CROSSED TRANSACTIONS

Following are alternative responses to the same statement. To the left of each response, indicate with a plus sign (+) if the response is a complementary and a minus sign (–) if it is a crossed transaction. Suggested answers may be found at the end of the chapter.

Situation A: A coworker says to you, "Why are you always late coming back from lunch?"

_____ "Look who's talking. You leave work early almost every day."

_____ "You're right. I take care of too many errands during lunch hour. Since it bothers you I will try to get back from lunch more promptly."

Situation B: Out of town on a company-sponsored trip, one worker says to the other, "Why don't we both eat at a sub shop tonight, and then charge the company for a fancy dinner."

_____ "I like the idea of having a little extra cash, but I am concerned that we would be violating company policy. Let's not do it."

_____ "Count me out. I dislike cheating, and I hate cheats."

on male-female differences in conversational style in the workplace. A book by John Gray, *Men Are from Mars, Women Are from Venus,* explores the same topic.

People who are aware of these differences face fewer communication barriers between themselves and members of the opposite sex. As we describe these differences, recognize that they are group stereotypes. Individual differences in communication style are usually more important than group (men versus women) differences. Here we will describe the major findings of sex differences in communication patterns.[8]

1. *Women prefer to use conversation for rapport building.* For most women, the intent of conversation is to build rapport and connections with people. Women are therefore more likely to emphasize similarities, to listen intently, and to be supportive.

2. *Men prefer to use talk primarily as a means to preserve independence and status by displaying knowledge and skill.* When most men talk they want to receive positive evaluation from others and maintain their hierarchical status within the group. Men are therefore more oriented to giving a *report* while women are more interested in establishing *rapport.*

3. *Women want empathy, not solutions.* When women share feelings of being stressed out, they seek empathy and understanding. If they feel they have been listened to carefully, they begin to relax. When listening to the woman, the man may feel blamed for her problems or that he has failed the woman in some way. To feel useful, the man might offer solutions to the woman's problems.

4. *Men prefer to work out their problems by themselves, whereas women prefer to talk out solutions with another person.* Women look upon having and sharing problems as an opportunity to build and deepen relationships. Men are more likely to look upon problems as challenges they must meet on their own. The communication consequence of these differences is that men may become uncommunicative when they have a problem.

5. *Women are more likely to compliment the work of a coworker, while men are more likely to be critical.* A communication problem may occur when a woman compliments the work of a coworker and expects reciprocal praise.

6. *Men tend to be more directive in their conversation, while women emphasize politeness.* Women are therefore more likely to frequently use the phrases "I'm sorry" and "Thank you," even where there is no need to express apology or gratitude. For example, a supermarket manager notices that the store has suddenly become busy. She would therefore say to a store clerk unpacking boxes, "I'm sorry Pedro, but we've become busy all of a sudden. Could you please open up a new lane up front? Thank you." A manager who is a stereotyped male might say, "Pedro, we need you to open a line up front, pronto. Put down the boxes and get up there."

7. *Women tend to be more conciliatory when facing differences, while men become more intimidating.* Again, women are more interested in building relationships, while men are more concerned about coming out ahead.

8. *Men are more interested than women in calling attention to their accomplishments or hogging recognition.* In one instance a sales representative who had already made her sales quota for the month turned over an excellent prospect to a coworker. She reasoned, "It's somebody else's turn. I've received more than my fair share of bonuses for the month."

9. *Men tend to dominate discussions during meetings.* One study of college faculty meetings found that women's longest turns at speaking were on the average, less than men's shortest turns. A possible explanation here is that women are still less assertive than men in the workplace.

How can the information just presented help overcome communication problems on the job? As a starting point, remember that these gender differences often exist. Understanding these differences will help you interpret the communications behavior of people. For example, if a male coworker is not as effusive with praise as you would like, remember that he is simply engaging in gender-typical behavior. Do not take it personally.

A woman can remind herself to speak up more in meetings because her natural tendency might be toward diffidence. She might say to herself, *I must watch out to avoid gender-typical behavior in this situation.* A man might remind himself to be more complimentary and supportive toward coworkers. The problem is that although such behavior is important, his natural tendency might be to skip the praise.

A woman should not take it personally when a male coworker or subordinate is tight-lipped when faced with a problem. She should recognize that he needs more encouragement to talk about his problems than would a woman. If the man persists in not wanting to talk about the problem, the woman might say: "It looks like you want to work out this problem on your own. Go ahead. I'm available if you want to talk about the problem."

Men and women should recognize that when women talk over problems, they might not be seeking hard-hitting advice. Instead, they may simply be searching for a sympathetic ear so they can deal with the emotional aspect of the problem.

SUMMARY

Communication is the basic process by which managers, customer-contact workers, and professionals accomplish their work, yet many communication problems exist in organizations. Communication among people is a complex process that can be divided into seven stages: ideation, encoding, transmission, receiving, decoding, understanding, and action.

SUGGESTED ANSWERS TO SKILL-DEVELOPMENT EXERCISE 3-3

Situation A: The first response will most likely result in a crossed transaction (–) because the second person is revengeful and insulting. The second response will most likely result in a complementary transaction (+) because the second person submits to the parental approach of the first person in a submissive, obedient-child manner.

Situation B: The first response will most likely result in a complementary transaction (+) because the childlike behavior of the first person is being controlled in a parental way. The second response will probably result in a crossed transaction (–) because the first person is insulted by the second.

Nonverbal communication plays an important part in sending and receiving messages and is especially important for imparting the emotional aspects of a message. The modes of nonverbal communication include the environment in which the message is sent, interpersonal distance, posture, gestures, facial expressions, voice quality, and personal appearance.

Nonverbal communication can be improved through such means as obtaining feedback, learning to relax, using gestures more discriminately, role playing, and mirroring. The latter refers to subtly imitating someone.

Methods of overcoming communication barriers include the following: (1) understand the receiver, (2) discuss differences in paradigms, (3) minimize defensive communication, (4) use multiple channels, (5) use verbal and nonverbal feedback, (6) use persuasive communication, (7) engage in active listening, (8) engage in complementary transactions with people, (9) recognize gender differences in communication styles.

QUESTIONS FOR DISCUSSION AND REVIEW

1. What are the reasons so many workers need improvement in communication skills?
2. How can knowing the steps in the communication process help a person become a more effective communicator?
3. How can people use their automobiles to send nonverbal messages?
4. What type of voice quality do you think would be effective in most situations?
5. What, if any, ethical problems are involved with mirroring?
6. Suppose your manager does not listen to your suggestions for job improvements. Explain this problem as a paradigm clash.
7. Should a person use power words when he or she is not in a powerful job? Explain.
8. Why is summarization such a powerful communication technique?
9. Why bother having a complementary transaction when you disagree with a person?
10. What are the implications of gender differences in communication for conducting meetings?

A HUMAN RELATIONS CASE PROBLEM

PROFESSIONALISM AT ABILENE HEALTH CENTER

Joan McKenzie, the health care administrator at Abilene Health Center (AHC), had become concerned about the casual behavior of nurses at the center. McKenzie observed that some of the RNs (registered nurses) and LPNs (licensed practical nurses) were dressing and acting in a manner that detracted from the professional image of the health center. McKenzie set up a meeting to deal with what she perceived to be a problem of professionalism. At the outset of the meeting, McKenzie distributed an agenda that described the goals and objectives for the nursing staff. She instructed the people present to read the memo, and then said, "After you have digested the information, we will have a full group discussion of the issues raised." A copy of her memo follows:

To: All members of the AHC nursing staff
From: Joan McKenzie, health care administrator
Re: Professionalism

We are *professional* adults and must behave accordingly. Professionalism can be achieved by keeping the following goals and objectives in mind.

1. Provide comprehensive health care of high quality in a cost-effective manner which provides satisfaction to those who receive and those who deliver services.
2. Assist, guide, and direct each nurse to his or her highest potential. Help each nurse be the best he or she can be.
3. Maintain and improve respect, pride, and dignity for coworkers.

In order to resolve existing problems, please observe the following rules:

1. Cursing will not be tolerated.
2. Screaming, yelling, or raising your voice is not acceptable.
3. Calling others names is not acceptable.
4. Everybody is to be at work from 8 A.M. to noon, and 1 to 5 P.M. If you have a problem with leaving at noon or 5 P.M., please call your supervisor one hour before that time.
5. If you are sick, you should call AHC before 8 A.M. at 442-0483. Lori Fanuco will answer the telephone and take your message. If there is no answer, please keep trying.
6. When you are asked to float to an area, please stay in that area and work appropriately.

(Continued) ►

7. There will be no nail-polishing in nurses' stations. Reading should be confined to nursing journals. Breaks must be taken in the break room.
8. As of May 1, the nursing staff is to wear white dresses or white pants or skirts with white or colored uniform-type tops. White nurses' shoes and sheer hose are also required. Name tags are to be worn by all employees at all times while at AHC.
9. A policies and procedures manual will be available in each nurses' station in the future.

As the nursing staff finished reading the memo, Joan McKenzie looked around the room to see if she could gauge reactions.

CASE QUESTIONS

1. How effective is the above memo from a communication standpoint?
2. What communication barriers might McKenzie be erecting?
3. What improvement in nonverbal communication is McKenzie seeking, as revealed by her memo?

A HUMAN RELATIONS ROLE PLAY

DISCUSSING A CONTROVERSIAL MEMO

The role play is a follow-up to McKenzie's memo and meeting. One of the nurses at the meeting initiates a discussion of his or her reaction to the memo and its implications. The nurse feels that McKenzie is putting the nursing staff on the defensive by using accusatory and hostile language. McKenzie believes that her memo is a useful communication vehicle and that the nurse is being too sensitive. One person plays the role of McKenzie; another person plays the role of the dissenting nurse. Several other people can play the roles of other meeting participants who want to express how they feel about McKenzie's written message.

Chapter 14

Resolving Conflicts with Others

Learning Objectives

After reading and studying this chapter and doing the exercises you should be able to

- Recognize your typical method of resolving conflict.
- Specify why so much interpersonal conflict exists in organizations.
- Understand your typical method of resolving conflict.
- Identify the five modes of handling conflict.
- Develop effective techniques for resolving conflict and negotiating.
- Understand how to combat sexual harassment in the workplace.

"Sorry, I can't let you take off three days to attend your friend's wedding in Indianapolis," said Gerry, the accounting supervisor, to Wendy, the accountant. "This is our busiest season and I just can't spare you."

"What do you mean you can't spare me?" asked Wendy. "My best friend is getting married and I'm the maid of honor. I have *to go."*

"You may think you have to attend the wedding," replied Gerry, "but we need you here to help us manage our peak workload. If you decide to take three unauthorized days from work, you will face company discipline."

The unfortunate incident between Gerry and Wendy illustrates several different meanings of **conflict.** A conflict is a situation in which two or more goals, values, or events are incompatible or mutually exclusive. Gerry wants Wendy to be present every day during the busy tax season, and Wendy wants to attend an out-of-town wedding. A conflict is also a strife, quarrel, or battle. Gerry and Wendy are in a quarrel. Finally, conflict is said to occur when one side interferes with, disrupts, or in some way makes the other side less effective. This aspect of conflict will occur only if Wendy is disciplined by a harsh measure such as suspension or termination.

The purpose of this chapter is to help you improve your ability to resolve conflicts with people at work. The same techniques are also useful in personal life. To improve your understanding of how to resolve conflict, we will present specific techniques and also explain why so much conflict exists. To get you started relating the topic of conflict to yourself, do Self-Assessment Exercise 4-1.

SOURCES OF INTERPERSONAL CONFLICT IN ORGANIZATIONS

Conflict between and among people has many sources, or causes. In this section we describe some of the leading sources. If you understand the cause of conflict, it can help you resolve the present conflict and help prevent a similar recurrence. For example, if you learn that much conflict on the job is caused by a series of little hurts (*pinches*) you can apologize for these hurts. You can also be on guard to avoid such pinches in the future.

Although specific sources of conflict can be identified, keep in mind an important fact. All conflict includes the underlying theme of incompatibility between your goals, values, or events and those of another person.

COMPETITION FOR LIMITED RESOURCES

An underlying source of job conflict is that few people can get all the resources they want. These resources include money, material, and personnel (or human resources). Conflicts arise when two or more people squabble over who should get the resources. Even in a prosperous organi-

SELF-ASSESSMENT

EXERCISE 4-1

STYLES OF CONFLICT MANAGEMENT

Directions: Check the alternative that most fits your typical reaction to the situation described.

Part I: The Quiz

1. When someone is overly hostile toward me, I usually:
a. ____ respond in kind
b. ____ persuade him or her to cool down
c. ____ hear the person out
d. ____ walk away

2. When I walk in on a heated argument, I'm likely to:
a. ____ jump in and take sides
b. ____ mediate
c. ____ keep quiet and observe
d. ____ leave the scene

3. When I suspect that another person is taking advantage of me, I:
a. ____ try to get the person to stop
b. ____ rely on persuasion and facts
c. ____ change how I relate to the person
d. ____ accept the situation

4. When I don't see eye to eye with someone, I typically:
a. ____ try to get him or her to see things my way
b. ____ consider the problem logically
c. ____ search for a workable compromise
d. ____ let the problem work itself out

5. After a run-in with someone I care about a great deal, I:
a. ____ try to make him or her see it my way
b. ____ try to work out our differences
c. ____ wait before renewing contact
d. ____ let it lie

6. When I see conflict developing between two people I care about, I usually:
a. ____ express disappointment
b. ____ try to mediate
c. ____ watch to see what develops
d. ____ leave the scene

(Continued) ▶

7. When I see conflict developing between two people who are relatively unimportant to me, I usually:
   a. ____ express disappointment
   b. ____ try to mediate
   c. ____ watch to see what develops
   d. ____ leave the scene
8. The feedback people give me indicates that I:
   a. ____ push hard to get what I want
   b. ____ try to work out differences
   c. ____ take a conciliatory stance
   d. ____ sidestep conflict
9. When having serious disagreements, I:
   a. ____ talk until I've made my point
   b. ____ talk a little more than I listen
   c. ____ listen and make sure I understand
   d. ____ listen passively
10. When someone does something that angers me, I generally:
   a. ____ use strong, direct language
   b. ____ try to persuade him or her to stop
   c. ____ go easy, explaining how I feel
   d. ____ say and do nothing

Part II: Score Analysis

When you've completed the questions, add all the As, Bs, Cs, and Ds to find where you collected the most responses. Then consider these profiles:

A. *Competitive.* If you picked mostly *A* responses, you feel best when you're able to direct and control others. Taken to extremes, you can be intimidating and judgmental. You are generally contemptuous of people who don't stand up for themselves, and you feel frustrated when you can't get through to someone.

B. *Collaborative.* If you scored high in this category, you may be from the "use your head to win" school of conflict management—strong-willed and ambitious, but not overbearing. You'll use persuasion, not intimidation, and are willing to compromise to end long-running conflicts.

C. *Sharing.* People who score high here don't get fired up. They listen to the opponent's point of view, analyze situations and make a factual pitch for their case. But in the end, they will defer to opponents in the interest of harmony.

D. *Accommodative.* A high score suggests that you avoid conflict and confrontation at all costs, suppress your feelings—strong as they may be—to keep peace.

Observation: No one style of conflict management is better than another. Most people use all four, depending on the situation. But if you rely too much on one, start shifting your approach.

Source: Adapted with permission from *Executive Strategies,* National Institute of Business Management, Feb. 20, 1990, p. 6.

zation, resources have to be divided in such a manner that not everybody gets what he or she wants.

Assume that you believe you need to have a personal computer immediately accessible the full workday. Yet the company has decided that three people must share one computer. As a result, you are likely to enter into conflict with the two others sharing the computer. The conflict will be intense if your two coworkers also think they need full-time access to a personal computer.

ROLE CONFLICT

A major source of conflict (and stress) on the job relates to being placed in a predicament. **Role conflict** is having to choose between two competing demands or expectations. If you comply with one aspect of a role, compliance with the other is difficult or impossible. An important example would be receiving contradictory orders from two people above you in your company. If you comply with the wishes of one person, you will antagonize the other.

A high-performing sales representative received a job offer from a manager in another division in her company. Her present boss told her she was not allowed to transfer, and made her a counteroffer. The sales representative found herself in conflict with the two managers. Distraught over the conflict, she found employment with a competitive firm in a comparable position to the internal job offer she had received.

Four types of role conflict have been identified. All are significant here because they can result in clashes with other people.

Intrasender conflict occurs when one person asks you to accomplish two objectives that are in apparent conflict. If your boss asked you to hurry up and finish your work but also decrease your mistakes, you would experience this type of conflict (plus perhaps a headache!).

Intersender conflict occurs when two or more senders give you incompatible directions. Your immediate superior may want you to complete a crash project on time, but company policy temporarily prohibits authorizing overtime payments to clerical help.

Interrole conflict results when two different roles that you play are in conflict. Your company may expect you to travel 50 percent of the time, while your spouse threatens a divorce if you travel over 25 percent of the time.

Person-role conflict occurs when the role(s) your organization expects you to occupy are in conflict with your basic values. Your company may ask you to fire substandard performers, but this could be in conflict with your humanistic values.

BUILDING STONE WALLS

The slow and steady growth of a conflict situation has been likened by Richard J. Mayer to the building of a stone wall. The seed of the conflict is a minor incident that is not dealt with openly, called a *pinch.* Next, the person pinched unconsciously gathers data to support his or her view of the situation because of a need to be right. Much of the data are subject to perceptual distortion (seeing things in a way that fits our needs). As a result, a wall of minor incidents is built. The incidents eventually become an insurmountable obstacle (or stone wall) preventing honest and candid interaction with the *pincher.*[1]

A typical pinch occurs when an employee fails to share credit for a good idea he or she received from a coworker. The coworker feels slighted and then looks for other incidents of the first person being dishonest. Communication breaks down between the two, and they are involved in frequent arguments. The employee who failed to share credit may be unaware of how or why the conflict began. If the pinched worker had confronted the issue early on, the conflict might not have festered. Have you ever been pinched psychologically and said nothing about it?

PERSONALITY CLASHES

Many workplace disagreements arise because people simply dislike each other. A **personality clash** is thus an antagonistic relationship between two people based on differences in personal attributes, preferences, interests, values, and styles. A personality clash reflects negative chemistry between two people, while personal differences are based more specifically on a value clash.

People involved in a personality clash often have difficulty specifying why they dislike each other. The end result, however, is that they cannot maintain an amiable work relationship. A peculiarity about personality clashes is that people who get along well may begin to clash after working together for a number of years. A contributing factor is that as both people change and as the situation changes, the two people may no longer be compatible.

AGGRESSIVE PERSONALITIES

Coworkers naturally disagree about topics, issues, and ideas. Yet some people convert disagreement into an attack that puts down other people and damages their self-esteem. As a result, conflict surfaces. **Aggressive personalities** are people who verbally, and sometimes physically, attack others frequently. Verbal aggression takes the form of insults, teasing, ridicule, and profanity. Furthermore, the aggression may also be expressed as attacks on the victim's character, competence, background, and physical appearance.[2]

Aggressiveness is so frequent in a work setting that verbal and physical assault is the second most frequent issue addressed by arbitrators.[3] (An *arbitrator* is an outside party who acts in the role of a judge in settling disputes.) Aggressiveness can also take the extreme form of shooting and knifing a former boss or colleague by a mentally unstable worker recently dismissed from the company. As companies continue to reduce their workforce, these incidents have increased in frequency.

CONFLICT-MANAGEMENT STYLES

The information presented so far is designed to help you understand the nature of conflict. Such background information is useful for resolving conflict because it helps you understand what is happening in a conflict situation. The next two sections offer more specific information about managing and resolving conflict. Before describing specific methods of resolving conflict, it is useful to present more details about five general styles, or modes, of handling conflict. You received preliminary information on four of these five styles when you completed Self-Assessment Exercise 4-1.

As shown in Figure 4-1, Kenneth Thomas identified five major styles of conflict management. Each style is based on a combination of satisfying one's own concerns (assertiveness) and satisfying the concerns of others (cooperativeness).[4]

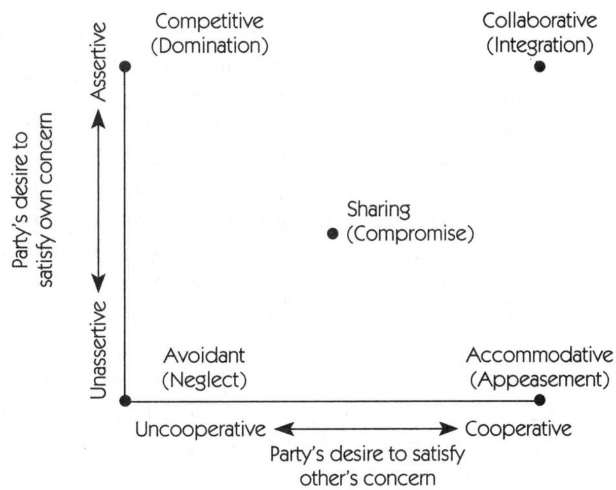

SOURCE: Kenneth W. Thomas, *Organizational Conflict,* in Steven Kerr, ed. Organizational Behavior (Columbus, Ohio: Grid Publishing, 1979, p. 156).

FIGURE 4-1 Conflict-Handling Styles According to Degree of Cooperation and Assertiveness

COMPETITIVE: The competitive style is a desire to win one's own concerns at the expense of the other party, or to dominate. A person with a competitive orientation is likely to engage in power struggles where one side wins and the other loses (an approach referred to as *win-lose*).

ACCOMMODATIVE: The accommodative style favors appeasement, or satisfying the other's concerns without taking care of one's own. People with this orientation may be generous or self-sacrificing just to maintain a relationship. An irate customer might be accommodated with a full refund, just to calm down the person. The intent of such accommodation might also be to retain the customer's loyalty.

SHARING: The sharing style is halfway between domination and appeasement. Sharers prefer moderate but incomplete satisfaction for both parties, which results in a compromise. The term *splitting the difference* reflects this orientation and is commonly used in such activities as purchasing a house or car.

COLLABORATIVE: In contrast to the other styles, the collaborative style reflects a desire to fully satisfy the desires of both parties. It is based on an underlying philosophy of **win-win,** the belief that after conflict has been resolved, both sides should gain something of value. The use of win-win approaches is genuinely concerned about arriving at a settlement that meets the needs of both parties, or at least does not badly damage the welfare of the other side. When collaborative approaches to resolving conflict are used, the relationships among the parties are built on and improved. The following example uses a win-win approach to resolve conflict.

> *Bruce is office assistant in a company that supplies food to restaurants, hospitals, and nursing homes. According to his budget analysis, Bruce needed a 5 percent salary increase to meet his monthly expenses. The company owner explained that there was no money in the budget for a salary increase. A cordial discussion about the issue led to a mutually acceptable solution. Bruce would receive the 5 percent salary increase as long as he increased his productivity enough to cover the increase. His target was to increase his productivity to the point that the company could decrease the hours worked by an office temporary. The amount of the decrease covered the 5 percent salary increase.*

Finding win-win solutions to problems (or options for mutual gain) is one of the most important conflict-resolution skills. To obtain practice in this skill, do Skill-Development Exercise 4-1.

AVOIDANT: The avoider is a combination of uncooperative and unassertive. He or she is indifferent to the concerns of either party. The person may actually be withdrawing from the conflict or be relying upon fate. The avoidant style is sometimes used by a manager who stays out of a conflict between two group members who are left to resolve their own differences.

SKILL-DEVELOPMENT EXERCISE 4-1

WIN-WIN CONFLICT RESOLUTION

The class organizes into small problem-solving groups. Each group spends about 10 minutes finding a win-win solution to one of following conflict situations:

1. Two coworkers want you to go to lunch with them more regularly, but you believe that you are too busy to go out to lunch regularly.
2. Deborah, a computer operator, wants workmates to call her "Deborah." Yet several people in the office persist in calling her "Deb" or "Debbie."
3. You are offered a transfer within your company to an exciting job that you want strongly. Your manager says he cannot let you go because you are too valuable.

In the following description of specific techniques for resolving conflict, attempt to relate most of them to these five key styles. For example, you will observe that the confrontation and problem-solving technique reflects the collaborative style.

GUIDELINES AND TECHNIQUES FOR RESOLVING CONFLICTS

Interpersonal conflict in organizations is inevitable. A career-minded person must therefore learn effective ways of resolving conflict. In this section we describe methods of conflict resolution that you can use on your own. All are based somewhat on the underlying philosophy of win-win. The five methods are as follows:

1. Confrontation and problem solving
2. Constructive handling of criticism
3. Image exchanging
4. Cognitive restructuring
5. Negotiating and bargaining

CONFRONTATION AND PROBLEM SOLVING

The ideal approach to resolving any conflict is to confront the real issue, and then solve the problem. Confrontation means taking a problem-solving approach to differences and identifying the underlying facts, logic, or emotions that account for them. When conflicts are resolved through confronting and understanding their causes, people feel responsible for finding the soundest answer.[5]

Confrontation can proceed gently, in a way that preserves a good working relationship, as shown by this example. Assume that Mary, the person working at the desk next to you, loudly cracks chewing gum while she works. You find the gum chewing both distracting and nauseating. If you don't bring the problem to Mary's attention, it will probably grow in proportion with time. Yet you are hesitant to enter into an argument about something that a person might regard as a civil liberty (the right to chew gum in public places).

A psychologically sound alternative is for you to approach her directly in this manner:

You: Mary, there is something bothering me that I would like to discuss with you.

She: Go ahead, I don't mind listening to other people's problems.

You: My problem concerns something you are doing that makes it difficult for me to concentrate on my work. When you chew gum you make loud cracking noises that grate on my nerves. It may be my hangup, but the noise does bother me.

She: I guess I could stop chewing gum when you're working next to me. It's probably just a nervous habit.

CONSTRUCTIVE HANDLING OF CRITICISM

Learning to profit from criticism is an effective way of benefiting from conflict. People who benefit from criticism are able to stand outside themselves while being criticized. It is as if they are watching the criticism from a distance and looking for its possible merits. People who take criticism personally anguish when receiving negative feedback. Following are several specific suggestions for dealing with criticism, including two methods that will often get the other party on your side.[6]

1. *See yourself at a distance.* Place an imaginary Plexiglas shield between you and the person giving the criticism. Attempt to be a detached observer looking for useful information.

2. *Ask for clarification and specifics.* Ask politely for more details about the negative behavior in question, so you can change if change is warranted. If your boss is criticizing you for being rude to customers, you might respond: "I certainly do not want to be rude. Can you give me a couple of examples of how I was rude? I need your help in working on this problem." After asking questions you can better determine if the criticism is valid.

3. *Decide on a response.* An important part of learning from criticism is to respond appropriately to the critic. Let the criticizer know what you agree with. Apologize for the undesirable behavior, such as saying, "I apologize for being rude to customers. I know what I can do differently now. I'll be more patient so as not to appear rude."

4. *Disarm the opposition.* As an extension of the point just made, you will often decide to agree with the criticizer because the person has a legitimate complaint about you. If you deny the reality of that person's complaint, he or she will continue to harp on that point and the issue will remain unresolved. By agreeing with that criticism of you, you may set the stage for true resolution of the problem.

Agreeing with criticism made of you by a superior is effective, because by doing so you are then in a position to ask for his or her help in improving the situation. Rational managers realize that it is their responsibility to help subordinates overcome problems, not merely to criticize them. Imagine that you have been chronically late with reports during the last six months. It is time for a performance review and you know that you will be reprimanded for your tardiness. You also hope that your boss will not downgrade all other aspects of your performance because of your tardy reports. Here is how disarming the opposition would work in this situation:

Your boss: Have a seat. It's time for your performance review, and we have a lot to talk about. I'm concerned about some things.

You: So am I. It appears that I'm having a difficult time getting my reports in on time. I wonder if I'm being a perfectionist. Do you have any suggestions?

Your boss: Well, I like your attitude. Maybe you *are* trying to make your reports too perfect before you turn them in. I think you can improve in getting your reports in on time. Try not to figure everything out to five decimal places. We need thoroughness around here, but we can't overdo it.

Disarming is effective because it takes the wind out of the other person's sails and has a calming effect. The other person is often waiting to clobber you if you deny guilt. If you admit guilt, you are more difficult to clobber. Skill-Development Exercise 4-2 gives you an opportunity to practice disarming the opposition.

IMAGE EXCHANGING

The essential point of **image exchanging** is that you and your antagonist make it clear that you understand the other person's point of view. Empathy of this kind may then lead to a useful and productive compro-

> **SKILL-DEVELOPMENT**
>
> **EXERCISE 4-2**
>
> ## DISARMING THE OPPOSITION
>
> In each of these two scenarios, one person plays the role of the person with more power in the situation. The other person plays the role of the individual attempting to disarm the criticizer.
>
> 1. A representative from a credit organization telephones you at work to inform you that you are 60 days behind schedule on your car payment. The agent wants a settlement as soon as possible. Unfortunately, the credit agent is correct. Run this happy scenario for about five minutes.
> 2. Your boss calls you into the office to discuss the 10-page report you just submitted. The boss says in a harsh tone, "Your report is a piece of trash. I counted 25 word-use mistakes such as writing *whether* for *weather* and *seen* for *scene.* (Your spell checker couldn't catch these errors.) Besides that I can't follow many of your sentences, and you left out the table of statistics. I'm wondering if you are qualified for this job."

mise. A convenient application of this method is for you to list on a sheet of paper (1) your side of the argument and (2) what you think is the other person's side of the argument. Next, he or she does the same for you. Exhibit 4-1 is an example of how images might be exchanged. Each person makes up an image sheet without consulting the other person. After the images are exchanged, discussion (and sometimes fireworks) begins.

COGNITIVE RESTRUCTURING

An indirect way of resolving interpersonal conflict is to lessen the conflicting elements in a situation by viewing them more positively. According to the technique of **cognitive restructuring,** you mentally convert negative aspects into positive ones by looking for the positive elements in a situation.[7] How you frame or choose your thoughts can determine the outcome of a conflict situation. Your thoughts influence your actions. If you search for the beneficial elements in the situation, there will be less area for dispute. Although this technique might sound like a *mind game* to you, it can work effectively.

Imagine that a coworker of yours, Jeff, has been asking you repeated questions about how to carry out a work procedure. You are about ready to tell Jeff, "Go bother somebody else, I'm not paid to be a trainer." Instead, you look for the positive elements in the situation. You say to yourself, "Jeff has been asking me a lot of questions. This does take time, but answering these questions is valuable experience. If I want to become a manager, I will have to help group members with problems."

After having completed this cognitive restructuring, you can then deal with the conflict situation more positively. You might say to Jeff, "I welcome the opportunity to help you, but we need to find a mutually convenient time. In that way, I can better concentrate on my own work." To get started with cognitive restructuring, do Skill-Development Exercise 4-3.

NEGOTIATING AND BARGAINING

Conflicts can be considered situations calling for **negotiating,** or conferring, with another person to resolve a problem. When you are negotiating a fair salary for yourself, you are trying to resolve a conflict. At first the demands of the two parties may seem incompatible, but through negotiation, a salary figure may emerge that satisfies both.

Managers and staff specialists must negotiate both internally (for example, with subordinates and bosses) and externally (for example, with suppliers and government agencies). Considerable negotiation also takes place among coworkers. Team members, for example, sometimes negotiate among themselves about work assignments. One might say to the other, "I'm willing to be note taker this year if there is some way I can cut back

EXHIBIT 4-1

AN IMAGE-EXCHANGING LIST BETWEEN YOU AND YOUR BOSS, BASED ON A CONFLICT ABOUT PUNCTUALITY

You: My side of the story	What I think is your side of the story
1. I'm usually on time for work. 2. I live on the other side of town. 3. Public transportation is unreliable in this city.	1. I'm not very dependable. 2. I live too far from the office. 3. I take the last possible bus.
Your boss: My side of the story	**What I think is your side of the story**
1. You are late too often. 2. If you cared more about your job. you would consider moving closer to the office. 3. If you got out of bed earlier, you could take an earlier bus.	1. I'm as punctual as most people in the office. 2. I think you don't take my transportation problems seriously. 3. I try hard to get here on time. It's not my fault that I'm late sometimes.

SKILL-DEVELOPMENT

EXERCISE 4-3

COGNITIVE RESTRUCTURING

The following are examples of negative statements about coworkers. In the space provided, cognitively restructure (reframe) each comment in a positive way.

Negative: Nancy is getting on my nerves. It takes her two weeks longer than anyone else on the team to complete her input.

Positive: ______________________________

____

____

____

Negative: My boss is driving me crazy. He is forever telling me what I did wrong and making suggestions for improvement. He makes me feel like I'm in elementary school.

Positive: ______________________________

____

____

____

on the amount of plant visits I make this year." Six leading negotiating tactics are presented here. Before studying them, do Self-Assessment Exercise 4-2.

Focus on Interests, not Positions

Rather than clinging to specific negotiating points, keep your overall interests in mind and try to satisfy them. Remember that the true object of negotiation is to satisfy the underlying interests on both sides. Here is how this strategy works:

> *Your manager asks you to submit a proposal for increasing productivity, and you see it as an opportunity to acquire an additional staff member. When you submit your ideas, you learn that management is really thinking about additional computerization, not additional staff. Instead of insisting on their hiring a new worker, be flexible. Ask to be included in the decision making for acquiring an additional computer. You will reduce your workload (your true interest), and you may enjoy such secondary benefits as having helped the company increase productivity.*[8]

SELF-ASSESSMENT

EXERCISE 4-2

THE NEGOTIATOR QUIZ

Directions: The following quiz is designed to give you tentative insight into your tendencies toward being an effective negotiator. Answer each statement Mostly true or Mostly false as it applies to you.

	Mostly true	Mostly false
1. Settling differences of opinion with people is a lot of fun.	______	______
2. I try to avoid conflict and confrontation with others as much as possible.	______	______
3. I am self-conscious asking people for favors they have not offered me spontaneously.	______	______
4. I am generally unwilling to compromise.	______	______
5. How the other side feels about the results of our negotiation is of little consequence to me.	______	______
6. I think very well under pressure.	______	______
7. People say that I am tactful and diplomatic.	______	______
8. I'm known for my ability to express my viewpoint clearly.	______	______
9. Very few things in life are not negotiable.	______	______
10. I always accept whatever salary increase is offered to me.	______	______
11. A person's facial expression often reveals as much as what the person actually says.	______	______
12. I wouldn't mind taking a few short-range losses to win a long-range battle.	______	______
13. I'm willing to work long and hard to win a small advantage.	______	______
14. I'm usually too busy talking to do much listening.	______	______
15. It's fun to haggle over price when buying a car.	______	______
16. I almost always prepare in advance for a negotiating session.	______	______
17. When there is something I need from another person I usually get it.	______	______
18. It would make me feel cheap if I offered somebody only two-thirds of his or her asking price.	______	______
19. People are usually paid what they are worth, so there's no use haggling over starting salaries.	______	______
20. I rarely take what people say at face value.	______	______
21. It's easy for me to smile when involved in a serious discussion.	______	______
22. For one side to win in negotiation, the other side has to lose.	______	______
23. Once you start making concessions, the other side is bound to get more than you.	______	______

(Continued) ►

24. A good negotiating session gets my competitive urges flowing. ______ ______

25. When negotiations are completed, both sides should walk away with something valuable. ______ ______

Total ______

Scoring and Interpretation: Score yourself plus one for each of your answers that agrees with the scoring key. The higher your score, the more likely it is that you currently have good negotiating skills, *providing your self-assessment is accurate.* It might prove useful to also have somebody who has observed you negotiate on several occasions to answer the Negotiator Quiz for you. Scores of 7 or lower and 20 or higher are probably the most indicative of weak or strong negotiating potential. Here is the scoring key:

1. Mostly true	7. Mostly true	13. Mostly true	19. Mostly false
2. Mostly false	8. Mostly true	14. Mostly false	20. Mostly true
3. Mostly false	9. Mostly true	15. Mostly true	21. Mostly true
4. Mostly false	10. Mostly false	16. Mostly true	22. Mostly false
5. Mostly false	11. Mostly true	17. Mostly true	23. Mostly false
6. Mostly true	12. Mostly true	18. Mostly false	24. Mostly true
			25. Mostly true

Compromise

The most widely used negotiating tactic is **compromise,** settlement of differences by mutual concessions. One party agrees to do something if the other party agrees to do something else. Compromise is a realistic approach to resolving conflict. Most labor-management disputes are settled by compromise. For instance, labor may agree to accept a smaller salary increase if management will subcontract less work to other countries.

Some people argue that compromise is not a win-win tactic. The problem is that the two parties may wind up with a solution that pacifies both but does not solve the problem. One example would be purchasing for two department heads half the new equipment each one needs. As a result, neither department really shows a productivity gain. Nevertheless, compromise is both inevitable and useful.

Begin with a Plausible Demand or Offer

The commonsense approach to negotiation suggests that you begin with an extreme, almost fanciful demand or offer. The final compromise will therefore be closer to your true demand or offer than if you opened the negotiations more realistically. A plausible demand is useful because it shows you are bargaining in good faith. Also, if a third party has to resolve a conflict, a plausible demand or offer will receive more sympathy than an implausible one will.

A judge listened to the cases of two people who claimed they were the victims of age discrimination by the same employer. The lawyer for the first alleged victim asked for $10 million in damages; the lawyer for the second *victim asked for $200,000. The first person was awarded $50,000 in damages, and the second person $150,000. An inside source reported that the judge was so incensed by the first lawyer's demands that she decided to teach him a lesson.*

Allow Room for Negotiation

Although it is advisable to begin with a plausible demand, one must allow room for negotiation. A basic strategy of negotiation is to begin with a demand that allows room for compromise and concession. If you think you need $5,000 in new software for your department, you might begin negotiations by asking for a $7,000 package. Your boss offers you $4,000 as a starting point. After negotiation, you may wind up with the $5,000 you need.

Make Small Concessions Gradually

Making steady concessions leads to more mutually satisfactory agreements in most situations. Gradually, you concede little things to the other side. The hard-line approach to bargaining is to make your concession early in the negotiation and then grant no further concession. The tactic of making small concessions is well suited to purchasing a new car. In order to reach a price you consider acceptable, you might grant concessions, such as agreeing to finance the car through the dealer or purchasing a service contract.

Effective negotiation, as with any other form of conflict resolution, requires extensive practice and knowledge of basic principles and techniques.

Know Your Best Alternative to a Negotiated Agreement (BATNA)

The reason you would probably negotiate would be to produce something better than the result obtainable without negotiating. The goal of negotiating is thus not just to agree, but to obtain more valuable results than would otherwise have occurred. When you are aware of your best alternative to a negotiated agreement (BATNA), it sets a floor to the agreement you are willing to accept. Your BATNA becomes that standard that can protect both parties from accepting terms that are too unfavorable. It also keeps you from walking away from terms that would be beneficial for you to accept.

What might a BATNA look like in practice? Suppose you are negotiating a starting salary for a full-time, professional position. The figure you have in mind is $32,000 per year. Your BATNA is $28,500 because this is the salary your future in-laws will pay you to enter the family business! You will therefore walk away from any offer less than $29,000—just taking salary into account.

Knowing the other side's BATNA is also important because it helps define the other participant's bargaining zone. Understanding each other's bargaining zones makes it profitable to arrive at mutually profitable trade-offs. In the preceding salary negotiations, the company's BATNA might be to hire a less well educated job candidate at $25,000 and then upgrade his or her knowledge on the job.

COMBATTING SEXUAL HARASSMENT: A SPECIAL TYPE OF CONFLICT

Many employees face conflict because they are sexually harassed by a supervisor, coworker, or customer. **Sexual harassment** is generally defined as unwanted sexually oriented behavior in the workplace that results in discomfort and/or interference with the job. It can include an action as violent as rape or as subtle as a sexually oriented comment about a person's body or appearance. Here we will focus on the types and frequency of sexual harassment, and guidelines for dealing with the problem.

TYPES AND FREQUENCY OF HARASSMENT

Two types of sexual harassment are recognized by the courts. In quid pro quo sexual harassment, the individual suffers job loss, or threatened loss of a job benefit, as a result of his or her responses to a request for sexual favors. The demands of a harasser can be explicit or implied. An example of quid pro quo harassment would be a manager promising an employee a promotion in exchange for sexual favors and then not promoting the employee because the employee refused.

The other form of sexual harassment is hostile-environment harassment. It occurs when someone in the workplace creates an intimidating, hostile, or offensive working environment. No tangible loss has to be suffered in this form of sexual harassment. An employee who is subjected to sexually suggestive comments, lewd jokes, or advances is a victim of hostile-environment harassment.

Sexual harassment through creating an intimidating environment received worldwide attention in 1991. The occasion was Congressional hearings to determine if Judge Clarence Thomas, a Supreme Court justice nominee, had sexually harassed a former employee, Professor Anita F. Hill. Although Congress subsequently approved Thomas as a Supreme Court justice, employers became more sensitive to the problem of sexual harassment. A long series of sexual harassment charges against U.S. Senator Robert Packwood two years later brought further attention to the problem.

Sexual harassment is also regarded as an expression of power by one individual over another, because the harasser has more formal power than the harassed. The harasser, following this logic, is a power abuser as well as a legal offender.[9]

Sexual harassment is widespread in the U.S. workplace and in other countries as well. A study by the U.S. Merit Systems Protection Board found that 42 percent of women and 15 percent of men have experienced some form of sexual harassment on the job within the last two years. According to the U.S. Equal Employment Opportunity Commission, more than 4,800 women filed harassment complaints in one year. More recently, 51 percent of the women surveyed responded yes to the question, "Have you experienced an incident of sexual harassment on the job?" The incidents reported included physical contact, off-color jokes, and demeaning comments about women. One manager complained that "filthy" pictures were continually left on her desk.[10]

GUIDELINES FOR PREVENTING AND DEALING WITH SEXUAL HARASSMENT

A starting point in dealing with sexual harassment is to develop an awareness of the type of behaviors that are considered sexual harassment. Often the difference is subtle. Suppose, for example, you placed copies of two nudes painted by Renoir, the French painter, on a coworker's desk. Your coworker might call that harassment. Yet if you took that same coworker to a museum to see the originals of the same nude prints, your behavior would usually not be classified as harassment. Following is a sampling of behaviors that will often be interpreted as environmental harassment[11]: If people refrain from doing them, many instances of sexual harassment will be avoided.

- *Inappropriate remarks and sexual implications.* Coworkers, subordinates, customers, and suppliers should not be referred to as sexual beings and their appearance should not be referred to in a sexual manner. Telling a coworker she has gorgeous feet, or he has fabulous biceps, is out of place at work.

- *Terms of endearment.* Refrain from calling others in the workplace terms such as "cutie," "sweetie pie," "honey," "dear," or "hunk." One might argue that these terms are simply *sexist* (different roles for men and women) and not sexual harassment. Nevertheless, some people find terms of endearment to have a sexual connotation. If you felt no physical attraction toward another adult would you call that person "cutie" or "hunk"?

- *Suggestive compliments.* It is acceptable to tell another person he or she looks nice, but avoid sexually tinged comments such as mentioning that the person's clothing shows off his or her body to advantage.

- *Physical touching.* To avoid any appearance of sexual harassment it is best to restrict physical touching to handshakes and an occasional sideways hug. Minimize such behaviors as adjusting a coworker's earring, touching hair, and tweaking the person's chin.

► *Work-related kissing.* It is best to avoid all kissing in a work context—except perhaps a light kiss at an office party. It is much more professional to greet a work associate with a warm, sincere handshake.

After sexual harassment has taken place, the victim will usually want to resolve the conflict. Two key strategies are to use either a formal complaint procedure or to resolve the conflict on your own. If you choose the latter course you will save yourself the time of going through a lengthy investigation procedure. Exhibit 4-2 presents details about the two key strategies for dealing with sexual harassment.

EXHIBIT 4-2

NOW TO DEAL WITH SEXUAL HARASSMENT

The potential or actual victim of sexual harassment is advised to use the following methods and tactics to deal with the problem.

Formal Complaint Procedure: Whenever an employee believes that he or she has encountered sexual harassment, or if an employee is suspected to be the perpetrator of sexual harassment, the complainant should report the incident to his or her immediate superior (if that person is not the harasser) or to the next higher level of management if the supervisor *is* the harasser. The supervisor contacted is responsible for contacting the equal employment opportunity officer immediately regarding each complaint. The officer will explain the investigative procedures to the complainant and any supervisor involved. All matters will be kept strictly confidential, including private conversations with all parties.

Dealing with the Problem on Your Own: The easiest way to deal with sexual harassment is to speak up before it becomes serious. The first time it happens, respond with a statement such as: "I won't tolerate this kind of talk." "I dislike sexually oriented jokes." "Keep your hands off me."

Write the harasser a stern letter shortly after the first incident. Being confronted in writing dramatizes your seriousness of purpose in not wanting to be sexually harassed.

Tell the actual or potential harasser: "You're practicing sexual harassment. If you don't stop, I'm going to exercise my right to report you to management." Or: "I think I heard you right. Would you like to accompany me to the boss's office and repeat what you said to me?"

SUMMARY

A conflict is a situation in which two or more goals, values, or events are incompatible or mutually exclusive. Interpersonal conflicts have many sources or causes. An underlying source of job conflict is that people compete for limited resources. Another leading cause of incompatibility is role conflict, having to choose between two competing demands or expectations. Other key sources of conflict are as follows: building of stone walls (the accumulation of minor hurtful incidents), personality clashes, and aggressive personalities.

Five major styles of conflict management have been identified: competitive, accommodative, sharing, collaborative, and avoidant. Each style is based on a combination of satisfying one's own concerns (assertiveness) and satisfying the concerns of others (cooperativeness).

Confrontation and problem solving is the ideal method for resolving conflict. Learning to benefit from criticism is an effective way of benefiting from conflict. People who benefit from criticism are able to stand outside themselves while being criticized. Another way to deal with criticism is to disarm the opposition by agreeing with his or her criticism. Image exchanging deals with conflict by enabling each party to understand the other's viewpoint. Cognitive restructuring lessens conflict by the person looking for the positive elements in a situation.

Negotiating is a major approach to resolving conflict. It includes focusing on interests rather than positions, compromise, beginning with a plausible demand or offer, allowing room for negotiation, and making small concessions gradually. It is also important to know your BATNA (best alternative to a negotiated agreement).

Sexual harassment is a form of interpersonal conflict with legal implications. The two forms of sexual harassment are (1) demanding sex in exchange for favors and (2) creating a hostile environment. A starting point in dealing with sexual harassment is to develop an awareness of the type of behaviors it encompasses. To deal directly with harassment, the harassed person can file a formal complaint or confront the harasser when the behavior first begins.

QUESTIONS FOR DISCUSSION AND REVIEW

1. How might conflict among students be seen as competition for limited resources?
2. Why does having family responsibility often place an individual in role conflict with his or her employer?
3. Can you describe an incident in which you have been *pinched* by a work associate or a friend? Share the details of this incident with classmates.

4. What good does it do for you to know a work associate's conflict style?
5. What are the disadvantages of having an accommodative style of handling conflict?
6. Experts have observed that it is difficult for most people to confront others. Why is confrontation so difficult for so many people?
7. Have you ever attempted to disarm the opposition? How effective was the tactic?
8. How might a student use cognitive restructuring to get over the anger of having received a low grade in a course?
9. Visualize yourself buying a new car of your choice. Which negotiating technique (or techniques) would you be the most likely to use?
10. Is inviting a coworker to dinner a second time a form of sexual harassment if the coworker refused the first invitation?

AN INTERPERSONAL RELATIONS CASE

SMOKERS' RIGHTS

Child-Decor, a manufacturer of children's furniture, recently placed a total smoking ban on employees. The official policy stated that company employees were not allowed to smoke on company premises, but they were allowed to smoke outside the building. If caught smoking inside the factory or office they would be subject to discipline, such as written documentation in their personnel files, suspension, or demotion. Repeated violators would be subject to dismissal.

Company president Bill Garrison, himself a former two-pack-a-day smoker, was proud of Child-Decor's new policy. In a speech to employees, he stated: "Our company has taken a giant step forward in creating a safe work environment. We are helping hundreds of our employees avoid the biggest job hazard they will ever face—passive smoking. It is much more dangerous than anything else you will inhale in a furniture factory. Every Child-Decor employee has a right to breathe air unpolluted with carcinogens. I am certain that the few remaining smokers among you will agree that the health and safety of the majority must take precedence over the addictions of the minority.

"My door is always open to discuss our new policy. And please keep your supervisors informed of any difficulties encountered in creating a smoke-free environment."

(Continued) ▶

Thirty days after the new policy began, Garrison asked his administrative assistant, Kathy Chang, to investigate how well the policy was working. While wandering around the office and the factory, Chang spoke to a number of Child-Decor employees to obtain a clear perspective on how well the smoking ban was being received.

"To be truthful," commented Bruce Garcia, a production scheduler, "this new policy is making me physically sick. And I intend to fight back. These smokers are revolting. They gather outside every doorway to smoke throughout the day. When you walk in on a still day you hit this wall of putrid smoke. It's as bad as the restrooms used to be when smoking was only allowed there. Smokers should not be allowed to smoke within 50 feet of a building entrance."

Inge Goldfarb, an office assistant, offered these observations with anger in her voice: "Never in my 15 years of working for this company have I been treated so shabbily. Forcing me to go outside my building to engage in a perfectly legal activity smacks of totalitarianism. What right do nonsmokers have to make smoking a crime? Show me the scientific evidence that smoking in a ventilated area is harming people who do not smoke. If you ask me, Mr. Garrison has gone overboard."

Terry McWorth, an industrial engineer, said to Chang: "It's too early to provide hard data, but I think the smoking ban is lowering productivity. I've heard a lot of complaints that the smokers are spending too much time outside the building smoking. They are missing time from work, and people have to be shifted around to cover for them. It's a tough sell to convince a nonsmoking worker to cover for a smoker who is outside the building puffing away.

"Another problem the smoking ban has created is that I see evidence of hard feelings between some smokers and nonsmokers. The smoking ban has been divisive. It shows up in little ways, like a smoker not cooperating with a nonsmoker. The reason seems to be that the smoker now feels like a second-class citizen."

Melody Lewis, a purchasing assistant, informed Chang: "I and a few other smokers are willing to put up with this policy for now. So far the weather has been cooperating. But can you imagine being forced to smoke outside the building when it's snowing, raining, sleeting, or freezing cold? Smoking outside in 100-degree weather wouldn't be too comfortable either. It's ludicrous. Give us back our smoking lounge, and treat us like human beings. This is a furniture factory, not a prison. I'm getting ticked off at these smug nonsmokers who have made life so uncomfortable for us."

Gil McAlister, a customer service representative, told Chang: "I like the policy. I was smoking a pack a day on the job. I'm now down to 10 cigarettes, and I enjoy the breaks outside. Since it's company policy to

(Continued) ▶

smoke outside, I don't have to feel guilty. I wish those other smokers would stop complaining. They may be killing off a good thing."

Chang reported back to Garrison that the ban on smoking inside the building was creating problems, and she wondered if something should be done about the situation. "There are more animosities created than is good for the company," said Chang.

CASE QUESTIONS

1. What actions, if any should the company take to resolve conflict between smokers and nonsmokers?
2. What methods of conflict resolution should smokers and nonsmokers use to resolve conflict among themselves?
3. What is your opinion about whether the rights of smokers are being violated?

AN INTERPERSONAL RELATIONS ROLE PLAY

IMAGE EXCHANGING

Assume that the company decides to resolve some of the conflict between smokers and nonsmokers using image exchanging. Several students play the role of representatives from the smokers, and another group plays the role of representatives of nonsmokers. Play out the image exchange, going through the steps outlined in Exhibit 4-2. The four key elements are as follows: (1) the nonsmokers' side of the story, (2) the nonsmokers' perception of the smokers' side of the story, (3) the smokers' side of the story, and (4) the smokers' perception of the nonsmokers' side of the story.

Chapter 15

Group Problem Solving

Learning Objectives

After reading and studying this chapter and doing the exercises you should be able to

- Understand why group problem solving is an important part of interpersonal relations in organizations.
- Use the general approach to problem-solving groups.
- Make effective use of brainstorming.
- Recognize the potential contribution of electronic brainstorming.
- Make effective use of the nominal group technique.
- Understand how to increase the efficiency of group problem solving through E-mail.

The vice president of human resources at a consumer products company announced to the human resources staff that they would be receiving an average raise of 5 percent for the year. "Sounds great," said Melissa Olsten, the director of training. "But how is management deciding who gets how much? I take it we are not all going to receive the same 5 percent raise."

With an excited expression, the vice president replied, "You people are an empowered group of professionals. You will decide how to divide up the pool of money available for raises." Surprised but delighted with the answer to her question, Melissa took the initiative to ask the group to set aside time for a three-hour meeting. The goal of the problem-solving session would be to decide how to divide up the money allocated for the raises. Several of the group members were apprehensive, but they realized here was a chance to engage in meaningful group decision making.

The case example just presented illustrates an increasingly important aspect of interpersonal relations in organizations: many key problems are solved by groups. Part of having high-level interpersonal skills is the ability to work closely with others in solving problems and making decisions. The purpose of this chapter is to enhance your group problem-solving skills. You will receive guidelines for applying several major group problem-solving methods. As a starting point in studying these techniques, first think through your present level of receptiveness toward group problem solving by doing Self-Assessment Quiz 6-1.

GROUP PROBLEM SOLVING IN WORK TEAMS

In the previous chapter we described various types of teams found in organizations. Some of the rapid growth of group problem solving in organizations can be attributed to a specific type of team called a *work team.* A work team is also referred to as a *self-managing team,* a *self-governing team,* an *autonomous work group,* and a *semiautonomous work group.* All these labels point toward the same idea. A **work team** is a group of employees who work somewhat independently and are responsible for an entire work process or the production of a good or service. Work teams are found in the factory as well as in the office.

Because a work team is given so much responsibility, the team members have to make a number of important decisions. Most of these decisions are made by the team, and team members receive training in group problem-solving techniques.

Members of the work team engage in such activities as setting their own goals, checking their own quality, hiring and training new members, and ordering materials. Table 6-1 presents a full list of activities engaged in by work teams. The more of these activities a given work team performs, the more autonomy it has. Group problem solving is the rule in carrying out these activities, because work teams are designed to be democratic.

SELF-ASSESSMENT

QUIZ 6-1

MY PROBLEM-SOLVING TENDENCIES

Directions: Describe how well you agree with the following statements. Use the following scale: Disagree strongly (DS); Disagree (D); Neutral (N); Agree (A); Agree strongly (AS).

	DS	D	N	A	AS
1. Before reaching a final decision on a matter of significance, I like to discuss it with one or more other people.	1	2	3	4	5
2. If I'm facing a major decision, I like to get away from others to think it through.	5	4	3	2	1
3. I get lonely working by myself.	1	2	3	4	5
4. Two heads are better than one.	1	2	3	4	5
5. Too many cooks spoil the broth.	5	4	3	2	1
6. To arrive at a creative solution to a problem it is best to rely on a group.	1	2	3	4	5
7. From what I've seen so far, group decision making is a waste of time.	5	4	3	2	1
8. Most great ideas stem from the solitary effort of great thinkers.	5	4	3	2	1
9. Important legal cases should be decided by a jury rather than by a judge.	1	2	3	4	5
10. Individuals are better suited than groups to solve technical problems.	5	4	3	2	1

Total Score ________

Scoring and Interpretation: Add the numbers you circled to obtain your total score.

46–50 You have strong positive attitudes toward group problem solving and decision making. You will therefore adapt well to the decision-making techniques widely used in organizations. Be careful, however, not to neglect your individual problem-solving skills.

30–45 You have neutral attitudes toward group problem solving and decision making. You may need to remind yourself that group problem solving is well accepted in business.

10–29 You much prefer individual to group decision making. Retain your pride in your ability to think independently, but do not overlook the contribution of group problem solving. You may need to develop more patience for group problem solving and decision making.

TABLE 6-1

PROBLEM-SOLVING AND DECISION-MAKING TOPICS FOR WORK TEAMS

Amount of empowerment		Topic
	High	Compensation for team members
	↑	Handling discipline
		Evaluating team member performance
		Product modification and development
		Budgeting
		Facility design
		Equipment purchase
		Choosing team leaders
		Vacation scheduling
		Setting up cross-functional teams
		Conducting job interviews
		Hiring team members
		Contact with external customers
		Dealing with suppliers
		Making continuous improvement
		Quality responsibility
		Production scheduling
		Equipment maintenance and repair
	↓	Training each other
	Low	Housekeeping

SOURCE: Based on information in Richard S. Wellins, William C. Byham, and Jeanne M. Wilson, *Empowered Teams: Creating Self-Directed Work Groups that Improve Quality, Productivity, and Participation* (San Francisco: Jossey-Bass, 1991), p. 26; Shari Caudron, "Team Staffing Requires New HR Role," *Personnel Journal,* May 1994, pp. 88–94.

GUIDELINES FOR USING GENERAL PROBLEM-SOLVING GROUPS

When team members get together to solve a problem, they typically hold a discussion rather than rely on formal problem-solving techniques. Several team members might attempt to clarify the true nature of the problem, and a search then begins for an acceptable solution. Although this technique can be effective, the probability of solving the problem well (and therefore making the right decision) increases when the team follows a systematic procedure. The following guidelines represent a time-tested way of solving problems and making decisions within a group.[1] You may recognize these steps as having much in common with the scientific method.

Assume that you are a team member of a small business that distributes food supplies to hospitals, nursing homes, and schools. Your business volume is adequate, but you have a cash-flow problem because some of your customers take over 30 days to pay their bills. Here is how problem solving would proceed following the steps for effective group problem solving and decision making:

1. *Identify the problem.* Describe specifically what the problem is and how it manifests itself. The surface problem is that some customers are paying their bills late. Your company's ultimate problem is that it does not have enough cash on hand to pay expenses.

2. *Clarify the problem.* If group members do not see the problem the same way, they will offer divergent solutions to their own individual perceptions of the problem. To some team members, late payments may simply mean the company has less cash in the bank. As a result, the company earns a few dollars less in interest. Someone else on the team might perceive the problem as mostly an annoyance and inconvenience. It is important for the group to reach consensus that the ultimate problem is not enough cash on hand to run the business, as explained in step 1.

3. *Analyze the cause.* To convert what is into what we want, the group must understand the cause of the specific problems and find ways to overcome the causes. Late payment of bills (over 30 days) can be caused by several factors. The customers may have cash-flow problems of their own, they may have slow-moving bureaucratic procedures, or they may be understaffed. Another possibility is that the slow-paying customers are dissatisfied with the service and are holding back on payments in retaliation. Research, including interviewing customers, may be needed to analyze the cause or causes.

4. *Search for alternative solutions.* Remember that multiple alternative solutions can be found to most problems. The alternative solutions you choose will depend on your analysis of the causes. Assume that you did not find customers to be dissatisfied with your service, but that they were slow in paying bills for a variety of reasons. Your team then gets into a creative mode by developing a number of alternatives. Among them are offering bigger discounts for quick payment, dropping slow-paying customers, sending out your own bills more promptly, and using follow-up phone calls to bring in money. Another possibility would be to set up a line of credit that would enable your firm to make short-term loans to cover expenses until your bills were paid.

5. *Select alternatives.* Identify the criteria that solutions should meet; then discuss the pros and cons of the proposed alternatives. No solution should be laughed at or scorned. Specifying the criteria that proposed solutions should meet requires you to think deeply about your goals. For example, your team might establish the following criteria for solutions: that they (1) improve cash flow, (2) do not lose customers, (3) do not cost much to implement, and (4) do not make the company appear desperate. The pros and cons of each proposed alternative can be placed on a flip chart, chalkboard, or computer screen.

6. *Plan for implementation.* Decide what actions are necessary to carry out the chosen solution to the problem. Suppose your group decides that establishing a bank line of credit is the most feasible alternative. The company president or the chief financial officer might then meet with a couple of local banks to apply for a line of credit at the most favorable rate. Your group also chooses to initiate a program of friendly follow-up telephone calls to encourage more rapid payment.

7. *Clarify the contract.* The contract is a restatement of what group members have agreed to do and deadlines for accomplishment. In your situation, several team members are involved in establishing a line of credit and initiating a system of follow-up phone calls.

8. *Develop an action plan.* Specify who does what and when to carry out the contract. Each person involved in implementing alternatives develops an action plan in detail that stems logically from the previous step.

9. *Provide for evaluation and accountability.* After the plan is implemented, reconvene to discuss progress and to hold people accountable for results that have not been achieved. In the situation at hand, progress will be measured in at least two objective ways. You can evaluate by accounting measures whether the cash-flow problem has improved and whether the average cycle time on accounts receivable has decreased.

The steps for effective group problem solving are best applied to complex problems. Straightforward problems of minor consequence (such as deciding on holiday decorations for the office) do not require all the steps. Nevertheless, remember that virtually every problem has more than one feasible alternative. For practice in using the steps just described, do Skill-Building Exercise 6-1.

GUIDELINES FOR BRAINSTORMING

In many work situations, groups are expected to produce creative and imaginative solutions to problems. When the organization is seeking a large number of alternatives to the problems, **brainstorming** is often the technique of choice. Brainstorming is a group problem-solving technique that promotes creativity by encouraging idea generation through noncritical discussion. The basic technique is to encourage unrestrained and spontaneous participation by group members. The term *brainstorm* has become so widely known that it is often used as a synonym for a clever idea.

Brainstorming is used as both a method of finding alternatives to real-life problems and as a creativity training program. In the usual form of brainstorming, group members spontaneously call out alternative solutions to a problem facing them. Any member is free to enhance or "hitchhike" upon the contribution of another person. At the end of the session, somebody sorts out the ideas and edits the more unrefined ones.

SKILL-BUILDING EXERCISE 6-2

BRAINSTORMING VERSUS BRAINWRITING

Half the class is organized into brainstorming groups of about six people. The rest of the class work by themselves. Groups and individuals then work on the same problems for 10 minutes. The brainstorming groups follow the aforementioned guidelines. Individuals jot down as many alternatives as come to mind without interacting with other people. After the problem-solving sessions are completed, compare the alternatives developed by the groups and individuals.

Groups and individuals choose one of the following problems so that solutions can be compared to the same problems:

1. How might we effectively utilize the senior citizens in our community?
2. How can we earn extra money, aside from holding a regular job?
3. How do we find new people to date?
4. How do we save money on food costs?
5. How can we save money on gasoline?

Evaluation apprehension means that many people are unwilling to come forth with some of their ideas because they fear being critically evaluated. This fear may be intensified when people are told that the group is being observed and rated, or that experts are in the group. (Did you notice any evaluation apprehension in the brainstorming exercise?) When people work by themselves—and do not have to present their ideas to the larger group—they will have less evaluation apprehension.

Free riding is just about the same behavior as social loafing. Free riders do not work as hard in a group as they would if they worked alone. They are willing to let the next person do the heavy thinking. A reason offered for free riding is that being an outstanding contributor in a group carries no larger reward than being a noncontributor. A person generating ideas alone would not have the opportunity to free ride.

An *inhibiting procedure* in verbal brainstorming is that only one person can speak at a time. This limits the idea generation and production time available to group members. As a result some people forget what they wanted to say because they were listening to others. They might also ignore the ideas of others because they are rehearsing what they want to say. Furthermore, they will hold back on ideas that are redundant.

THE ELECTRONIC BRAINSTORMING PROCEDURE

A recent development designed to overcome the problem of production blocking in brainstorming is **electronic brainstorming.** Using this method, group members simultaneously enter their suggestions into a computer, and the ideas are distributed to the screens of other group members. Although the group members do not talk to each other, they are still able to build on each other's ideas and combine ideas.

Electronic brainstorming allows members to enter their ideas whenever they want, while sending along their ideas anonymously. These two features reduce the inhibitions caused by waiting for other people and by fear of negative evaluations.

During electronic brainstorming, individuals work in face-to-face groups, typically seated around a U-shaped table. Each group member has a computer terminal connected to all the other terminals, and a monitor. *Electronic Brainstorming* is the title of representative software for this activity. The software enables individuals to anonymously enter their ideas as those ideas occur to them. (Good keyboarding skills are essential to keep up with the group.)

Every time an individual enters an idea, a random set of the group's ideas is entered on the individual's monitor. Individuals can access other random sets of ideas by pressing a specified function key. Accessing the other ideas can stimulate the person's own generation of new ideas and also allows for piggybacking.

An experiment with electronic brainstorming indicated that, with large groups, the method produces more useful ideas than does verbal (the usual type) of brainstorming. For example, a four-person electronic brainstorming group produced more nonredundant ideas than verbal groups (traditional brainstorming). The group also produced more ideas than nonelectronic groups who did not interact with people.[3]

If your school or employer is equipped with an electronic brainstorming capability, you are encouraged to try the procedure. Setting up such a capability is costly. Next, we describe a low-cost manual (nonelectronic) procedure that offers many of the advantages of electronic brainstorming. In addition, you will be able to test the procedure yourself.

GUIDELINES FOR THE NOMINAL GROUP TECHNIQUE

A team leader or other manager who must make a decision about an important issue sometimes needs to know what alternatives are available and how people would react to them. In such cases, group input may be helpful. Verbal brainstorming is not advisable because the problem is still in the exploration phase and requires more than a list of alternative solutions.

A problem-solving technique called the **nominal group technique (NGT)** has been developed to fit the situation. The NGT is a group problem-solving technique that calls people together in a structured meeting with limited interaction. The group is called *nominal* (in name only) because people first present their ideas without interacting with each other, as they would in a *real* group. (This aspect of the nominal group technique is incorporated into electronic brainstorming.) However, group discussion does take place at a later stage in the process.

A STEP-BY-STEP EXAMPLE OF THE NOMINAL GROUP TECHNIQUE

A problem that is an appropriate candidate for NGT is a decision about which suppliers or vendors should be eliminated. Many companies are shrinking their number of suppliers because they believe that working with a smaller number of suppliers can lead to higher-quality components. It is easier to train a small number of suppliers, and it is also possible to build better working relationships when fewer people are involved.

A decision of this type can lead to hurt feelings and breaking up of old friendships. Suppose Pedro Ortiz, the team leader, is empowered to make this decision about reducing the number of suppliers. The nominal group technique is followed by using a six-step decision process.

1. Work-team members are assembled because they will all participate in the decision to reduce the number of companies that serve as suppliers to the team. All team members are told in advance of the meeting and the agenda. The meeting is called, and an office assistant is invited to help take care of the administrative details of the meeting.

2. The team leader presents a specific question. Ortiz tells the group, "Top management says we have to reduce our number of suppliers by two-thirds. It's too difficult to keep track of all these different suppliers and train them to meet our quality specs. I dislike terminating a supplier as much as anybody, but I can understand the logic of top management. Right now our team is doing business with 12 suppliers, and we should shrink that number to four. Your assignment is to develop criteria for choosing which suppliers to eliminate. I also need to know how you feel about the decision you make on supplier reduction and how it might affect the operations of our team."

3. Individual team members write down their ideas independently, without speaking to other members. Using notepads, the five team members write down their ideas about reducing the number of suppliers by two-thirds.

4. Each team member in turn presents one idea to the group. The group does not discuss the ideas. The office assistant summarizes each idea by writing it on a flip chart. Here are the ideas submitted by each team member:

Alternative A. We'll carefully study the prices offered by all twelve suppliers. The eight suppliers with the highest average prices for comparable goods are given the boot. I like this idea because our team will save the company a bundle of money.

Alternative B. Let's keep the four suppliers who have the best quality record. We'll ask each supplier if they have won a quality award. If a supplier has won a quality award, the company is put on the retained list. We'll include awards from their customers or outside standards such as ISO 9000. If we find more than four of the suppliers have won awards, we'll retain those with the most impressive awards.

Alternative C. I say we reward good service. We keep the four suppliers among the twelve who have been the most prompt with deliveries. We'll also take into account how good the suppliers have been about accepting returns of damaged or defective merchandise.

Alternative D. Here's an opportunity to get in good with top management. Stop kidding each other. We know that the plant's general manager [Jake] has his favorite suppliers. Some of them are his fishing and golfing buddies. The suppliers who are friends with Jake get our vote. In this way, Jake will think our team shows really good judgment.

Alternative E. Let's reward the suppliers who have served us best. We'll rate each supplier on a 1-to-10 scale on three dimensions: the quality of goods they have provided us, price, and service in terms of prompt delivery and returns policy. We could do the ratings in less than one hour.

5. After each team member has presented his or her idea, the group clarifies and evaluates the suggestions. The length of the discussion for each of the ideas varies substantially. For example, the idea about rating suppliers on three criteria might precipitate a 30-minute discussion. The discussion about retaining the plant manager's political connections might last only five minutes.

6. The meeting ends with a silent, independent rating of the alternatives. The final group decision is the pooled outcome of the individual votes. The team members are instructed to rate each alternative on a 1-to-10 scale, with 10 being the most favorable rating. The ratings that follow are the *pooled ratings* (the sum of the individual ratings) received for each alternative. The maximum score is 50 (10 points × 5 raters).

Alternative A, price alone: 35

Alternative B, quality-award record: 30

Alternative C, good service: 39

Alternative D, plant manager's favorites: 14

Alternative E, combination of quality, price, and service: 44

Team leader Ortiz agrees with the group's preference for choosing the four suppliers with the best combination of quality, price, and service. He schedules a meeting to decide which suppliers meet these standards. Ortiz brings the team's recommendations to the plant manager, and they are accepted. Although the team is empowered to make the decision, it is still brought forth to management for final approval. To practice the nominal group technique, do Skill-Building Exercise 6-3.

USING E-MAIL TO FACILITATE GROUP DECISION MAKING

A recurring theme in the subject of interpersonal relations in organizations is that teams are deeply entrenched in the modern workplace. The presence of teams means that people must work collectively and that they must make decisions together. An obvious requirement of group decision making is that group members have to engage in collective effort. In turn, collective effort usually translates into meetings. Without any meetings, people are working primarily on their own, and thus not benefiting from working in teams. Yet with too many meetings it is difficult to accomplish individual work such as making telephone calls, analyzing information, and preparing reports.

SKILL-BUILDING EXERCISE 6-3

THE NOMINAL GROUP TECHNIQUE

With a clear understanding of the mechanics of the NGT as described in the text, the technique can be demonstrated in about 50 minutes. The class is divided into groups of about seven. One person plays the role of the team leader who can also assume the responsibility of the office assistant (recording information on flip charts).

You are the key members of a motion picture and television film production company. You have a contract to produce a series of four action films. The problem you face is which North American (the United States, Canada, or Mexico) city to choose as the film site. The president has ruled out Hollywood because expenses are too high. Solve this problem using the NGT, and make a decision about which city to choose for your film sites.

Appropriate use of electronic mail can facilitate interaction among team members and group decision making, while at the same time minimizing the number of meetings.[4] By using E-mail, team members can feed important information to all other members of the team without the ritual of entering a meeting and passing around handouts. The typical use of E-mail is to send brief memos to people on a distribution list. Yet a more advanced use of E-mail is to distribute word processing documents as well as spreadsheets and graphics.

Think back to the decision reached by the team using the NGT. As a follow-up to the meeting, the team was to get together to rate all 12 suppliers on quality, price, and service. Using E-mail, the group could cut down substantially on the amount of time they would have to spend in a group meeting. They might even be able to eliminate a group meeting. Pedro Ortiz might instruct the team members to send their ratings and explanations to each other within 10 working days.

Each team member would then rate all 12 suppliers on quality, service, and price. The ratings would then be sent to all other team members by E-mail. Pedro could tally the results and report the final tally to each team member by E-mail. Since all team members could have performed the same calculation themselves, there would be no claims of a biased decision. A team meeting could be called to discuss the final results if Pedro or the other team members thought it was necessary.

Pushing the use of E-mail too far can inhibit rather than enhance group decision making and teamwork. If people communicate with each other almost exclusively by E-mail, the warmth of human interaction and facial expressions is lost. Piggybacking of ideas is possible by reading each other's ideas on a computer monitor. Nevertheless, the wink of an eye, the shared laughter, and the encouraging smiles that take place in a traditional meeting make an important contribution to team effort, including group problem solving.

SUMMARY

An important aspect of interpersonal relations in organizations is that many key problems are solved by groups. Some of the rapid growth of group problem solving in organizations can be attributed to the growth of work teams. These teams, working somewhat independently, are responsible for an entire work process or the production of a good or service. Work teams make a number of important decisions by themselves.

General problem-solving groups are likely to arrive at better decisions when they follow standard guidelines for group problem solving. The guidelines are as follows: identify the problem, clarify the problem, analyze the cause, search for alternative solutions, select alternatives, plan for implementation, clarify the contract, develop an action plan, and provide for evaluation and accountability.

When the organization is seeking a large number of alternatives to problems, brainstorming is often the technique of choice. Brainstorming is used as both a method of finding alternatives to real-life problems and as a creativity-training program. Using the technique, group members spontaneously call out alternative solutions to the problem. Members build on the ideas of each other, and ideas are not screened or evaluated until a later stage. Brainstorming by working alone, or brainwriting, is also effective in generating alternative solutions.

Electronic brainstorming is a recent development designed to overcome the problem of production blocking in brainstorming. Using this method, group members simultaneously enter their suggestions into a computer, and the ideas are distributed to the screens of other group members. Building on each other's ideas is allowed. Experiments with electronic brainstorming have been favorable.

The nominal group technique (NGT) is recommended for a situation in which a leader needs to know what alternatives are available and how people will react to them. In the NGT, a small group of people contribute written solutions to the problem. Other members respond to their ideas later. Members rate each other's ideas numerically, and the final group decision is the sum of the pooled individual votes.

Electronic mail can be used to facilitate group decision making because members can feed information to each other without having to meet as a group. Memos, spreadsheet analyses, and graphics can be distributed through the network. Too much emphasis on E-mail, however, results in losing the value of face-to-face human interaction.

QUESTIONS FOR DISCUSSION AND REVIEW

1. Why are group decision-making skills so important for members of a work team?
2. Based on any experience you have had at school or at work, what process or method is usually followed in making group decisions?
3. Most textbook mentions of brainstorming are neutral to unfavorable. What do you suppose the textbook authors tend to dislike about brainstorming?
4. Identify several problems on or off the job for which you think brainstorming would be effective.
5. In your experience with brainstorming, what evidence have you found of "production blocking"?
6. What, if any, accommodations should be made in electronic brainstorming for group members who have poor keyboarding skills?

7. Textbook writers and researchers make very favorable comments about the nominal group technique. For what reasons do you think the NGT is looked upon so favorably?
8. Can you identify two work-related problems for which the NGT is particularly well suited?
9. What advantage does E-mail offer over paper memos and phone calls as a contributor to group decision making?
10. Which group decision-making technique described in this chapter do you think members of top management are the most likely to use? Why?

AN INTERPERSONAL RELATIONS CASE

THE TORPEDOED SUBMARINE ROLLS

Chad Davis is the sales manager for Guarino's Bakery, a supplier of bread products, cakes, and pastries to local restaurants and stores. He enjoys the challenge of his job and welcomes the opportunity to practice the skills and techniques of a professional manager. Chad has acquired some of these techniques through experience and many others through reading business books and through course work.

One management technique Chad has featured is to organize activity into production teams. The sales effort is organized into a team of outside and inside salespeople and a customer service representative. The service rep responds to customer problems such as late deliveries. Chad has also influenced the plant superintendent to organize manufacturing into teams. Two examples are the "Sub Kings and Queens," and the "Pastry Gang." Both teams run their operation with minimum supervision by management. The teams report to the plant superintendent, who reports to the president and owner, Angelo Guarino.

During the last three months, five accounts have stopped ordering from Guarino's the Italian bread that they use for submarine sandwiches. Angelo Guarino told Chad, "Our submarine sales have been torpedoed. Our reputation is getting so bad that we'll soon be out of business. Find out by next week what has gone wrong with our line of bread. Max [the head baker] swears the bread hasn't changed. Laura [the customer service rep] has received loads of complaints over the phone. Talk to her."

"Angelo, I've been trying hard to find the right answer," responded Chad. "So far, the only clue I have is that our submarine rolls just don't

(Continued) ▶

taste right. Something is wrong, but our customers don't know what it is. Several of them have complained that their customers say the bread is just not as good as in the past."

Angelo retorted, "Then go back and investigate some more. We've got to know what is wrong."

Chad said to himself, *Now is the time for action. But I'm not sure which action. Should I take a survey of dissatisfied customers? Should I increase the advertising budget?*

Just before leaving the office early that evening, Chad checked his E-mail. As he scanned his in-box index, Chad noticed a message from Michelle Bastian, the sub roll team leader. The message said, "We heard you're hard at work trying to find out what, if anything, has gone wrong with the quality of the subs. Our team stands ready to cooperate fully in your investigation. As you probably know, everybody on this team is supposed to have good problem-solving skills."

Chad thought to himself, "Here's another angle I hadn't thought of. We shouldn't overlook the manufacturing process in trying to figure out what has gone wrong with the rolls."

CASE QUESTIONS

1. Why is this case included in a chapter about group problem solving?
2. Which technique should Chad use to solve the problem of customer resistance to the submarine rolls?
3. What is the underlying, or true, problem facing Guarino's bakery?

Chapter 16

Becoming an Effective Leader

Learning Objectives

After reading and studying this chapter and doing the exercises you should be able to

- Identify key leadership traits for personal development.
- Develop several attitudes and behaviors that will help you appear charismatic.
- Develop your team leadership skills.
- Understand how you can develop your leadership potential.

The manager of administrative services at one of the regional telephone companies invited Sara Arnetti, a data processing technician, to her office. "Sara, we're asking you to be the data processing team leader," said the manager. "It's been obvious to us that you have good leadership potential, so we're giving you the opportunity."

Quite pleased, Sara responded that she was flattered. Yet Sara asked what she had done that suggested leadership potential. The manager answered, "You have a great work ethic, and you have expert knowledge of data processing. Besides that, you get along fabulously with people. For those reasons, we know you will be an outstanding team leader."

Sara's invitation to become a team leader illustrates two key points about developing leadership capability. You need the *right stuff* (effective personal characteristics) for leadership. You also need to carry out the right actions (such as getting along well with people). Leadership in the workplace deals with influencing and persuading people to achieve worthwhile goals. It also involves helping to bring about constructive change such as increasing sales or streamlining work.

In working toward improving your leadership ability, the following definition is a goal to strive for. **Leadership** is the ability to inspire support and confidence among the people who are needed to achieve company goals. A company president might have to inspire thousands of people, while a team leader such as Sara is concerned with inspiring about six people. Both these leaders play an important role.

Becoming a leader does not necessarily mean that the company has to put you in charge of others (or assign you a formal leadership position). Rising to leadership can also happen when people come to respect your opinion and personal characteristics, and are thus influenced by you. Your greatest opportunity for exerting leadership will come about from a combination of these methods of influence. An individual with appealing personal characteristics and expertise who is placed in a position of authority will find it relatively easy to exert leadership.

The purpose of this chapter is twofold. One is to make you aware of the basic concepts you will need to become a leader. The other purpose is to point you toward developing skills necessary for leadership effectiveness. As a starting point in thinking about your leadership skills, do Self-Assessment Quiz 8-1.

KEY LEADERSHIP TRAITS TO DEVELOP

An important part of being an effective leader is to have the *right stuff.* In this section and the following one about charisma we describe personal attributes that help a person lead others in many situations. Recognize, however, that radically different situations require a different set of leadership characteristics. For example, a leader might have to be more

SELF-ASSESSMENT

QUIZ 8-1

TEST YOUR LEADERSHIP SKILLS

Rate yourself on basic leadership characteristics:

	Always	Sometimes	Rarely
1. I'm a good listener.	❑	❑	❑
2. I'm accessible.	❑	❑	❑
3. I'm decisive.	❑	❑	❑
4. I'm gracious.	❑	❑	❑
5. I keep it simple.	❑	❑	❑
6. I'm optimistic.	❑	❑	❑
7. I give credit where due.	❑	❑	❑
8. I confront problems.	❑	❑	❑
9. I speak directly.	❑	❑	❑
10. I acknowledge mistakes.	❑	❑	❑
11. I have a can-do attitude.	❑	❑	❑
12. I'm enthusiastic.	❑	❑	❑
13. I seek strong subordinates.	❑	❑	❑
14. I have a positive attitude.	❑	❑	❑

To Score:
Number of responses in Always column × 5 = ____________
Number of responses in Sometimes column × 3 = ____________
Number of responses in Rarely column × 1 = ____________
Total score (add the three totals): ____________

Analyze Your Score:
More than 50: You have a great deal of natural leadership ability!
30 to 50: You have a good base of leadership characteristics.
Less than 30: Underdeveloped leadership skills may be hampering your ability to manage and supervise successfully. It will be helpful for you to study leadership and attend a leadership development course.

SOURCE: Pryor Resources Inc., P.O. Box 2951, Shawnee Mission, KS 66201. Reprinted with permission.

assertive with group members performing distasteful work versus those whose work is enjoyable.

Each of the seven leadership traits described next can be developed. For such development to take place, you need to be aware of the importance of the personal characteristic, and then monitor your own behavior to make progress. To assist you with such development, the description of each trait is accompanied by a suggestion for improvement.

SELF-CONFIDENCE

In virtually every leadership setting, it is important for the leader to be realistically self-confident. A leader who is self-assured without being bombastic or overbearing instills confidence in group members. Self-confidence was among the first leadership traits researchers identified. Recent research with leaders in many situations has continued to underscore the importance of this trait. In addition to being self-confident, the leader must project that self-confidence to the group.[1]

Self-confidence is not only a personality trait. It also refers to the behavior a person exhibits in a number of situations. It is similar to being cool under pressure. We can conclude that a person is a self-confident leader when he or she retains composure during a crisis such as flood damage during a busy season.

You can appear more self-confident to the group by using definitive wording, maintaining good posture, and making appropriate gestures such as pointing an index finger outward. Developing self-confidence is a lifelong process of performing well in a variety of situations. You need a series of easy victories to establish self-confidence. Further development of your self-confidence requires performing well in challenging circumstances.

HONESTY, INTEGRITY, AND CREDIBILITY

Group members consistently believe that leaders must display honesty, integrity, and credibility. Leaders themselves believe that honesty makes a difference in their effectiveness. Being honest with team members helps to build trust, which in turn leads to good cooperation and team spirit. One study showed that leaders who rise to top positions generally championed the following formula: "I will do exactly what I say I will do when I say I will do it. If I change my mind, I will tell you in advance so you will not be harmed by my actions."[2]

Chapter 13 about ethical behavior provides details about honesty on the job. A starting point in developing a strong sense of honesty is to follow a variation of the Golden Rule: Be as honest with others as you want them to be with you.

ASSERTIVENESS

A widely recognized leadership trait is **assertiveness,** being forthright in expressing demands, opinions, feelings, and attitudes. If you are self-confident, it is easier to be assertive with people. Assertiveness helps leaders perform many tasks and achieve goals. Among them are confronting group members about their mistakes, demanding higher performance, and setting high expectations. An assertive leader will also make legitimate demands on higher management, such as asking for equipment needed by the group.

To be assertive differs significantly from being aggressive or passive. Aggressive people express their demands in an overly pushy, obnoxious, and abrasive manner. Passive people suppress their own ideas, attitudes, feelings, and thoughts as if they were likely to be perceived as controversial.

Developing assertiveness is much like attempting to become less shy. You must force yourself to take the opportunity to express your feelings and demands. For example, if something a teammate does annoys you, make the statement, "I enjoy working with you in general, but what you are doing now annoys me." You can also practice expressing positive emotion, such as telling a coworker, "I'm happy that you and I are working on this project together, because I like your approach to work."

Expressing demands is easier for most people to practice than expressing feelings. People who do start expressing their demands are often surprised at the result. For example, if you are contemplating the purchase of an item that is beyond your budget, try this statement: "I like this product very much. Yet all I have to spend is $45 below your asking price. Can we do business?"

For a reading on your own level of assertiveness, do Self-Assessment Quiz 8-2.

EMOTIONAL STABILITY

Anyone who has ever worked for an unstable boss will attest to the importance of emotional stability as a leadership trait. (As described in Chapter 2, emotional stability is one of the Big Five personality traits.) Emotional stability is important for a leader because group members expect and need consistency in the way they are treated.

A sales representative had this to say about her boss, the major-accounts team leader: "It was difficult to know whether to bring problems to Jerry's attention. Some days he would compliment me for taking customer problems seriously. Other times he would rant and rave about the ineffectiveness of my sales techniques. We all worry about having our performance appraised on one of Jerry's crazy days."

Emotional stability is difficult to develop, but people can learn to control many of their emotional outbursts. People who cannot control their emotions, yet still want to become leaders, should seek assistance from a mental health professional.

SENSE OF HUMOR

A sense of humor is borderline between being a trait or a behavior. However you classify it, the effective use of humor is considered an important part of a leader's role. Humor serves such functions in the workplace as relieving tension and boredom and defusing hostility. Because humor

SELF-ASSESSMENT

QUIZ 8-2

THE ASSERTIVENESS SCALE

Directions: Indicate whether each of the following statements is Mostly true or Mostly false as it applies to you. If in doubt about your reaction to a particular statement, think of how you would generally respond.

	Statement	Mostly true	Mostly false
1.	It is extremely difficult for me to turn down a sales representative when that individual is a nice person.	______	______
2.	I express criticism freely.	______	______
3.	If another person were being very unfair, I would bring it to his or her attention.	______	______
4.	Work is no place to let your feelings show.	______	______
5.	No use asking for favors; people get what they deserve.	______	______
6.	Business is not the place for tact; say what you think.	______	______
7.	If a person looked as if he or she were in a hurry, I would let that person in front of me in a supermarket line.	______	______
8.	A weakness of mine is that I'm too nice a person.	______	______
9.	If my restaurant bill is even 50¢ more than it should be, I demand that the mistake be corrected.	______	______
10.	If the mood strikes me, I will laugh out loud in public.	______	______
11.	People would describe me as too outspoken.	______	______
12.	I am quite willing to return merchandise that I find has a minor blemish.	______	______
13.	I dread having to express anger toward a coworker.	______	______
14.	People often say that I'm too reserved and emotionally controlled.	______	______
15.	Nice guys and gals finish last in business.	______	______
16.	I fight for my rights down to the last detail.	______	______
17.	I have no misgivings about returning an overcoat to the store if it doesn't fit me right.	______	______
18.	After I have an argument with a person, I try to avoid him or her.	______	______
19.	I insist on my spouse (or roommate or partner) doing his or her fair share of undesirable chores.	______	______
20.	It is difficult for me to look directly at another person when the two of us are in disagreement.	______	______
21.	I have cried among friends more than once.	______	______
22.	If someone near me at a movie kept up a conversation with another person, I would ask him or her to stop.	______	______
23.	I am able to turn down social engagements with people I do not particularly care for.	______	______

(Continued) ▶

24. It is in poor taste to express what you really feel about another individual. ______ ______

25. I sometimes show my anger by swearing at or belittling another person. ______ ______

26. I am reluctant to speak up at a meeting. ______ ______

27. I find it relatively easy to ask friends for small favors such as giving me a ride to work while my car is being repaired. ______ ______

28. If another person were talking very loudly in a restaurant and it bothered me, I would inform that person. ______ ______

29. I often finish other people's sentences for them. ______ ______

30. It is relatively easy for me to express love and affection toward another person. ______ ______

Scoring Key

1. Mostly false	11. Mostly true	21. Mostly true
2. Mostly true	12. Mostly true	22. Mostly true
3. Mostly true	13. Mostly false	23. Mostly true
4. Mostly false	14. Mostly false	24. Mostly false
5. Mostly false	15. Mostly true	25. Mostly true
6. Mostly true	16. Mostly true	26. Mostly false
7. Mostly false	17. Mostly true	27. Mostly true
8. Mostly false	18. Mostly false	28. Mostly true
9. Mostly true	19. Mostly true	29. Mostly true
10. Mostly true	20. Mostly false	30. Mostly true

Interpretation: Score yourself a plus one (+1) for each of your answers that agrees with the scoring key. If your score is 15 or less it is probable that you are currently nonassertive. A score of 16 through 24 suggests that you are assertive. A score of 25 or higher suggests that you are aggressive. Retake this quiz about 30 days from now to give yourself some indication of the stability of your answers. You might also discuss your answers with a close friend to determine if that person has a similar perception of your assertiveness.

helps the leader dissolve tension and defuse conflict, it helps him or her exert power over the group.

Self-effacing humor is the choice of comedians and organizational leaders alike. When you are self-effacing, nobody else is insulted or slighted, yet a point can be made. A vice president of marketing at Sun Microsystems once said, "I want you people to design a workstation so uncomplicated that even managers at my level could learn how to use it."

Creativity is required for humor. Because creativity can be enhanced with practice, so can a sense of humor. To gather some experience in making humorous comments in the workplace, do Skill-Building Exercise 8-1.

SELF-AWARENESS AND SELF-OBJECTIVITY

Effective leaders are aware of their strengths and limitations. This awareness enables them to capitalize upon their strengths and overcome their weaknesses. A leader, for example, might realize that he or she is naturally

SKILL-BUILDING EXERCISE 8-1

THE WITTY LEADER

Groups of about five students gather in problem-solving groups to invent humorous comments a leader might make to the following scenarios. After the problem-solving groups have formulated their witty comments, the comments can be shared and compared.

Scenario 1: A store manager wants to communicate to employees how bad business has been lately. Sales have declined about 20 percent for three consecutive weeks.

Scenario 2: A leader has to communicate to the group that salaries have been frozen for another year due to limited business. The leader knows that group members have been eagerly awaiting news about the salary increase.

Scenario 3: Due to an unprecedented surge in orders, all salaried personnel will be required to work about 65 hours per week for the next 10 weeks. Furthermore, the office and factory must be staffed on Saturdays and Sundays.

distrustful of others. Awareness of this problem cautions the leader to not distrust people without good evidence. Another leader might realize that he or she is adept at counseling team members. This leader might then emphasize that activity in an effort to improve performance.

You can enhance your self-awareness and self-objectivity by regularly asking for feedback from others. You then compare the feedback to your self-perception of your standing on the same factor. You might, for example, think that you communicate in colorful, interesting terms. In speaking to others about your communication style, you might discover that others agree. You can then conclude that your self-awareness is accurate about your communication skills.

Another technique for improving self-awareness and self-objectivity is to take a goodly number of the type of self-examination exercises found in this text. Even if they do not describe you exactly, they stimulate you to reflect on your characteristics and behaviors.

COGNITIVE SKILLS

Mental ability as well as personality is important for leadership success. To inspire people, bring about constructive changes, and solve problems creatively, leaders need to be mentally sharp. Problem-solving and intellectual skills are referred to collectively as **cognitive factors.** The term *cognition* refers to the mental process or faculty by which knowledge is gathered. Two cognitive skills were discussed in Chapter 2: mental ability and the personal factor of openness to experience.

Another cognitive skill of major importance is *knowledge of the business,* or technical skill. An effective leader has to be technically or professionally competent in some discipline, particularly when leading a group of specialists. It is difficult for the leader to establish rapport with group members when he or she does not know what they are doing. A related damper on leadership effectiveness is when the group does not respect the leader's technical skill.

Increasing one's mental ability, or raw intelligence, may not be easy to accomplish. Yet people can develop their cognitive skills by continuous study and by working on challenging problems. The mere act of keeping up with developments in your field can keep you mentally sharp.

SUGGESTIONS FOR DEVELOPING CHARISMA

The study of leadership in recent years has emphasized the importance of inspirational leaders who guide others toward great heights of achievement. Such leaders are said to possess **charisma,** a special quality of leaders whose purposes, powers, and extraordinary determination differentiate them from others.[3] An important fact about charisma is that it reflects a subjective perception on the part of the person being influenced. A leader such as U.S. Attorney General Janet Reno (during the Clinton administration) was regarded as powerful and inspirational by many. Yet she was also disliked by many people and was the recipient of derogatory cartoons in newspapers.

The term *charisma* is most frequently used in association with nationally and internationally known leaders. Yet first-level supervisors, team leaders, and minor sports coaches can also be charismatic. Possessing a naturally dynamic personality is a major contributor to charisma, but a person can engage in many tangible actions that also contribute to charisma. Here we list a number of suggestions for behaving charismatically, all based on characteristics and behaviors often found among charismatic leaders. If you are not currently a leader, remember that being perceived as charismatic will help you become one.

1. *Communicate a vision.* A charismatic leader offers an exciting image of where the organization is headed and how to get there. A vision is more than a forecast because it describes an ideal version of the future of an entire organization or an organizational unit such as a department. The supervisor of paralegal services might communicate a vision such as, "Our paralegal group will become known as the most professional and helpful paralegal group in Arizona." Skill-Development Exercise 8-2 will give you a chance to develop visioning skills (a new buzzword in business).

2. *Use masterful communication skills.* To inspire people, the charismatic leader uses colorful language and exciting metaphors and analogies. An aspiring or current leader can then enhance his or her charisma by using more colorful language. The president of Compaq Computers has been quoted as using phrases such as "I know we can build outrageously good machines at outrageously low cost" and "We can accomplish what other computer manufacturers can only fantasize."

3. *Exhibit energy and an action orientation.* Charismatic leaders are energetic and serve as models for getting things done on time. People can therefore enhance their charisma by displaying these behaviors. Speaking rapidly and forcefully, when combined with vigorous hand movements, will make you appear energetic.

4. *Be emotionally expressive and warm.* A key characteristic of charismatic leaders is the ability to express feelings openly. Assertiveness is therefore an important component of charisma. In dealing with team members, refer to your feelings at the time, such as "I'm excited because I know we are going to hit our year-end target by mid-October." Nonverbal emotional expressiveness, such as warm gestures and frequent touching (nonsexual) of group members, also exhibits charisma.

5. *Be willing to take personal risks.* Charismatic leaders are typically risk takers, and risk taking adds to their charisma. Risks you might take would include extending additional credit to a start-up business, suggesting a bright but costly idea, and recommending that a former felon be given a chance in your firm.

SKILL-DEVELOPMENT
EXERCISE 8-2
CREATING A VISION

The class organizes into small problem-solving groups. Each group constructs a vision for a unit of an organization or for a total organization of its choosing. Students can choose an organization with which they are familiar or choose a well-known business firm or government agency. The vision should be approximately 25 words long and depict a glorious future. A vision is not simply a straightforward goal, such as "In 2001 our firm will gross $10 million in sales." Remember, the vision statement you draw should inspire people throughout the organization.

6. *Be self-promotional.* Charismatic leaders are not shy. Instead, they toot their own horns and allow others to know how important they are. Without appearing self-absorbed, you, too, might let others know of your tangible accomplishments. Explain to others the key role that you played on your team or how you achieved a few tough goals.

7. *Make everybody you meet feel that he or she is quite important.* For example, at an office picnic shake the hand of every person you meet.

8. *Multiply the effectiveness of your handshake.* Shake hands firmly, without creating pain, and make enough eye contact to notice the color of the other person's eyes. By doing so you project care and concern. Think a positive thought about the person whose hand you shake.

9. *Thank people frequently, especially your own group members.* Thanking others is still infrequently practiced, thus adding to your distinctiveness and giving you a charismatic edge.

10. *Smile frequently, even if you are not in a happy mood.* A warm smile seems to indicate a confident, caring person, which contributes to a perception of charisma.[4]

DEVELOPING TEAM LEADERSHIP SKILLS

As organizations continue to increase the use of teams, some of the best opportunities for practicing leadership occur as a team leader. A team leader typically reports to a higher-level manager. The team leader is not a boss in the old-fashioned sense, but a facilitator or coach who shares decision making with team members. (A facilitator is a person who helps make things happen without taking control.) A team leader practices **participative leadership,** or sharing authority with the group. Self-Assessment Quiz 8-3 gives you an opportunity to gauge your attitudes toward being a participative leader. Here we describe six techniques that would contribute to your effectiveness as a team leader, as outlined in Figure 8-1.

BUILD A MISSION STATEMENT

A starting point in developing teamwork is to specify the team's mission. The mission should contain a specific goal and purpose, and it should be optimistic and uplifting. Here is an example from a service team at a Cadillac dealership:

> *To plan and implement a level of automobile service and repair of the highest quality, at a competitive price, that will delight customers and retain their loyalty.*

The leader can help develop the mission statement when the team is first formed or at any other time. Developing a mission statement for a

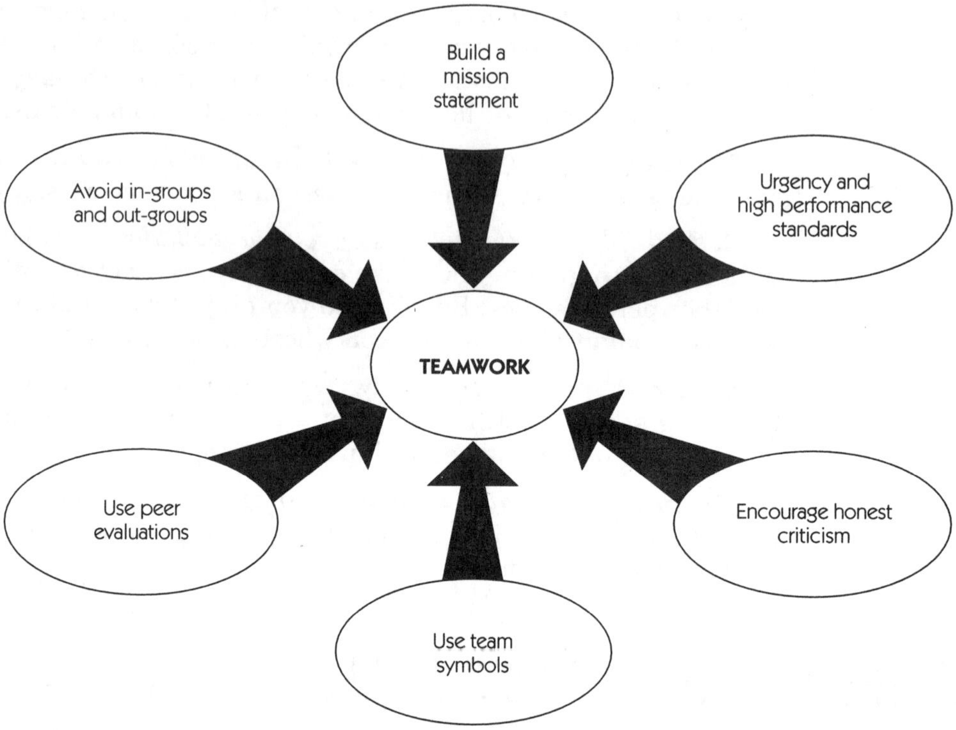

FIGURE 8-1 Developing Teamwork

long-standing team breathes new life into its activities. Being committed to mission improves teamwork, as does the process of formulating a mission statement. Skill-Building Exercise 8-2 gives you practice in developing a mission statement for a team.

ESTABLISH A SENSE OF URGENCY AND HIGH PERFORMANCE STANDARDS

To build teamwork, members need to believe that the team has urgent, constructive purposes. A demanding performance challenge helps create and sustain the team. Team members also want to know exactly what is expected of them. The more urgent and relevant the rationale, the more likely the team will perform well.[5] Based on this information, as a team leader you might project a sense of urgency and encourage setting high goals.

ENCOURAGE HONEST CRITICISM

A superficial type of camaraderie develops when team members avoid honestly criticizing each other for the sake of group harmony. Avoiding criticism

SELF-ASSESSMENT

QUIZ 8-3

HOW PARTICIPATIVE IS YOUR LEADERSHIP STYLE?

Directions: The purposes of this quiz are to (1) specify what kind of behaviors are represented by an ideal participative leader and (2) give you an opportunity to compare your behavior (or potential behavior) to that ideal. Be more concerned about giving yourself the gift of candid self-appraisal than attempting to give the "right" answer. Grade your leadership style by rating the frequency with which you use (or *would* use if placed in the situation) the behaviors listed: 3 = Almost always; 2 = Sometimes; 1 = Never.

	AA	S	N
1. I believe that employee involvement is critical to my work group's success.	3	2	1
2. I hardly ever review our corporate mission statement with our group.	3	2	1
3. My work group develops their own measurable goals.	3	2	1
4. I communicate how my work group contributes to the success of the entire organization.	3	2	1
5. I allow my group to establish its own performance measures.	3	2	1
6. I provide informal performance feedback to my group.	3	2	1
7. My group members play an active role in determining their own recognition and rewards.	3	2	1
8. I appropriately delegate my responsibilities to my work group.	3	2	1
9. I support my work group by providing the resources they need.	3	2	1
10. I emphasize the importance of work.	3	2	1

Scoring and Interpretation: Subtract your answers to questions 2, 3, 5, and 7 from the sum of your remaining questions.

11–14	You are already a participative leader (or already think and act like one).
7–10	You are well on your way to becoming a participative leader.
4–6	You have begun the shift to participative leadership (or you are beginning to think in that direction).
0–3	You are still leading in a traditional manner (or are thinking like one who does).

SOURCE: Adapted from a quiz from Suzanne W. Zoglio, *The Participative Leader* (Doylestown, Pa.: Tower Hill Press, 1994).

can result in groupthink. As a team leader you should therefore explain that being a good team player includes offering honest feedback on mistakes and flawed ideas. The team benefits from mutual criticism. A stronger team spirit will develop because team members realize they are helping each other through honest feedback. An example of honest criticism took place in the shipping department of a manufacturer of small kitchen appliances:

SKILL-BUILDING EXERCISE 8-2

DEVELOPING A TEAM MISSION STATEMENT

The class organizes into teams of about six people and appoints a team leader. Each team plays the role of a specific team within a company, government agency, or hospital. An example would be the customer service team at a utility. The task is to develop a mission statement approximating the type described in the text. The team leader might also take notes for the group.

Remember that a mission statement contains a goal and a purpose, and it is uplifting and optimistic. Allow about 30 minutes for preparing the mission statements. The groups then compare mission statements. One representative from each group presents the mission statements to the rest of the class.

One member of a quality-improvement team had designed a satisfaction survey to mail to customers. The purpose of the survey was to investigate whether the packing materials were of satisfactory quality. Another member said, "Are you sure you want to do this? Would we just annoy our customers by asking about packing ingredients? Why waste more paper? We've never had a complaint about packing materials."

The person whose idea was challenged was miffed at first, but then expressed appreciation. She said, "I guess I went a little overboard on trying to measure customer satisfaction. Maybe we should save our survey dollars for a more important issue."

USE TEAM SYMBOLS

Teamwork on the athletic field is enhanced by team symbols such as uniforms and nicknames. The term "Fighting Irish," for example, deserves some credit for contributing to the mystique of the Notre Dame football team. Symbols can also be an effective team builder in business. Trademarks, logos, mottoes, and other indicators of products both advertise the company and signify a joint effort. Company jackets, caps, T-shirts, mugs, ballpoint pens, and business cards can be modified to symbolize a work unit. As a team leader, you might therefore invest part of your team's budget in an appropriate symbol. Use the opportunity to practice participative leadership. Conduct a group problem-solving session to develop a team logo to place on a T-shirt or cap.

CAUTION: Screen team logo suggestions carefully. A member of a production team at a Harley-Davidson plant suggested that each team member tatoo his or her arm with a drawing of an armadillo!

USE PEER EVALUATIONS

In the traditional performance-evaluation system, the manager evaluates group members at regular intervals. With peer-evaluation systems, the team members contribute to the evaluation by submitting evaluations of each other. The evaluations might consist of filling out rating forms about each other's performance. Sometimes brief essays are written about each other and then synthesized by the team leader.

Peer evaluations contribute to teamwork because team members realize that helping each other becomes as important as helping the boss. Similarly, team members recognize that pleasing each other counts as much as pleasing the boss.

As a team leader you might not have the authority to initiate a peer-evaluation system without first checking with your manager. Making a recommendation for peer input into evaluations might demonstrate that you are committed to participative leadership.

MINIMIZE FORMATION OF IN-GROUPS AND OUT-GROUPS

An established leadership theory, the **leader-exchange model,** provides useful information for the aspiring team leader. According to this theory, leaders establish unique working relationships with group members. By so doing, they create in-groups and out-groups. The in-groups become part of a smoothly functioning team headed by the leader. Out-group members are less likely to experience good teamwork.[6] Figure 8-2 depicts the major concept of the leader-exchange model.

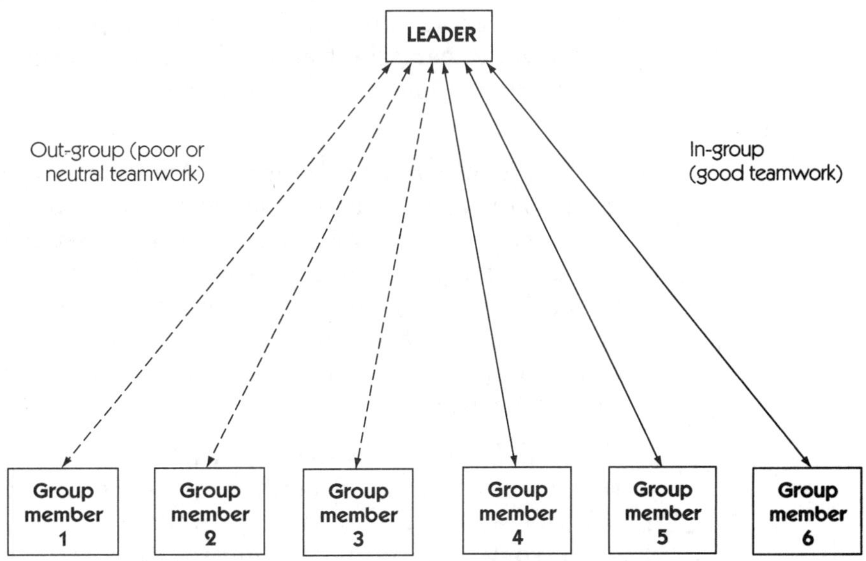

FIGURE 8-2 The Leader-Member Exchange Model

The in-group may come about because the leader prefers certain group members and therefore is motivated to form good working relationships with them. Conversely, the leader may neglect to form good relationships with people with whom he or she has limited rapport. Team leaders should therefore guard against the formation of out-groups just because they are not fond of a few team members.

DEVELOPING YOUR LEADERSHIP POTENTIAL

Much of this book deals directly and indirectly with information that could improve your leadership effectiveness. Chapter 3 on communications is a case in point. Improving your communications effectiveness would be one way to enhance your ability to lead people. Formal education and leadership development programs also contribute to enhancing leadership potential. (Many such programs include some of the activities found in this chapter.) Here we describe four strategies for developing your leadership potential, in addition to studying and participating in formal programs.

1. *Acquire broad experience.* Because leadership varies somewhat with the situation, a sound approach to improving leadership effectiveness is to attempt to gain supervisory experience in different settings. A person who wants to become an executive is well advised to gain supervisory experience in at least two different organizational functions, such as marketing and operations.

First-level supervisory jobs are an invaluable starting point for developing your leadership potential. It takes considerable skill to manage a fast-food restaurant or direct a public playground during the summer. A first-level supervisor frequently faces a situation where group members are poorly trained, poorly paid, and not well motivated to achieve company objectives.

2. *Model effective leaders.* Another strategy for leadership development is to observe capable leaders in action and then model some of their approaches. You may not want to copy a particular leader entirely, but you can incorporate a few of the behavior patterns into your own leadership style. For instance, most inexperienced leaders have difficulty confronting others. Observe a skilled confronter handle the situation, and try that person's approach the next time you have unfavorable news to communicate to another person.

3. *Self-develop leadership traits and behaviors.* Study the leadership traits and behaviors described earlier in this chapter. As a starting point, identify several attributes you think you could strengthen within yourself, given some determination and perhaps combined with the right training program. For example, you might decide that with some effort you could improve your sense of humor. You might also believe that you could remember to encourage honest criticism within the team. It is also helpful to obtain feedback from valid sources (such as a trusted manager) about which traits and behaviors you particularly need to develop.

4. *Become an integrated human being.* A philosophical approach to leadership suggests that the model leader is first and foremost a fully functioning person. According to William D. Hitt, mastering the art of leadership comes with self-mastery. Leadership development is the process of self-development. As a result, the process of becoming a leader is similar to the process of becoming an integrated human being. For example, you need to develop values that guide your behavior before you can adequately guide the behavior of others.

The model (or ideal) leader, according to Hitt, must possess six character traits: identity (know thyself), independence, authenticity, responsibility, courage, and integrity.[7] All of these traits have everyday meanings, but can also have personal meanings. Part of becoming an integrated person is to answer such questions as "What do I mean when I say I have integrity?"

SUMMARY

Effective leadership depends on having the right personal characteristics and taking the appropriate actions. Leadership is the ability to inspire support and confidence among the people who are needed to achieve company goals. People can exercise leadership whether or not they occupy a formal leadership position.

Certain traits contribute heavily to leadership effectiveness. Among them are self-confidence; honesty, integrity, and credibility; assertiveness; emotional stability; sense of humor; self-awareness and self-objectivity; and cognitive skills (including intelligence).

Although charisma depends heavily on personal characteristics, people can work toward being charismatic. Suggestions for behaving charismatically include: (1) communicate a vision, (2) communicate masterfully, (3) be action-oriented, (4) be emotionally expressive and warm, (5) take personal risks; (6) be self-promotional, (7) make others feel important, (8) shake hands effectively, (9) thank others frequently, and (10) smile frequently.

A team leader acts as a facilitator or coach who shares decision making with team members, thus practicing participative leadership. Techniques for effective team leadership include:

1. Build a mission statement.
2. Establish a sense of urgency and high performance standards.
3. Encourage honest criticism.
4. Use team symbols.

5. Use peer evaluations.
6. Minimize forming in-groups and out-groups.

In addition to participating in formal leadership development programs, four strategies for developing leadership potential are as follows: acquire broad experience; model effective leaders; self-develop leadership traits and behaviors; and become an integrated human being (a fully functioning person).

QUESTIONS FOR DISCUSSION AND REVIEW

1. Visualize a work associate or fellow student whom you think has good leadership potential. On what basis did you conclude that this person would be effective as a leader?
2. How do you explain the fact that a person can be a leader even though he or she lacks a job that includes responsibility for others?
3. What does it mean to say that a person has the "right stuff" for being a leader?
4. Assume that you worked for a manager who was dishonest with customers and suppliers, yet honest with employees. How would that affect your perception of the manager's leadership effectiveness?
5. Assertiveness is said to be important for leadership effectiveness. Yet can you give an example of an effective leader who is downright aggressive and obnoxious?
6. A sense of humor is important for leadership effectiveness, yet telling rehearsed jokes is not considered effective. How do you account for this discrepancy?
7. What does the term *self-objectivity* mean to you, and why is it important for leadership?
8. In what way do the concepts of charismatic leadership and participative leadership differ substantially from each other?
9. What is the difference between a vision and a mission?
10. Assume that a student obtains a part-time job as an assistant store manager. What can this person do to capitalize on this position for leadership experience?

AN INTERPERSONAL RELATIONS CASE PROBLEM

HOW CAN I INSPIRE MY TEAM?

Jacques Renfert considered himself fortunate to be chosen as team leader for one of the newly formed work teams at the insurance company where he worked. The purpose of forming teams was to improve customer service. Each team now had the authority to issue policies and settle claims, within limits, for specific geographic regions. Before the organization into teams, separate departments existed for sales administration, underwriting, and claims. Although the company was profitable, it received too many criticisms about poor service. Many complaints were made by external customers indicating that it took too long to settle claims. Company sales representatives contended that the underwriting department took too long to approve and issue policies.

One of Renfert's early initiatives was to call frequent team meetings to discuss how service was going to be improved. He emphasized to the group that the company had moved into the modern era and that teams were empowered to look for ways to improve efficiency. Renfert also emphasized that each team member had more responsibility than under the previous structure. Each team member would be doing some sales administration, some underwriting, and some claims work.

Molly Goldwin, a team member, commented during one of Renfert's meetings: "Just think of it, three jobs in one and being paid just the same as before."

At the same meeting, another team member asked, "What's so special about calling us a team? I had a nice job in the underwriting department before these teams were formed. I enjoyed that work. Now my job is more confusing."

Renfert replied, "The company decided this was the way to go. Trust me, everything will work out fine in the end. Just go along with the team idea for now."

Four months after the work teams were formed, Renfert's boss, Nancy Wong, met with him to discuss progress. Wong told Renfert, "Your team isn't making as much progress as I would like. Policies are not being issued any faster. Customer complaints about slow claims settlements are at the same level as before we converted into teams. The other teams are making more progress. Does your team have a problem?"

"We have a problem," said Renfert. "Everyone comes to work just as in the days before teams. They do most of their work alone, but they get together when needed. It just seems to be business as usual. So far, the idea of being a high-producing team hasn't caught on."

(Continued) ▶

"Are you being an effective team leader?" asked Wong.

"I think I am," said Renfert. "I do everything I'm supposed to. I hold meetings. I take care of the paperwork and answer electronic mail. I try to settle problems."

"I'll be back with you in three months to discuss your team's progress. I want to see some improved results in terms of better customer service."

CASE QUESTIONS

1. How can Jacques Renfert be a more effective team leader?
2. What can Jacques do to inspire his team?
3. Based on whatever information you have found in the case, how would you rate Renfert's charisma?

AN INTERPERSONAL RELATIONS ROLE PLAY

INSPIRING THE TEAM

One student plays the role of Jacques Renfert and calls a meeting designed to inspire the team toward new heights of productivity and customer service. Be dramatic. Use whatever inspirational approaches you think might work. Five other students play the role of a team member, none of whom were expecting an inspirational meeting. If Renfert inspires you, act accordingly. If he fails to inspire you, demonstrate your lack of inspiration.

Chapter 17

Customer Satisfaction Skills

Learning Objectives

After reading and studying this chapter and doing the exercises you should be able to

- Enhance your ability to satisfy customers.
- Describe general principles and guidelines for satisfying customers.
- Create bonds with present or future customers.
- Have a plan for dealing effectively with customer dissatisfaction.

Purchasing agent Hal said to Cynthia, a sales representative calling on his firm, "Our company has decided to take advantage of your volume discount. We want to order one gross of print cartridges, model number 7PL89. You said we would receive a 25 percent discount by buying in bulk."

"That's exactly what I said last week, Hal. Our company would like to sell you 144 cartridges in one shot. But I have some new information that suggests you should limit your purchase to two dozen for now. Those two dozen are the older cartridges. The manufacturer recently shifted to a new components supplier. Some quality problems have been found with the latest ribbons. Let's hold off on that big order until we can be sure you will receive the quality that your company needs and deserves."

"It's a pleasure doing business with you, Cynthia," said Hal. My company and I are happy to know that you are looking out for our best interests."

The conversation between Hal and Cynthia may sound idealistic, but it represents an important new thrust in relationships between buyers and sellers. Many companies today emphasize total customer satisfaction over short-range profits. An important reason is that excellent customer service leads to goodwill, repeat business, and referrals. In this chapter we present information and exercises that can enhance your ability to satisfy both external and internal customers at a high level.

External customers fit the traditional definition of customers that includes clients, guests, and patients. External customers can be classified as retail or industrial. The latter represents one company buying from another, such as purchasing steel or a gross of printer cartridges. *Internal customers* are the people you serve within the organization or those who use the output from your job. Our emphasis, however, is on satisfying external customers.

Customer satisfaction skills are required by all workers in contact with customers, including sales representatives, customer service representatives (those who back up sales and take care of customer problems), and store associates. Various aspects of developing customer satisfaction skills are divided here into three parts: general principles, bonding with customers, and dealing with customer dissatisfaction. To reflect on your attitudes toward satisfying customers, do Self-Assessment Quiz 12-1.

GENERAL PRINCIPLES OF CUSTOMER SATISFACTION

Knowing how to satisfy customers is a subset of effective interpersonal relations in organizations. Nevertheless, there are certain general principles that will sharpen your ability to satisfy customers and thereby improve customer retention. Six key principles for satisfying customers are presented in this section. Remember, however, that *satisfaction* is considered a minimum expectation. If you do an outstanding job of satisfying customers, they will experience *delight,* as shown in Figure 12-1.

SELF-ASSESSMENT

QUIZ 12-1

WOULD YOU BUY FROM YOU?

One of the most effective ways to assess your effectiveness in handling customers is via the question: "If you were the customer, would you buy from yourself?" You would if you scored well on the following quiz. Answer each question by checking the appropriate Yes or No blank. If you do not deal with external customers, take this quiz in relation to your handling of internal customers. If you are not currently working, just imagine how you would handle the situations described.

	Yes	No
1. Is your image one of honest and straightforward sincerity?	___	___
2. Based on your experience with customers over the past year or so, *from the buyer's point of view,* would you be classified as reliable?	___	___
3. Could you say your customers obtained special benefits dealing with you they wouldn't have obtained from others?	___	___
4. Do you think you come off as an expert in the eyes of your customers?	___	___
5. Have you been effective in helping to solve customer problems?	___	___
6. Wherever possible, would you say you handled customer complaints to the buyer's satisfaction?	___	___
7. Is *integrity* one of the most important words in your vocabulary?	___	___
8. Do you think customers believe you have their personal welfare and well-being at heart with respect to business?	___	___
9. Can you honestly say most of your company's customers believe you have their personal welfare and well-being at heart, even outside of business?	___	___
10. Do customers look upon you as a good, reliable source of product and industry information?	___	___
11. Has doing business with you contributed positively to most of your customers' profit performance?	___	___
12. Would most of your company's customers continue dealing with you even if a competitor approached them with a price that's a little bit lower?	___	___

Total number of Yes answers ________

Your Rating: Multiply the sum of your Yes answers by 5. If you achieved a score of 55 or higher, it's a privilege to do business with you. Fifty is well above average; 40 to 45 is mediocre to fair.

Source: Adapted from "Making . . . Serving . . . Keeping . . . Customers," Dartnell Corporation, Chicago, 1995.

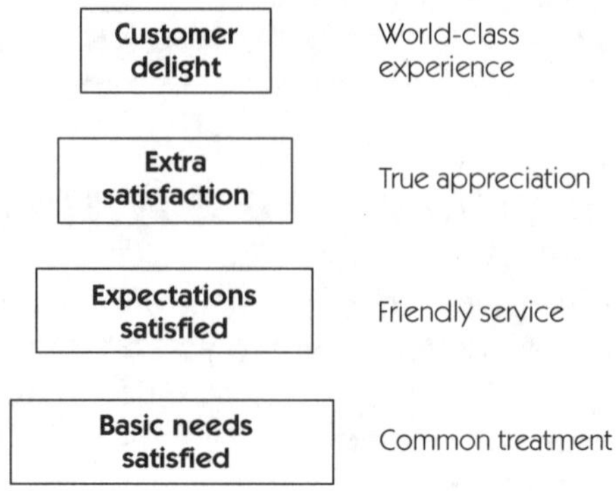

FIGURE 12-1 Levels of Customer Satisfaction

SATISFIED EMPLOYEES PROVIDE BETTER CUSTOMER SERVICE

Researchers have observed frequently that employees who are happy with their jobs are the most likely to satisfy customers. Treating employees well puts them in a better frame of mind to treat their customers well. One example of this relationship was found at the Metropolitan Property and Casualty Insurance Company.[1] The company recognized that the difference between success and failure in the property and casualty insurance field is often the quality of service and speed of handling transactions.

Human resources specialists at Metropolitan observed that customer service and employee satisfaction were closely related to each other. Customers, for example, expect outstanding customer service. Employees want recognition and compensation that relates to the achievement of customer service goals. Customers want to deal with knowledgeable customer-contact personnel who can make decisions. Employees want to be led, inspired, and recognized.

Acting alone, you cannot improve company conditions that contribute to job satisfaction. What you can control to some extent, however, is attitudes of yours that are related to job satisfaction. A checklist of attitudes and beliefs related to job satisfaction, and over which you can exert some control, follows.

- *Interest in the work itself.* Job satisfaction stems directly from being interested in what you are doing. People who love their work experience high job satisfaction and are therefore in the right frame of mind to satisfy customers.

- *A feeling of self-esteem.* If you have high self-esteem you are more likely to experience high job satisfaction. High-status occupations contribute more to self-esteem than do those of low status. Feelings of self-esteem also stem from doing work the individual sees as worthwhile. This perception is less influenced by external standards than is the status associated with a particular job or occupation.

- *Optimism and flexibility.* An optimistic and flexible person is predisposed to be a satisfied employee. A pessimistic and rigid person will most likely be a dissatisfied employee. Every company has its share of "pills" who always find something to complain about. Some evidence suggests that a tendency toward optimism versus pessimism is inherited.[2] If you have a predisposition toward pessimism it does not mean that with self-discipline you cannot become more optimistic. You can, for example, look for the positive aspects of a generally unpleasant situation.

- *Positive self-image.* People possessing a positive self-image are generally more satisfied with their jobs than are those possessing a negative self-image. One explanation is that the people who view themselves negatively tend to view most things negatively. You have to like yourself before you can like your job.

- *Positive expectations about the job.* People with positive expectations about their jobs are frequently more satisfied than are those with low expectations. These expectations illustrate a self-fulfilling prophecy. If you expect to like your job, you will behave in such a way that those expectations will be met. Similarly, if you expect your job not to satisfy your needs, you will do things to make your expectations come true. Assume that a worker expects to earn low commissions in a sales job. The person's negativism may come through to customers and prospective customers, thus ensuring low customer satisfaction and low commissions.

UNDERSTAND CUSTOMER NEEDS AND PUT THEM FIRST

The most basic principle of selling is to identify and satisfy customer needs. One challenge is that many customers may not be able to express their needs clearly. To help identify customer needs, you may have to probe for information. For example, the associate in a camera and video store might ask: "What uses do you have in mind for a video camera?" Knowing such information will help the associate identify which camcorder will satisfy the customer's needs.

After customer needs have been identified, the focus must be on satisfying them rather than those of oneself or the company. Assume that the customer says, "The only convenient time for me to receive delivery this week would be Thursday or Friday afternoon." The sales associate should not respond, "On Thursday and Friday our truckers prefer to make morning deliveries." Instead, the associate should respond, "I'll do whatever is possible to accommodate your request."

FOCUS ON SOLVING PROBLEMS, NOT JUST TAKING ORDERS

Effective selling uses sales representatives to solve problems rather than merely taking orders. An example is the approach taken by Kraft U.S.A.'s sales representatives, who no longer restrict their efforts to devising promotions in supermarkets. Now they also offer information for improving a store's profits, such as suggestions on store displays.

The focus on problem solving enables sales representatives to become partners in the success of their customers' businesses. By assisting the customer solve problems, the sales representative enhances the value of the supplier-customer relationship to the customer. The customer is receiving consulting services in addition to the merchandise or service being offered. In some situations, a store associate can capitalize on the same principle. If the customer appears unsure about a purchase, ask him or her what problem is being faced that the product will solve. The following scenario in a computer store illustrates this point:

Customer: I think I would like to buy this computer. I'm pretty sure it's the one I want. But I don't know too much about computers.

Store Associate: I am happy you would like to purchase a computer. But could you tell me what problems are you facing that you want a computer to help you solve?

Customer: Right now I feel I'm not using the information superhighway. I want to join those fancy networks like Internet so I can communicate with people of similar interests all over the world.

Store Associate: To solve your problem, you will need a more powerful computer than the one you are looking at. I would like you to consider another model that is about the same price as the one you have chosen. The difference is that it has just the memory you need to communicate with people all over the world.

RESPOND POSITIVELY TO MOMENTS OF TRUTH

An effective customer contact person performs well during situations in which a customer comes in contact with the company and forms an impression of its service. Such situations are referred to as **moments of truth.** If the customer experiences satisfaction or delight during a moment of truth, the customer is likely to return when the need for service arises again. A person who is frustrated or angered during a moment of truth will often not be a repeat customer.

You can probably visualize many moments of truth in your experiences with services. Reflect on how you were treated by a store associate when you asked for assistance; the instructions you received when an airplane flight was canceled; or how you were treated when you inquired about financial aid. Each business transaction has its own moment of truth. Yet they all follow the theme of a key interaction between a customer and a company employee.

One way you can track moments of truth is to prepare a cycle-of-service chart, as shown in Figure 12-2. The **cycle-of-service chart** summarizes

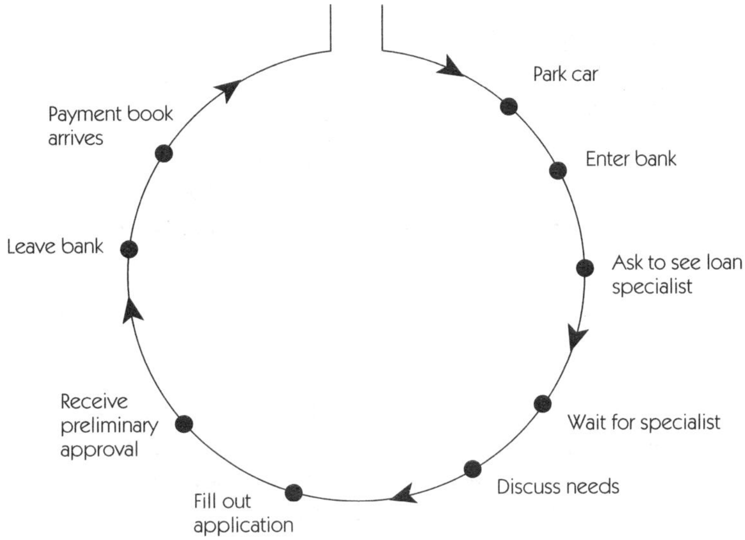

FIGURE 12-2 A Cycle-of-Service Chart for Obtaining a Car Loan at a Bank

the moments of truth encountered by a customer during the delivery of a service.[3] To gain insight into these charts, do Skill-Building Exercise 12-1.

BE READY TO ACCEPT EMPOWERMENT

A major strategy for improving customer service is to empower customer-contact employees to resolve problems. **Empowerment** refers to managers transferring, or sharing, power with lower-ranking employees. In terms of customer relations it means pushing decision making and complaint resolution downward to employees who are in direct contact with customers. The traditional method of dealing with all but the most routine

SKILL BUILDING EXERCISE 12-1

MOMENTS OF TRUTH

The class organizes into small groups to discuss what can go right versus what can go wrong during customer moments of truth. First refer to the cycle-of-service chart shown in Figure 12-2. Discuss what can go right or wrong at each moment of truth. Second, the team develops its own cycle-of-service chart for another service, using your own experience and imagination.

After making the two analyses, discuss the usefulness of a cycle-of-service chart for improving customer satisfaction.

customer problems is for the customer-contact worker to refer them to the manager. An excellent example of empowerment took place at the typewriter division of IBM. A company executive describes what happened:

> *A customer called one of our IBM administrators with a problem. He had been sent a bill for the repair of a typewriter that he thought was covered under a maintenance agreement and therefore should have been fixed at no charge. The customer fully expected an argument. Instead, the empowered employee made the decision to credit the invoice.*
>
> *A week later, the pleased customer converted his entire system to an IBM maintenance agreement for three years without being asked to do so.*[4]

The IBM executive explains that empowerment is not giving away the store. Instead, it is taking a reasonable risk based on company principles to provide meaningful customer service. For empowerment to work, the company must grant decision-making latitude to employees. The employees, in turn, must be willing to accept empowerment (or decision-making authority). Imagine yourself in a customer-contact position. For empowerment to work effectively, you should be able to answer affirmatively to the following statements:

- ▶ I am willing to arrive at a quick decision as to whether the company or the customer is right.
- ▶ I would be willing to admit to a customer that the company has made a mistake.
- ▶ I would be willing to take the risk that at times I will lose money for the company on a given transaction.
- ▶ I would be comfortable making an out-of-the ordinary decision about a customer problem without consulting a manager.

AVOID RUDENESS

We have reserved the most frequently violated principle of good customer service for last: avoid being rude to customers. Although rudeness to customers is obviously a poor business practice, the problem is widespread. Rudeness by customer-contact personnel is a major problem from the employer's standpoint. Rude treatment creates more lost business than does poor product quality or high prices.

A representative example of the importance of not being rude to customers took place at Alamo Rent A Car. To overcome customer complaints (and to improve coworker relationships) the company initiated a Best Friends program, explained as follows:

> *Make your customers your best friends; treat them that way all the time, and they will always be your customers. And they will always be your best*

friends. Extend this concept to your fellow Alamo family members. Make each one with whom you come in contact your best friend.

What happens then? Our work environment becomes a happy place with a caring, family atmosphere. It becomes a pleasure to come to work every day. Moreover, because you *have a caring attitude, because* you *have created a family atmosphere, the customer senses it and responds accordingly.*

The idea of actually making your customers your best friends may seem far-fetched; nevertheless, the Best Friends program did show good results. After one year, business transactions increased 30 percent, and the number of repeat customers rose 70 percent. Complaints about sales and service both decreased about 15 percent.[5]

To elevate your awareness level about rudeness among customer-contact personnel, do Self-Assessment Quiz 12-2.

CREATING A BOND WITH YOUR CUSTOMER

Another key perspective on achieving customer satisfaction and delight is to create a bond—or emotional relationship—with customers. The rationale is that if you form warm, constructive relationships with your customers, they will keep buying. Staying focused on the importance of customers will help provide the motivation for forming such a bond. Exhibit 12-1 explains how employees at a famous consumer-products company are requested to regard customers.

Creating a bond is aimed at increasing sales, but also enhances service. If the customer relies on and trusts the sales representative, the customer will perceive the service to be of high quality. Similarly, people perceive medical and legal services to be of high quality if they trust the physician or lawyer.

Virtually all of the principles and techniques presented in this chapter will help form a bond with customers. However, five key principles are as follows:

1. Provide exceptional service.
2. Show care and concern.
3. Smile at every customer.
4. Make the buyer feel good.
5. Build a personal relationship.

1. *Provide exceptional service.* The best-accepted axiom about keeping customers is to provide exceptional service. Many successful companies contend that their competitive advantage is good service. An excellent example is USAA, the fourth-largest insurer and financial services firm in the United States. The company has a much lower than industry average

SELF-ASSESSMENT

QUIZ 12-2

AM I BEING RUDE?

Directions: Following is a list of behaviors of customer-contact workers that would be interpreted as rude by many customers. Indicate whether you have engaged in such behavior in your dealings with customers, or whether you are likely to do so if your job did involve customer contact.

	Yes	No
1. I talk to a coworker while serving a customer.	___	___
2. I conduct a telephone conversation with someone else while serving a customer.	___	___
3. I address customers by their first names without having their permission.	___	___
4. I chew gum or eat candy while dealing with a customer.	___	___
5. I laugh when customers describe an agonizing problem they are having with one of our company's products or services.	___	___
6. I minimize eye contact with customers.	___	___
7. I say the same thing to every customer, such as "Have a nice day," in a monotone.	___	___
8. I accuse customers of attempting to cheat the company.	___	___
9. I hurry customers when my break time approaches.	___	___
10. I comment on a customer's appearance in a flirtatious, sexually oriented way.	___	___

Interpretation: The more of these behaviors you have engaged in, the ruder you are and the more likely that you are losing potential business for your company. If you have not engaged in any of these behaviors, even when faced with a rude customer, you are an asset to your employer. You are also tolerant.

percentage of customer defectors, and its business grows primarily through referrals. USAA has no external salespeople and does not use insurance agents. Most customer concerns and inquiries are settled within minutes by calling an 800 number. The mission of the firm is expressed in one word: *service.*

Exceptional service includes dozens of customer transactions, including prompt delivery, a fair-returns policy, accurate billing, and prompt attention to a customer's presence. Exceptional service also includes giving customers good advice about using the product or service.

2. *Show care and concern.* During contacts with the customer, the sales representative should show concern for the customer's welfare. The

EXHIBIT 12-1

WHAT IS A CUSTOMER?

- A Customer is the most important person ever in this office . . . in person or by mail.
- A Customer is not dependent on us . . . we are dependent on him.
- A Customer is not an interruption of our work . . . he is the purpose of it. We are not doing a favor by serving him . . . he is doing us a favor by giving us the opportunity to do so.
- A Customer is not someone to argue or match wits with. Nobody ever won an argument with a customer.
- A Customer is a person who brings us to his wants. It is our job to handle them profitably to him and ourselves.

Source: L.L. Bean, Freeport, Maine.

representative should ask questions such as: "How have you enjoyed the laser printer you bought a while back?" "How are you feeling today?" After asking the question, the sales representative should project a genuine interest in the answer.

3. *Smile at every customer.* Smiling has many benefits, including lowering stress, decreasing wrinkles, and making a person more photogenic and telegenic. Smiling is also a natural relationship builder and can help you bond with your customer. Smile several times at each customer meeting, even if your customer is angry with your product or service.

Seminars for both sales and customer service skills often coach people on how to smile. In addition, you might practice smiling in front of a camcorder and play back the results. Smiling over the telephone is also recommended because it helps you achieve a warmer voice tone.

4. *Make the buyer feel good.* A fundamental way of keeping a relationship going is to make the buyer feel good about him- or herself. Also, the customer should be made to feel good because of having bought from the representative. Offer compliments about the customer's appearance or about a report that specified clearly vendor requirements. An effective feel-good line is: "I enjoy doing business with you."

5. *Build a personal relationship.* Building a good working relationship with a customer often leads to a positive personal relationship. A bold approach is to do the reverse—build a working relationship based on an authentic personal relationship. You gather personal facts about the interests of your customers and then appeal to those interests. A case history of a bank manager, Jack Foxboro, shows the potential effectiveness of this technique:

> *Several years ago Foxboro was a commercial loan officer. He acquired a base of existing accounts from the previous officer and gradually increased his base. Jack invested considerable time telephoning existing loan holders. He collected facts about them, such as birthdays, the names of family members, golf handicaps, hobbies, and favorite sports teams. Jack entered all this information into a computer.*
>
> *Jack would send cards to customers in recognition of their birthdays and special accomplishments. When a customer visited the bank to talk about an existing loan or to apply for a new one, he would retrieve relevant personal facts from the computer. Jack's clients were so impressed that he enlarged existing accounts and received substantial referral business.*

Skill-Building Exercise 12-2 will give you an opportunity to practice techniques for bonding with customers.

SKILL-BUILDING EXERCISE 12-2

BONDING WITH CUSTOMERS

Role players in this exercise will demonstrate two related techniques for bonding with customers: show care and concern, and make the buyer feel good.

Scenario 1: Show Care and Concern. A sales representative meets with two company representatives to talk about installing a new voice mail system. One of the company representatives is from the human resources department and the other from the telecommunications department. The sales representative will attempt to show care and concern for both company representatives during the same meeting.

Scenario 2: Make the Buyer Feel Good. A couple, played by two role players, enters a new-car showroom to examine a model they have seen advertised on television. Although they are not in urgent need of a new car, they are strongly interested. The sales representative is behind quota for the month and would like to close a sale today. The rep decides to use the tactic "make the buyer feel good" to help form a bond.

DEALING WITH CUSTOMER DISSATISFACTION

Most companies put honest effort into preventing customer dissatisfaction. In addition to employing many of the principles and techniques already cited, many companies routinely survey customers to detect problem areas that could lead to dissatisfaction. A representative survey is shown in Exhibit 12-2. Despite all these efforts to achieve total customer satisfaction, some customer dissatisfaction is inevitable. One reason is that mistakes in serving customers are almost inevitable; for example, a piece of equipment may have a faulty component unknown to the seller. Second, some customers have a predisposition to complain. They will find something to complain about with respect to a product or service. Here we describe approaches to handling customer dissatisfaction from three aspects: dealing with complaints and anger, involving the customer in resolving a problem, and handling unreasonable requests.

DEAL CONSTRUCTIVELY WITH CUSTOMER COMPLAINTS AND ANGER

In an era when customer satisfaction is so highly valued, both retail and industrial customers are likely to be vocal in their demands. When faced with an angry customer, use one or more of the following techniques recommended by customer satisfaction specialists.[6]

1. *Acknowledge the customer's point of view.* Make statements such as "I understand," "I agree," and "I'm sorry." Assume, for example, a customer says: "The accounts payable department made a $1,000 overcharge on my account last month. I want this fixed right away." You might respond, "I understand how annoying this must be for you. I'll work on the problem right away."

2. *Avoid placing blame.* Suggesting that the customer is responsible for the problem intensifies the conflict. With the customer who claims to have been overcharged, refrain from saying: "Customers who keep careful accounts of their orders never have this problem."

3. *Use six magic words to defuse anger.* The magic words are: *I understand* [that this is a problem]; *I agree* [that it needs to be solved]; *I'm sorry* [that this happened to you].

4. *Apologize for the problems created by you or your company.* To recover from a breakdown in customer service, it is best to acknowledge error immediately. Apologies are most effective when stated in the first person (such as "I created the problem"). The corporate "we're sorry" sounds less sincere than when one specific person accepts responsibility for what went wrong.

5. *Follow up on the resolution of the problem.* Following up to see if the resolution to the problem is satisfactory brings closure to the incident. The follow-up also helps the service deliverer know that he or she can rebound from an episode of customer dissatisfaction. One useful form of

EXHIBIT 12-2

A RETAIL STORE CUSTOMER SATISFACTION SURVEY

HOW ARE WE DOING?
DICK'S CLOTHING & SPORTING GOODS

NAME (OPTIONAL) ____________ ADDRESS ____________

PHONE NUMBER ____________ CITY ____________

DATE AND TIME OF VISIT ____________ NAME OF ASSOCIATE WHO HELPED YOU ____________

	EXCELLENT	GOOD	AVERAGE	NEEDS IMPROVEMENT	POOR
PROMPT AND COURTEOUS GREETING	❑	❑	❑	❑	❑
KNOWLEDGEABLE SALESPEOPLE	❑	❑	❑	❑	❑
STORE CLEANLINESS	❑	❑	❑	❑	❑
STORE DISPLAYS	❑	❑	❑	❑	❑
PRICES	❑	❑	❑	❑	❑
SPEEDY CHECKOUTS	❑	❑	❑	❑	❑
HOW DO YOU RATE US OVERALL?	❑	❑	❑	❑	❑

	NEWSPAPER	TV	RADIO	OTHER
WHAT BROUGHT YOU TO DICK'S?	❑	❑	❑	❑

DID YOU MAKE A PURCHASE? ____________

ITEMS YOU WANTED THAT WE DID NOT HAVE? ____________

GENERAL COMMENTS: ____________

SOURCE: Dick's Clothing & Sporting Goods, Corporate Park Drive, P.O. Box 206, Conklin, NY 13748-9984.

follow-up is to telephone the customer whose problem was repaired. For example, a representative from the service department at an automobile dealership might telephone a customer whose new car required substantial warranty repairs. "Hello, this is Jill Gordon from Oak Street Automotive. We replaced your original transmission last month. How is the new transmission working?"

A less personal, and usually less effective, form of follow-up is to send a customer satisfaction questionnaire to the person with the problem. The questionnaire will often be interpreted as a company procedure that does not reflect specific concern about the individual's problem.

INVOLVE THE CUSTOMER IN WORKING OUT THE PROBLEM

Mistakes and problems in serving customers are inevitable, however hard the customer-contact worker strives for perfection. To minimize the perception of poor service, the customer should be involved in deciding what should be done about the problem. By involving the customer in the solution to the problem, the customer is more likely to accept a deviation from the service promised originally. The following case history illustrates the technique of customer involvement:

Seth Bradbury is a sales promotion specialist at an advertising agency. A furniture store hired the agency to prepare and mail 3,000 postal cards advertising a new line of furniture. One side of the postal card contained a photograph of the furniture, and the other side contained product details and space for addressing and stamping the card. After the cards were mailed, Seth received an urgent call from the client. "The photograph of the furniture is printed vertically. It looks horrible. We agreed on a horizontal shot. This means 3,000 cards have been mailed with a mistake."

After allowing the client to finish his complaint, Seth responded, "You're right, it is a vertical shot. Perhaps we misinterpreted your directions. However, I think your furniture still looks beautiful. The extra white space the vertical shot provides creates an interesting effect. "It's unfortunate that the cards have already been mailed. What would you like us to do? It's important that you are satisfied."

The client responded, "I guess there is nothing we can do to change the photograph. Would you be willing to give us a discount off the price we agreed on?"

Seth checked with his boss, and the agency agreed to a 15 percent discount on the job. The client accepted these terms and was doubly pleased because the mailer achieved his targeted response rate. Seth had impressed his client because he listened fully to the complaint and involved the client in achieving a workable compromise to settle the problem.

ANTICIPATE HOW TO HANDLE AN UNREASONABLE REQUEST

No matter how hard the customer contact worker attempts to provide outstanding customer service, at some point a customer comes along with an unreasonable request. Or the customer may raise an unfair objection. Speak to any experienced store associate to obtain a case history of a "customer from Hell." For example, a small-business owner demanded that a store associate grant him exchange credit for six printer ribbons. The ribbons were purchased four years previously and were now obsolete.

Recognize that the customer who makes an unreasonable demand is usually aware of the unreasonableness. The customer may not expect to be fully granted the request. Instead the customer is bargaining by beginning with an unreasonable demand. The small-business owner who brought in the printer ribbons was probably looking to salvage whatever he could.

Sales representatives and other customer-contact workers who stand their ground with dignity and courtesy will generally not lose the customer with the unreasonable request. The suggestions presented next will help you deal with unreasonable demands while retaining the business.[7]

- Let your customers retain their dignity by stating your position politely and reasonably.
- Avoid arguing with an upset customer. As the adage says, "You never win an argument with a customer."
- Appeal to your customer's sense of fair play and integrity. Explain that your intention is to do what is right and fair.
- Be firm by repeating the facts of the situation, but keep your temper under control.
- Accept responsibility for your decision rather than blaming company policy or your manager. Making somebody else the villain may intensify the problem.
- Be willing to say no to a customer when it is justifiable. Saying yes to an outrageous demand opens the door for a series of outrageous demands.

Dealing diplomatically and effectively with difficult customers requires an awareness of the type of tactics described in the previous several pages. Practice on the firing line is also indispensable. The type of experience provided by Skill-Building Exercise 12-3 is also helpful.

SUMMARY

Many companies today emphasize total customer satisfaction because it leads to goodwill, repeat business, and referrals. Customer satisfaction skills are required by all workers in contact with customers. Six key principles for satisfying customers are as follows:

SKILL-BUILDING EXERCISE 12-3

DEALING WITH DIFFICULT CUSTOMERS

The following scenarios require one person to play the role of the customer-contact worker and another person to play the difficult customer. As usual, the role players project their feelings into the role play by imagining how they would behave in the situation.

Scenario 1: One person is a store associate in a high-fashion women's clothing store. A woman who bought a $900 gown the previous week brings back the gown today. She claims that she is returning the gown because it doesn't fit comfortably. The store associate strongly suspects the woman bought the gown originally with the intent of wearing it for a special occasion and then returning it.

Scenario 2: One person plays the role of a customer service representative in a consumer-electronics store. Another person plays the role of a customer who purchased a $3,500 giant-screen television receiver three months ago. He comes up to the service rep's counter ranting about the store's ineptitude. The customer claims that the TV has broken down three times.

After the first repair, the TV worked for two weeks and then broke down again. The second repair lasted two weeks, only for the TV to break down during a Super Bowl party at his house. The customer is red in the face and shouting loudly. The service rep wants to resolve the customer's problem and prevent him from bad-mouthing the store.

1. Satisfied employees provide better customer service. (Some of your own attitudes, such as optimism and flexibility, influence your job satisfaction.)
2. Understand the customer needs and put them first.
3. Focus on solving problems, not just taking orders.
4. Respond positively to moments of truth (points at which the customer forms an impression of company service).
5. Be ready to accept empowerment. (Being empowered enables you to solve customer problems.)
6. Avoid rudeness. (Rude treatment of customers creates lost business.)

Another key perspective on achieving customer satisfaction and delight is to create a bond—or emotional relationship—with customers.

Almost any act of good customer service helps create a bond, but five principles are highlighted here: provide exceptional service; show care and concern; smile at every customer; make the buyer feel good; and build a personal relationship.

Despite the best efforts on the company's part, some customer dissatisfaction is inevitable. One approach to dealing with customer dissatisfaction is to deal constructively with customer complaints and anger. Tactics for achieving this end include the following: acknowledge the customer's point of view; avoid placing blame; defuse anger; apologize for the problem created; and follow up on the problem resolution.

Another approach to dealing with customer dissatisfaction is to involve the customer in working out the problem. The customer contact worker must sometimes deal with an unreasonable request. Remember that the customer probably recognizes that he or she is being unreasonable. Do not to argue with an unreasonable customer, yet at times you must say no.

QUESTIONS FOR DISCUSSION AND REVIEW

1. Visualize Billy, whose job it is to prepare French fries at a McDonald's. Who are Billy's internal customers?
2. For what reason is a satisfied employee more likely to provide better customer service?
3. Describe a situation in your life when you experienced customer delight. What made the experience delightful?
4. Imagine any sales situation involving a major purchase. Describe how you might identify customer needs.
5. Describe several customer moments of truth you have experienced this week. What made you classify them as moments of truth?
6. At the Hampton Inn hotel chain, every hotel employee is authorized to give a dissatisfied guest a voucher for a free night of lodging. What customer service principle does this voucher system illustrate?
7. Identify several typical ways in which customers are rude to customer-contact workers.
8. What do you think of the ethics of forming a bond with customers?
9. Can you identify any ways in which a customer-contact worker has made you feel good?
10. How effective is the principle "the customer is always right" when dealing with dissatisfied customers?

AN INTERPERSONAL RELATIONS CASE

THE TROUBLESOME BIG SCREEN

The Chavez nuclear family consists of Maria, an office manager at a hospital; Tony, an ambulance medic; and their daughter Jennifer, an eighth-grade student. A happy family, they share many activities. Among their joint activities is watching MTV (music television). The family regularly scrunches down to watch their favorite music shows on a 10-year-old, 13-inch color television.

One Thursday evening, Jennifer sighed, "Mom and Dad, I have a great idea. Let's do something exciting with some of your money. Let's buy a giant TV so we can have more fun watching the rock channel."

Maria and Tony thought that Jennifer's idea had merit. However, they both agreed that a giant-screen TV was a luxury item they could ill afford right now. Just before they fell asleep, the issue surfaced again. Maria said to Tony, "Deep down, we both agree with Jennifer. For less than $1,000 we could bring much joy into our home."

Friday night the Chavez family visited Appliance City to look at television sets. Maria spotted a 29-inch TV that seemed ideal. A store associate, however, convinced them that the model they were inspecting was of mediocre quality. Instead, he recommended a domestic brand with a 32-inch screen that he claimed was the highest-quality model in its class. Spearheaded by Jennifer's exuberance, the Chavez family was convinced. The cost, including a three-year complete service warranty, was $1,157.

The television set was delivered Monday evening as scheduled. For several days the Chavez family enjoyed watching MTV and other favorite programs on their new big-screen set. Friday evening, however, Maria, Tony, and Jennifer were mystified by an image that appeared on their screen. Shortly after Jennifer punched the menu button, an advertisement appeared on the screen touting the features of the set. Among the messages was one indicating that if the owner of this set were in a noisy room, he or she could mute the audio and watch the video.

Tony laughed as he explained that the demonstration mode was somehow triggered, and that the solution would be to just punch a few buttons. Next, Maria and he punched every button on the receiver and the TV remote. The demonstration mode remained. Tony then pulled the plug and reinserted it, only for the demonstration mode to reappear. Maria, Tony, and Jennifer than searched the owner's manual, but found no information about the problem.

Maria telephoned the dealer and got through to the service department after six minutes of being placed on hold. The service

(Continued) ▶

department said they knew nothing about the problem, but that she should speak to the sales department. After Maria explained her problem to a sales associate, she was told to speak to the service department.

Maria called back the service department and explained the problem again. A customer service specialist said that the store relied on an outside TV-appliance-repair firm to handle such problems. She said she would call the repair firm on Monday and that the firm would contact the Chavez family. By Tuesday morning the Chavez family still had not heard from the repair firm.

In desperation, Tony scanned a customer information booklet that came with the TV receiver. He found a list of 10 authorized service centers throughout the United States and Canada that repaired his brand of television. Tony telephoned a service center in California. A cheerful woman answered the phone and listened to Tony's problem. With a sympathetic laugh, she said, "We get lots of calls like this. No problem. Just push the volume-up and volume-down buttons at the same time. The demo mode will disappear. The mode was activated when somebody pressed the menu up and down buttons at the same time." Tony raced into the living room, and triumphantly restored the TV set to normal functioning.

Friday, a representative from the local television repair shop called. She said, "This is Modern TV and Appliance. Do you still need service on your set?" With anger in her voice, Maria explained how the problem was finally resolved.

Later that night as the family gathered to watch MTV, Maria said, "I guess we all love our new giant-screen TV, but I wouldn't go back to Appliance City to buy even an electric can opener."

QUESTIONS

1. What mistakes in customer satisfaction principles did Appliance City personnel make?
2. What mistakes in customer satisfaction principles did Modern TV and Appliance make?
3. What would you have done if you experienced a similar problem with an expensive TV receiver?
4. Should the manufacturer of the giant-screen TV set have any responsibility for the problem faced by the Chavez family?

Appendix A

EVALUATION SHEETS FOR APLED 121

Remove evaluation sheet and turn in with technical description

Technical Description Evaluation Name__________________________

1.	**Heading and Overall Format** Date, To, From, Subject (Topic + focus, all in capitals, and initialed) Accessibility (white space, indentation, headings, bullets, italics, windowing, all caps, bold face) Conciseness Clarity	
2.	**Introduction** - Title noting your topic's name (and any identifying numbers). Introduction a. state the topic b. mention its functions or purpose of the mechanism c. list the components	
3	**Discussion** – (describe topic clearly and accurately) Weight materials (composition) size (dimensions) Identifying numbers color shape density Make/model texture capacity Provide graphics that are correctly labeled, appropriately placed, neatly drawn or reproduced, and appropriately sized.	
4.	**Conclusion** – (Use one or more of the following) Sales uses guarantees testimony compare/contrast reiteration of introductory comments	
5.	**Technical writing communication standards** Audience analysis Multicultural awareness Avoid sexist language Correct spelling Correct grammar Correct punctuation Correct capitalization	
		TOTAL POINTS

**SCC Ability COMMUNICATION

write an effective well developed technical description

Remove evaluation sheet and turn in with completed travel/trip report

Trip Report Evaluation

Name________________________________

1.	**Heading and Overall Format** Date, To, From, Subject (Topic + focus, all in capitals, and initialed) Accessibility (white space, indentation, headings, bullets, graphics, italics, windowing, all caps, bold face) Conciseness Clarity	
2.	**Introduction** (overview, background) *Purpose*: document the date(s) and destination of travel. State objectives or rationale (what motivated the trip, what did you plan to achieve, what were your goals, why were you involved in job-related travel) *Personnel:* With whom did you travel? *Authorization:* Who recommended or suggested that you leave your work site for job-related travel?	
3	**Discussion (body, findings, agenda)** Using subheadings document activities include a review of your observations, contacts, seminars attended, or difficulties encountered.	
4.	**Conclusion/Recommendations** *Conclusion:* What did you accomplish-what did you learn, who did you meet, what sales did you make, what benefit to yourself, colleagues, and/or your company occurred? *Recommendations:* What do you suggest next? Should the company continue on the present course (status quo) or should changes be made in personnel or in the approach to a particular situation? Would you suggest that other colleagues attend this conference in the future, or was the job-related travel not effective? In you opinion, what action should the company take?	
5.	**Technical writing communication standards** Audience analysis Multicultural awareness Avoid sexist language Correct spelling Correct grammar Correct punctuation Correct capitalization	
		TOTAL POINTS

**SCC Ability COMMUNICATION

Write an effective well-organized technical travel report

Remove evaluation sheet and turn in with completed summary

Summary Evaluation Name________________________________

1.	**Heading and Overall Format** Date, To, From, Subject (Topic + focus, all in capitals, and initialed) Accessibility (white space, indentation, headings, all caps, graphics, bullets, italics, windowing, all caps, bold face) Conciseness Clarity	
2.	**Introduction** - Cite information for the article. Clearly state the author's primary focus.	
3	**Discussion** - Explain the author's primary view and omit secondary side issues. Explain facts and figures while avoiding lengthy technicalities.	
4.	**Conclusion**--Reiterate the author's primary contentions, reveal the author's value judgment, or state the author's recommendations for future action.	
5.	**Technical writing communication standards** Audience analysis Multicultural awareness Avoid sexist language Correct spelling Correct grammar Correct punctuation Correct capitalization	
		TOTAL POINTS

**SCC Ability COMMUNICATION

Write an effective well-organized summary

Remove evaluation sheet and turn in with completed progress report

Progress Report Evaluation Name______________________________

1.	**Heading and Overall Format** Date, To, From, Subject (Topic + focus, all in capitals, and initialed) Accessibility (white space, indentation, headings, bullets, graphics, italics, windowing, all caps, bold) Conciseness Clarity	
2.	**Introduction** (overview, background) *Objectives:* These can include the following þ Why are you working on this project (what's the rationale?) þ What problems motivated the project? þ What do you hope to achieve? Who initiated the activity? *Personnel:* With whom are you working on this project (i.e., (work team, liaison, contacts)? *Previous activity:* If this is the second, third, fourth report in a series, summarize what work has already been accomplished..	
3	**Discussion (findings, body, agenda)** *Work accomplished: Using* subheadings, itemize work accomplished either through a chronological list or a discussion organized by importance. *Work remaining:* explain what work you plan to accomplish next. List these activities for easy access. Visual aids, such as Gantt charts or pie charts, fit well in these two sections. The charts will graphically depict both work accomplished and work remaining. *Problems encountered:* Inform the reader(s) of any difficulties encountered (scheduling, interviews, research, etc.) not only to justify your possibly being behind schedule but also to show the readers where you'll need help to complete the project.	
4.	**Conclusion/Recommendations** *Conclusion:* Sum up what you've achieved during this reporting period and provide your target completion date. *Recommendations:* If problems were presented in the discussion, you can recommend changes in scheduling, personnel, budget, or materials that will help you meet your deadlines.	
5.	**Technical writing communication standards** Audience analysis Multicultural awareness Avoid sexist language Correct spelling Correct grammar Correct punctuation Correct capitalization	
		TOTAL POINTS

SCC Ability COMMUNICATION

Write an effective well-organized, technical progress report

Remove evaluation sheet and turn in with completed lab report.

LAB REPORT EVALUATION

Name______________________________

1.	**Heading and Overall Format** Date, To, From, Subject (Topic + focus, all in capitals and initialed) Accessibility (white space, indentation, headings, bullets, **graphics**, italics, windowing, all caps, bold face) Conciseness Clarity	
2.	**Introduction/Objectives** Why is report written—what will the report prove? Who authorized the report? List of equipment--	
3	**Discussion** WHO, WHAT, WHEN, WHERE, WHY, HOW How was the test performed? What equipment/approach/theory did you use to perform the test? Procedure—what steps were followed to perform the test?	
4.	**Conclusion –** Present the findings—what was learned/discovered? What are the implications? How do you interpret the findings?	
5.	**Technical writing communication standards** Audience analysis Multicultural awareness Avoid sexist language Correct spelling Correct grammar Correct punctuation Correct capitalization	
		TOTAL POINTS

**SCC Ability COMMUNICATION

Write an effective well-developed lab report

Remove evaluation sheet and turn in with completed technical instructions

Instruction Evaluation

Name______________________________

1.	**Heading and Overall Format** Date, To, From, Subject (Topic + focus, all in capitals, and initialed) Accessibility (white space, indentation, headings, bullets, graphics, italics, widowing, all caps, bold face) Conciseness Clarity	
2.	**Introduction** *1. Does the instruction have an effective title?* ■ Is the topic mentioned? ■ Is the reason for performing the instruction mentioned? *2. Does the instruction have an effective introduction?* ■ Is the topic mentioned? ■ Is the reason for performing the instruction mentioned? ■ Is the ease of use or capabilities mentioned? ■ Have the number of steps been listed? Has a list of required tools or equipment been provided?	
3	**Discussion** *1. Are hazard alert messages used effectively?* ■ Are the hazard alert messages placed correctly? ■ Is the correct term used (Danger, Warning, Caution, or Note)? ■ Is the correct color used with the appropriate term? ■ Does the hazard alert text identify the hazard, provide the consequences, and suggest avoidance steps? ■ Is an effective icon used to depict the hazard? *2. Is the instruction's discussion effective?* ■ Is the instruction organized chronologically? ■ Does each step avoid overloading by presenting one clearly defined action? ■ Does each step begin with a verb? Does the instruction's discussion contain the same number of steps mentioned in the introduction?	
4.	**Conclusion** *Is the conclusion effective?* ■ Have warranties been mentioned? ■ Is a sales pitch provided showing ease of use? ■ Has the conclusion reiterated a reason for performing these steps? Are disclaimers provided?	
5.	**Technical writing communication standards** Audience analysis Multicultural Awareness Avoid sexist language Correct spelling Correct grammar Correct punctuation Correct capitalization	
		TOTAL POINTS

**SCC Ability COMMUNICATION

Write and effective, organized set of instructions

Remove evaluation sheet and turn in with completed incident report

INCIDENT REPORT EVALUATION

Name________________________________

1.	**Heading and Overall Format** Date, To, From, Subject (Topic + focus, all in capitals, and initialed) Accessibility (white space, indentation, headings, bullets, graphics, italics, windowing, all caps, bold face) Conciseness Clarity	
2.	**Introduction** *Purpose:* document when, where, and why you were called to perform maintenance. Include what motivated your visit to the scene of the problem	
3	**Discussion (body, findings, agenda, work accomplished)** Using subheadings to Itemization/ quantify what you saw (the problems motivating the activity) Include what you did to solve the problem.	
4.	**Conclusion** Explain what caused the problem. **Recommendations** Relate what could be done in the future to avoid similar problems.	
5.	**Technical writing communication standards** Audience analysis Multicultural awareness Avoid sexist language Correct spelling Correct grammar Correct punctuation Correct capitalization	
		TOTAL POINTS

**SCC Ability COMMUNICATION

Write and effective, well-organized technical incident report

Remove evaluation sheet and turn in with completed feasibility report

FEASIBILITY REPORT EVALUATION

Name______________________________

1.	**Heading and Overall Format** Date, To, From, Subject (Topic + focus, all in capitals, and initialed) Accessibility (white space, indentation, headings, bullets, graphics, italics, windowing, all caps, bold face) Conciseness Clarity	
2.	**Introduction** (overview, background) *Objectives*—Rationale, motivating problems, achievement goal, and/or who initiated study *Personnel*—team members, liaison, contact person(s)	
3	**Discussion** (accessible and objective documentation) *Criteria*-State criteria on which your decision will be based *Analysis*-Compare findings against the criteria --Along with the written analysis, include a visual aid to organize the criteria and provide easy access	
4.	**Conclusion** - State the significance of your findings **Recommendations** - Recommend a course of action	
5.	**Technical writing communication standards** Audience analysis Multicultural awareness Avoid sexist language Correct spelling Correct grammar Correct punctuation Correct capitalization	

**SCC Ability COMMUNICATION

Write an effective, organized technical feasibility report

Remove evaluation sheet and turn in with completed memo assignment.

MEMO EVALUATION

Name_______________________________

1.	**Heading and Overall Format** Date, To, From, Subject (Topic + focus, all in capitals, and initialed) Accessibility (white space, indentation, headings, bullets, graphics, italics, windowing, all caps, bold face,) Conciseness, Clarity,	
2.	**Introduction –** Why you are writing. What you are writing about.	
3	**Discussion** - Exactly what you want to say. Answer questions *who, when, why, what, where,* and *how*	
4.	**Conclusion** - What's next? Provide either a complimentary or a directive close.	
5.	**Technical writing communication standards** Audience analysis Multicultural awareness Avoid sexist language Correct spelling Correct grammar Correct punctuation Correct Capitalization	
		TOTAL POINTS

**SCC Ability COMMUNICATION

Write an effective, organized well-developed technical memo

Remove evaluation sheet and turn in with completed letter assignment.

SALES LETTER EVALUTION

Writer's address—company's address a. Street address (do not abbreviate street, avenue, road, drive,...) b. City, state, zip code (state may be abbreviated with appropriate two-letter abbreviation)	
Date—placement depends on style of paper (letterhead) a. January 14, 1999 or 14 January 1999 b. Placed 2 spaces below writer's address	
Inside address—placed 2 spaces below the date a. Reader's name and title b. Company's name c. Company street address d. Company city, state, and zip code	
Salutation—placed 2 spaces below the inside address a. Begin with a capital letter—*Dear...*+ reader's name b. Use Mr., Mrs., Ms., or first name if appropriate c. Use a colon at the end of the name	
Introduction—1st paragraph placed 2 spaces below the salutation a. State why you are writing (increase happiness--reduce anxieties) b. Explain what you are writing about (the product---the service) c. Use a good lead-in (an anecdote—a question—a quotation—data	
Discussion—each new paragraph placed 2 spaces below the last a. Specify **exactly** what you are offering to benefit your reader b. OR—how you'll solve your reader's problems c. Provide data—document your credentials give testimony from satisfied customers d. Use action verbs—power writing e. Show ease of use—*easy, simple to operate,*	
Conclusion—last paragraph a. Make your readers act give directions to your place of business provide a tear-out to send back for further information supply a self-addressed, stamped envelope for customer reply b. Give your name and phone number c. Set up a potential appointment—*now, today, don't delay, 10% off*	
Complimentary Close—last paragraph a. *Sincerely* followed by a comma b. Go down 4 spaces and type your name c. Sign your name between the close and the typed name	
Technical writing communication standards Audience analysis—multicultural awareness Avoid sexist language Correct spelling Correct grammar Correct punctuation	
TOTAL POINTS	

SCC Ability COMMUNICATION

Write an effective, organized, well-developed sales letter

Remove evaluation sheet and turn in with completed letter assignment.

INQUIRY LETTER EVALUATION

Writer's address a. Street address (do not abbreviate street, avenue, drive, road) b. City, state, zip code (state may be abbreviated with appropriate two-Letter abbreviation)	
Date—placement depends on style of paper (letterhead) a. January 12, 1999 or 12 January 1999 b. Placed 2 spaces below writer's address if the letter is long c. Place 3-8 spaces below the writer's address if the letter is short	
Inside address—placed 2 spaces below the date a. Reader's name and title b. Company name c. Company street address d. Company city, state, and zip code	
Salutation—placed 2 spaces below the date a. Begin with a capital letter—*Dear…*+ reader's name b. Use Mrs., Ms., Mr., or first name if appropriate c. Use a colon at the end of the name	
Introduction—1st paragraph placed 2 spaces below the salutation a. Tell the reader why you are writing—intent b. Tell the reader what you are writing about—subject matter	
Discussion—each new paragraph 2 spaces below the last a. Specify your needs—ask precise questions b. State all available information—size, specifications	
Conclusion—last paragraph a. Explain when you need the response b. Explain why the date is important	
Complimentary Close—place 2 spaces below the conclusion a. *Sincerely* followed by a comma b. Go down 4 spaces and type your name c. Sign your name between the close and the typed name	
Technical writing communication standards Audience analysis—multicultural awareness Avoid sexist language Correct spelling correct grammar correct punctuation	
Total Points	

* SCC Ability—COMMUNICATION

write an effective, organized, well-developed

Remove evaluation sheet and turn in with completed letter assignment.

COMPLAINT LETTER EVALUATION

Writer's address—personal address or company's address a. street address(do not abbreviate street, avenue, road, drive) b. city, state, zip code (state may be abbreviated with appropriate two-letter abbreviation) c. DO NOT INCLUDE YOUR NAME	
Date—placement depends on style of paper (letterhead) a. January 14, 1999 or 14 January 1999 b. Place 2 spaces below writer's address if the letter is long c. Place 3-8 spaces below the writers address if the letter is short	
Inside address—placed 2 spaces below the date a. Reader's name b. Reader's title c. Company name d. Company street address e. Company city, state, and zip code	
Salutation—placed 2 spaces below the inside address a. Begin with a capital letter—*Dear…*+Reader's name b. Use Mr., Mrs., Ms., or first name if appropriate c. Use a colon at the end of the name	
Introduction—1st paragraph placed 2 spaces below salutation a. politely state the problem b. politely state how the problem affected you/your company c. include supporting documents serial numbers— dates of purchase—invoice numbers—check numbers— names of salespeople	
Discussion—each new paragraph 2 spaces below the last a. explain in detail the problems experienced—be specific b. include dates—contact names—info about shipping—breakage—list of defects—etc. c. **state what you want done and when you want it done**	
Conclusion—last paragraph a. end letter positively (you want the cooperation of the vendor) b. include phone number—and time you can be reached	
Complimentary Close—place 2 spaces below the conclusion a. *Sincerely* followed by a comma b. Go down 4 spaces and type your name c. Sign your name between the close and the typed name	
Technical writing communication standards audience analysis—multicultural awareness avoid sexist language correct spelling correct grammar correct punctuation	
Total points	

- SCC Ability—COMMUNICATION

  Write an effective, organized, well-developed problem/solution letter

Remove evaluation sheet and turn in with completed letter assignment.

ADJUSTMENT LETTER EVALUATION

Writer's address a. street address (do not abbreviate street, avenue road, drive) b. city, state, zip code (state may be abbreviated with 2 letter abb.)	
Date—placement depends on style of paper (letterhead) a. March 21, 1999 or 21 March 1999 b. Place 2 spaces below the writer's address	
Inside address—placed 2 spaces below the date a. Reader's name b. Reader's address including city, state, and zip code	
Salutation—placed 2 spaces below the inside address a. Begin with a capital letter—*Dear* + Reader's name b. Use Mr., Mrs., Ms., or first name if appropriate c. Place colon after the nme.	
Introduction—1st paragraph placed 2 spaces below salutation politely state your decision 100%-agree with the writer's complaint and agree to the adjustment 100%-disagree and begin with a buffer (a positive statement) partial-be diplomatic—state the good news first	
Discussion—each new paragraph 2 spaces below the last 100%-agree and explain what happened—why it occurred—how problem will be avoided in the future 100%-disagree and explain precisely what happened—facts--figures, then politely state the bad news partial- explain precisely what happened, then state the bad news	
Conclusion—last paragraph 100%-agree end with upbeat tone—resell the audience 100%-disagree end with upbeat tone—provide reader with choice partial-resell the audience (win back the reader's faith)	
Complimentary Close—place 2 spaces below the conclusion a. *Sincerely* followed by a comma b. Go down 4 spaces and type your name c. Sign your name between the close and typed name	
Technical writing communications standards Audience analysis—multicultural awareness Avoid sexist language Correct spelling correct grammar correct punctuation	
TOTAL POINTS	

* SCC Ability COMMUNICATION
Write an effective, organized well-developed adjustment letter

Appendix B

EVALUATION SHEETS FOR APLED 123

Effective Listening Exercise

Name ________________________________

1.	**Format** Name, Course, Format, Typed, Length	
2.	**Introduction** Purpose: State the purpose of the assignment	
3.	**Discussion:** Part 1: How did your use of active listening impact the conversation? Was the other individual more responsive? Part 2: How did your friend/family member rate you in terms of listening? Do you agree or disagree with their assessment? If you disagree, what would you rate yourself and why?	
4.	**Conclusion:** What did you learn from this exercise? What can you apply to your work environment?	
		TOTAL POINTS:

MIDTERM ARTICLES

Name ________________________________

1.	**Technical Writing Format** Name, course, typed, spelling & grammar Use headings, white space, bullets, & highlighting	
2.	**Articles Attached (3)** Cite Article Location—magazine name etc. Sources listed in APA format at the end of paper	
3.	**Content** Summary of articles: What did the author say? How does it relate to what you have learned/observed? What new insights did you gain from the articles? Did the members of your group have differing views? If so, what were their thoughts? How will this help you on the job?	
		TOTAL POINTS:

FINAL PROJECT
ORAL PRESENTATION (Individual)

Name: ______________________________

1.	**Voice** Could everyone hear you? Did you use variety in your intonation (or were you sound monotone)?	
2.	**Gestures and Body Language** Did you use appropriate gestures and body language to communicate your ideas? Did you use Facial expressions? Did you maintain eye contact with the audience?	
3.	**Visual Aids** Were the visual aids appropriate? Were they large enough to be seen? Did you use them at the right time? Were a variety of visual aids used?	
4.	**Content** Clear presentation of ideas Addressed all areas thoroughly Appropriately researched Charts/graphs included as needed Discussion progresses to a conclusion	
5.	**Transitions and Cohesiveness** Transitions between members was smooth The entire presentation was cohesive	
		TOTAL POINTS:

FINAL PROJECT
WRITTEN REPORT

Names: ______________________________
____
____
____

1.	**Technical Writing Format** Cover page, Table of Contents, Topics Covered, Resources, Page Numbers, Spelling, Grammar, Typed	
2.	**Content—Part 1** **Cover Page and Resources** All team members have initialed cover page References cited in APA format	
3.	**Content—Part 2** **Main Body** **Introduction--** Explains the problem background **Discussion--** Documented steps of the problem-solving process Topics discussed thoroughly Appropriately researched Charts/graphs included as needed Discussion progresses to a conclusion **Conclusion--** Recaps discussion and provides a basis for a decision	
		TOTAL POINTS: